WHAT MAKES BEHAVIOR
CHANGE POSSIBLE?

What Makes Behavior Change Possible?

Edited by
ARTHUR BURTON

BRUNNER/MAZEL, *Publishers* • New York

Library of Congress Cataloging in Publication Data

Main entry under title:
What makes behavior change possible?
  Includes bibliographies and index.
  1. Psychotherapy. 2. Personality change.
  I. Burton, Arthur, 1914-   [DNLM: 1. Behavior therapy—Methods.
WM420 W555]
RC480.5.W4   616.8'914   76-22752

ISBN 0-87630-131-6

Published by
BRUNNER/MAZEL, INC.
19 Union Square
New York, New York 10003

MANUFACTURED IN THE UNITED STATES OF AMERICA

Preface

No book I have written or edited has given me the satisfaction of this one. For more than three decades I have met with countless patients, offering them my person and my therapeutic techniques to resolve their pain, displeasure, and internal conflicts. And this has involved both the patient sequestered in the mental hospital with the more fateful prognosis and the patient from the community, of high intelligence, culture, and achievement. With each such patient, I, sometimes like Don Quixote, galloped forth to bring them the special succor and cure I totally believed in and that I had found most effective.

But this is a time of universal challenge to the basic myths and premises of institutions, cultures, and existence. The business of healing others has similarly no privileged immunity from self- and public examination. It follows then that we should give some research thought to what it is that makes behavior change possible in our patients, and this is precisely the subject matter of this book. Was I really helping my patients in the way it appeared to me? Was there perhaps a more efficient way? Or could it even be that it was all a complex charade of a sort and that, as some believe, psychotherapy is no more effective than simple self-regeneration? Out of such questions this book was formulated.

Whether one should be encouraged or discouraged by the findings is left for my own reflections in the final summary chapter. But one assurance can immediately be given: that the liberal, humanizing, and caring tendency of men everywhere—away from cruelty, perverseness, and sadism—has had its major phenomenal social manifestation in the worldwide psychotherapeutic movement. The dialogue of men, often where none seemed possible, is the true example of the ideal of testamentary brotherhood, and counseling and psychotherapy are therefore now as indigenous to our culture as pizza and apple pie. Universities are full of students busily learning to become healers, and everyone today wants to help others.

In this book we attempt to investigate how professional methods of helping work, and precisely what in them comprises the effective medium of help. In this way we hope to come to some better understanding of the process of healing we are so emotionally involved with, and to better distinguish that procedure which helps from that which does not. Perhaps out of this will come as well a more unified field of psychotherapy with fewer forms of practice and stronger supporting theories. By raising the science of psychotherapeutic practice slightly above the art of it, we may give it the foundation it has so sorely lacked.

ARTHUR BURTON

Contents

Contributors

ALBERT BANDURA, Ph.D.
Professor of Psychology, Stanford University; Past President, American Psychological Association.

REUVEN BAR-LEVAV, M.D.
Head, Bar-Levav and Associates, Detroit, Michigan.

ARTHUR BURTON, Ph.D.
Professor Emeritus of Psychology, California State University, Sacramento.

ALBERT ELLIS, Ph.D.
Executive Director, Institute for Advanced Study in Psychotherapy, New York, New York.

JEROME D. FRANK, M.D.
Professor Emeritus of Psychiatry, The Johns Hopkins University School of Medicine, Baltimore, Maryland.

JUDD MARMOR, M.D.
Franz Alexander Professor of Psychiatry, University of Southern California School of Medicine; President, American Psychiatric Association.

IVAN BOSZORMENYI-NAGY, M.D.
Director, Family Psychiatry Department, Eastern Pennsylvania Psychiatric Institute; Clinical Professor of Psychiatry, Hahnemann Medical College, Philadelphia, Pennsylvania.

JOHN WEIR PERRY, M.D.
Jungian Psychoanalyst, San Francisco; Assistant Clinical Professor of Psychiatry, University of California School of Medicine, San Francisco.

ERVING POLSTER, Ph.D.
Director, Gestalt Training Center, San Diego, California.

MIRIAM POLSTER, Ph.D.
Co-Director, Gestalt Training Center, San Diego, California.

VICTOR RAIMY, Ph.D.
Professor of Psychology, University of Colorado, Boulder, Colorado.

LEON SALZMAN, M.D.
Professor of Clinical Psychiatry, Georgetown University School of Medicine, Washington, D.C.

HANS H. STRUPP, Ph.D.
Professor of Psychology, Vanderbilt University, Nashville, Tennessee.

ELIZABETH VALERIUS, Ph.D.
Staff Psychotherapist, Atlanta Psychiatric Clinic, Atlanta, Georgia.

JOHN WARKENTIN, M.D., Ph.D.
Staff Psychotherapist, Atlanta Psychiatric Clinic, Atlanta, Georgia.

JOSEPH WOLPE, M.D.
Professor of Psychiatry, Temple University; Director, Behavior Therapy Unit, Eastern Pennsylvania Psychiatric Institute, Philadelphia, Pennsylvania.

Introduction

Everyone subscribes to the idea of behavior change. But it is only when troubled individuals realize that such change is necessary—even mandatory— and cannot make the behavior alterations themselves that they look to professional behavior changers. By designation and consensus, such professionals are called "psychotherapists"; but this is merely the generic term for a large number of species of healers who change behavior using different sets of principles and diverse techniques. All the healers claim that they treat successfully, but some have better-entrenched positions in the public and scientific mind than others.

As the pioneer in the field, with Sigmund Freud and C. G. Jung as Founding Fathers, psychoanalysis is the beginning and end of all current healing theories. The idea that the inner mental life of the patient had medical status and could therefore be changed; that patients had unconscious conflicts which made them unhappy and diverted their soma in bizarre ways;

and that a neurosis, as they called it, could be changed by a definite technique of "talking it out"—this was the signal and well-nigh incredible contribution of psychoanalysis.

Today we believe even more firmly in behavior change, attempting of course first to change ourselves, and psychotherapy has become a social institution on a par with education, political forms, religious practices, etc. Psychotherapeutic scientists are more or less determinists in philosophical outlook, but very few of them believe we are imprinted to the point where we must behave automatically against our reason and emotions. Even the most instinctual pattern is surrounded by a learning penumbra which mitigates its expression. While there is much to criticize in the founding psychoanalytic theory as the panacea we seek for our lives—and the critique of psychoanalysis has been both fair and unfair—it was Freud and Jung who added a new dimension to our social existence, whose magnificent insights into the psyche changed society and individual persons so thoroughly.

All of the authorities represented in this book believe in behavior change. Indeed, they have devoted their professional lives to changing behavior in the apparently unchangeable, and have made it their special research preoccupation as well. A very high percentage of the middle-class members of English-speaking societies have had counseling or psychotherapy or behavioral modification of some kind, so that psychotherapy is no novelty and is a part of the fabric of socialized living. For the wealthy, in every culture of record, the extent of participation is even greater. For the less privileged we can still claim that analytic concepts—the complex, inferiority feelings, life-style, ego, archetypes, psychosis, neurosis, dream analysis, depression, anxiety, and the like—are part and parcel of daily living, if only because the mass media dramatize them daily on television and radio, in the cinema and the press. This is a psychological world and psychology has become incorporated in all of us as ways of thinking, feeling, and behaving. Where a psychiatric concept has so broad a base in society, it is not then only a treatment form but a style of living, of coping, and of adjustment—a way of interpersonal relationships by which we grow and survive. Not many today escape the psychoanalytic shadow, although we all like to think we are immune from it or above it. But it does not take much in the way of hunger or sex deprivation to demonstrate a regression to precisely what Freud and Jung were talking about. Each of our fifteen contributors to this volume owes a debt of gratitude to the Founding Fathers, even if all of them do not always graciously acknowledge it.

We expect more today from psychotherapy than we did 10, 20, 50, or 100 years ago. In the old days, just to stay out of the mental hospital, to forestall a divorce, or to arrive at some kind of family amity between parent and child was sufficient proof of successful treatment. This is no longer true. Successful psychotherapy must now bring with it a newer and focal creative consciousness, a considerable quantum of joy, more sensitized and intimate interpersonal relationship, and a new hope and spirit about existence itself. To be free from tension and anxiety is not enough.

Not only can therapists no longer assume the passive analytic posture, but they must also demonstrate some healing properties of a guru, be a modern-day Socrates, be conversant with Pavlovian conditioning, have a thorough knowledge of perception-cognition, and be themselves crowning models of a life worth living. Some even claim that a therapist must be a friend, a kind of lover, or a Christian brother, and longer-term therapy is certainly a temporary marriage-analogue of sorts. The "romantic" family model is both losing out and gaining ground, if such a paradox can be countenanced. But whatever the case, pleasure in the Freudian sense is no longer sufficiently viable as the touchstone of a healing system, and Jung's archetypes, symbols, and collective unconscious have somehow not caught on in the way expected. We are in a sense desperate for a new theory of health, a new philosophy of existence, a feeling of what individuation is, a new vision of man. For this we have in our need looked for relief to analytic apostates like Frederick Perls, to massage, to primal screams, to ancient Hindu and other Eastern texts for meditation, yoga, satori, and the like. Murder, violence, and suicide have never been more prevalent in the United States. There is much more sex and pleasure around for the taking, and Freud would have been puzzled at the fact that the absence of sexual repression has not resulted in more joy. Indeed, joyless sex is the new problem we see. We are caught up socially in a state of expressive violence and expressive love but we do not know how to integrate them. Spock out of Freud omitted this crucial bit of information!

I have never been able to accept Eysenck's (1) claim that psychotherapy did not help overall, nor the antipodal conclusion that all psychotherapies, regardless of their nature, help equally (2). In the first instance, Eysenck is emotionally involved with denying psychotherapy, and does not admit clinical data, demanding instead as proof a kind of experimentation that cannot be done and never will be done in the face of the phenomenology of the healing process. And how can we say that all methods are interchangeably good when we do not even know what the cure is? The hazards of evaluating the outcome of a treatment are, as I see it:

1. The therapist is passionately involved in showing positive results with the methods he or she uses.

2. Most treated patients in private practice are never heard from again after they leave.

3. We have no systematic or agreed-upon procedure of follow-up.

4. We ignore the patients who come once, twice, or thrice and fail to return, as not in the experiment. But they are our failures.

5. Patients are "persuaded" that they feel better and are fearful of going against the complex of healing forces. We condition them to approve of what we do!

6. The placebo effect operates unevenly to help precisely those we do help.

7. There are no data on patients who suicide in treatment, and it is considered bad taste to include them in the statistics.

8. For those patients not made worse, the recovery baseline is not zero but 25% or more, representing those who would spontaneously regenerate themselves.

9. We have failed to agree on a concept of the good or fulfilled life. Without it, only the absence of discomfort can be taken as recovery. This obviously has limitations.

If we believe that psychotherapy is effective, as I do—and how can one say otherwise in the face of the millions treated by it—and if we further believe that one healing method must be superior or more economical than another on the principle of parsimony, then we should make a serious attempt to discover what it is that heals and sharpen it to a fine point. No one to my knowledge has asked a considerable sample of outstanding researchers what it is specifically that heals in their own healing systems and in others. This book attempts precisely such a research examination.

On the basis of their published research, their affiliations, and their clinical skills, I selected fifteen research authorities on behavior change and asked them the question: *What Makes Behavior Change Possible?* These authorities represent not only the apogee of therapeutic ability and knowledge but a diversity of treatment that covers today's broad spectrum of approaches. To this I offered five queries for each (at the end of each chapter) to challenge the point of view expressed.

Dr. Judd Marmor and Dr. Leon Salzman discuss the psychoanalytic position; behavioral conditioning approaches are handled by Dr. Albert Bandura and Dr. Joseph Wolpe; Dr. Jerome D. Frank and Dr. Hans H. Strupp can perhaps be called universalist-eclectic-analytic; humanistic-experiential approaches are in the hands of Dr. Arthur Burton, Dr. Elizabeth Valerius, and Dr. John Warkentin; the cognitive-rational are worked through by Dr. Albert Ellis and Dr. Victor Raimy; family therapy is the province of Dr. Ivan

Boszormenyi-Nagy; gestalt therapy is clarified by the Drs. Polster; crisis intervention therapy by Dr. Reuven Bar-Levav; and, last but not least, behavior change, as it occurs in schizophrenia, by Dr. John W. Perry.

In the chapters which follow, let us then see what for these research and healing scientists "makes behavior change possible." And, of course, in a concluding chapter, I attempt to put some design and order to the variegated approaches, hoping that some unity of concept and method is possible in today's world.

ARTHUR BURTON

REFERENCES

1. EYSENCK, H. J.: The effects of psychotherapy. *J. Couns. Psychol.*, 1952, 16, 319-324.
2. LUBORSKY, L., et al.: Comparative studies of psychotherapy. *Arch. Gen. Psychiat.*, 1975, 32, 995-1008.

Acknowledgments

1. DR. FRANK'S chapter includes material from "Therapeutic Factors in Psychotherapy (*American Journal of Psychotherapy*, 1971, 25, 350-361), "Psychotherapy: The Restoration of Morale" (*American Journal of Psychiatry*, 1974, 131, 271-274) and "An Overview of Psychotherapy" (Chapter 1, pp. 3-21 in G. Usdin (Ed.), *Overview of the Psychotherapies*, New York: Brunner/Mazel, 1975).
2. DR. RAIMY'S chapter is a revision and adaptation of Chapter IV of Victor Raimy, *Misunderstanding of the Self: Cognitive Psychotherapy and the Misconception Hypothesis*, San Francisco: Jossey-Bass, 1975.
3. DR. BANDURA'S chapter arose from research supported by Public Health Research Grant M-5162 from the National Institute of Mental Health. Some of the material was presented at a Conference on the Behavior Basis of Mental Health, Galway, Ireland. It is also a chapter in a symposium edited by J. D. Krumboltz and C. E. Thoreson, *Counseling Methods*, and published by Holt, Rinehart, and Winston, 1976.
4. DR. STRUPP'S chapter includes material from "On the Basic Ingredients of Psychotherapy" in *Psychotherapy and Psychosomatics*, edited by Jurgen Ruesch, A. H. Schmale, and Th. Spoerri, and published by S. Karger; and from "Therapeutic Influence," *Arch. Gen. Psychiat.*, 1972, 32, 133-135.

This material is used with permission.

WHAT MAKES BEHAVIOR
CHANGE POSSIBLE?

Judd Marmor

1

Common Operational Factors in Diverse Approaches to Behavior Change

by JUDD MARMOR, M.D.

The view that human psychological disorders could be modified via the deliberate psychological influence of another person gained its first important foothold in Western medical thinking with the advent of Mesmerism in the late eighteenth century. Prior to that time the medical approach to such disturbances was predominantly a somatic one—purges, bleedings, and various medicaments. By the second half of the nineteenth century, the influence of suggestion in the treatment process had begun to achieve wide recognition, at least in France. The Nancy school under Bernheim coined the term "psychotherapeutics" to describe the overall process. Other French psychiatrists, influenced by the Nancy group, elaborated on its theme and incorporated various techniques of persuasion and indoctrination to supplement the use of suggestion.

3

Countervailing currents also began to appear, however. Paul Dubois (1848-1918) in Switzerland developed a method he called rational psychotherapy, that strongly abjured the use of suggestion, which he considered to be of only transitory value. His approach was a strongly rationalistic one that focused on modifying the "erroneous ideas" of the patient "by means of proof, by demonstration, by logical induction, and by reason which touches the heart" (1). And in France Pierre Janet (1858-1947) described unconscious psychodynamic mechanisms and developed a system of treatment that he called "psychological analysis."

It was Freud, however, who gave the greatest impetus to a system of rational psychotherapy. His approach was based on giving the patient "insights" into the unconscious memories and affects that presumably were the basis for the psychopathology. Freud believed that most psychoneurotic disorders had their origin in traumatic vicissitudes, generally of a sexual nature, in the first six years of life, and was convinced that if patients could be enabled to recall and understand the importance of these repressed, conflict-laden experiences they would be cured.

It is notable that this fundamental tenet of Freudian psychotherapeutic theory—namely, that the cure lies in giving the patient cognitive insight into the origin and meaning of his disorder—has never been seriously questioned by other psychoanalytic schools however much they may differ with basic Freudian theory in other respects. It was not until the late 1950's, when some analysts began to study the nature of the psychotherapeutic process experimentally, that this basic assumption began to be seriously questioned within the ranks of analysis itself.

Outside of analytic circles, however, other psychotherapeutic approaches began to develop that rested on different theoretical assumptions. Perhaps the most prominent of these is that encompassed by the term "behavior therapy." The behavior therapies are rooted in theories of learning, primarily Pavlovian, Hullian, or Skinnerian, and employ a wide variety of conditioning techniques: desensitization, reward-punishment, aversive conditioning, implosion, social reinforcement, and the like. In contrast to the psychoanalytic schools, proponents of behavior therapy generally minimize the importance of cognitive insight, and place their emphasis strictly on altering the behavioral manifestations or symptoms presented by the client-patient. Subjective attitudes, feelings, fantasies, dreams, and transference-countertransference reactions are considered by them to be essentially irrelevant to or outside of the treatment process.

Another major current trend in psychotherapy bypasses both cognitive and behavioral factors and focuses instead on emotional abreaction. This approach, utilizing mainly group techniques, involves methods such as sensitivity training, Gestalt therapy, massage and other forms of body-contact therapy, and marathons (nude or clothed), all designed to break down conventional controls, heighten emotional awareness, and facilitate the expression of repressed feelings. These techniques have mushroomed in recent years into a variety of widely advertised and well-promoted public offerings.

Many other psychotherapeutic approaches have developed in recent years. Indeed, there has been a veritable explosion of them. The noteworthy fact about all of these current practices is that each endeavors to explain its therapeutic successes in terms of a unitary factor that uniquely distinguishes it from all others and makes it presumably superior. Thus, each psychoanalytic school attributes its results to its special brand of cognitive insights and transference interpretation; behavioral therapists, to the specific conditioning techniques they employ; Rogerians, to releasing the patient's own self-actualizing mechanisms; transactional analysts, to identifying the particular interpersonal "game-patterns" being employed by their patients; etc.

My own researches (2, 3, 4, 5) over the past twenty years into the nature of the psychotherapeutic process have firmly convinced me that *in no instance* can the results achieved, in these or any other psychotherapeutic approach that I have studied, be attributed simply to such unitary factors. I fully share Strupp's view that "there is not, and it is doubtful that there ever will be, a pure technical intervention analogous to a particular surgical procedure or the injection of a specific drug" (6).

What, then, are the relevant operational factors in the psychotherapeutic process? In actuality, a substantial number of interacting variables enter into this process. These variables encompass the personalities of the patient and the therapist (including both conscious and unconscious elements); the nature of the patient's problem; the degree of his or her motivation; the social role of the therapist, and the faith, hope, and expectancy that it engenders in the patient; the favorable or unfavorable potentials that the actual life situation of the patient presents; and the type of *relationship* that develops as a result of the specific patient-therapist interaction.

In the usual psychotherapeutic transaction patients seek help because of some degree of behavioral maladjustment, discomfort, or unhappiness. They generally go to persons whose social role defines them as help-givers. The hope and expectancy that accompanies this action, coupled with the release of tension experienced in discussing the problem with a presumptive help-giver, usually results in some initial feelings of relief. The greater the trust in the therapist, and the greater the hope and expectancy, the greater will be this initial improvement. In the subsequent course of events *all* therapists then begin to convey to the patient their therapeutic objectives, value systems, and conceptual frames of reference. They do this, whether they consciously intend to or not, by virtue of the questions they ask, what they emphasize or ignore in their comments, and their nonverbal as well as their verbal reactions. Many nondirective therapists labor under the illusion that because they endeavor to be deliberately neutral in their reactions to the patient's statements, they can avoid communicating their objectives or values to patients, but this is a myth. In actuality, *all* therapists, dynamic, behavioral, or other, inevitably communicate these matters to their patients, wittingly or unwittingly, if only by what they react to as "healthy" or "neurotic." This does not even necessarily involve direct verbal comments, although it usually does. It can and often does take place nonverbally in the form of facial reactions, pregnant silences, even the timing and tonal qualities of an "mm-hmm" (7, 8, 9). Moreover, the inference of approval or disapproval, either by such nonverbal cues or by verbal ones, acts as a powerful operant conditioning factor for change in the patient.

Another nonverbal influence on the patient takes place when the therapist's reactions to patients' verbal productions and behavior are different from what the patients have previously experienced from significant authority figures in their lives. Franz Alexander labeled these "corrective emotional experiences" and in the course of therapy such experiences act as additional operant conditioning factors.

Finally, the element of suggestion is present in every psychotherapeutic process. The fact that patients come expecting to be helped, the implicit or explicit message they receive that this help will be forthcoming if they comply with the therapist's treatment plan, and the indications they receive that certain patterns of behavior are more desirable or "healthy" than others, all involve elements of suggestion and persuasion. The greater the degree of trust, faith, and expectancy on the part of the patient, the greater will be the impact of these suggestive processes.

Although it seems increasingly clear, therefore, that psychotherapy involves a learning procedure, it is of the utmost importance to recognize the complexity of the factors that enter into this process. On the basis of my own studies and research, it is my conviction that at least eight major factors are present as common operational factors in all psychotherapeutic approaches. These can be summarized as follows:

(1) *A good patient-therapist relationship.* The basic matrix of any psychotherapeutic process consists of a good patient-therapist relationship, resting heavily on the trust and rapport engendered by the therapist's social role as well as his or her genuine interest in, and respect and empathy for, the

patient. An essential additional element is the patient's motivation to be helped. This matrix includes both conscious and unconscious elements, and encompasses concepts such as "rapport" and "therapeutic alliance" as well as transference and countertransference aspects of the patient-therapist relationship.

(2) *Release of tension.* Given the basic matrix, the second element that takes place in all psychotherapies is an initial release of tension by virtue of the patients' being able to "unburden" themselves by discussing their problems with a helping person within the context of hope and expectation that help will be forthcoming.

(3) *Cognitive learning.* A greater or lesser degree of cognitive learning then begins to take place, based on the therapist's efforts to assist patients in achieving a better understanding of the reasons for their difficulty. This serves to correct various misconceptions about themselves or their problems that the patients may have. This cognitive learning may be an integral part of the therapeutic plan, as in the psychodynamic or transactional analysis models, or it may take place unwittingly or coincidentally, as in the behavioral, Gestalt, or other "noncognitive" approaches, but careful observation will reveal that some cognitive learning inevitably tends to occur.

(4) *Operant conditioning.* This may occur deliberately as in some of the behavioral therapies, or by means of approval-disapproval cues that are either implicitly or explicitly communicated in other forms of therapy. It also occurs, as already noted, by virtue of corrective emotional experiences in the relationship with the therapist.

(5) *Suggestion and persuasion.* These may be implicit, as in most nondirective therapies, or explicit, as in the more directive ones.

(6) *Identification with the therapist.* An interesting and unexpected consequence of the observation of diverse psychotherapeutic approaches has been the discovery that most patients to a greater or lesser degree unconsciously tend to model themselves after the therapist by imitating or adopting the therapist's patterns of thought and behavior. This, of course, is a well-known form of social learning (10).

(7) *Repeated reality testing.* This involves the practicing or rehearsal of new adaptive techniques, and is the essence of the so-called "working through" process of analytically oriented techniques.

(8) *Emotional support from the therapist.* For reality testing to be persisted in, despite occasional setbacks, and for behavior change to ultimately become internalized, the final component that is demonstrable in all successful psychotherapies is sustained and consistent emotional support from the therapist, implicit or explicit.

Although these eight elements are present in all psychotherapies, I am not implying that they are present in the same proportions in all therapies. The particular mix of these elements varies with different therapeutic problems, different patients, different therapists, and different therapeutic approaches. Psychoanalysts tend to place a greater emphasis on the cognitive learning aspects of their process; behavior therapists, on the reconditioning aspects; Gestalt therapists and others of similar persuasion, on the release of repressed emotional tension; Rogerians, on the good patient-therapist relationship, etc. —but a careful observation of each of these techniques will inevitably reveal that all of the other elements are present and operative also, albeit in varying degrees. No therapy actually operates in the pure form that its theoretical framework leads its proponents to believe.

Certain adjuvant techniques can sometimes facilitate the operation of these eight factors, but without altering their ultimate importance. Thus, the use of psychopharmacological medication may reduce an overwhelming anxiety that is paralyzing the patient, and thus may make the patient more accessible both to the relational and the communicative aspects of the therapeutic process. Similarly, placing the patients on the couch, the use of relaxation techniques, or other techniques that tend to limit the sensory input of the patients and restrict it to the communicative process between them and the therapist all serve to heighten the suggestive aspect of the therapeutic process, and may thus facilitate the operation of the other therapeutic factors that are involved.

The fact that similar basic factors are involved in all psychotherapeutic approaches does not, however, mean that all psychotherapeutic approaches are interchangeable. One of the great problems that faces the student of the psychotherapeutic process is that of elucidating the nature of the conditions under which one particular kind of emphasis or "mix" of these factors may be more suitable than another. The challenging question is not which technique is better than all others, but under what circumstances and for what conditions is a particular technique or a particular kind of therapist more suitable than another. If we can succeed in elucidating this, perhaps some day we can achieve the Utopian goal of a unified science of psychotherapy that will put an end to partisan proclamations of superiority by competing techniques with restricted perspectives.

ADDENDUM QUERIES

I

DR. BURTON: One of the eight factors which you state are present in every operational psychotherapy is a "good patient-therapist relationship." Can you define with greater precision how you use the word "good" here? Does this mean a patient with a certain programmed readiness, a special compliance, a built-in set of predisposing traumas, or the wherewithal to purchase undeviating friendships in a society which no longer listens?

DR. MARMOR: There are two major facets to a "good patient-therapist relationship." The one usually described in the psychoanalytic literature is the *unconscious* one—i.e., a capacity for positive transference on the part of the patient and a strong motivation that will make it possible to overcome his or her unconscious resistances to achieve the therapeutic objectives.

My own conception, however, also includes *conscious* factors. The *real attributes* of both patient and therapist are involved— the way in which their personality attributes mesh, their liking and respect for one another—as well as the actual qualities of the therapist—personal style, knowledge, intelligence, assurance, objectivity, integrity, and empathy. The issue of the patient's ability to pay has unfortunately been greatly overemphasized by classical analysts. In private practice it is a factor because that is how the therapist earns his or her living. But by now we have an extensive experience in free clinics that clearly indicates that good therapy is possible in the absence of a monetary exchange, so long as the other requisite factors mentioned above and in my chapter are present.

II

DR. BURTON: At times it seems that *conceptually* we have not advanced very far from the basic ideas of Dubois, Bernheim, Janet, and Freud in 100 years. Would you on the other hand say that our *technical* proficiency has improved remarkably and that the rate of cure or improvement through psychotherapy is much more efficient than it was?

DR. MARMOR: I would put it just the other way around. I think that our *understanding* of the nature of the therapeutic process has progressed considerably—we *have* made progress conceptually. I'm not sure, however, that our psychotherapeutic *results* in general are necessarily much better than those of the pioneers you've named. We are more efficient, however, in some areas. For example, the development of behavioral techniques for the treatment of phobias and sexual dysfunctions represents a distinct advance over what we were able to accomplish previously. I am, of course, excluding from my remarks the great advances that have been made in the psychopharmacological treatment of the psychoses.

III

DR. BURTON: You touch on the importance of drugs and medication in the treatment of the patient. With any single patient there is not only the question of what form of psychotherapy to provide (if it is to be given) but whether a totally psychopharmacological approach is not more certain, less expensive, and at any rate maintaining the central function of medicine. How do you decide this question for any single patient who consults you?

DR. MARMOR: This is really too major a question to deal with in a simple paragraph except in general terms. There are a variety of medications that may be indicated as adjuvants in the psychotherapy of depressive reactions or severe anxiety states. I would say in general that when tension or depressive symptoms are so great that they make it difficult for a patient to cooperate in the therapeutic process, medication can be helpful in alleviating the severity of the symptoms and thus facilitating psychotherapy. Its use in such situations, therefore, should be seriously considered. Medication, however, is not a *substitute* for psychotherapy, and should not be used as a means of enabling patients to avoid coping adaptively with their life problems.

IV

DR. BURTON: Since it appears from your discussion that the psychotherapeutic approach necessary for a patient must be carefully selected by the therapist and then applied in a perspicacious way, would you make training institutes less doctrinaire and more all-purpose than they are at present? Would the well-trained analyst (or therapist) be then conversant with a broad panoply of concepts and technical possibilities?

DR. MARMOR: This is something that I have been advocating for many years. Psychotherapeutic training must not become a producer of monolithic, rigid, Procrustean techniques that are applied to all patients indiscriminately. The well-trained analyst or psychotherapist ideally should be one who is capable of utilizing psychodynamic understanding in a variety of techniques, and who can flexibly adapt therapeutic techniques to the specific needs of the patient. Hopefully, such capability should encompass individual and group therapies, conjoint marital and family therapies, and psychodynamic as well as behavioral techniques. At the very least, the therapist should be open-minded enough to know whether his or her own skills are what the particular patient's problem requires, and if not, to be able to make an appropriate referral.

V

DR. BURTON: As one who has been at the fountainhead of psychoanalysis and psychiatry for a half century, can you make some projections about the future of mental healing? Do you sense a professional and cultural shift in the healer and what it is that requires healing?

DR. MARMOR: I'm going to beg off from answering this one. I've indicated what I would like to see happen, but I am not a soothsayer and I hesitate to make predictions of this kind. The only prediction about which I feel reasonably confident is that the growing trend toward health insurance is going to place a greater premium on shorter, less expensive techniques—crisis therapies, one- to two-times-a-week psychotherapies, and group therapies—in contrast to long-term intensive analytic techniques.

REFERENCES

1. Quoted by Lewis, N. D. C. in Historical roots of psychotherapy. In Masserman, J. and Moreno, J. (Eds.), *Progress in Psychotherapy*, Vol. III. New York: Grune and Stratton, 1958, p. 25.
2. MARMOR, J.: Psychoanalytic therapy as an educational process. In Masserman, J. (Ed.), *Science and Psychoanalysis*, Vol. V. New York: Grune and Stratton, 1962.
3. MARMOR, J.: Psychoanalytic therapy and theories of learning. In Masserman, J. (Ed.), *Science and Psychoanalysis*, Vol. VII. New York: Grune and Stratton, 1964.
4. MARMOR, J.: The nature of the psychotherapeutic process. In Usdin, G. (Ed.), *Psychoneurosis and Schizophrenia*. Philadelphia: Lippincott, 1966.
5. MARMOR, J.: The nature of the psychotherapeutic process revisited. *Canadian Psych.*, 1976.
6. STRUPP, H. H.: Toward a reformulation of the psychotherapeutic influence. *Int. J. Psych.*, 11:263-365, 1973.
7. KRASNER, L.: Studies of the conditioning of verbal behavior. *Psych. Bull.*, 55:148-70, 1958.

8. MANDLER, G., and KAPLAN, W. K.: Subjective evaluation and reinforcing effect of a verbal stimulus. *Science*, 124:582-3, 1956.
9. SALZINGER, K.: Experimental manipulation of verbal behavior: a review. *J. Gen. Psychol.*, 61:65-94, 1959.
10. MILLER, N. E., and DOLLAR, J. C.: *Social Learning and Imitation.* New Haven: Yale U. Press, 1941.

Leon Salzman

2

The Will to Change

by LEON SALZMAN, M.D.

It is only in the last century that human behavior has been viewed as a complex integration of basic biological needs and essential cultural adaptations. Previously man was understood as having animal needs and a spiritual nature endowed by God which gave him the capacity to choose between right and wrong and good and bad.

Developments in science, particularly the theory of evolution, brought to the foreground an explanation for man's behavior which supplanted the theological conception. While it did not alter the notion of man's rationality, the biological instinct hypothesis de-emphasized man's freedom of choice and action, and attributed most of his behavior to preformed, naturalistic, unchangeable, and instinctual forces. Man was unable to control this behavior; it occurred without his choice or decision. According to this explanation, man's behavior was viewed as entirely free, entirely directed, or as a combination, dichotomized into mind-body or natural vs. spiritual man. Thus it was to be

13

expected that disorders of behavior were seen in terms of a hereditary taint or organic defect or as a deliberate opposition to the rational pursuit of God's will.

Another explanation for certain types of behavior was possession by the devil or some hostile force that had entered the body through magic or malevolence. Except for the notion of possession, it was presumed that the demented person behaved the way he did because of some purpose or design, in order to get something he wanted. Most theologians and physicians believed that a person could abandon or alter his course of action if he really wanted to. This idea persisted until the late nineteenth century, when it was demonstrated beyond dispute that behavior could be influenced by thoughts, attitudes, and experiences not immediately apparent to the person involved. The unconscious had been suspected and described by philosophers and theologians prior to Freud, but its role in human functioning had not been systematically and intensively studied.

Freud's discoveries enabled us to see that irrational, discrepant, or ego-alien behavior was not due to possession or invasion by demonic forces. Nevertheless it is still widely believed that distorted behavior is deliberately conceived, stubbornly and wittingly maintained, and subject to termination by volitional means. This notion persists not only because of our Judeo-Christian heritage but because of the difficulty of demonstrating the role of unconscious factors. The need to rationalize our behavior subtly but perceptibly influences our perceptions of others and attributes volitional elements to their activity. Freud's influence helped dissipate the devil theory of mental illness and this notion of rationality, but his instinct theories helped sustain the belief that behavior is ultimately beyond choice and control.

The concept of psychic determination dispelled the idea that behavior is random or accidental and emphasized the idea that elements in any piece of behavior are associated with other elements, and that the significance of the behavior is dependent upon these associations. One's behavior and thinking are always reasonable and rational because they represent a coherent attempt to pursue a need or goal, even if a maladaptive one.

The concept of determinism and the wish-fulfilling hypothesis reinforce the idea that one behaves the way one does because one chooses to do so. For example, if an individual is annoying or irritating it must be because he wishes to alienate or antagonize others, and therefore his behavior reflects this wish. He may have some deep need to be rejected or some masochistic wish to be humiliated which is ultimately related to his death instinct. Consequently his behavior, though seemingly contradictory and irrational, is, according to classical psychoanalytic theory, consistent with his unconscious desires. In this motivational description of behavior, it is assumed that the consequences of the behavior are precisely what the person intended and designed.

Without abandoning any portion of the concept of the unconscious, we may view the consequences of behavior in a different framework, one that takes into account a person's intent and also examines the state of mind, expectations, and needs of the recipient of the behavior. This approach reflects the interactional view of human behavior; it acknowledges that one may be annoying to others not because of wishing to irritate or antagonize, but because of the manner in which one attempts to curry favor. The need for acceptance may be so intense that one becomes overly aggressive and persistent, ultimately irritating and annoying the other person and causing the very opposite effect of the one intended.

We could say that the individual who is annoying, irritating, or hostile is so because he is trying too hard to be pleasing and accepted. He overdoes it by excessive catering and by obsequious, toadying, and fawning behavior. Instead of a deep Ucs* need to be rejected, he has an exaggerated need for acceptance because of his underlying feelings of worthlessness. His behavior is not wish-fulfilling because the anxiety involved in his neurotic needs promotes a failure in his performance. Both this view and the wish-fulfilling hypothesis support the concept of an Ucs or a state of unawareness. One view underlines the role of anxiety in distorting efforts made to fulfill one's needs, and the other maintains that one's overt behavior is always a clear statement of one's Ucs desires. This is an essential issue in our philosophy and technique of therapy. We can direct our attention to discovering what the Ucs really wants us to do, or we can explore our behavior in terms of its intent and its effects. Thus we can have an interactional, interpersonal model of human behavior or an interpersonal, instinctual model. Mostly we have both because many therapists are unclear as to which model they are using.

Freud was covertly supporting the concept of willfulness and choice in human behavior when he pointed out that the dominating goals of behavior are the pursuit of pleasure and the avoidance of pain, except in cases where realistic requirements demand some modification. Yet in his discovery and illumination of the unconscious and his attribution of instincts in human activity he was at the same time suggesting that not all behavior was volitional, or consciously organized and directed.

Do we really freely choose the defenses we employ in dealing with the demands of our instincts or our anxieties? At a particular moment, when

---

* Unconscious

person of the same sex. This is notably true in the relationship of patient and therapist. The mere fact that the consequences of behavior are so often opposite to what one wishes is evidence supporting Freud's view that the distortions of behavior are based on the effects and manifestations of anxiety.

The ability to distinguish between the intent and the consequence of behavior plagues the entire practice of psychotherapy, from the untrained worker in counseling and helping situations to the trained psychoanalyst searching for covert and disguised evidence of instinctual wishes. An endless search ensues to establish the underlying wish that promoted the behavior and produced the neurotic symptoms. Often the relentless and persistent efforts of the psychoanalyst may produce the very effects that he insists were already present in the patient's wishes. The patient may be pressed to examine and acknowledge aggressive elements in a piece of behavior in which he insists they are not present. The therapist's tenacious demand and his refusal to accept the patient's denial of such feelings may make the patient restive, annoyed, and ultimately irritated and angry. Outbursts of anger which may then follow fail to prove that the anger was originally present or that the patient is truly aggressive. Instead, it may indicate that if pushed hard enough he can become annoyed and angry even though he started out with feelings of some tenderness and warmth. This is a common enough drama acted out in the "who's angry" game, in which a person is accused by another of being angry. Since he is not angry, he responds with irritation and somewhat caustically says, "Who's angry?" The other then retorts, "You see! I was right in the first place. You are angry." This is an example of the "wish-fulfilling prophecy" in which we produce what we already expect to find in an interpersonal situation.

Neurotics often stir up anger and resentment in others when really wishing to promote goodwill toward themselves. When this is manifest in the extreme, it is labeled "negative therapeutic reaction." It is often the therapist who goes into therapeutic negativism in his inability to handle this type of masochistic personality structure. The patient is behaving in the only way he knows, pressed by the dictates of his neurotic character structure. Certainly annoyance and despair are often stirred up in the therapist when he sees his potentially useful interpretations being distorted by the patient in destructive ways instead of the ways he, the therapist, intended. In some cases the therapist may feel so frustrated and helpless that he will terminate the therapeutic relationship and provide ample rationale and justification for the decision. In despair and disappointment the therapist describes the situation as the patient's unconscious need to fail. This allows him to overlook the factors in himself and in his own response to the patient's neurotic style that produced the impasse. He therefore does not explore the neurotic bind into which he was drawn in his earnest desire to be helpful.

If the therapist is unaware of and insensitive to the effect the patient's behavior has on him, he may assign the major responsibility for the difficulty and the failures in the therapeutic process to the patient. This conveniently overlooks the fact that it is the patient who is neurotic and needs therapy for his unsuccessful behavioral patterns. Surely he should not be blamed for behaving according to the dictates of his distorted thinking. The therapist's failure to distinguish the patient's intent from his own reactions to the patient's patterns leads to a curious paradox. The patient, who needs and wants treatment because of his repetitive tendency to fail, is pushed out of therapy because this pattern is also present in the therapeutic process. The term "negative therapeutic reaction" should be applied to a situation created by therapeutic despair in the therapist rather than the patient. It represents a failure on the part of the therapist to be adequate to the task, whatever the reason may be.

The confusion between the intent and the consequences of children's behavior often produces misunderstanding and may cause considerable psychological damage to the child. The child's cry may be a bid for attention, but it may also be a response to pain, need, or discomfort. To fulfill its needs the infant must first obtain the attention of others. Thus the cry is always an interpersonal communication. The plea for attention should not be viewed as an invalid or disruptive activity; because adults may experience the infant's plea as annoying and willful, they assume it can be turned off at will. When it continues they view it as a deliberate, mischievous provocation and treat it with disinterest or avoidance.

How can the matter of will, choice, or intention involve the therapeutic process when the philosophy of mental disorder is centered on the theory of unconscious drives and conflicts? Since the essence of a psychic defense is to avoid, deny, and make unavailable the real meaning and goal of behavior, how can we alter it by volitional means? If Ucs motivations do exist, then simple willfulness will not suffice to alter the behavior, since one may not even be aware of which elements need to be altered. How can one control a dangerous impulse when one may not be able to identify its source or know what may trigger the response? Unless one knows the how and why as well as the nature of the impulse, one still cannot direct intentional capacities to prevent its appearance.

In spite of these apparent impediments to the volitional control of their impulses, some patients have a strong drive and determined interest in overcoming them. Most people, however, prefer to remain as they are, in spite of discomfort and limited productivity, and display little interest in altering their way of life except at times of crisis or great stress. Even then they wish only to eliminate the anxiety and not their way of reacting to it. They do not want to abandon their neuroses; they want bigger and better neuroses, but without anxiety. This is a striking feature in the obsessional disorders where anxiety and distress come from the unrealizable demand that the person be perfect and beyond human limitations. The recognition of weakness and fallibility produces the anxiety which may bring such a person to the psychiatrist.

Instead of trying to overcome their demands for superhuman performance, patients want the psychiatrist to perfect their neurotic structure so they will be immune to anxiety. If a more drastic change can be brought about in some magical fashion or moment of illumination without struggle or turmoil, and with only momentary discomfort, they might be agreeable to such a plan. Since therapists are advocating change, they often find themselves in the position of being viewed as unacceptable and unwelcome authority figures. They appear to be encouraging change in areas in which the patients are only vaguely interested. When people are motivated toward change, there are many subtle, covert, and indefinable obstacles which may sabotage the process. Most striking is the evidence that, though patients may be strongly motivated to change, they cannot alter their behavior or use their positive impulses for change in a constructive way, because those aspects of their living that require alteration are beyond their conscious control and influence. Those compulsive elements in their behavior are precisely the ones they cannot alter by deliberate intent.

It has long been noted that insight alone is not enough to effect change in a patient's behavior. This observation led to a distinction between intellectual and emotional insight. Only the latter was assumed to have the power of altering neurotic behavior. Now we are aware that change requires an additional dimension. What makes the difference is whether the insight is used, and the degree of motivation that lies behind the efforts to use it. The therapeutic process must focus on the dual role of discovery and action, not merely on insight or understanding. Emotional insight may be viewed in this framework as decisive willfulness or committed intention. Change should be the ultimate goal in therapy. Unfortunately, it is not true that when patients recognize their neurotic pattern and uncover its roots they will be free to experience their new powers and will do so. The "working through," or the utilization of insight, is a crucial aspect of therapy and frequently the most difficult one. This fact must be understood early in therapy, preferably through an actual experience in which self-discovery did bring about a favorable change in the patient's living. When the goal of therapy is change and not *just* insight, a more rational and organized treatment plan can be formulated.

This recognition raises the question of how much activity is justified in promoting and expanding the volitional interests and wishes of patients to effectuate a change in their living. Do such efforts have destructive possibilities in the ultimate resolution of the patients' neuroses? This, in turn, raises the equally controversial question of the value of resolutions, determined decisions, and fervent promises in the achievement of one's goals.

The therapist's activity or passivity in the therapeutic process and the reliance on uncovering—in contrast to the exertion of will—as an instrument for change are questions that still need to be extensively investigated. Recent developments in ego psychology have directed attention to the issue of activity, on the part of both patient and therapist. These modalities include direct therapy, reality therapy, radical therapy, behavioral therapy, and a host of others. Developments in existentialism as it relates to the psychotherapeutic process, such as daseinanalysis, existential analysis, phenomenology, and the like, point to the need for definitive action and commitment in the process of therapy.

Some psychotherapeutic theories have insisted that while in treatment patients should refrain from taking any steps or making any decisions or commitments about their lives. They require that patients talk out their desires or intentions in the therapy sessions and refrain from "acting out." There are various justifications and rationalizations for this viewpoint, ranging from the need to allow the patients to arrive at their own goals after they have fully explored all the neurotic obstacles and impediments in their living, to the notion that if acting out is prevented, the data that need to be discovered about these neurotic conflicts and anxieties will not be dissipated. This injunction implies that acting out or living and behaving according to one's neurotic patterns will interfere with the process of studying these patterns, since the emotional elements in them will be expressed outside of the therapeutic sessions. Those who hold to this theory believe that the quality of the transference with the therapist is thereby reduced.

This viewpoint is justified if the theoretical assumptions which underlie it are valid. However, psychoanalysts do not universally agree that activity on the part of the patient or therapist disturbs or distorts the transference relationship. Neither is it agreed that willful or decisive behavior in the course of treatment is always a neurotic device to avoid confrontation with one's unconscious. At times, the activity of patients outside the therapeutic sessions may indeed be a way of frustrating treatment by avoiding a confrontation with their feelings and attitudes. This activity must be dealt with as a necessary part of understanding the patients instead of merely forbidding it to happen. The therapist's failure to interrupt impulsive and destructive behavior which may be an acting out of fleeting and transient feelings and attitudes can be most detrimental to the therapeutic process and ultimately to the patients' existence. On the other hand, patients must continue to function during the course of their prolonged therapy, and some decisions can grow out of the encouragement and understanding achieved, long before a grasp of the total neurotic process is possible. It takes mature judgment on the part of the therapist to interrupt behavior when it is inappropriate, and to allow it to proceed when it is useful. Rigid rules in this regard can be most detrimental, particularly in the therapy of the obsessive-compulsive character disorders.

At some point in the process of therapy patients must act on their new understanding and insight; activity must follow insight if progress is to occur. This understanding necessitates a reexamination of the role of will in the therapeutic process, obliging the therapist to restore its status as a force in human behavior which the concept of the unconscious has tended to minimize. It does not imply that the unconscious as a factor in human mentation should be abandoned, or that one should resort exclusively to willful or conscious motivational factors in the therapy of the mental disorders. Some recent theorists have taken extreme positions in their zeal for behavioral alterations. Contrariwise, an awareness of the function of the will in human affairs will make it possible to avoid the excesses of those who advocate an exclusively unconscious origin to mental dysfunction and who see treatment as a process of mutual attunement and communication of the unconscious of patient and therapist.

The problem is extremely complicated because in most neurotic states the will or capacity for committed intentionality is weakened. Patients are therefore handicapped in expressing their will at a time when their therapy requires them to exert it in order to make the necessary progress in undoing their neurotic, incapacitating patterns in living. On the other hand, many therapeutic approaches depend entirely on the ability of patients to mobilize their willfulness to effect behavioral changes without any alteration of their underlying character structure. These behavioral changes can be of the utmost importance in some circumstances, but we must not confuse manipulations of patients' behavior with therapy of their neurotic or psychotic patterns of functioning.

Behavioral therapy is currently enjoying some acclaim in this regard, since it alters behavior by a variety of deconditioning processes such as desensitization, aversion, rewards, and other operant procedures. By applying these techniques, a therapist can alter or terminate specific items of behavior without affecting in any way the character structure of which these items may be minor or major manifestations. In doing this the therapist calls on the willful and intentional capacities of the person to press toward change in an area of living that is capable of being changed without additional understanding or insight. Thus, behaviorists can alter responses that are derived from the conditioning process, even though they are incapable of altering some of the complicated symbolic transformations and other complex, defensive, intellectual, and emotional issues that interpose between the stimulus and response in neurotic or psychotic disorders. In fact, we do need to understand the role and function of a piece of behavior that is part of the individual's character structure before we can exert the will required to alter it. Behavior therapy is conducted on the assumption that there is a direct correlation between behavior and inner subjective life. There is often, however, no such direct one-to-one correlation, but rather a set of interrelated hypersensitivities or other intervening variables. Other behavioral therapies or charismatic techniques, regardless of the skill and personality of the healer, cannot overcome a disorder in which understanding is a prerequisite, just as one cannot be a good musician by the simple exercise of will and determination.

Other volitional or behavioral therapies, such as the rational or Gestalt, can be understood in the same light. They emphasize the willful elements in human behavior and attempt to strengthen them by a rational examination of the effects of neurotic behavior on one's own living. Patients are encouraged to explore the ways in which their behavior affects others. Then the therapist tries to alter their maladaptive behavior through a rational process of explanation or ethical exploration. Encouragement for behavior alteration comes in the forms of active support, exhortation, suggestion, and persuasion, accompanied by emotional support and empathic understanding of the difficulties. The process overlooks the fact that many of the obstacles underlying the continuation of the neurotic patterns are out of awareness and require uncovering techniques to bring them into the open. The rational therapies focus on the power of will to effectuate change but overlook those elements in the neurotic structure that are outside of immediate awareness. While focusing on change, these therapies often overlook the prior requirement of insight, which is necessary for change to occur.

The utilization of the patient's positive powers and will to cooperate and participate can only enhance the therapeutic process when wisely applied. This is the dilemma of the psychotherapy process: if it is to be effective it requires active participation of patient and therapist, although such activity may often distort the therapeutic process. By focusing on the areas of therapeutic interest one can negate the value of a free-floating, unfocused attention on the part of patient and therapist. Awareness of this problem does not mean that it is necessary to establish rigid technical rules; rather one must be free and flexible in one's attempts to artfully utilize both horns of the dilemma. Neurotic patients who are encouraged to "do" something about their distorted way of functioning are also warned against "acting out" or trying to alter their behavior by doing rather than talking. Sometimes this is good advice. Some people try to solve all their difficulties by action, and until they have learned enough about themselves their activities will only repeat previous failures. On the other hand, refusal to take action in the face of new insight does not allow patients to test out their discoveries. Unless the role of will in human functioning is taken into account, this contradictory situation will continue to plague psychotherapeutic theory and practice.

How can we overcome this dilemma? At the outset, we must acknowledge that the removal of obstacles, physical or mental, is only the first step and not the ultimate goal in the resolution of a mental disorder. The notion that people, motivated by positive pressures for fulfillment and creative achievement, will become productive when the way is cleared of psychological impediments is a romantic delusion and not a scientific fact. People pursue goals that are beyond mere survival at great physical and emotional cost. These goals fill creative urges and are culturally rewarding. Yet the motivations to achieve them are not as omnipresent as the urge to achieve relief of pain and discomfort. The additional factors of will, creativity, striving for higher values, etc., must be present to push people to objectives and goals beyond the biological necessities. Even if sufficient motivation is present there must be some feeling of assurance that newly discovered insight and understanding can work in the real world. Patients must have some willingness to confront the difficulties and the possible rebuffs which may result when the newly acquired patterns of behavior are attempted. Encouragement and support from a friendly, interested helper may stimulate these efforts to explore hitherto closed areas of experience and to attempt to put new understanding into action.

How can change be achieved if we acknowledge out-of-awareness factors in the production of personality and mental illness? In spite of Freud's unfortunate metaphor, personality development is not based on the freedom of passage of libido through a series of canals. If one canal gets clogged, the whole system will not be relieved by unclogging it. Even if a traumatic situation sets off widespread changes because of anxiety or other threats to one's integrity, the passage of years has rearranged and realigned the patterns based on these traumas, and they are now used to ward off present-day threats and dangers. A revivification of these events may illuminate why a particular way of dealing with the world was developed, but it does not help us understand why it continues today. The present patterns may be the only way the patient knows how to confront the world, even though they may be defective, painful, or inadequate. One cannot simply discard the patterns, even with encouragement and support. Such a change requires determination, patience, and motivation based on the assumption that the change will be an *improvement* on one's present way of living.

If, on the other hand, theories of personality development and psychopathology are determined by a multiple set of variables and a repeated set of experiences in a malevolent cultural environment, one's expectations of a magical, immediate transformation of one's established patterns will be less likely. The therapeutic situation then becomes a partnership of two or more people (group or family therapy), and the process is one of attempting to understand how and why individuals came to be what they are, how their present way of living is maladaptive and unsatisfactory, and how it can be altered without compromising or giving up valid goals and ideals. The individuals are not required to adjust to a defective culture, but to adapt their skills and capacities to functioning more productively within it.

Because behavioral patterns tend toward stability and rigidity when successful in achieving their purpose, patients must be helped to develop positive motivations for change. To do this we must increase the individuals' self-esteem by a positive awareness of their true capabilities, divorced from neurotic idealizations and impossible expectations. Then they can see alternatives and choices, heretofore blocked by compulsive necessity. The expansion of their will through therapy enables them to choose. Such a process is long and arduous. It requires considerable skill on the part of therapists to encourage patients to utilize their resolve and will where the possibility of a successful outcome can reasonably be expected. We cannot wait for *ideal* circumstances; they may never occur. Yet this is often the patient's justification for postponing action. The therapist must take a calculated risk, based on a reasonable understanding of the situation and the knowledge that, if failure occurs, the patient will not suffer devastating effects, but may have a useful and necessary learning experience. This does not mean that we should encourage willful activity when the risks of failure seem too great or when failure might serve to confirm the patients' deprecated view of themselves as ineffective personalities. To ask the homosexual to decide whether he wishes to live a heterosexual life before he has grasped any of the factors that produced his homosexuality will be useless. Though he may wish to change in theory, pressure to get him to change before he is able to make a valid choice will only serve to strengthen his notions of inadequacy and incompetency.

We must always take into account the factors operating in people's lives that are beyond them. The elements of compulsion which exist and operate in all mental illnesses as well as in so-called normal living must be taken into account in any attempts to alter inadequate patterns of functioning. If one's capacity for decisive action is interfered with by the compulsive need to behave otherwise, no amount of persuasion or encouragement, however rewarding or punishing, will alter it.

How can we utilize our professional skills to formulate interpretations to patients whose disease patterns employ intellectualizing, philosophizing, and conceptual thinking to defeat understanding? How can we focus on the concrete when the patients' defenses insist on generalization or when they concretize to such a minute degree as to destroy the value of the observation? How can we ask people whose disease prevents them from letting go or giving up control to abandon themselves to free association of "whatever comes to mind"? How can we manage to overcome a compulsion that is the essence of a rigid resolve by asking patients to abandon all resolution and behave in a random, unplanned fashion, which they then turn into a new compulsion? How can we encourage the development of a less ego-preoccupied self, when the process of therapy demands some ego-focusing and introspection?

These contradictions can be managed only when we recognize that our patients' behavior under these circumstances is *not* volitional and therefore cannot be terminated at will. While we must not yield to, or become enmeshed in, their neurotic patterns neither can we become irritated, disappointed, or rejected because these patterns continue. We must present patients with a view of their behavior and its consequences without rancor or criticism, and not assume that the behavior is the outcome of a conscious choice. They are victims in the sense that there are influences outside their awareness that determine their behavior. Patients can experience some freedom in exploring different or more useful patterns of reacting only after these elements are clarified through the psychotherapeutic process, and it is recognized that their rigid patterns are not necessary. Only then can we call on their will and their conscious efforts.

Existentialism and some Eastern philosophies, particularly Zen, have much to offer in clarifying this matter. Existentialism developed from the desire to understand man as he "is," not as he "should be" in some ideal sense. Existentialism focused on the inevitable conflicts, contradictions, and dichotomies produced by man, the transcendent animal capable of making choices and decisions and of acting through intention and will initiated through cortical desires for experiences beyond physiological necessity. Zen is an Oriental philosophico-religious system which attempts to get at the heart of the ultimate truth through the process of "direct action."

These philosophical systems speak directly to the excesses of a compulsive, power-oriented, activity-dominated culture which believes that one can do anything one wants, that one can succeed at anything if only one wishes, and that the possibility of achievement and fulfillment is limited only by one's desires and capacity for work. Insufficient account is taken of the physiological and existential barriers and limits to man's capabilities. By focusing on man's mortality, for example, existentialism has forced man to acknowledge some of his limitations, especially with regard to aging and its physiological accompaniments.

It is in the treatment of the compulsive disorders and other disorders of the will, such as catatonia, apathy, and resignation, that these philosophies have been most useful in offering clues for therapeutic management.

Existentialism concerns itself with the problems that confront man in his real, conscious existence. It is a philosophy of action, as opposed to speculation. It demands an understanding of man as he *is* and as he experiences the problems of his existence, such as loneliness, self-consciousness, choice, decision, and death. Existential philosophy, with its recognition of the role of commitment in the living of a full and productive life, touches directly on the psychiatric conception of the obsessional state, in which commitment is avoided because of the fear of consequences. The avoidance of any commitment and the consequent effects—nonbeing, nonidentity, rootlessness, and isolation—is a constellation that has been familiar to the behavioral scientist for the past three decades. The epidemic of rootlessness and meaninglessness of existence with the accompanying feelings of powerlessness is the psychiatric disease of our times. Its technical name is obsessive-compulsive neurosis. Interest in existentialism and related philosophies is indicative of this development and of the response to it.

Our culture is overwhelmed by compulsions, imperatives, shoulds, and musts, and there is little freedom or possibility of choice. A philosophy that states that commitment is a prelude to freedom and choice, and that a responsible view of man's limitations is necessary for authentic living is very intriguing to us. Zen is a practical application of the need to remove oneself from the active, distracting world of doing and producing. It advocates meditation and a confrontation with one's inner self, a confrontation that can only be reached when one can divest oneself of the *compulsive* need to perform. The interest in existential philosophy and, subsequently, existential analysis grew out of the relevance of the existentialist's speculations about the psychoanalytic problems of will and consciousness and the issues of loneliness and meaninglessness. As existentialism developed its own methodology and technology, and attempted to deal with mental disorder, it became a cumbersome, ineffective, and heavily intellectualized instrument.

Zen as a philosophical and theological system has concerned itself with many of the same questions that interested the existentialists. Zen practitioners established rituals which put many of their philosophical ideas into action. Psychotherapeutic techniques, especially as they apply to the obsessional disorders, can be considerably enriched by a study of Zen and its practice by Zen masters. By firmly refusing to accept all theories and speculations about the self, and by focusing on the concrete and avoiding the abstract, the Zen master, through the koan, forces the student to respond in a natural, spontaneous fashion. The student comes to recognize that the natural *cannot* be reached through conscious effort, but only through spontaneous living. This is a major goal in the therapy of the obsessional, a therapy that attempts to free the patient from the compulsive necessity to act and leads him to spontaneously and freely choosing his course of action.

The Zen master attempts to develop naturalness by avoiding preparedness and preoccupation, and by an attitude of constant, vigilant anticipation. The student is encouraged to remain in a fluid state from which spontaneity, freedom, and naturalness can ensue.

Zen philosophy has illustrated the dilemma: one achieves understanding only when one can stop working toward it. This validates the cardinal principle in the therapy of the obsessional. The therapist encourages patients to examine their behavior and focus on it without trying too hard or becoming too preoccupied with it. The process follows the well-known maxim: "Let yourself go and it will come." To conquer the inability to act or the compulsion toward action, the element of necessity must be removed and the notion of spontaneity introduced. Yet when the compulsive recognizes the need to be spontaneous, he turns *that* into a compulsion, and now has a "bigger and better" compulsion. Zen deals with this problem by the principle of WU-WEI, or *not doing*, just letting be, which resolves the dilemma.

Recently, in our culture, too, we have been called to come to grips with the special qualities of experiential knowledge. How can one really understand what it's like to be black, to be a drug addict, or to be on an L.S.D. trip unless one has experienced it? We are beginning to realize the inadequacy of words in translating these intensely personal and private experiences into public and communicable discourse.

The developments in psychoanalytic theory and practice have also been in the direction of encouraging such therapeutic techniques as alpha bio-feedback training, relaxation training, techniques for inducing altered states of consciousness, and meditative techniques. These developments in general reduce verbalization and conceptualization and reduce the interpersonal relevance of the therapy. Drugs also fit into this category.

Meditation, because it is compatible with the psychoanalytic process in many respects, may ultimately serve as a facilitator or adjuvant to therapy. Transcendental meditation is quickly mastered and involves no special beliefs or life-style. Effort or sustained focus is discouraged and spontaneity encouraged. It is similar to free association, but it has no goal or purpose and should be effortless. There is a predominance of alpha-waves and other hypo-metabolic physiological functions.

In many instances there is a reduction in tension and anxiety, and openness to one's feelings. A strong sense of a self, a separateness, and a oneness all appear to develop. Significantly, many addictive and compulsive tendencies seem to be abandoned as a result of meditative practices. These addictions include smoking, drinking, and overeating.

As I view it, its value is based on the freedom that one achieves to explore and examine one's living after the rigid constraints and dictates of the compulsive tendencies are relieved by letting go and allowing one's thoughts to move about freely. In contrast to traditional psychoanalytic approaches, conscious, deliberate efforts to arrive at understanding are avoided, since in the compulsive the very disorder mitigates against this by the techniques of displacement and isolation of affect. The rational elements likewise are avoided since these require willful deliberateness in their problem-oriented focusing. Clearly this is only a prelude to change since enlightenment can only clear the way for newer patterns of living and functioning. Consequently, more tranquility need not be associated with positive change. Change requires doing, not just seeing or experiencing in the abstract.

Not only can meditation be valuable to the patient, it can also benefit the therapist who undoubtedly has numerous compulsive tendencies in his own life-style.

ADDENDUM QUERIES

I

DR. BURTON: You seem to stress the point that the search for psycho-dynamic factors in psychoanalysis and psychoanalytic psychotherapy has been overdone and even, at its worst, leads to projections upon the patient. Do you therefore advocate a primarily ego psychology in which wish fulfillment and the analysis of the unconscious drives play only a minor part?

DR. SALZMAN: The exploration of psychodynamic factors in the resolution of neurotic difficulties is an essential element in the restructuring of one's personality. However, such elucidation is not sufficient to motivate or initiate action which would result in characterological changes. The concepts of wish fulfillment and the analyses of unconscious drives, attitudes, and needs are involved in the psychoanalytic exploration of personality development and psychopathologic formations. They do not occupy a minor part, but an integral part of the process of constructive change of a characterological structure. However, my point is that the therapist must be an active participant and facilitant in the process instead of an objective, anonymous researcher whose task is simply to illuminate. Consequently, I am a strong advocate of a primarily ego psychology which is dependent upon the total comprehension of human behavior as deriving from sources often beyond the individual's awareness.

II

DR. BURTON: Somewhat in common with humanistic/existential thinking you seem to minimize transferential relationships in psychotherapy and stress the interpersonal and intercurrent. You even claim error on the part of therapists in that they may attempt to unconsciously actualize their theoretical bent. What value do you therefore ascribe to the transference, to historical parental models, in your style of treatment?

DR. SALZMAN: One cannot function in any realm of human interaction without acknowledging, comprehending, and utilizing the concepts of transference, historic parental models, and the determining influence of unconscious or out-of-awareness elements in one's existence. The way one utilizes those elements in exploring and elucidating the individual's characterological difficulties or neurotic traits differs among therapists. Transference enables us to understand why an individual responds to another in an interpersonal context in a distorted, excessive, contradictory fashion. The patient's understanding of this distortion allows him or her not only to explain the "strange" or inexplicable attitude, but lays the groundwork for change. It is only by grasping the patient's interpersonal experiencing, introspective and fantasied ruminations, minor or major parapraxes, dreams, and the like that we recognize those distorted items of behavior as growing out of transferential or role-model issues. Thus it is not an either/or, but a utilization of all these concepts that advance our understanding as to why individuals behave the way they do today and how it has grown out of their background and development. The next step is to institute change, which requires techniques and therapeutic concepts over and above those involved in the uncovering processes.

III

DR. BURTON: That insight development which is effective in changing behavior you call emotional insight and then define it as "decisive willfulness" or "committed intention." Can you explain in somewhat greater detail what you mean by these terms?

DR. SALZMAN: I believe that change occurs when an individual recognizes the benefits from altered behavior and is willing to accept the discomforts and uneasiness of moving from familiar, established ways of functioning to newer, untried, and uncertain patterns. However, understanding of an intellectual nature, called intellectual insight, is not enough except in the most trivial or tangential aspects of one's behavior. What is required is a determined conviction of the need for change and a willful determination to attempt it and accept the difficulties along the way. Sometimes this is called emotional insight to indicate that the understanding was accompanied by a profound emotional reaction to the discovery of the insight or an emotional reenactment of the issues involved in the distorted behavior. Rather than "Yes, I see what you mean," it is "My God! I see what I have been doing. I was furious at the time it happened and have always resented, etc., etc. . . . This *must* change!" (accompanied by tears or genuine emotional reaction).

The term "emotional insight," however, did not necessarily subsume any planned or determined program for change.

My point is to stress the therapeutic necessity of adding an additional dimension and impetus to the concept of emotional insight since even such insight may fall short of the persistence and patience required for decisive change. Consequently, the insight process is a preliminary to the more difficult "working through," or "working out," program which needs a determined and committed interest in change. It involves the patient's understanding of the difficulties in changing and accepting the early, inevitable clumsiness and potential failures and disappointments in the process of change. It requires some recognition of the important magic expectation element in neurotic

Albert Bandura

3

Social Learning Perspective on Behavior Change

by ALBERT BANDURA, Ph.D.

Social learning principles can be implemented in many different ways, some of which are more effective than others. The optimal procedures for achieving enduring changes in behavior include induction through modeling, refinement through enactment, and reinforcement through successful use. The treatment approach combining modeling with guided reinforced performance has therefore yielded the most impressive results with diverse psychological conditions. This chapter analyzes the method of participant modeling as applied to the treatment of behavioral deficits and defensive behavior. Let us first consider the principal components.

Modeling

Desired activities are repeatedly modeled, preferably by different models who demonstrate progressively more difficult performances. In competence training, complex patterns of behavior are broken down into the requisite subskills and organized hierarchically to ensure optimal progress. In eliminating inappropriate fears and inhibitions, anxious individuals observe models engaging in threatening activities without experiencing any adverse consequences.

Guided Performance

After the demonstration, individuals are provided with necessary guidance and ample opportunities to enact the modeled behaviors under favorable conditions at each step until they perform them skillfully and spontaneously. Various response induction aids are used whenever needed to assist participants through difficult performances.

Success Experiences

Modeling and guided performance are ideally suited for inducing psychological changes, but the resultant behaviors are unlikely to endure unless they prove effective when put into practice in everyday life. People must therefore experience sufficient success in using what they have learned. This is best achieved by a transfer program in which newly acquired skills are first tried in natural situations likely to produce favorable results, and then extended to more unpredictable and risky circumstances.

In the weakest treatment approaches, those relying upon conversational influences, all three components are typically lacking. Therapists favoring such techniques tend to model a restricted range of conduct, and what they do exemplify most prominently may have limited functional value for those seeking help. In addition, clients are, for the most part, left to their own devices to develop and to try new styles of behavior in their daily lives. Modeling is now increasingly employed, but in many instances its potential is not fully realized because the treatment either fails to provide sufficient practice in the modeled activities or it lacks an adequate transfer program that helps clients become adept in their new conduct under advantageous conditions.

Given appropriate demonstration, guided practice, and success experiences, the multiform method achieves excellent results. Since, in participant modeling, people learn and perfect effective ways of behaving under lifelike conditions, problems of transfer of learning are largely obviated. An additional advantage of this approach is that a broad range of resource people can be enlisted to serve as therapeutic models.

ERADICATING DYSFUNCTIONAL FEARS AND
DEFENSIVE BEHAVIOR

In modifying fearful and defensive behavior, therapists tend to focus their efforts primarily on eliminating emotional arousal. The desensitization approach devised by Wolpe (1) is conducted on the principle of minimization of anxiety arousal. Treatment strategies are therefore keyed to this factor. Aversive stimuli are presented in small doses and promptly withdrawn whenever the clients experience anxiety. Should disturbing emotional reactions be evoked, there are essentially two things the therapist can do: relax the client and reduce the threat value of the aversive scenes. As emotional responses to weaker threats are eliminated, more stressful situations are progressively introduced.

More recently, avoidance behavior has been treated by flooding procedures, which rely upon maximization of anxiety arousal (Gath, 2; Watson and Marks, 3). In this approach, intense anxiety is elicited by prolonged exposure to the most threatening situations. The therapist's main efforts are aimed at inducing and sustaining anxiety at high levels without relief until the reactions are extinguished.

Coupled with the focus on anxiety is a heavy reliance upon symbolic renditions of aversive events. In both desensitization and flooding treatments, emotional responses are typically extinguished to visualized representations of feared situations. Results of numerous laboratory studies reveal that elimination of anxiety to imagined threats improves behavioral functioning. However, there is a notable transfer loss of therapeutic effects from symbolic to real-life threats (Agras, 4; Barlow, Leitenberg, Agras and Wincze, 5). It is not at all uncommon for clients to respond fearfully when confronted with intimidating situations after the imaginal counterparts have been thoroughly neutralized. Such transfer decrements are understandable considering that complete generalization rarely occurs when treated events differ significantly from the natural ones.

The arousal-oriented treatments are based on the assumption that anxiety activates defensive reactions. To eliminate defensive responding it is therefore considered necessary to eradicate its underlying anxiety. This theory, though still widely accepted, has been found wanting (Bandura, 6). Autonomic arousal, which serves as the principal index of anxiety, may facilitate, but is not required for, defensive learning. Maintenance of avoidance responses is even less dependent upon autonomic feedback. The overall evidence indicates that anxiety and defensive behavior are coeffects rather than causally related. Aversive experiences, either of a personal or vicarious sort, create expectations of injury that can activate both fear and defensive conduct. Being coeffects, there is no fixed relationship between arousal and action. Until effective means of securing reality testing. There is nothing more persuasive But after people become adept at self-protective behaviors they perform them in potentially threatening situations without having to be frightened. Should their habitual modes fail, they reexperience heightened arousal until new defensive learning reduces their vulnerability.

The participant modeling approach favors successful performance as the primary vehicle of psychological change. Avoidance of subjectively real but objectively unwarranted threats keeps behavior out of touch with existing conditions of reinforcement. Participant modeling provides a dependable and effective means of securing reality testing. There is nothing more persuasive than the experience of successful action in feared situations.

Persons suffering from intractable inhibitions, of course, are not about to do what they dread. The therapist must therefore arrange the environment in such a way that, despite themselves, the incapacitated clients can perform successfully. This is achieved by enlisting a variety of supportive aids and protective controls. To begin with, the threatening *activities are repeatedly modeled* to show the clients how they can be best performed and that the consequences they fear do not in fact occur. By weakening inhibitions, modeling influences facilitate the use of other performance inducements should they be needed. *Joint performance* with the therapist, who offers physical assistance when required, further enables apprehensive clients to engage in threatening activities that they would not consider doing on their own. Highly demanding or intimidating performances are reduced to *graduated subtasks* of increasing difficulty so that at any given step participants are asked only to do what is clearly within their immediate capabilities. Treatment is conducted in this stepwise fashion until eventually the most difficult activities are performed skillfully and fearlessly.

Another method for overcoming response inhibition is to have the client practice the avoided behavior over *graduated temporal intervals*. As will be shown later, obsessive-compulsives who wash repeatedly to avoid contamination can be led to handle dirty objects without ritualistic washing for manageable short periods, but they would refuse if required from the outset to endure distress over a long time. By gradually extending the time interval, clients perform with equanimity activities that earlier would have produced intolerable distress.

Arrangement of *protective conditions* that reduce the likelihood of feared consequences is a further means of weakening dysfunctional restraints that retard change. Thus, for example, snake phobics are willing to touch snakes, which ordinarily they refuse to do, provided the model holds the snake securely by the head and tail (Bandura, Blanchard, and Ritter, 7); and acrophobics will climb scary heights given the security of the therapist's physical support (Ritter, 8).

Most of the preceding methods attenuate the fear-arousing potential of a threat while keeping it at a high level. Animal phobics, for example, are exposed to scary animals but performance supports and safeguards are temporarily introduced so that participants can do what they previously were too frightened to even contemplate. If such environmental arrangements prove insufficient to induce the desired behavior, incapacitating restraints can be overcome by *reducing the severity* of the threat itself. Weaker threats are presented.

During the early phases of treatment, therapists use whatever supplementary aids are necessary to initiate behavioral changes. As treatment progresses, however, the supportive aids and protective controls are gradually removed until clients function effectively without assistance. The provisional supports undoubtedly attenuate emotional arousal, but performance is not deferred until anxiety reactions have been extinguished. Successful action is considered to be the best eradicator of anxiety.

Accelerating Change through Response Induction Aids

The manner in which provisional induction aids influence the rate of therapeutic progress is revealed in a study by Bandura, Jeffery, and Wright (9). Adult phobics received participant modeling with either a low, moderate, or high number of performance aids. Clients given the same amount of treatment progressed rapidly when therapists had recourse to an array of performance aids, whereas progress was slow and arduous when therapists had only a few induction aids at their disposal. In subsequent assessments, clients who had the benefit of high and moderate induction procedures surpassed their minimally aided counterparts in behavioral improvement, in attitudinal changes, and in reductions in anticipatory fears.

When induction procedures are used to ensure continuous progress, the severity of clients' debilities determines the number of response facilitators that will be required, but not the level of attainment. Given sufficient aid even the severely incapacitated can eventually gain full benefit. These findings indicate that, in the development of powerful treatments, attention might be more profitably directed at the scope of therapists' serviceable skills than at the clients' limiting characteristics.

Generalizing Change through Self-Directed Performance

Social learning theory distinguishes among three basic change processes, namely, the *induction, generalization,* and *maintenance* of behavior (Bandura, 10). Analysis of treatment in terms of these processes provides a more informative basis for evaluating and improving therapeutic methods than do undifferentiated assessments of outcome.

The table below depicts different patterns of effects that might obtain for any given treatment. Pluses and minuses signify successes and failures, respectively. From this perspective, the general issue of therapeutic efficacy is

Processes	Treatment Accomplishments				
	1	2	3	4	5
Induction	—	+	+	+	+
Generalization	—	—	+	—	+
Maintenance	—	—	—	+	+

divided into the more analytic questions of whether a method induces psychological changes, whether the changes generalize across situations and response systems (behavioral, affective, attitudinal), and whether the changes are maintained over time.

Applying this multiprocess analysis, the first treatment shown in the table above fails on all counts. The second induces changes, but they are circumscribed and transitory. This does not necessarily mean that the method is inadequate. Quite the contrary. It may be effective for creating changes, but it requires a supplemental transfer program and proper maintaining conditions. The third treatment produces generalized changes that are short-lived. Here the deficiencies lie in the maintenance component of the approach. The fourth treatment achieves enduring but circumscribed changes, thus requiring supplementary procedures to enhance transfer effects. The fifth, and most powerful treatment, succeeds on all indices—induction, generality, and durability. Just as therapists do not rely upon unplanned influences to initiate psychological changes, generalization and maintenance should not be left to fortuitous circumstances.

Aided participant modeling is a demonstrably powerful way of creating psychological changes. Although the positive effects generalize across both stimuli and responses, there is room for improvement in the amount of transfer achieved (Bandura, Blanchard, and Ritter, 7; Bandura, Jeffery and Wright, 9; Blanchard, 11). When disinhibition is facilitated by extensive supports, clients may attribute their performances to external aids rather than to restored capacity. Generalization may also be reduced by judgments that the probable consequences of feared activities differ under circumstances varying in safeguards. As a result, clients may behave boldly under secure conditions but remain somewhat fearful in less protected situations.

In applications of participant modeling erroneous attributions and discriminations can be minimized by fading the response aids and having clients repeatedly engage in the activities unassisted. Any lingering doubts they may have either about their capabilities or about probable response consequences can be easily dispelled in this manner.

Self-directed performance can enhance the efficacy of participant modeling in several ways. It serves to extinguish residual fears. Observable success disconfirms erroneous attributions concerning the source of the attainments. And it reinforces a sense of personal efficacy in coping with threatening situations. People who feel less vulnerable and expect to succeed in what they do will behave more boldly and persistently than if they harbor self-doubts.

Evidence bearing on these issues is provided in a study of the generality and durability of therapeutic changes achieved through participant modeling as a function of the amount and variety of self-directed performance (Bandura, Jeffery, and Gajdos, 12). Adults whose functioning was adversely affected by snake phobias were matched in triads on strength of phobic behavior and administered aided participant modeling until they completed all the therapeutic tasks. This method achieves terminal performances within a relatively short period, requiring on the average only one hour of treatment time. Clients who received *participant modeling* alone were tested after they successfully performed all the therapeutic tasks. Those assigned to the *self-directed performance* condition spent an additional hour interacting freely by themselves with the same snake (boa constrictor) used in treatment. A third group, that had the benefit of *varied self-directed performance,* spent the additional hour handling not only the familiar boa, but also an unfamiliar king snake markedly different in color and activity level.

Results of this study attest to the therapeutic benefits of a brief period of self-directed performance. It thoroughly extinguished clients' fears and substantially boosted their self-confidence in dealing with snakes under diverse circumstances. It produced similar gains in behavioral functioning. Figure 1 depicts the percent of clients in each of the three treatment conditions who were able to achieve terminal performances with the snake used in treatment and with an unfamiliar corn snake. Those who received participant modeling supplemented with self-directed performance behaved fearlessly toward the treatment snake and showed virtually complete transfer of boldness toward the generalization threat. Most clients who received par-

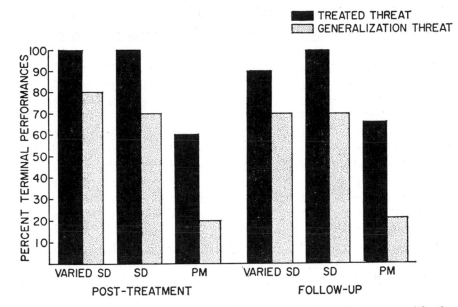

FIGURE 1. Percent of clients who achieved terminal performances with the treatment and generalization snakes depending upon whether they received participant modeling alone or supplemented with either similar or varied self-directed performance.

ticipant modeling alone likewise behaved fearlessly toward the treatment snake, but they displayed transfer losses in coping with the generalization threat.

The absence of differences between the two self-directed conditions indicates that it is the experience of independent success rather than the diversity of extinction experiences that accounts for the therapeutic benefits. These, and other findings (Bandura, Blanchard, and Ritter, 7), corroborate the view that positive transfer involves at least two intervening processes. The first includes generalization of fear extinction on the basis of stimulus similarity. The greater the likeness between treated and subsequently encountered events, the greater the transfer. The second process relies upon reinforcement of personal capability through success. By instilling success expectations, action-oriented treatments can enhance transfer of boldness toward dissimilar threats. Durable and generalized changes are thus best achieved by using aided participant modeling to restore formerly inhibited behavior followed by self-directed performance to extinguish residual fears and to reinforce personal efficacy.

Comparative Effectiveness of Participant Modeling

The comparative effectiveness of participant modeling for producing behavioral, affective, and attitudinal changes was initially evaluated in an elaborate design by Bandura, Blanchard, and Ritter (7). The participants in this project were adolescents and adults who suffered from snake phobias that, in most cases, adversely affected their lives or restricted their occupational functioning in troublesome ways.

One group received the standard form of desensitization by pairing relaxation with snake scenes of increasing aversiveness. A second group participated in a self-administered symbolic modeling treatment in which they observed a film depicting children and adults engaging in progressively more intimidating interactions with a snake. They reviewed threatening scenes repeatedly under self-induced relaxation until the depicted events were thoroughly neutralized.

The third group of phobics received the treatment combining live modeling with guided performance. This earlier version of the method, however, did not include the full array of induction aids or the self-directed component. After observing the therapist interact closely with the snake, clients were aided through other induction procedures to perform progressively more frightening responses. At each step the therapist himself performed the activities fearlessly and gradually led clients into touching, stroking, and holding the midsection of the snake's body with gloved and then bare hands for increasing periods. After clients could touch the snake under these secure conditions, anxieties about contact with the snake's head area and entwining tail were similarly extinguished. The therapist again performed the responses fearlessly and then they both performed them jointly. As clients became more courageous the therapist gradually reduced his level of participation and control over the snake until eventually clients were able to tolerate the squirming snake in their laps without assistance, to let the snake loose in the room and retrieve it, and to let it crawl freely over their bodies.

As depicted graphically in Figure 2, nontreated controls remained unalterably fearful. Symbolic modeling and desensitization produced substantial reductions in phobic behavior, while participant modeling proved to be unusually powerful, eliminating phobic behavior with substantial transfer after approximately two hours of treatment. These procedures not only eliminated defensive behavior of long standing but also altered attitudes and reduced fears in other areas of functioning. The extent of the collateral changes was roughly proportional to the potency of the treatments.

In order to demonstrate that in cases achieving only partial improvement

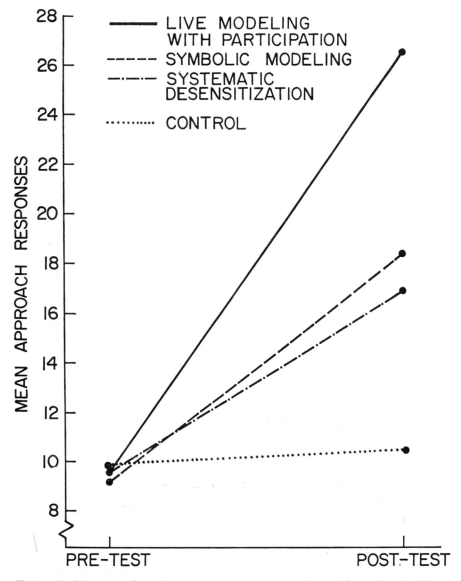

FIGURE 2. Mean number of approach responses performed by individuals before and after receiving different forms of treatment, and by nontreated controls (Bandura, Blanchard, and Ritter, 7).

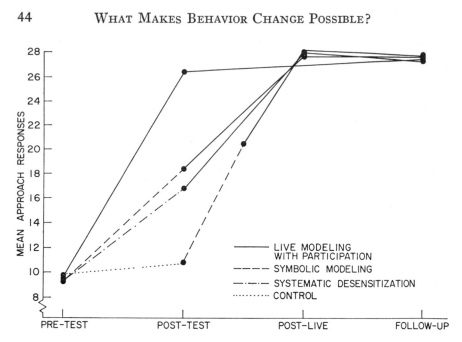

FIGURE 3. Mean number of approach responses performed by individuals before and after (post-test) receiving different treatments. Controls were subsequently given symbolic modeling without relaxation. All individuals in the
desensitization, symbolic modeling, and treated control conditions who failed
to perform the terminal tasks then received the treatment combining live
modeling with guided participation (post-live). Approach behavior was measured again in a follow-up study conducted one month later (Bandura, Blanchard, and Ritter, 7).

the major deficits reside in the method rather than in the client, those who
failed to attain maximum performances, including the controls, were subsequently administered the participant modeling treatment. Phobic behavior
was thoroughly extinguished in all of these cases within a brief period regardless of their age, sex, anxiety proneness, and severity of avoidance behavior
(Figure 3).

Other Clinical Applications

Hardy (13) has evolved a highly promising method for treating agoraphobia, a condition that has been highly refractory to change. The treatment
essentially involves joint performance of activities during graduated massive
exposure to feared situations until the clients' anxieties and phobic behavior
are eliminated. Clients accompany the therapist into the avoided situations

over a period of several days. The longer they are exposed to the aversive events, the more dramatic is the experience that what they dread does not happen. Since a variety of things may produce fear, the specific performance tasks differ from case to case. Transportation phobics ride trains and buses; those who dread automobile travel drive freeways and mountain roads; those with flying phobias board planes during servicing and then make regular flights with the therapist to neighboring places; clients who fear bridges repeatedly cross bridges; those who shun supermarkets or department stores accompany the therapist on shopping trips; acrophobics ride elevators and climb scary heights; claustrophobics visit enclosed places, while those who become apprehensive in crowds walk through busy city streets; clients who dread public speaking deliver simulated talks; and obsequious individuals who invite maltreatment through their passivity are given self-assertive training.

As the clients' anxieties diminish, the therapist reduces his support and guided participation. He sends the clients on gradually longer missions alone while he stands by and waits for them. Later, solo excursions are arranged for clients to carry out on their own. They are asked to perform previously threatening activities that bring them to specific locations from which they call after completing their missions. To reinforce and extend therapeutic changes, alumni functions are scheduled. Ex-phobics regularly engage as a group in activities they formerly dreaded. They convene social gatherings, automobile jaunts, mountain excursions, shopping trips, and theatre outings.

Hardy reports that of 100 severe phobics treated by this method, 80 percent achieve extinction of their phobic behavior after several days of intensive treatment. Of these cases, approximately half require some supplementary treatment in the form of additional performance assignments or modification of family interactions to ensure continued improvement.

Participant modeling with ritual prevention has been recently applied to chronic obsessive-compulsives who remained incapacitated for many years by their incessant rituals (Rachman, Hodgson, and Marks, 14; Rachman, Hodgson, and Marzillier, 15). Most dreaded contamination and spent countless hours each day scrubbing themselves and their households. Their lives were further constricted by avoidance of situations in which the feared contamination might occur. Others suffered from ruminations about safety that prompted repetitious checking rituals. Not only did they make life miserable for themselves, they also imposed intolerable restrictions on others. Neither insight therapies, nor drug treatment, nor relaxation training brought them any relief.

Rachman, Marks, and Hodgson (16) compared the relative efficacy of modeling, in which clients perform increasingly disturbing behavior demonstrated by the therapist, and flooding, in which they are encouraged to perform the most disturbing activities from the outset without prior modeling. Both methods proved equally successful. In some comparisons, however, the treatment that has produced the best results combines modeling with performance of the most uncomfortable activities and prevention of rituals. Therapists first demonstrate the repugnant behavior. Clients are then asked to engage in the same activities and to refrain from performing their compulsive rituals for increasing periods of time. They are also asked to resist rituals between sessions. Assessments based on a variety of measures reveal enduring reductions in compulsive behavior. Success rates of different versions of the multiform approach indicate that ritual prevention, a method originally reported by Meyer (17), plays a vital role in the extinction process.

The following report provides a detailed description of how the procedures and the transfer program were implemented in treating a 38-year-old woman whose fear of contamination ruled the household.

She had a 20-year history of compulsive handwashing and other rituals centering round a fear of tuberculosis infection. Her rituals had worsened since the birth of her son two years previously. She was unable to feed him for fear of contaminating him and the husband had to spend hours daily boiling bottles and feeding utensils to feed the child. The child was not allowed to play outside his playpen and was confined to it most of the day. The patient's mother, who lived nearby, had never been allowed to play with the child for fear of infecting him and indeed had never held him. The home was not swept because dust was thought to contain TB germs so that a thick layer of dust accumulated in most of the house. On returning home from work, if dirty, the husband sometimes had to strip naked outside the home before he was allowed to enter and don clean clothes inside.

The patient was admitted to hospital and did not improve during three weeks of control relaxation treatment. She was then given exposure *in vivo* with modeling (e.g., she watched her therapist rub a biscuit on the floor and then eat it and was asked to follow suit). She was asked to rub her hands in dirt and to hold stained slides of bacteria without subsequent washing. The patient was most cooperative and rapidly lost all her rituals. However, it was feared that improvement would not transfer from hospital to her home 200 miles away, so the husband and son were brought to London to lodge near the hospital. The son was brought into the ward, and the patient was required to feed him after touching the food on the floor first. The husband was asked to participate. In the ward the patient soon lost her rituals concerning her son. At discharge the precaution was taken of sending a nursing sister with her and the family on the train home. As soon as the patient went on the train further rituals appeared such as avoidance of touching handles on doors and windows. The nurse prevented this avoidance on the train. On arrival at home the nurse ensured that the patient swept the house so that it was 'contaminated.' The husband had to be taught to desist from cleaning rituals his wife had engrained in him over the years. After 36 hours the nurse left the family, but regular contact was maintained by telephone and by further home visits. The patient remained free of most of her rituals over two years' follow-up. . . . (Marks, 19, p. 424).

The authors suggest that supervised home treatment, in which clients perform disturbing activities but refrain from compulsive rituals, can augment the therapeutic benefits. Since compulsives tend to impose burdensome restrictions on those around them, family members can expedite changes by withdrawing reinforcement of compulsive behavior and substituting rewarding activities as clients become freed of their time-consuming rituals.

Durability of Therapeutic Changes

If defensive behavior can be removed by corrective experiences, is it likely to be easily reinstated by a few adverse incidents? Not necessarily. There are several factors that favor persistence of changes long after treatment has been discontinued. Removal of unwarranted anxieties alleviates distress and enables people to participate in rewarding activities they formerly avoided. A compulsive who spent inordinate amounts of time scrubbing and avoiding contact with "dirty" objects, for example, was able to hold a job, to go swimming and to walk on grass for the first time in many years after his compulsive rituals were eliminated (Rachman, Hodgson, and Marzillier, 15). Reinstated behaviors are thus supported by favorable conditions of reinforcement without requiring a special maintenance program. Moreover, reinforcement of personal competence often improves functioning in nontreated areas (Bandura, Blanchard and Ritter, 7; Bandura, Jeffery and Gajdos, 12). The benefits of restored competencies can counteract the effects of occasional distress.

The capacity of adverse events to reinstate fears and defensive behavior depends upon the total pattern of experience in which they occur. Occasional mishaps among many positive or neutral experiences have little negative effect (Rescorla, 18). Favorable experiences curtail inappropriate generalization of fear as well as neutralize aversive events (Hoffman, 20). Therefore, an effective way to reduce people's vulnerability to mishaps is to have them perform extensively the formerly threatening activities under advantageous conditions after treatment has been terminated. A dog-phobic who, following treatment, has had many benign interactions with different dogs will not be much affected by a few unpleasant encounters. At most, such experiences will establish discriminative avoidance of realistic threats, which has adaptive value. By contrast, for persons who have had limited contact with previously feared objects after treatment, a few unfavorable experiences are likely to reestablish defensive behavior that generalizes inappropriately.

The oft-repeated dictum that maintenance of change depends upon environmental contingencies conveys the impression that behavior is at the mercy of fortuitous circumstances. This belief has retarded research on how supplemental experiences can be arranged in the immediate post-treatment phase to reduce vulnerability to defensive relearning. Findings based on studies of self-directed performance and rate of reconditioning under varying experiences indicate that sustaining therapeutic benefits can be achieved at the point at which treatments are usually terminated. Among procedures that eliminate avoidance behavior, some leave subjects more susceptible to aversive relearning than others (Polin, 21). The therapeutic value of a given treatment should therefore be judged in terms of vulnerability to defensive relearning as well as success in the initial elimination of defensiveness.

If disinhibited behavior frequently results in punishing consequences, then therapeutic changes will be short-lived unless the adverse social conditions are modified. No psychological methods exist that can render an organism insensitive to the consequences of its actions. Nor would imperviousness be desirable, were it possible, because individuals who remained unaffected by the consequences of their behavior would function in a grossly maladaptive way.

It might also be noted in passing that persons whose unwarranted fears have been extinguished do not behave recklessly. Elimination of an automobile phobia does not dispose unimpeded clients to saunter heedlessly into onrushing traffic on busy thoroughfares. Rather, stereotyped avoidance is replaced by flexibly adaptive behavior that is cognitively controlled by judgments of probable consequences resulting from prospective actions.

PARTICIPANT MODELING AND BEHAVIOR DEFICITS

Participant modeling figures even more prominently in the modification of problems arising from behavioral deficits. Fears can be overcome without the aid of models, but competence learning would be exceedingly laborious, not to mention perilous, if it proceeded solely on the basis of trial-and-error experiences without the guidance of models who exemplify the patterns. For this reason, most competencies, whether they involve social or vocational skills, are acquired and perfected by the combined influence of instructive example and reinforced practice. In the treatment program devised by Lovaas (22), behavioral repertoires are established in autistic children, who display little functional behavior, through reinforced modeling. Complex skills are gradually elaborated by modeling activities in small steps of increasing difficulty and by rewarding matching performances. Manual prompting and other induction aids are used when children fail to respond. The provisional supports are then gradually withdrawn to promote natural responsiveness.

Although all children improve during the course of treatment, their subsequent level of functioning, as assessed one to four years later, varies depending upon environmental circumstances (Lovaas, Koegel, Simmons, and Stevens, 23). Those whose parents are trained to conduct the treatment at home maintain their gains or improve further. By contrast, those who are discharged to a state hospital, for lack of a better alternative, abandon most of what they had learned and revert to their former autistic conduct. The skills they had acquired are not lost, however. Brief reinstatement of the therapeutic conditions restores the original gains in the institutionalized children.

Development of assertiveness provides another illustration of clinical application of participant modeling (Bandura, 24). People who are unable to behave assertively, a not uncommon problem, are likely to suffer considerable mistreatment. In teaching people how to behave affirmatively, assertive styles of conduct must be modeled for them. Depending upon individual needs, these might include such things as complaining about inadequate service, returning purchases, refusing arbitrary or unreasonable demands, responding to unfair criticism, making rightful claims to goods and facilities, defending one's position in the face of opposition, and in other ways standing up for one's rights.

Clients then practice by behaving assertively and receiving feedback that rewards their successes and corrects their errors. Fear of revealing one's inadequacies creates initial reluctance to engage in behavior rehearsals even under simulated conditions. There are several ways in which such resistances can be reduced. First, participant modeling is structured in a nonthreatening manner aimed at fostering new competencies and confidence rather than exposing deficiencies. Concern over poor performance is further decreased by noting that in all successful skill learning initial efforts are awkward; hence, it is progressive improvement with practice rather than instant proficiency that is expected. In an optimistic, forward-looking program clients more readily accept and profit from their mistakes. Prior modeling provides a helpful guide for new styles of behavior. Participants therefore do not have to grope around for appropriate responses, which reduces needless failure experiences. In addition, assertion tasks are graduated, beginning with relatively easy performances. As apprehensions are diminished through repeated practice, progressively more difficult encounters demanding more assertive actions are introduced.

In a comprehensive treatment, clients must also learn when and where assertiveness is appropriate. And they need positive reinforcement for asserting themselves in their daily interactions. Transfer of assertiveness from the training situation to the natural environment should be an integral part of the treatment rather than being left to chance. A transfer program might proceed as follows: After the clients have perfected their social skills and overcome their timidity they accompany the therapist on excursions into the field where they witness further demonstrations of how to handle situations calling for assertive action. The therapist then reduces his or her level of participation to background support and guidance as the clients try their skills in situations likely to produce favorable results. By careful selection of encounters of increasing difficulty the assertion requirements can be adjusted to the clients' momentary capabilities to bolster their sense of confidence. As a final step in the program, clients would be assigned a series of assertive performance tasks to carry out on their own.

COMPONENT ANALYSIS OF PARTICIPANT MODELING

The influence of some of the factors contained in participant modeling has been examined singly, especially in modifying defensive behavior. Observation of bold models can, by itself, produce substantial reductions in phobic behavior both in children and in adults (Bandura, 6). Similarly, repeated performance of frightening activities without untoward effects can eventually eliminate fears and inhibitions (Bandura, 10).

Some efforts have been made to assess the relative contribution of the constituent influences in the multiform procedure. The proportional weights furnished by a given study must be accepted with reservation, however, because only a single value of each component is assessed, whereas other versions of the same factor may have different efficacy. In a study comparing the outcomes associated with various component combinations, Blanchard (26) found that modeling accounted for approximately 60 percent of behavior change, and 80 percent of changes in attitude and fear arousal; guided participation contributed the remaining increment. Factual information about what is feared, on the other hand, had no significant effect on any of the measures.

The guided participation component of the treatment under discussion can be further analyzed into separable elements. When clients are assisted in performing the desired behavior the protection afforded by the model may facilitate changes by reducing behavioral restraints. As participants engage in the feared activities part of the changes are undoubtedly attributable to feedback. In evaluating the contribution of protective guidance and response performance, Ritter (8) reports that modeling accompanied by physically guided performance decreased acrophobic behavior more effectively than modeling with verbally guided enactment, which, in turn, was superior to a brief demonstration alone.

Numerous studies have also been conducted on the relative contribution of modeling, performance, and reinforcement influences to development of new modes of behavior or to facilitation of responsiveness that is unencumbered by restraints (Bandura, 25). The evidence generally shows that modeling plays a paramount role in the acquisition of novel and complex behavior, whereas learning is difficult to achieve through response consequences alone. In enhancing conduct that is already learned, modeling serves a secondary function, while response inducements and reinforcing consequences emerge as prominent determinants. Regardless of whether deficit or defensiveness is the problem of concern, modeling supplemented with guided performance and reinforcing consequences is the most powerful means of effecting psychological change.

MECHANISM OF OPERATION

According to social learning theory, changes in defensive behavior, regardless of the methods used to achieve them, derive from a common cognitive mechanism (Bandura, 27, 28). Psychological procedures alter the level and strength of self-efficacy. The strength of convictions in one's own effectiveness determines whether coping behavior will be attempted to begin with. People fear and avoid threatening situations they believe exceed their abilities to cope with, whereas they behave affirmatively when they judge themselves capable of handling successfully situations that would otherwise intimidate them.

Perceived self-efficacy not only reduces anticipatory fears and inhibitions but, through expectations of eventual success, affects coping efforts once they are initiated. Efficacy expectations determine how much effort people will expend, and how long they will persist in the face of obstacles and aversive experiences. The stronger the perceived self-efficacy, the more active the efforts. Those who persist in activities that are subjectively threatening but are in fact relatively safe will gain, through their actions, corrective experiences that further reinforce their sense of mastery and thereby eventually eliminate their fears and defensive behavior. Those who cease their coping efforts prematurely will retain their self-debilitating expectations and fears for a long time.

Expectations of personal efficacy are based on several sources of information. *Performance accomplishments* provide the most dependable source of self-efficacy because they are based on one's own personal experiences. Successes raise mastery expectations; repeated failures lower them. Once established, enhanced self-efficacy tends to generalize to other situations in which performance was previously self-debilitated by preoccupation with personal inadequacies (Bandura, Jeffery, and Gajdos, 12).

Many expectations are derived from *vicarious experience*. Seeing others perform threatening activities without adverse consequences can create expectations in observers that they too will improve if they intensify and persist in their efforts. Indeed, a number of modeling variables likely to affect mastery expectations have been shown to enhance the disinhibiting power of modeling procedures.

In attempts to influence human behavior, verbal persuasion is widely used because of its ease and ready availability. People are led through suggestion, verbal interpretation, or exhortation into believing they can cope successfully with what has overwhelmed in the past. The impact of verbal persuasion on perceived self-efficacy will vary depending upon the credibility of the persuaders, their prestige, trustworthiness, expertness, and assuredness. Expectations of personal efficacy induced vicariously or through verbal persuasion are likely to be weaker than those arising from one's own accomplishments because they do not provide an authentic experiential base for them.

Emotional arousal can affect perceived self-efficacy in coping with threatening situations. People rely partly upon their state of physiological arousal in judging their anxiety and vulnerability to stress. Because high arousal usually debilitates performance, individuals are more likely to expect success when they are not beset by aversive arousal than if they are tense, shaking, and viscerally agitated. Fear reactions generate further fear of impending threatening situations through anticipatory self-arousal. By conjuring up fear-provoking thoughts, individuals can rouse themselves to elevated levels of anxiety that far exceed the actual threats. In the social learning analysis, treatments aimed at reducing physiological arousal improve performance because they raise expectations of personal efficacy rather than by eliminating a drive that instigates defensive behavior.

Empirical tests of this theory (Bandura, Adams, & Beyer, 29) confirm that the more authentic the experiental sources, the greater are the changes in self-efficacy. Thus, for example, treatments based on performance accomplishments through the aid of participant modeling produce higher, stronger, and more generalized expectations of personal efficacy than do vicarious experiences alone. Behavioral changes correspond closely to level of self-efficacy regardless of the mode of treatment. The stronger the mastery expectations, the higher the likelihood that clients will cope successfully with threatening situations. The theory also accounts for variations in behavioral change produced by the same method of treatment.

ADDENDUM QUERIES

I

DR. BURTON: In your social learning approach to personality change the model seems of central importance, if not critical. Can you discuss the qualities of a model in greater depth?

DR. BANDURA: The social learning approach favors successful performance as the primary vehicle of psychological change. Without the aid of models, the change process would be more protracted, stressful, and unpredictable in outcome. If models are to be of much help, they must exemplify the types of competencies and coping skills that will have functional value for their clients in their everyday life. In addition, models must be adept at using the diverse performance aids in ways that ensure clients will experience continuous progress and develop a strong sense of personal efficacy.

Findings of studies we have conducted show that, after gaining proficiency in implementing social learning procedures, models who differ widely in personality characteristics achieve equally good results. Weak methods place heavy demands on personal qualities of therapists to sustain clients' interest in treatment. When clients have the benefit of powerful methods, progress toward desired goals provides a strong and reliable source of motivation.

II

DR. BURTON: Isn't modeling at least as old as Sigmund Freud, who had a great deal to say about identification and introjection, and about transference in general?

DR. BANDURA: Freud, the ancient Greeks, and their predecessors all assigned a prominent role to modeling processes in human development. As regards the psychological analyses of the phenomenon, psychoanalytic and social learning theories differ in several important respects. From the psycho-analytic perspective, modeling is a global unitary process that is regulated by a few determinants, namely, nurturance withdrawal and anxiety arising from Oedipal conflicts.

Social learning theory distinguishes between observational learning and performance of modeled patterns of behavior. Learning by observation is governed by four component processes; these include attentional, cognitive, ideomotor, and motivational processes. This conceptual scheme not only posits a different type of learning process, but a more complex set of determinants of whether observationally learned patterns will be expressed in action. A detailed analysis of the phenomena subsumed under the term identification is provided in the following publication:

> Bandura, A. Social-learning theory of identificatory processes. In D. A. Goslin, ed. *Handbook of Socialization Theory and Research.* Rand McNally, 1969, pp. 213-262.

III

DR. BURTON: You put great stress upon "success" as a reinforcer. But you fail to mention "failure" which can be common in these conditions. Does "failure" dynamically block "success"?

DR. BANDURA: Failures impede rather than block change, especially if they occur during early phases of treatment. After a strong sense of personal efficacy is developed through repeated success, occasional failures will have little negative impact. Indeed, in later phases of treatment occasional failures that are overcome by determined effort strengthen coping behavior. The effects of failures therefore partly depend upon the timing and the total pattern of experiences in which they occur.

IV

DR. BURTON: Lasting personality change following social learning seems highly dependent upon a reinforcing environment, and perhaps the continuous presence of a favorable model: sort of a "good mother." Can we say that the results of a successful psychoanalytic psychotherapy are more stable and independent of the environment than would be true for social learning?

DR. BANDURA: Not if one respects evidence.

This question raises the basic issue concerning the doctrine of determinism upon which different theories are based. On conceptualizing causal processes, radical behaviorists subscribe to environmental determinism. According to this view, behavior is controlled by the environment. Maintenance of personality change therefore depends upon the existence of reinforcing environmental conditions.

Humanistically oriented theorists tend to favor personal determinism. People presumably determine their environment through their perceptions and actions. The ample evidence of environmental determination of behavior disputes the extreme form of this view of causality.

Social learning theory conceives of regulatory processes in terms of reciprocal determinism. The environment is not an autonomous force that automatically shapes and controls behavior. Environments have causes as do behaviors. It is true that behavior is regulated by environmental contingencies, but the contingencies are partly of a person's own making. Thus, for example, people who acquire, through social learning therapy, effective coping skills will create different environments for themselves than they did when they were less adept. After passive individuals master assertive skills that enable them to exercise some control over their environment, they are no longer dependent upon the continued presence of assertive models, nor are they adversely affected by seeing ineffectual models. Once competencies have been transmitted, the "good mother" can be retired without loss. Success in managing events that affect one's well-being provides the most powerful reinforcement for behavior. To the oft-repeated dictum, "change the contingencies and you change behavior," social learning theory adds the reciprocal side, "change behavior and you change the contingencies."

The notion that behavior is regulated by its consequences is often interpreted to mean that actions are at the mercy of situational influences. External consequences, influential as they often are, are not the sole determinants of human behavior. Most behavior is under self-reinforcement control. In this process, people adopt certain standards of conduct and respond to their own actions in self-reinforcing or self-punishing ways. As a result behavior is regulated by the interplay of self-generated and external sources of influence. Because of their symbolizing and self-reactive capacities people are less dependent upon immediate external supports for their behavior.

V

DR. BURTON: Would you allow that social learning is only one way among many to behavior change, or would you insist that it is the method *par excellence* or even the sole way—at least for the phobias?

DR. BANDURA: I shall resist the temptation to deliver a commercial on the relative efficacy of social learning approaches and brand X. I would prefer to rest the case on objective outcome data.

REFERENCES

1. WOLPE, J.: *The Practice of Behavior Therapy.* New York: Pergamon Press, 1969.
2. GATH, D. H.: Implosion therapy (flooding) for phobic patients: Results of a controlled trial. Unpublished manuscript, Oxford University, 1973.
3. WATSON, J. P., and MARKS, I. M.: Relevant and irrelevant fear in flooding: A cross-over study of phobic patients. *Behavior Therapy,* 1971, 2, 275-293.
4. AGRAS, W. S.: Transfer during systematic desensitization therapy. *Behavior Research and Therapy,* 1967, 5, 193-199.
5. BARLOW, D. H., LEITENBERG, H., AGRAS, W. S., and WINCZE, J. P.: The transfer gap in systematic desensitization: An analogue study. *Behavior Research and Therapy,* 1969, 7, 191-196.
6. BANDURA, A.: Psychotherapy Based upon Modeling Principles. In Bergin, A. E., and Garfield, S. L. (Eds.), *Handbook of Psychotherapy and Behavior Change.* New York: Wiley, 1971, pp. 653-708.
7. BANDURA, A., BLANCHARD, E. B., and RITTER, B.: The relative efficacy of desensitization and modeling approaches for inducing behavioral, affective, and attitudinal changes. *J. Personality and Social Psychol.,* 1969, 13, 173-199.
8. RITTER, B.: The use of contact desensitization, demonstration-plus-participation, and demonstration alone in the treatment of acrophobia. *Behavior Research and Therapy,* 1969, 7, 157-164.
9. BANDURA, A., JEFFERY, R. W., and WRIGHT, C. L.: Efficacy of participant modeling as a function of response induction aids. *J. Abn. Psychol.,* 1974, 83, 56-64.
10. BANDURA, A.: *Principles of Behavior Modification.* New York: Holt, Rinehart & Winston, 1969.
11. BLANCHARD, E. B.: The generalization of vicarious extinction effects. *Behavior Research and Therapy,* 1971, 8, 323-330.
12. BANDURA, A., JEFFERY, R. W., and GAJDOS, E.: Generalizing change through self-directed performance. *Behavior Research and Therapy,* 1975, 13, 141-152.
13. HARDY, A. B.: Exposure therapy as a treatment for agoraphobia and anxiety. Unpublished manuscript, Palo Alto, California, 1969.
14. RACHMAN, S., HODGSON, R., and MARK, I. M.: The treatment of chronic obsessive-compulsive neurosis. *Behavior Research and Therapy,* 1971, 9, 237-247.
15. RACHMAN, S., HODGSON, R., and MARZILLIER, J.: Treatment of an obsessional compulsive disorder by modeling. *Behavior Research and Therapy,* 1970, 8, 385-392.
16. RACHMAN, S., MARKS, I. M., and HODGSON, R.: The treatment of obsessive-compulsive neurotics by modeling and flooding *in vivo. Behavior Research and Therapy,* 1973, 11, 463-471.
17. MEYER, V.: Modification of expectations in cases with obsessional rituals. *Behavior Research and Therapy,* 1966, 4, 273-280.
18. RESCORLA, R. A.: Pavlovian conditional inhibition. *Psychol. Bull.,* 1969, 72, 77-94.

19. MARKS, I. M.: New approaches to the treatment of obsessive-compulsive disorders. *J. Nerv. Ment. Dis.*, 1973, 156, 420-426.
20. HOFFMAN, H. S.: Stimulus Factors in Conditioned Supression. In Campbell, B. A. and Church, R. M. (Eds.), *Punishment and Aversive Behavior.* New York: Appleton-Century-Crofts, 1969, pp. 185-234.
21. POLIN, A. T.: The effects of flooding and physical suppression as extinction techniques on an anxiety motivated avoidance locomotor response. *J. Psychol.*, 1959, 47, 235-245.
22. LOVAAS, O. I.: A Behavior Therapy Approach to the Treatment of Childhood Schizophrenia. In Hill, J. P. (Ed.), *Minnesota Symposia on Child Psychology*, Vol. 1. Minneapolis: U. of Minnesota Press, 1967, pp. 108-159.
23. LOVAAS, O. I., KOEGEL, R., SIMMONS, J. Q., and STEVENS, J.: Some generalization and follow-up measures on autistic children in behavior therapy. *J. Applied Behavior Anal.*, 1973, 6, 131-166.
24. BANDURA, A.: *Aggression: A Social Learning Analysis.* Englewood Cliffs, N. J.: Prentice-Hall, 1973.
25. BANDURA, A. (Ed.): *Psychological Modeling: Conflicting Theories.* Chicago: Aldine-Atherton, 1971.
26. BLANCHARD, E. B.: The relative contributions of modeling, information influences, and physical contact in the extinction of phobic behavior. *J. of Abn. Psychol.*, 1970, 76, 55-61.
27. BANDURA, A.: *Social Learning Theory.* Englewood Cliffs, N.J.: Prentice-Hall, 1976a.
28. BANDURA, A.: Divergent trends in behavioral change: towards a unifying theory. Unpublished manuscript, Stanford University, 1976b.
29. BANDURA, A., ADAMS, N. E., and BEYER, J.: A common mechanism mediating behavioral change. Unpublished manuscript, Stanford University, 1976.

Joseph Wolpe

4

Conditioning Is the Basis of All Psychotherapeutic Change

by JOSEPH WOLPE, M.D.

The general goal of psychotherapy is to change, and if possible eliminate, learned habit patterns that are unadaptive and to replace them with adaptive ones. As is clear from the other chapters of this book, there are many ways of setting about to accomplish this kind of task; and it is well known that almost all therapists can record substantial numbers of successes, especially in treating the commonest category of unadaptive learned habits—the neuroses. It will be argued in this chapter that the distinctive procedures employed to treat neuroses by therapists other than behavior therapists rarely have much to do with successful outcomes, that such outcomes usually depend on a process that often occurs inadvertently in all kinds of psychotherapeutic interviews, and that this process is a mode of conditioning—conditioned inhibition based on reciprocal inhibition (Wolpe, 1, 2, 3). Behavior therapists, by contrast, not only profit from this inadvertently occurring reciprocal inhibition, but also make extensive deliberate use of it, as well as of other retraining procedures such as contingencies of reinforcement (e.g., Ullmann and Krasner, 4).

Since in behavioristic parlance it is customary to use the words "conditioning" and "learning" synonymously, it might be wondered why I prefer in the title of this chapter to use the less widely accepted term. The answer is that the word "learning" is used by people of many orientations and in a variety of different senses; while the word "conditioning" refers quite precisely to the establishment or disestablishment of stimulus-response relationships.

COGNITIVE AND OTHER HABITS

Habits are conveniently subdivided according to response modality—autonomic, cognitive, or motor; though most habits actually involve all three modalities. When a previously unrelated stimulus and response repeatedly occur in conjunction, and it is afterwards found that the stimulus reliably elicits the response, a habit can be said to have been established by learning. This is true no matter in what modality the response lies. There is one nervous system, and it is reasonable to believe that the physiological mechanism of learning is essentially the same for all the modalities—whether it is a phrase or a doctrine that is being learned, or a reflex response like salivation.

The last point needs to be more explicitly made, because the idea is widespread that cognitive learning involves different processes from those applying to "lower" levels of the organism. Many of my co-contributors write as if they believe that cognitive events belong to a domain that is distinct from the bodily. Ryle (5) called this presumed domain "the ghost in the machine." He showed that its separation from the body is due to a "radical category mistake"—the mistake of regarding different aspects of the same thing as different entities. An example of this is the case of the foreigner who goes to a football game between two teams: he see the 11 men on each team, then asks, "Where is the team?"—not comprehending that in the particular context the men are the team. How the "ghost in the machine" is a category mistake clearly emerges in the following passage:

". . . When a person talks aloud, ties knots or sculpts . . . he is bodily active and he is mentally active, but he is not being synchronously active in two different 'places' or with two different 'engines.' There is the one activity, but it is one susceptible of and requiring more than one kind of explanatory description" (Ryle, 5, pp. 50-51).

Expanding on Ryle's demonstration of the organic unity that underlies all the functions of human beings, Taylor (6) showed in substantive detail how physiological events and experience are related. He showed how a person's conscious life is an emergent of complex learned intercompensating integrations of proprioceptive with other sensory inputs. On the basis of studies of the long-term effects on visual perception of the constant wearing of distorting prisms, Taylor solved some of the fundamental problems that have baffled men for centuries—one of which is the problem of perceptual constancy. Visual perception develops in the young child on the basis of the manner in which its incursions into the physical world either reinforce or correct, by sensory feedback, the information from visual stimulation. One of the results of a multitude of such experiences is the establishment of perceptual constancy—our remarkable ability to perceive an object, e.g., a kettle, as the same despite the different visual inputs it delivers from different angles and distances. The intercompensating integrations mentioned above make this possible (and at the same time provide the simultaneous readiness for action towards all objects in the perceptual field—a characteristic of perceptual fields).

Thus, not only particular cognitive habits, but the very existence of cognition is based on learning. That values and philosophies are habits, no less than fears or grimaces, is evident from the fact that they are restated again and again by the person who holds them, each time he or she is presented with a relevant social stimulus.

In the *formation* of habits, there is abundant evidence that the mechanism of reinforcement operates in all three modalities. Each time a stimulus-response sequence is followed by "reward," the strength of the habit increases, until an asymptote is reached. The relevance of reinforcement in the establishment of motor and autonomic habits has been repeatedly documented since the time of Pavlov (7), and more extensive and precise studies of autonomic habit formation have appeared in recent years (e.g., Kimmel, 8; Miller and Di Cara, 9). It has been found that conditioning of the "second-signaling system," which includes words, images, and ideas, obeys the same laws as the formation of "primary" conditioned responses (Pavlov, 10; Razran, 11). For example, Cautela (12) has shown that the probability of a motor response can be increased by having the subject imagine a reinforcing state of affairs after *imagining* the response. There are, of course, numerous studies of the operant control of verbal behavior (e.g., Greenspoon, 13).

In many of the foregoing studies, the reinforcing agent has been social approval, sometimes as simple as the experimenter uttering "Uh-huh." Social reinforcement has, not surprisingly, proved to be a potent therapeutic agent.

It plays a part in almost all psychotherapy, in ways that are usually unnoticed by both patient and therapist, but that have been precisely demonstrated in behavioral studies, again and again. For example, Ayllon and Haughton (14) showed how psychotic talk could be increased or decreased at will according to whether demonstrating an active interest in the patient's verbalizations followed psychotic or normal talk. The fact that the source of reinforcement lies in the behavior of other people, and is often subtle and difficult to define, makes no fundamental difference to the way the learning process operates within the subject.

Important as is the reinforcement of new behavior in many cases who come to the psychotherapist's office, the central problem in the commonest of cases —the neuroses—is the *overcoming of unadaptive anxiety response habits.* There are many neuroses in which anxiety is immediately prominent; and in most of the others its central role becomes apparent from the behavior analysis (Wolpe, 2, p. 22 ff). For example, though anxiety is not often a presenting complaint in stuttering, most cases of stuttering are shown by behavior analysis to be based on anxiety that is evoked in specifiable social contexts; and the stuttering can almost always be overcome or markedly improved by deconditioning the anxiety, without applying any treatment to the speech disturbance as such—though this does call for attention in certain cases. There are a few neurotic syndromes in which anxiety is not an integral component—notably classical hysteria with *la belle indifférence* (see Wolpe, 1, p. 85). As we shall see, it is likely that reciprocal inhibition, which occurs in a large variety of ways, underlies practically every instance of the overcoming of unadaptive anxiety response habits.

RECIPROCAL INHIBITION AND ITS ROLE IN BREAKING HABITS

On the matter of breaking habits, everybody is familiar with experimental extinction—the progressive diminution in the strength of a response that is repeatedly elicited without reinforcement. The best-known explanation of extinction is that it is due to conditioned inhibition that develops on the basis of reactive inhibition—a fatigue-associated inhibition of response (Hull, 15). Another explanation is that non-reward leads to frustration responses which compete with the original response (e.g., Gleitman, Nachmias, and Neisser, 16)—a form of reciprocal inhibition. Whether or not extinction is based on competition between response systems, reciprocal inhibition is an enormously important mechanism for the breaking of habits.

Sherrington (17) was the first explicitly to recognize the phenomenon of reciprocal inhibition. He noted that the reflex excitation of muscles automatically involves the inhibition of their antagonists. For example, percussion of the patellar tendon leads both to reflex excitation of the extensors of the knee and to inhibition of the flexors. Conversely, excitation of the flexors is accompanied by inhibition of the extensors. Reciprocal excitation and inhibition are found in every modality of nervous function and at all levels of neural integration. In the words of Wendt (18), ". . . Anything an animal may be doing at the moment, be it sleeping, playing, groaning, vocalizing . . . is reciprocally related to anything else it would otherwise have been doing at the same moment. . . ." We are unable to say, or even to think, of a word without simultaneously inhibiting the formulation of all other words. Our laughter is inhibited by sadness or anxiety, and may, in turn, inhibit them. The findings of laboratory research on the autonomic nervous system (Gellhorn, 19) confirm our emotional experience that reciprocal inhibition complements almost every excitation.

The reciprocal coordination of inhibitions and excitations has the profound consequence for learning that when a stimulus is being conditioned to a response, it is at the same time being conditioned to the inhibition of any other response already elicitable by that stimulus (Pavlov, 7; Hilgard & Marquis, 20). If, for example, an animal has developed a right-turning habit in an alley because that response has been repeatedly followed by food, the habit will extinguish if food is no longer delivered; but will do so more rapidly if left-turning is now rewarded. With each actual left turn, there is an inhibition of the tendency to turn right, which inhibition leads the old habit to undergo conditioned inhibition when the new one is reinforced. *Reciprocal interactions apply equally to the breaking of cognitive habits.* Osgood (21) recognized that retroactive inhibition, on which ordinary forgetting depends, is an instance of conditioned inhibition based on reciprocal inhibition. Even though Osgood's subject matter was nonsense syllables, it can scarcely be doubted that in the same nervous system the process of elimination of complex cognitive response habits is fundamentally the same.

RECIPROCAL INHIBITION IN BEHAVIOR THERAPY

The distinguishing feature of behavior therapy is that all of its formal techniques are based on experimentally established paradigms. The experimental paradigm for reciprocal inhibition therapy was derived from observations on the treatment of experimental neuroses—habits of severe anxiety induced by shocking an animal in a small cage, habits as strangely persistent as the neuroses of man. So severe is the anxiety conditioned to the experimental environment that it inhibits the neurotic animal from eating there even if it is starving. But the animal will eat in a place remotely similar to that in which it was shocked, a place where the anxiety is relatively weak; and repeated helpings of food will diminish this anxiety to zero, since the act of eating reciprocally inhibits the weak anxiety. Environments increasingly resembling the experimental environment can then be similarly treated in ascending rank order, until finally even the experimental cage where the shocks were once delivered is deprived of its ability to elicit any anxiety.

The foregoing paradigm has been applied in many ways (Wolpe, 2) to the treatment of human neuroses. Among the many counteranxiety responses in current use, the commonest are relaxation, assertive, and sexual responses. Deep muscle relaxation has autonomic accompaniments that are the opposite of those of anxiety (Jacobson, 22; Paul, 23). Jacobson, the originator of deep muscle relaxation, taught his patients to be as relaxed as possible at all times, including in disturbing situations. To the extent that patients can achieve this, they weaken their anxiety response habits. In the now widely-used technique of systematic desensitization (Wolpe, 2, 24), anxiety-evoking situations are presented to the imagination of the deeply relaxed patient in rank order of their capacity to disturb, each image being repeated until it totally fails to evoke anxiety. The real stimuli correspondingly lose their power to evoke anxiety.

Assertive training, the overt expression of spontaneous and appropriate feelings *other than anxiety,* is used especially to treat the anxiety underlying timidity. The patient is encouraged and coached in the verbal expression, in interpersonal situations, of customarily inhibited feelings such as anger or affection. Each expressive act, by reciprocally inhibiting anxiety to some extent, weakens the anxiety-response habit.

Sexual responses are mainly used for overcoming anxiety responses that have been conditioned to sexual situations. Since penile erection is subserved by the parasympathetic division of the autonomic nervous system, it tends to be reciprocally inhibited by the sympathetic manifestations of anxiety. The behavior therapist enables the parasympathetically dominated sexual arousal to inhibit the anxiety by regulating the patient's sexual approaches so that the level of anxiety is always kept low.

While the reciprocal inhibition paradigm is most often applied to anxiety response habits, it is also used to treat unadaptive motor and cognitive habits. For example, by reinforcing a school-avoiding child for leaving home, his habits of staying at home was eliminated (Ayllon, Smith, and Rogers, 25). Similarly, when a person terrified by attacks of dizziness that he interpreted

matically evoked when and only when the stimulus conditions to which it is the learned response occur; and it will in turn automatically evoke *its* learned consequents. What Bandura is suggesting sounds perilously like a renascence of the ghost in the machine.

As noted above, nonbehavioristic psychotherapists can expect about half of their neurotic patients to recover or improve markedly. Since the level of good results is unaffected by their widely varying procedures, one must conclude that there is a common therapeutic factor that works in like measure for all of them, and that their distinctive procedures have very little to do with the outcomes. Though the reality of this common factor is beyond doubt, it has not yet received much objective study, especially psychophysiological study. What we now know about it is a step or two removed from what direct observation might tell us. Truax and Carkhuff (34) found that there is some correlation between favorable outcomes and the therapist's "accurate empathy, nonpossessive warmth and genuineness." The more the patient feels a responsive warmth towards the therapist, the more likely to be inhibited are those of his anxieties that are evoked during the interview. I have frequently noted that patients who improve in the course of a few sessions *before* any specific procedures have started are those in whom a high degree of positive feeling is aroused by the therapeutic situation. Such emotions are the probable reason for most of the therapeutic effects that are common to therapeutic transactions of all kinds.

Only evidence of favorable results significantly in excess of the common baseline can justify a claim for the therapeutic potency of the distinctive procedures of a mode of psychotherapy. At present, behavior therapy alone has convincingly provided such evidence (see above). However, there are indications (Meichenbaum, 35) that the interventions of rational emotive therapy (Ellis, 36) also have therapeutic effects superior to the common baseline; and, not surprisingly, this seems related to the extent that these interventions are similar to those of behavior therapy in the areas of cognitive and emotional change. (For a discussion, see Wolpe, 37.)

It is not to be inferred from the foregoing that nonbehavioristic therapists do not change the thinking and attitudes of their patients by their deliberate interventions. It would be strange if close communion with an authoritative figure failed to do this. The point is that the direction of the induced changes, frequently dictated by empirically unsubstantiated theorizing, is not usually towards overcoming the emotional difficulties that are the core of neurotic patients' suffering. If the direction were relevant, this would be reflected in superior outcomes.

As long as we interact with the world, we learn. Experience constantly modifies us, and frequently towards enhancing our adaptiveness. It is not only in the offices of therapists that psychotherapeutic changes take place. Many neuroses recover without psychotherapy of any kind, especially in children (e.g., Jersild and Holmes, 38; MacFarlane, Allen, and Honzik, 39). In such cases it is often possible to elicit a history of the occurrence of emotional events that could have provided reciprocal inhibition of anxiety.

I know that many people will not take kindly to the proposition that the changes they obtain in their patients are all due to "conditioning," a label evocative of images of salivating dogs and bar-pressing rats. However, as stated at the start of this chapter, "conditioning" equals "learning." To respond with an image of flame to the word "fire" is based on the same kind of "chaining" in the nervous system as to respond with salivation to a bell. If conditioning is the basis of therapeutic change, it is likely that all therapists would have better control of change within their own frameworks, if, like the behavior therapists, they made use of available knowledge of the learning process and the factors that influence it. To those who deny that learning is the mechanism on which therapeutic change depends, the question must be put: If it is not learning, what is it?

ADDENDUM QUERIES

I

DR. BURTON: In your chapter you give a central position to the concepts of adaptation and habit, as though in our modern world they were still the ideal motifs of existence. But some of the best adapted people I have seen, and those without troublesome habits in a clinical sense, were also by self-admission restless and unhappy and unfulfilled. Does reciprocal inhibition properly account for such observations?

DR. WOLPE: I did not, in my chapter, refer to adaptation and habit as "motifs of existence." It is an incontestable fact that we form habits, of which, fortunately, most are adaptive, but some not. The changing of concepts in "our modern world" cannot spirit habits out of existence.

Apart from actual personal deprivation and humanitarian *Weltschmerz,* if a person is unhappy and unfulfilled, how can he be described as "well-adapted to his world"? When I do behavior analyses of cases that "dynamic" psychotherapists have previously evaluated as being "without troublesome habits," I usually discover that such habits do in fact exist. The reason for the difference is that behavior therapists make a searching study of each patient's day-to-day reactions, while "dynamic" therapists do not.

In some cases, unhappiness is the result of learning *deficits*, and then positive conditioning procedures are indicated. Patients with neuroses or with learning deficits must be differentiated from so-called "borderline cases," who are actually pseudo-neurotic schizophrenics. That they are really schizophrenic is shown either immediately by such special means as pupillography studies (Rubin, 40), or later by their clinical evolution. Since schizophrenia is a biological condition (see Wolpe, 41), psychotherapeutic interventions are of little avail except in those cases in whom unadaptive learned habits are a secondary feature (e.g. Ayllon, 42).

II

DR. BURTON: You claim that psychotherapy is successful only insofar as it covertly employs conditioning and reciprocal inhibition principles which, of course, the psychotherapist fails to recognize at the time. But I have heard it said on the other hand that behavioral therapies are covertly successful only insofar as the human aspects of the person modifier come through in his dialogue with the patient. How would you reconcile such philosophical antinomy?

DR. WOLPE: I agree that the "human aspects of the person modifier," the therapist, have an emotional impact on the patient and believe that this accounts for the marked beneficial effects obtained in about 50% of patients in the general range of therapies. The fact that about 90% of patients who receive behavior therapy improve markedly indicates that its specific procedures have therapeutic effects additional to the common effects that all therapies share. It seems reasonable to attribute the superior results to the procedures of behavior therapy; or would you contend that behavior therapy has twice the "human" impact of other therapies? In practice, one of the most satisfying aspects of behavior therapy is observing change in a target area in quantitative correlation with the interventions directed to that area.

III

DR. BURTON: Ryle's conception of the "ghost in the machine" makes a needed scientific correction in the tendency to divide mind from body. But I have yet to see an acceptable description by behavioral therapists of the psychosomatic clinical response where the will or mind, as in a case of anorexia nervosa I am treating, leads the patient to the point of a seeming willful death. Is there no room in your approach for an overriding heroic or death impulse which at rare moments takes over the body's biology?

DR. WOLPE: The seemingly willful death-seeking activity that is sometimes noted does not pose for the behaviorist the difficulties you suggest. It is quite possible for a person to be conditioned to the performance of self-injurious and even self-destructive behavior, and there are experimental models for this (e.g. Wolpe, 1, p. 53). The "masochistic" behavior persists be-cause its harmful consequences are too delayed to have impact on the stimulus-response bonds of the crucial behavior. Smoking and overeating behaviors provide commonplace examples.

Apart from such habitual behaviors, if life is filled with unbearable suffer-ing, death will often seem a natural solution. Suicide is then where motiva-tion leads. The same applies to self-sacrifice for a "cause."

IV

DR. BURTON: In my own chapter in this book I make the statement that anxiety is no longer the modern psychopathological problem and those clin-icans who insist on treating or modifying it as the central focus are clinging to an outmoded psychiatry. More and more patients, I may say almost all of them, have neuroses of existence and meaning in which anxiety is only a minor part. The human condition is anxiety itself. Would you still feel the same about reciprocal inhibition if you had to give up the controlling aspects of anxiety?

DR. WOLPE: I do not know the grounds for your contention that "anxiety is no longer the modern psychopathological problem." I agree that anxiety is "the human condition," but in that context it is adaptive anxiety, related to the real dangers that menace us. As stated in my answer to Ques-tion I, a thorough behavior analysis almost invariably reveals that unadaptive anxiety is central to neuroses even though the patient may have arrived with an "existential" problem. Clinging to our strategy of overcoming unadaptive anxiety response habits is justified by the superior results across the neurotic board obtained by effective anxiety-eliminating methods (Wolpe, 1; Paul, 43). In certain cases the predominant emotional tone is some kind of reactive depression, but even then, what we seem to have is really a variant of anxiety—as psychophysiological studies show (Wolpe, 1). However, despite its dominant importance, anxiety is not the basis of all problems based on learning. Behavior analysis is designed to lead to the retraining appropriate to the particular problem.

V

DR. BURTON: Classical approaches to behavior change, including behavioral modification, are now under severe strain from secular and nonmedical interests. What do you see in the future for the styles of healing now prevalent in our society? Is that society itself shifting in its basic premises away from disease as you and I know it?

DR. WOLPE: The widening popular disenchantment with "classical approaches to behavior change" seems to me to be related to widening awareness of their relative ineffectiveness, coupled often with their long duration and high expense. The criticisms of behavior therapy have a different basis. They are largely the result of misinformation, much of which comes from the films *The Manchurian Candidate* and *The Clockwork Orange,* which misrepresent behavioral methods and portray the behavior therapist as controlling and callous. Considerable damage to the image of behavior therapy has also been done by the misuse of aversion therapy in prisons by inadequately trained people. Good training in behavior therapy is still scarce.

I do not know if it is true about society "shifting in its basic premises away from disease as you and I know it," and even if it is, it should not influence the thinking of scientists. The mechanisms of the unadaptive behavior that is the basis of the suffering that interests us are not functionally related to the views of "society."

REFERENCES

1. WOLPE, J.: *Psychotherapy by Reciprocal Inhibition.* Stanford: Stanford U. Press, 1958.
2. WOLPE, J.: *The Practice of Behavior Therapy* (2nd ed.). New York: Pergamon Press, 1973.
3. WOLPE, J.: *Theme and Variations: A Behavioral Therapy Case Book.* New York: Pergamon Press, 1976.
4. ULLMANN, L. P., and KRASNER, L.: *A Psychological Approach to Abnormal Behavior.* Englewood Cliffs, N.J.: Prentice-Hall, 1969.
5. RYLE, G.: *The Concept of Mind.* London: Hutchinson, 1949.
6. TAYLOR, J. G.: *The Behavioral Basis of Perception.* New Haven: Yale U. Press, 1962.
7. PAVLOV, I. P.: *Conditioned Reflexes.* (Trans. by G. V. Anrep.) New York: Liveright, 1927.
8. KIMMEL, H. D.: Instrumental conditioning of autonomically mediated behavior. *Psychol. Bull.,* 1967, 67, 337.
9. MILLER, N. E., and DI CARA, L. V.: Instrumental learning of vasomotor

responses by rats: learning to respond differentially in the two ears. *Science*, 1968, 159, 1485.

10. PAVLOV, I. P.: *Selected Works*. Moscow: Foreign Language Publishing House, 1955.
11. RAZRAN, G.: *Mind in Evolution: An East-West Synthesis of Learned Behavior and Cognition*. Boston: Houghton Mifflin, 1971.
12. CAUTELA, J.: Covert reinforcement. *Behav. Ther.*, 1970, 1, 33.
13. GREENSPOON, J.: Verbal conditioning and clinical psychology. In Bachrach, A. J., (Ed.), *Experimental Foundations of Clinical Psychology*. New York: Basic Books, 1962.
14. AYLLON, T., and HAUGHTON, E.: Control of the behavior of schizophrenic patients by food. *J. Exp. Anal. Behav.*, 1962, 5, 343.
15. HULL, C. L.: *Principles of Behavior*. New York: Appleton-Century, 1943.
16. GLEITMAN, H., NACHMIAS, J., and NEISSER, U.: The S-R reinforcement theory of extinction. *Psychol. Rev.*, 1954, 61, 23.
17. SHERRINGTON, C. S.: *The Integrative Action of The Nervous System*. New Haven: Yale U. Press, 1906.
18. WENDT, G. R.: An interpretation of inhibition of conditioned reflexes as competition between reaction systems. *Psychol. Rev.*, 1936, 43, 258.
19. GELLHORN, E.: *Principles of Autonomic-Somatic Integrations*. Minneapolis: U. of Minnessota Press, 1967.
20. HILGARD, E. R., and MARQUIS, D. G.: Acquisition, extinction, and detention of conditioned lid responses to light in dogs. *J. Comp. Psychol.*, 1935, 19, 29.
21. OSGOOD, C. E.: Meaningful similarity and interference in learning. *J. Exp. Psychol.*, 1946, 38, 132.
22. JACOBSON, E.: *Progressive Relaxation*. Chicago: U. of Chicago Press, 1938.
23. PAUL, G. L.: Physiological effects of relaxation training and hypnotic suggestion. *J. Abnorm. Psychol.*, 1969, 74, 425.
24. WOLPE, J.: Reciprocal inhibition as the main basis of psychotherapeutic effects. *Arch. Neur. Psychiat.*, 1954, 72, 205.
25. AYLLON, T., SMITH, D., and ROGERS, M.: Behavioral management of school phobia. *J. Behav. Ther. Exp. Psychiat.*, 1970, 1, 125.
26. KNIGHT, R. P.: Evaluation of the results of psychoanalytic therapy. *Amer. J. Psychiat.*, 1941, 98, 434.
27. EYSENCK, H. J.: Learning theory and behavioral therapy. *J. Ment. Sci.*, 1959, 105, 61.
28. WOLPE, J.: The prognosis in unpsychoanalyzed recovery from neurosis. *Amer. J. Psychiat.*, 1961, 117, 35.
29. SLOANE, R. B., et al.: Short-term analytically oriented psychotherapy versus behavior therapy. *Amer. J. Psychiat.*, 1975, 132, 373.
30. BURTON, A.: *The Patient and the Therapist*. Sacramento: Hamilton Psyche Press, 1975.
31. BERLYNE, D. E.: *Conflict, Arousal and Curiosity*. New York: McGraw-Hill, 1960.
32. BERLYNE, D. E.: *Aesthetics and Psychobiology*. New York: Appleton-Century-Crofts, 1971.
33. BANDURA, A.: Behavior theory and the models of man. *Amer. Psychol.*, 1974, 29, 859.
34. TRUAX, C. B., and CARKHUFF, R. R.: *Toward Effective Counseling and Psychotherapy*. Chicago: Aldine, 1962.
35. MEICHENBAUM, D. H.: Self Instructional Methods. In Kanfer, F. H., and

Goldstein, A. P. (Eds.), *Helping People Change*. New York: Pergamon Press, 1975.

36. ELLIS, A.: *Reason and Emotion in Psychotherapy*. New York: Lyle Stuart, 1962.

37. WOLPE, J.: Behavior therapy and its malcontents: II. Multimodal eclecticism, cognitive exclusivism and exposure empiricism. *J. Behav. Ther. Exp. Psychiat.*, (in press).

38. JERSILD, A. T., and HOLMES, F. B.: Methods of overcoming children's fears. *J. Psychol.*, 1935, 1, 75.

39. MACFARLANE, J. M., ALLEN, L., and HONZIK, M.: *A Developmental Study of the Behavior Problems of Normal Children*. Berkeley: U. of California Press, 1954.

40. RUBIN, L. S.: Pupillary reflexes as objective indices of autonomic dysfunction in the differential diagnosis of schizophrenia and neurotic behavior, *J. Behav. Ther. Exp. Psychiat.*, 1970, 185.

41. WOLPE, J.: The discontinuity of neurosis and schizophrenia. *Behav. Res. Ther.*, 1970, 8, 179.

42. AYLLON, T.: The practical modification of deviant behavior through operant techniques. *Comparative Psychopathology*, 1967, 240.

43. PAUL, G. L.: Outcome of systematic desensitization. II. Controlled investigations of individual treatment, technique variations, and current status. In C. M. Franks (ed.), *Behavior Therapy: Appraisal and Status*, New York. McGraw-Hill, 1969.

Jerome D. Frank

5

Restoration of Morale and Behavior Change

by JEROME D. FRANK, M.D.

INTRODUCTION

A person's morale markedly affects all aspects of his or her functioning. Demoralization is accompanied by apathy and other dysphoric emotions, low self-confidence, and lack of initiative. The thesis of this chapter is that loss of morale is a necessary, and often a sufficient, reason for a person to seek psychotherapy, and that, therefore, a major function of all schools of psychotherapy is to restore morale. Successfully treated psychiatric patients, whatever their symptoms, regain their zest, self-confidence, and initiative.

The field of psychotherapy seems more chaotic today than ever. For many decades psychoanalysis and its modifications dominated the therapeutic scene, and conflicting claims were confined to proponents of variants of dyadic interview therapy growing out of the theories of Freud, his disciples, and his opponents. Then group therapies entered the picture, also dominated for a long while by psychoanalytic thinking, although many were influenced from the beginning by the theories and methods of Moreno. Recently, group methods have exploded into a kaleidoscopic and still expanding spectrum that defies any simple classification. Concomitant with this development, psychologists have introduced a growing repertory of behavior therapies based on the work of Pavlov and Skinner. Finally, abreaction in various guises is being vigorously promulgated by new therapeutic schools. The explosion of psychotherapeutic methods has been accompanied by a proliferation of healers with all types of training, or even none at all.

Research efforts to clarify the principles and modes of effectiveness of some of these approaches have also expanded but, as always, they have not begun to keep pace with the innovations of practitioners, all of whom are no less insistent than their forebears that their particular method surpasses all others.

The bulk of the clinical and research literature on psychotherapy has focused on detailed analysis of different methods or on the relative effectiveness of their outcomes. In both cases the center of attention has been features which distinguish the particular therapy under study from other therapies. Features which are shared by all therapies have been relatively neglected, since little glory derives from showing that the particular method one has mastered with so much effort may be indistinguishable from other methods in its effects.

My own preoccupation has been an effort to isolate, in the psychotherapeutic relationship and the context of the therapeutic situation common to all forms of psychotherapy, those features which may contribute to their success. Once the part played by these shared features has been identified, we may be better able to determine the differential effects of different techniques with different types of patients. This question may be first approached from historical and cultural perspectives.

A brief historical overview of Western psychotherapy since Freud highlights two points. The first is that the dominant psychotherapeutic approach of an era reflects the cultural attitudes of its time and place; the second, that the same techniques keep recurring under different guises, suggesting that, despite their superficial differences, they all may be variations of a few underlying themes.

Freud developed psychoanalysis, the fountainhead of Western psychotherapy, within a competitive culture which placed a high value on individual integrity and achievement. Its ideal person would be an inner-directed one, guided by high moral principles, striving for success, and resistant to social pressures that might lead to violating principles and ideals. Such a person would be fearful of too much openness. For one thing, it might give others knowledge of one's weaknesses, which they could then exploit to their own advantage. Furthermore, if one allowed oneself to become too concerned with the welfare of others, this might hamper one in achieving one's own goals, which necessarily involved hindering others from reaching theirs.

Success depended on maintenance of a righteous, self-confident facade, which required denying or suppressing inner impulses that, if admitted to consciousness, could create self-doubts. Freud postulated that self-deception and repression of unacceptable impulses and feelings were major sources of psychic distress, disturbances in intimate relationships, and poor work performance.

The family structure of Freud's society was authoritarian, and intimacies were confined within the family circle, but openness was unilateral, not mutual. Children were expected to have no secrets from their parents, but not the reverse.

A form of therapy modeled on this pattern of child-parent relationship, that aimed to help patients become more accepting of their hidden feelings so that they could drop their facade and thus become more successful in both love and work, and one, furthermore, that was conducted in the strictest privacy, would be fully in keeping with Freud's cultural setting as a member of a Western industrial society. (For completeness, one would have to add, as Bakan (1) has shown, that much of psychoanalysis also derives from Freud's Jewish heritage, but that would lead too far afield.)

Psychoanalysis also accorded well with the nineteenth-century faith in science as holding the solution to all problems, a belief which Freud, as a medical scientist, fully shared. He insisted that the information about the patient's past revealed by psychoanalysis had the status of scientific fact because it was elicited by an impartial, trained observer, the psychoanalyst. We now know, of course, that this was to some extent erroneous, because the patient's productions are so strongly influenced by the analyst's expectations. But the scientific method is not the only path to truth, and there is no doubt that, with all its sources of error, psychoanalysis has greatly increased our knowledge of human nature.

PSYCHOTHERAPY AND THE AMERICAN CULTURE

As a cultural offshoot of Europe, with more stress on competition and a greater faith in science, America was highly sympathetic to both the goals and scientific pretensions of psychoanalysis, so that it was readily transplanted to American soil.

Two distinctive features of American society, however, contributed to new developments—its pragmatism and its gregariousness. The pragmatic outlook is action-oriented, therefore sympathetic to attempts to modify feelings and behavior by direct assault rather than through the leisurely, roundabout way of free association, leading to the still mushrooming growth of so-called behavior therapies. Like psychoanalysts, proponents of these methods claim them to be scientific, often with some justification. Behavioral phenomena can be counted and measured, so goals and outcomes of behavior therapy can be stated with far more specificity and objectivity than those of psychoanalysis. But it must be remembered that, despite the name, many behavior therapies rely heavily on the patient's imagery and fantasies, which cannot be measured directly, and their theoretical underpinning seldom is as rigorous as it appears. I concur with those behavior therapists who maintain that the central contribution of behavior therapy is methodological (2). All forms force therapists to make specific predictions and modify their own behavior in accordance with the outcome. This encourages flexibility of approach, permits the formulation of questions that are amenable to precise research, and makes possible experimentation with a single case, leading to real gains in knowledge of the limitations of behavior therapies as well as the sources and nature of their therapeutic effects.

The second relevant feature of American culture, as contrasted with European, is its greater gregariousness, which may be related to the popularity of group therapies. Gregariousness has always existed along with, and to some extent has ameliorated, the American stress on competitiveness and individualism. The isolation and hardships of frontier life, for example, were periodically relieved by religious revival meetings, characterized by intense emotional outbursts, public confession of sins and, for many participants, intimate sexual activities.

American sociability, however, too often is the servant of competitiveness rather than a genuine expression of liking for others. While nineteenth-century Western man had to maintain a mask of righteousness, his modern counterpart, at least in America, feels impelled to wear one of affability, behind which may lurk considerable hostility and suspiciousness. To get ahead, one must be likable; so the need to be liked has replaced the need to appear righteous as an important source of inner conflicts.

With the increasing complexity and interdependence of modern life, a value system holding that the good of society as a whole emerges from the free competition of its members in pursuit of their individual goals is proving to be increasingly inappropriate. As a result, more and more Americans question the goal of worldly success and seek instead, among other aims, enhanced capacity to give and receive genuine affection, often through participation in groups.

Another cultural contributor to the popularity of group therapies, itself probably a response to the hunger for greater intimacy, has been the emphasis in mass media, including especially TV and radio, on revelation of intimate details of personal lives. An extreme manifestation of this trend has been the broadcasting of live group therapy sessions.

Privacy, in some circles, has become almost a vice. To quote Dr. Ross Speck, the originator of network therapy: "Many individuals who would not consider going to private or individual treatment are quite willing to discuss their problems in the presence of members of the immediate social field" (3).

Network therapy involves inclusion not only of the patient's family but of neighbors and friends, and Speck points out its similarity to tribal healing rituals in which the extended family, and usually other members of the tribe, join to heal a sick member by participating with him in time- and energy-consuming rites that stress mutual confession and mutual aid, conducted by a healer and his acolytes (4).

The newer group approaches, however, reflect more than a hunger for honest, intimate relationships to combat the sense of isolation behind false affability. They also may be responses to other stressful characteristics of American society. These include bureaucratization with its fragmentation of persons into roles, a sense of dislocation from the past because of rapid changes in the conditions of life, and the widespread suspicion that Science may be a false god luring mankind to destruction.

The result of these forces is a weakening of the sense of identity coupled with pessimism about the future. To combat identity diffusion and despair, many are turning away from the outer world to explore the inner one, through two apparently opposed routes. One involves immersion in the present and search for revelations about oneself through highly charged emotional interactions with others. This route is typified by marathon groups, about which one commentator has remarked: "The frenetic liaison comes to stand as the acme of interpersonal achievement" (5). The other path involves detachment from the outer world altogether and looking inward, with or without the help of drugs, for new experiences that will give meaning to life. This is the age-old route of mysticism. It, too, be it noted, often involves participation in group exercises, as in Zen.

These activities still embody the nineteenth-century therapeutic goal of discarding one's mask, in the hope of gaining greater self-awareness and more rewarding relationships with others. They have abandoned the goal of enhanced ability to work, which is no longer essential in an affluent society and which plays into competitiveness and careerism. With this, however, often goes also a rejection of the values of self-discipline and long-term responsibility for the welfare of others. (Members of marathon groups may be deeply involved in each other's troubles during the life of the group, but not afterwards.)

The efforts of encounter groups to stir their members emotionally is paralleled in dyadic therapy by the revival of interest in emotional abreaction. The arousal of intense emotions has always characterized healing rituals in a religious context and played a large part in Mesmerism, the precursor of modern psychotherapy. Its rediscovery by Freud is not as easily traced to cultural influences as are some other features of psychoanalysis, but seems to have been the result of his ability to grasp the therapeutic potential of an unexpected occurrence in therapy. Initially he viewed it as the essence of psychoanalysis. Then it gradually receded in interest, except for a few hypnotherapists (6) and mavericks like Wilhelm Reich. Possibly this was because it ran counter to the values of a science-worshiping culture. Nothing is less appealing to the scientific mentality than uncontrolled emotion. In any case, the same disenchantment with science, coupled with the search for intense experiences, that has fostered encounter groups may also be related to the sudden reemergence of therapies devoted to producing abreactions, among them implosion therapy (7), primal scream therapy (8), and reevaluation counseling (9).

In short, in psychotherapy, as in so many other fields, it appears that there is nothing new under the sun. Innovations that at first glance seem revolutionary turn out to be modified applications of newly rediscovered principles of learning and healing. Behavior therapies systematically use modeling, reward and punishment, and extinguishing of fears through repeated exposure to the feared situation in the absence of reinforcement. New methods of facilitating emotional release, and thereby resolving pathologic feeling states, are variants of abreaction, while most, if not all, of the novel methods of encounter groups are ingenious applications of well-established principles of learning, of abreaction, and of the utilization of group pressures to change the attitudes of group members. Some of these techniques will probably become permanent additions to the psychotherapeutic armamentarium, but their apparent novelty should not be permitted to obscure their shared features or their historical origins.

The facts that the prevalent method of psychotherapy in any given era is strongly influenced by the prevailing cultural standards and values, that no one method has succeeded in eliminating its rivals, and that many forms of contemporary treatment embody rediscoveries of age-old healing principles, all suggest that features common to all forms of treatment contribute importantly to their effectiveness.

Beneath the din of conflicting claims and the kaleidoscopic panorama of activities, it is possible to discern certain characteristics which all share. That these may account for more of their effectiveness than the features which distinguish them is suggested by the persistent difficulty in demonstrating significant differences in their outcome (10, 11). All therapies attract a loyal following, and I have yet to hear of a school that has disbanded because it became convinced of the superiority of its rivals.

To be sure, behavioral modification techniques seem more effective than open-ended interview therapies in relieving certain circumscribed phobias (12, 13) and encouraging obese patients to maintain their diets (14), but these account for a very small percentage of persons seen by psychotherapists (15). Many schools of therapy claim to reconstruct the patient's personality, although recent data from the Menninger psychotherapy research study suggest that this rarely occurs, even after extensive psychoanalysis (16). It probably happens occasionally, but its frequency is probably no greater than that of religious conversions, which have similar effects.

THE DEMORALIZATION HYPOTHESIS

In any case, the least common denominator of all therapies, and the one on which their claims to success must depend, is their ability to combat a destructive state of mind which characterizes persons who seek psychotherapy, whatever their specific symptoms. This state may be termed demoralization. It results from persistent failure to cope with internally or externally induced stresses which the patients and those close to them expect them to handle (17, 18). Its characteristic features, not all of which need be present in any one person, are feelings of helplessness, hopelessness, impotence, and isolation. They feel rejected by others because of failure to meet their expectations. Insofar as they feel their symptoms or problems to be unique— a surprisingly common attitude—these expectations contribute to their sense of alienation. Since the meaning of life derives from the ties of individuals with persons whose values they share, alienation may contribute to a sense of meaninglessness.

Of course, patients seldom present themselves to therapists with the complaint that they are demoralized; rather, they seek relief for an enormous variety of symptoms and behavior disorders, and both patients and therapists see relief or modification of these as the prime goal of therapy. However, surveys of general populations (19), confirmed by clinical experience, indicate that only a small proportion of persons with psychopathological symptoms come to therapy. That is, persons do not seek psychotherapy *solely* because of their symptoms. Apparently they must also be demoralized.

The demoralization hypothesis is consistent with many other observations, of which only a few can be mentioned here. These include the facts that, as already mentioned, with rare exceptions no good evidence exists that one therapy produces better results than another, and that, whatever the form of therapy, improved patients show a greater sense of inner control, independence, or self-determination (20). Moreover, the most significant prognostic sign, regardless of the form of treatment, is the patient's ego-strength, a term referring to ability to cope and to form rewarding personal relationships (21, 22).

The demoralization hypothesis also accounts for the growing recognition that persons with similar problems can be very helpful to each other, as witnessed by the mushrooming of peer self-help psychotherapy groups (23, 24). A fellow sufferer who has encountered and conquered the same problem is especially effective in restoring hope and combating isolation, particularly if the condition carries a social stigma, as does drug addiction, alcoholism, epilepsy, or obesity.

The most frequent symptoms of patients in psychotherapy—anxiety and depression—are direct expressions of demoralization. The causes of other symptoms, such as disorders of thinking or mood swings, may be primarily genetic, while still others, such as conversion reactions or obsessions, may be combinations of oblique expressions of inner conflicts and disguised efforts to control the attitudes of others. Whatever their sources, however, symptoms interact in two ways with demoralization. First, the more demoralized people are, the more severe their symptoms tend to be. Thus patients troubled with obsessions find them becoming worse when they are depressed. Secondly, by crippling people and intensifying their sense of alienation, symptoms reduce their coping capacity, thereby aggravating their feelings of failure.

In any case, the claims for success of all therapies must rest on their ability to overcome the patient's sense of isolation, helplessness, and hopelessness.

SHARED FEATURES OF PSYCHOTHERAPIES
THAT COMBAT DEMORALIZATION

Let us now look more closely at features of all therapies that contribute to these ends. These are:

1. An intense, emotionally charged, confiding *relationship* with a helping

person, often with the participation of a group. In this relationship patients let themselves become dependent on the therapist for help, because of their confidence in the therapist's competence and goodwill. The patients' dependence on the therapist is reinforced by their knowledge of the therapist's training, the setting of treatment (see below), and the congruence of the therapist's approach with the patients' expectations. While these attributes determine the therapist's ascendancy initially, after they are face to face the main source of the therapist's power increasingly becomes his or her personal qualities, especially the ability to convince the patients that the therapist can understand and help them; that is, the ability to establish what has been termed a therapeutic alliance.

For Rogerian and existentialist therapists (25), the therapeutic relationship or encounter is the therapy; it is both a necessary and a sufficient cause of the patients' progress. They leave the patients free to structure it as they wish and confine their own activities to facilitating the exploration and expression of the patients' feelings, to which the therapist responds by freely revealing his or her own reactions. Such encounters are believed to promote personal growth, the ultimate aim of therapy. Therapies in the psychoanalytic tradition also foster openness by the patient, but make the therapeutic relationship itself an object of scrutiny. To this end, analytic therapists do not reveal themselves, since to do so would interfere with the emergence and analysis of transference reactions. Behavior therapists, by contrast, regard the relationship simply as a means for persuading the patient to cooperate in the techniques of behavior modification.

2. A *healing setting* which reinforces the relationship by heightening the therapist's prestige through symbolizing the role of healer, such as a clinic in a prestigious hospital or a private office complete with bookshelves, impressive desk, couch, and easy chair. The setting often contains evidences of the therapist's training such as diplomas and pictures of his teachers.

3. A *rationale,* conceptual scheme, or myth that explains the cause of the patient's symptoms and prescribes a *ritual* or procedure for resolving them. I have used the provocative word "myth" to emphasize that, although many rationales of Western psychotherapies do not invoke supernatural forces, they resemble the myths of primitive ones in that they cannot be shaken by therapeutic failures. That is, they are not subject to disproof.

The rationale must be convincing to both patient and therapist; hence, as mentioned above, it is validated by being linked to the dominant worldview of their culture. In the Middle Ages the conceptual scheme underlying what we today call psychotherapy was demonology. In many primitive societies it is witchcraft. In the United States today it is science. This was beautifully demonstrated at a symposium of leading proponents of various psychotherapeutic schools. Each introduced his presentation by invoking symbols of science: one showed anatomical charts, another displayed polygraphic tracings, and a third referred to experimental work with mice. Now, as a reflection of the growing disenchantment with science, therapies are emerging that are validated by religious or mystical cosmologies.

4. Linked to the rationale is a *ritual* which requires active participation of both patient and therapist and which is believed by both to be the means for restoring the patient's health.

Proponents of all schools of psychotherapy agree that they offer essentially the same kind of therapeutic relationship, but each claims special virtues for their particular rationales and procedures. To oversimplify vastly, therapeutic schools, whether they use individual or group approaches, can be classified with respect to whether they conceptualize the causes of the patient's problems as lying primarily in the past, the present, or the future, and link their rituals to this. Psychoanalytically oriented therapies stress unresolved inner conflicts or arrests in development resulting from destructive early life experiences, and seek to undo their effects by procedures which lead the patients to relive them emotionally in a context that enables them to be resolved or otherwise dispelled. Many of the newer abreactive techniques, although based on a variety of rationales, seem to belong in this category. Behavior therapies view the patients' distress as resulting from their present behavior, which is maintained by current environmental contingencies, and seek to overcome their difficulties primarily by showing them they can change their reactions on the spot, thereby also changing the responses of others that have maintained them (26). Existential therapies, finally, stress the patients' view of their future as closed and seek to enable them to widen their options through their encounter with a therapist who combats their feelings of meaninglessness and despair.

Therapeutic rationales and their associated rituals may also be classified as to whether they view psychopathology as lying within the patients' skin or in their interactions with others. Existentialist, psychoanalytically oriented and abreactive therapies, including those which foster altered states of consciousness, assume that resolution of inner conflicts will lead to improvement in behavior. Behavior therapies hold that appropriate changes in behavior, by eliciting more favorable responses from others, will reduce disturbing thoughts and feelings, which they regard as outside their purview.*

---

* Recently a group of behavior therapists have announced, with considerable fanfare, their rediscovery of attention, imagery and other mental processes, which they include in what they term "cognitive-behavior therapy."

Many group and family approaches carry this conceptualization a step further by viewing the patients' psychic distress as resulting from disturbance in a pathological communication network in which they are immersed, whether it be the family, a neighborhood network, or a therapy group. These therapies focus on resolving the pathology of the network as a whole as the means of reducing the patients' disturbed behavior and feelings (27).

THERAPEUTIC FUNCTIONS OF COMMON FEATURES OF PSYCHOTHERAPIES

Despite marked differences in *content,* all therapeutic myths and rituals, reinforced by the setting, share six therapeutic *functions.*

1. They *strengthen the therapeutic relationship,* thereby combatting the patient's sense of isolation. The therapeutic ritual serves as a vehicle for maintaining the therapeutic relationship, especially over stretches when nothing much seems to be happening. It keeps both patient and therapist interested and interacting.

Being irrefutable, and shared by a group to which the therapist adheres, rationale and ritual protect his or her self-esteem, especially in the face of lack of therapeutic progress. As one young adherent of a psychotherapeutic school remarked: "Even if the patient doesn't get better, you know you are doing the right thing."

Mastery of the rationale and procedure gives therapists a feeling of competence, which indirectly strengthens patients' confidence in them as people who know what they are doing.

Since the therapists represent the larger society, their mere acceptance of the patients as worthy of help helps to combat the latter's sense of isolation and reestablish their sense of connectedness with their group. This is further reinforced by the fact that therapist and patient adhere to the same belief system, a powerful unifying force in all groups.

2. They inspire and maintain the patients' *hope for help,* which not only keeps them coming but is a powerful healing emotion in itself (28). Hope is sustained by being translated into concrete expectations. Thus experienced therapists of all schools spend considerable time early in therapy in teaching patients their particular therapeutic game and shaping the patients' expectations to coincide with what they will actually receive (29, 30).

In this connection, despite their conviction that the effectiveness of behavior therapies depends primarily on specific techniques, experienced behavior therapists implicitly recognize that arousal of their patients' hopes is important by going to considerable lengths to accomplish it. A group of research psychotherapists who spent five days observing two leading behavior therapists (incidentally, one of the great virtues of the behavior therapists is that they allow their work to be studied by others) state that they were amazed at the amount of suggestion involved during the orientation period.

"The therapist tells the patient at length about the power of the treatment method, pointing out that it has been successful with comparable patients and all but promising similar results for him too. The patient . . . is given a straightforward rationale for the way in which the specific treatment procedures will 'remove' his symptoms. . . . The explicit positive and authoritarian manner in which the therapist approaches the patients seems destined, if not designed, to establish the therapist as a powerful figure and turn the patient's hopes for success into concrete expectations" (31).

3. They give patients opportunities for both *cognitive and experiential learning* by providing them with new information about their problems and possible ways of dealing with them, or new ways of conceptualizing what they already know.

Thus insight therapies teach patients about the link between their present attitudes or behavior and previous life experiences, while behavior therapies clarify the immediate instigators and consequences in the patients' current life situation. Some of this information is transmitted cognitively, but probably the more important part comes through the patients' directly experiencing it, through, for example, transference reactions or the emotions aroused by attempts to change the contingencies governing their behavior. Much of this information is gained through self-discovery, but a lot also comes from the therapist and, in therapy groups, from the group members. The patients use both as models as well as sources of knowledge. In any case, the information is typically formulated in terms of the therapeutic rationale.

All therapeutic schools agree that intellectual insight is not sufficient to produce change. Patients must also have a new experience, whether this be related to reliving of their past, discovering symptom-reinforcing contingencies in their environment, or becoming aware of distortions in their interpersonal communications.

4. Experiential learning implies *emotional arousal,* which supplies the motive power for change in attitudes and behavior (32). The revelations emerging in psychotherapy may be pleasant surprises, but more often are unsettling shocks, as patients discover features of themselves which they had not let themselves face. Some therapies deliberately cultivate emotional arousal, which they see as central to therapy. As already mentioned, these therapies are currently riding the crest of popularity.

5. Perhaps the central therapeutic effect of all psychotherapies is enhance-

ment of the patients' sense of mastery (33), self-control (34), competence, or effectiveness. Ability to control one's environment starts with ability to master one's own impulses and feelings, an achievement which in itself overcomes anxiety and strengthens self-confidence. Nothing is more frightening than feeling oneself to be at the mercy of inchoate and mysterious forces. A powerful source of a sense of mastery is being able to name and order one's experiences, a function performed by the therapeutic rationale. That naming a phenomenon is a way of gaining dominance over it is a frequent theme in folklore and religion as in, for example, the fairy tale of Rumpelstiltskin and the first task God assigns Adam in Genesis, to name the animals.

The sense of mastery is reinforced by *success experiences,* which all therapies provide in one form or another. These keep the patients in therapy by maintaining their hopes, enhancing their sense of mastery over their feelings and behavior, and reducing their fear of failure. The role of success experiences is most obvious in behavior therapies, which are structured to provide continual evidence of progress and aim to have every session end in a sense of success. Emotional flooding therapies, by showing patients that they can survive the full impact of feelings they feared would destroy them, powerfully enhance their feelings of self-mastery. Psychoanalytically and existentially oriented therapies, being less clearly structured, yield more subtle but equally potent successes. Patients who favor these approaches master problems through verbalization and conceptualization, so the achievement of a new insight or ability to formulate a hitherto inchoate state of mind can powerfully enhance their self-confidence.

6. Finally, all therapies tacitly or openly encourage patients to digest or "work through" (35) and apply what they have learned in their daily living, thereby fostering generalization of the therapeutic gains beyond the therapeutic situation itself. Some therapies actually assign "homework" and require the patients to report back how well they have carried out their assignment. For others, this remains a tacit, but nevertheless strong, expectation.

In short, evidence available to date strongly suggests that in treating most conditions for which persons get into psychotherapy the shared functions of different rationales and rituals, not their differing contents, supply most of the therapeutic power. These functions, which are interwoven, all contribute to reestablishment of the patients' morale by combatting their sense of isolation, reawakening their hopes, supplying them with new information as a basis for both cognitive and experiential learning, stirring them emotionally, providing experiences of mastery and success, and encouraging them to apply what they have learned.

The great differences in lengths of therapies practiced by different schools depend in part on the expectations they inculcate in both patients and therapists. Behavior therapies are expected to be brief; psychoanalytically oriented ones, long. Within each school, differences may depend primarily on how long it takes to establish a genuine therapeutic alliance—i.e., win the patients' trust—and how much practice they need to unlearn old attitudes and habits and ingrain new, healthier ones.

A NOTE ON TRANSCENDENTAL THERAPIES

A potent source of extensive and enduring behavior change is joining a tightly knit group which believes passionately in a transcendental value system that offers a solution for all life's problems—in other words, a religious conversion. This has not been considered to be a form of psychotherapy but today, reflecting the disillusionment with science and the waning consolatory power of traditional religions, persons who formerly sought naturalistic forms of psychotherapy flock to quasi-religious groups, and the lines between psychotherapeutic schools and religious sects are blurred. Scientology, an outgrowth of Dianetics, has officially become a religion, and the messianic zeal of adherents to Transactional Analysis and Re-evaluation Counseling, to mention only two, is indistinguishable from that of members of proselytizing religions. Furthermore, many currently flourishing religio-mystical cults, while not aimed at relieving specific symptoms, offer their acolytes the hope of achieving inner peace by the practice of rituals believed to enable them to escape from the tyranny of the individual ego and achieve union with the cosmic consciousness. Foreshadowed by Christian Science, current examples are Oscar Ichazo's Arica Institute, Maharishi Mahesh's Transcendental Meditation, and the Divine Light Mission of Guru Maharaj ji.

In the light of this analysis, the therapeutic benefits of transcendental cults appear identical with those of naturalistic therapies: formation of a strong dependent, emotionally-charged tie to a healing leader and group with a shared myth linked to a ritual which is believed to solve all problems. In conjunction, myth and ritual restore the converts' sense of group solidarity, arouse their hopes, and instill them with confidence.

What the transcendental component adds must remain open. The apparent power of religious healing, however, warrants more sympathetic attention to phenomena which have hitherto been considered beyond the pale by most scientists, notably those in the realm of the paranormal such as telepathy, the study of auras, and spiritual healing. Pursuing these further here would lead too far afield. Suffice it that some of these phenomena are apparently receiving scientific confirmation (36).

CATEGORIES OF RECEIVERS OF PSYCHOTHERAPY

To retreat to safer ground, viewed from the standpoint of the demoralization hypothesis, those who seek or are brought to psychotherapy can be loosely grouped into five categories with reference to the sources and manifestations of their difficulties in coping with problems of living: the psychotic, the shaken, the unruly, the neurotic, and the discontented. Regardless of the category into which they most nearly fit—and most fit in several—all commonly suffer from the generic manifestations of demoralization—anxiety, depression, resentment, and feelings of isolation—to which may or may not be added specific psychotic, neurotic, and behavioral symptoms.

At one end of the spectrum are the psychotics, whose demoralization is based on vulnerabilities arising from genetic defects or damaging early life experiences, the effects of which are so deeply ingrained in the nervous system that they cannot be undone by psychologic means. These patients are analogous to the chronically medically ill. Their management requires a medical regime but, since their bodily defects usually account for less of their suffering and disability than does loss of morale, medical treatment alone is not adequate. Schizophrenics, like diabetics, may require drugs, but they also need long-term psychotherapeutic support to enable them to function to the limit of their capacities. Professional skills often must be employed in managing the medications and in the use of behavioral reinforcement methods with some of them. The basic functions of psychotherapy with these patients, however, are to offer support and help them to adjust to their limitations or to avoid situations to which they are especially vulnerable. These functions can be effectively performed by nonprofessionals under professional supervision.

The same is true of the psychologically shaken, who are unable to cope with aspects of their immediate life situations, including marital disharmonies, misbehaving children, and crises which temporarily overtax their adaptive capacities. Relatively brief interventions usually suffice to restore them to emotional equilibrium. Since persons shaken by current life stresses can manifest the entire gamut of neurotic and psychotic symptoms (37) and, since all respond gratifyingly to any form of psychotherapy, they fan the competitiveness between different therapeutic approaches.

Much of the caseload of community mental health centers and psychiatric clinics consists of patients of these two types, so these agencies will probably be staffed increasingly by nonprofessionals. To the extent that patients' symptoms are crisis responses on the one hand or expressions of constitutional weaknesses on the other, there is no evidence that any one specialized technique is more effective than any other as long as it helps restore and maintain the patient's morale. Since group methods do this very effectively and also are economical of the therapist's time, more and more of these patients will probably be treated in groups.

The third category, who may be termed the unruly, try to combat their demoralization by resort to deviant behavior or excessive use of drugs or alcohol. Here belong "acting-out" children and adolescents, husbands or wives whose spouses cannot stand their behavior and, of course, addicts, alcoholics, and antisocial personalities. Some of these merge with the preceding category. The difference lies in the severity of the disturbance, the extent to which they disturb those about them, and the motivation for help. The shaken seek treatment themselves; the unruly are brought to treatment by others.

The fourth category, the neurotics, suffer from specific maladaptive interpersonal strategies called neurotic symptoms, presumably resulting from deprivations or traumata in early life that warped the normal processes of maturation and learning. Depending on their personal attributes and the specific nature of their symptoms and life experiences, some may respond best to abreactive approaches, others to long-term therapy, still others to behavioral methods tailored to their particular problems. Some may be more accessible to group approaches; others may need the privacy of the dyad.

Finally, we come to the discontented—the legions in today's confusing world who are struggling with problems of identity, alienation, and what has been termed existential despair. Searching for a meaning and purpose for their lives, including a sense of connectedness with others, many gravitate to psychotherapies which promulgate well-articulated, strongly-held belief systems, such as Freudian and Jungian psychoanalysis, or to quasi-religious therapeutic cults mentioned earlier. Others seek to integrate their lives and overcome their sense of isolation by the intense bursts of emotional intimacy cultivated by some encounter groups.

TOWARD THERAPEUTICALLY RELEVANT DIAGNOSIS

Implicit in this brief categorization of persons seeking or brought to psychotherapy is the recognition that clinical diagnoses in themselves do not determine which psychotherapy would be most helpful. Persons in all five categories have been successfully and unsuccessfully treated by practitioners of all schools.

Diagnosis is necessary to determine in the first instance which complaints are modifiable by psychotherapy and which are not. For treatment of constitutional disabilities, accurate descriptive diagnosis is crucial in determining appropriate medications. Diagnosis would also include determination of the modifiability of environmental stresses contributing to the person's demoralization. The best psychotherapy can do with respect to unmodifiable environmental pressures is help the patients to endure what they cannot change (38).

Persons who are appropriate candidates for psychotherapy can be relieved by symbolic communications with a help-giver, and these include most persons who come to psychotherapy. For them, the conventional diagnostic categories are indeed probably irrelevant, but another diagnostic approach could be helpful. This would be to determine the form of help or kind of help-giver to which they are most accessible by exploration of the expectations they bring to therapy, their preferred type of success experience (39), their arousability, and the like (40).

Expectations could be determined through inquiry about the psychotherapeutic experiences of the patients' social circle (41) or their own previous therapeutic contacts. Characteristic modes of care-eliciting behavior (42) might also yield clues. Persons who seek aid by verbalizing their feelings and have strong motivation for insight (43) would probably respond to a verbally oriented approach; those who convey their need by somatic complaints might do better with a behavioral one; and patients with a strong sense of inadequacy might respond best to techniques providing early and obvious evidences of success.

Degree and nature of arousability might yield clues as to which patients would profit most from emotional flooding procedures. Would they be the most easily aroused, the most phlegmatic, or perhaps those who maintain a placid exterior while seething underneath? This approach to diagnosis obviously remains to be systematized.

CONCLUSION

If the analysis offered in this presentation is valid, it raises questions about the goals of training programs in psychotherapy. Until we have a rational basis for choice of specific therapies, one may well ask whether there is any point in mastering any particular one, especially since all have so much in common. The apparent interchangeability of rationales and rituals, however, does not mean that they are unimportant or unnecessary. Such an unwarranted conclusion confuses the content of therapeutic conceptualizations and procedures with their functions. Some therapeutically gifted persons, to be sure, can be effective with very little formal training, but most of us need to master some conceptual framework to enable us to structure our activities, maintain our confidence, and provide us with adherents of the same school to whom we can turn for support. If any moral can be drawn from this survey, it is that therapists' choices should be guided by their personal style. Some therapists are effective hypnotists, others are not; some welcome emotional displays, others shy away from them; some work best with groups, others in the privacy of the dyad; some enjoy exploring psyches, others prefer to try to change behaviors. Ideally, a therapist should master as many rationales and procedures as possible and try to select those which are most appropriate for different patients. Most of us are capable of some flexibility, but very few can effectively handle all procedures. Training programs should expose trainees to several approaches so that they can select and master those most congenial to their own personality (44). The greater the number of approaches one can handle, the wider the range of patients one will be able to help.

ADDENDUM QUERIES

I

DR. BURTON: In your chapter you relate the specifics of a culture to the form which a psychic healing approach takes. Thus we recognize that this is not *fin de siècle* Vienna where psychoanalysis was created and that psychoanalysis does not apply in the United States exactly as Freud enunciated it. But are there not some deep psychoanalytic truths which cut across every culture and can even be said to be timeless? Are you perhaps carrying cultural relativism too far?

DR. FRANK: Regardless of the generalizability of any concepts or findings concerning human mental functioning, their acceptability, and hence their usefulness, for psychotherapy depends to a large extent on their resonance with the culture in which they are promulgated. In suggesting some aspects of nineteenth-century Vienna and twentieth-century America which seem related to the popularity of Freudian psychoanalysis, I intended to leave open the extent to which its concepts are generalizable across cultures and times. Since the data base on which Freud built his theories is very small, it is a tribute to his genius that they are as widely applicable as they seem to be, but how far each extends is a matter for further transcultural research to determine. For example, some of the Freudian concepts may prove to have universal applicability. The existence of unconscious thought processes, although he was not the first to note them, does probably apply to all humans, but his particular concept of the Unconscious remains an interesting speculation. Other concepts, such as the Oedipus complex, have already been found not to be universal.

II

DR. BURTON: You discuss psychoanalysis and psychotherapy as science in your chapter. This is still the academic pecking order of the acceptability of a psychotherapy and comes up in every consideration of the adequacy of a treatment. But no psychotherapeutic approach can be said to be scientific if experimental quantification and replication are the modes. Indeed, the greater the controlled artistry the better seem the results. Shall we therefore give up our quest to be scientific as a chimera?

DR. FRANK: I agree that psychotherapy of all sorts is primarily an art, and that much of it may therefore always elude scientific analysis. However, scientific method is in essence a systematic search for relationships that can be replicated, and I do not believe that the limits of this approach for advancing the theory and practice of psychotherapy have yet been reached.

My point, incidentally, was not that psychoanalysis and behavior therapies are fully scientific but that in Western society they have gained acceptance largely because of their claim to be so. For us, Science has replaced God or the Spirit World as the ultimate source of credibility and power.

III

DR. BURTON: The benefits of group therapy are of course well known and are no doubt important. But I have never found that group therapy can replace dyadic therapy for most people unless of course dyadic therapy is practiced in the group. Family therapy is perhaps the most useful of them across a broad spectrum. What do you see as the place of group therapy in our current arsenal?

DR. FRANK: Since most therapists have been trained in dyadic therapy, they see it as the primary modality, with group therapy as a supplement which cannot fully replace it. Many group therapists see group therapy as the primary form of treatment and assert that dyadic therapy cannot completely replace it. Both are correct.

Dyadic, group, and family therapies and combinations thereof all have a place. Ideally all should be used, depending on the nature of the patient's problem or the phase of therapy. Most group therapists prepare their patients for group therapy by individual interviews and in the course of treatment individual sessions may be used, for example, to enable a patient to test out a sensitive topic in privacy, as it were, before raising it in the group. In family therapy, dyadic sessions with individual members may get the family to approach an issue which is too disruptive to tackle first in the family.

If one holds that the most useful concept of neurotic symptoms is that they arise from and are perpetuated by persistent failures of communication and that the symptoms themselves are miscarried interpersonal strategies, then treating the patient in the company of others so that these distortions can be directly exposed and corrected would be the treatment of choice. When these problems arise in and are perpetuated by family interactions, family or marital therapy would seem to be the most appropriate means of resolving them.

In the same connection, since humans are group creatures, group forces can exert particularly strong pressures for change. For these reasons, group or family therapy should be considered to be the central modality, with dyadic as supplementary.

IV

DR. BURTON: You seem attracted by the patient's helplessness, isolation, and lack of basic hope. But these states are similarly found in convicts, residents of convalescent hospitals, and certain college students. What distinguishes such, shall we say, normal demoralization from that which accompanies or is a part of a mental disease? Or are all such states psychopathological in your opinion?

DR. FRANK: Demoralization is a normal response to strong or persistent frustration or failure. In itself it is not psychopathological. Its relief becomes the goal of psychotherapy only when one has been unable to recover one's morale by one's own efforts or the informal help of others. In the absence of severe environmental obstacles such as incarceration, this failure may be the result of high vulnerability to stress, reduced or absent adaptive powers, as with chronic illness, fear of initiating new behavior (itself a result of demoralization), or resort to behaviors which perpetuate and intensify the failure through the responses they elicit from others. Most neurotic and many psychotic symptoms fall into this category. Demoralization is a major source of the distress and disability of the chronically ill, who are from this standpoint appropriate candidates for psychotherapy.

V

DR. BURTON: Your chapter may be disturbing to the professional in that it tends to equate all approaches without due attention to investment and history. It seems also to accept the supposed modern bankruptcy of science and to mildly approve of non-objective approaches. Would you therefore advise a student who wanted to become a psychotherapist to become an M.D. or Ph.D., or simply seek the company of healers and learn tutorially after the A.B. degree?

DR. FRANK: The purpose of all formal training is to enable therapists to master one or more psychotherapeutic conceptual schemes and procedures. The resulting sense of competence is necessary for their own self-confidence, especially in the face of the many failures experienced by psychotherapists of all schools. It also gives them the support of a like-minded group and the status attached to an advanced academic degree. Such a degree also enhances the therapists' credibility with their patients, while mastery of a theory and procedure helps maintain the patients' faith in the therapist when treatment is not going well. Formal training also enhances the therapist's sense of responsibility and accountability.

On the other hand, for some patients, such as addicts, alcoholics, and some slum dwellers, an academic degree, by increasing the therapist's social distance from the patient, may impede the patient's ability to use the therapist as a model of someone who has experienced and overcome a similar problem, often the major therapeutic source of the therapeutic effect. Thus I would advise most students to seek an advanced degree, while recognizing that there are important therapeutic roles for those who do not have one.

REFERENCES

1. BAKAN, D.: *Sigmund Freud and the Jewish Mystical Tradition.* Princeton: Van Nostrand, 1958.
2. YATES, A. J.: *Behavior Therapy.* New York: Wiley, 1970.
3. SPECK, R. V., and OLANS, J.: The social network of the family of a schizophrenic: Implications for social and preventive psychiatry. Unpublished manuscript, p. 10.
4. SPECK, R. V., and RUEVENI, U.: Network therapy—A developing concept. *Family Process,* 1969, 8, 182-191.
5. ANTHONY, E. J.: Discussion of Stoller, F. H., Accelerated interaction: A time-limited approach based on the brief, intensive group. *Int. J. Group Psychother.,* 1968, 18, 249-254.
6. ROSEN, H.: The hypnotic and hypnotherapeutic unmasking: Intensification and recognition of an emotion. *Amer. J. Psychiat.,* 1952, 109, 120-127.
7. STAMPFL, T. G., and LEVIS, D. J.: Essentials of implosion therapy: A learn-

ing-theory-based psychodynamic behavioral therapy. *J. Abn. Psychol.*, 1967, 72, 496-503.

8. JANOV, A.: *The Primal Scream.* New York: Putnam, 1970.
9. JACKINS, H.: *The Human Side of Human Beings: The Theory of Reevaluation Counseling.* Seattle: Rational Island Publishers, 1965.
10. BERGIN, A. E.: The Evaluation of Therapeutic Outcomes. In Bergin, A. E. and Garfield, S. L., (Eds.), *Handbook of Psychotherapy and Behavior Change: An Empirical Analysis.* New York: Wiley, 1971, pp. 217-270.
11. SLOANE, R. B., STAPLES, F. R., CRISTOL, A. H., et al.: *Psychotherapy versus Behavior Therapy.* Cambridge: Harvard U. Press, 1975.
12. BANDURA, A.: Psychotherapy Based upon Modeling Principles. In Bergin, A. E., and Garfield, S. L. (Eds.), *Handbook of Psychotherapy and Behavior Change: An Empirical Analysis.* New York: Wiley, 1971, pp. 653-708.
13. PAUL, G.: *Insight vs. Desensitization in Psychotherapy.* Stanford: Stanford U. Press, 1966.
14. LEVITZ, L. S., and STUNKARD, A. J.: A therapeutic coalition for obesity: Behavior modification and patient self-help. *Amer. J. Psychiat.*, 1974, 131, 423-427.
15. MARKS, I. M.: *Fear and Phobias.* New York: Academic Press, 1969.
16. VOTH, H. M., and ORTH, M. H.: *Psychotherapy and the Role of the Environment.* New York: Behavioral Publications, 1973.
17. GRUENBERG, E. M.: The social breakdown syndrome—some origins. *Amer. J. Psychiat.*, 1967, 123, 1481-1489.
18. ENGEL, G.: A life setting conducive to illness: The Giving-Up—Given-Up Complex. *Annals Int. Med.*, 1968, 69, 293-300.
19. SROLE, L., LANGER, T. S., MICHAEL, S. T., et al.: *Mental Health in the Metropolis: The Midtown Manhattan Study.* New York: McGraw-Hill, 1962.
20. LORR, M., McNAIR, D. M., MICHAUX, W. M., et al.: Frequency of treatment and change in psychotherapy. *J. Abnorm. Soc. Psychol.*, 1962, 64, 281-292.
21. KERNBERG, O. F., BURSTEIN, E. D., COYNE, L., et al.: Psychotherapy and psychoanalysis: Final report of the Menninger Foundation's Psychotherapy Research Project. *Bull. Menninger Clinic*, 1972, 36, Nos. 1/2, whole issue.
22. LUBORSKY, L., AUERBACH, A. H., CHANDLER, M., et al.: Factors influencing the outcome of psychotherapy. *Psychol. Bull.*, 1971, 73, 145-185.
23. SCHEFF, T. J.: Re-evaluation counseling: Social implications. *J. Humanistic Psychol.*, 1972, 12, 58-71.
24. HURVITZ, N.: Peer self-help psychotherapy groups and their implications for psychotherapy. *Psychotherapy: Theory, Research and Practice*, 1970, 7, 41-49.
25. HAVENS, L. L.: The existential use of the self. *Amer. J. Psychiat.*, 1974, 131, 1-10.
26. LIBERMAN, R. P., KING, L. W., DeRISI, W. J., and McCANN, M.: *Personal Effectiveness: Guiding People to Assert Themselves and Improve their Social Skills.* Champaign, Ill.: Research Press, 1975.
27. SPECK, R. V., and RUEVENI, U.: Network therapy—A developing concept. *Family Process*, 1969, 8, 182-191.
28. FRANK, J. D.: The role of hope in psychotherapy. *Int. J. Psychiat.*, 1968, 5, 383-395.

29. LENNARD, H. L., and BERNSTEIN, A.: *The Anatomy of Psychotherapy: Systems of Communication and Expectation.* New York: Columbia U. Press, 1960.
30. HOEHN-SARIC, R., FRANK, J. D., IMBER, S. D., et al.: Systematic preparation of patients for psychotherapy: I. Effects on therapy behavior and outcome. *J. Psychiat. Res.*, 1965, 2, 267-281.
31. KLEIN, M. H., DITTMAN, A. T., PARLOFF, M. R., and GILL, M. W.: Behavior therapy: Observations and reflections. *J. Consult. Clin. Psychol.*, 1969, 33, 259-266, p. 262.
32. HOEHN-SARIC, R., LIBERMAN, B., IMBER, S. D., et al.: Arousal and attitude change in neurotic patients. *Arch. Gen. Psychiat.*, 1972, 26, 51-56.
33. FRANK, J. D.: Psychotherapy and the sense of mastery. In Spitzer, R. L. and Klein, D. F. (Eds.), *Evaluation of Psychological Therapies.* Baltimore: Johns Hopkins University Press, 1976, pp. 47-56.
34. LOW, A. A.: *Mental Health through Will-Training.* Boston: Christopher Publishing House, 1950.
35. MENDEL, W. M.: Interpretation and working through. *Amer. J. Psychiat.*, 1975, 29, 409-414.
36. KRIPPNER, S.: *Song of the Siren: A Parapsychological Odyssey.* New York: Harper & Row, 1975.
37. TYHURST, J. S.: The role of transition states—including disasters—in mental illness. In *Symposium on Preventive and Social Psychiatry.* Washington, D. C.: Walter Reed Army Institute of Research, 1957, pp. 149-169.
38. FRANKL, V. E.: *The Doctor and the Soul: From Psychotherapy to Logotherapy.* New York: Knopf, 1965.
39. LIBERMAN, B. L., HOEHN-SARIC, R., FRANK, J. D., et al.: Mastery: Prescriptive treatment and maintenance of change in psychotherapy. Submitted for publication.
40. LAZARUS, A.: *Behavior Therapy and Beyond.* New York: McGraw-Hill, 1972.
41. KADUSHIN, C.: *Why People Go to Psychiatrists.* New York: Atherton, 1969.
42. HENDERSON, A. S.: Care-eliciting behavior in man. *J. Nerv. Ment. Dis.*, 1974, 159, 172-181.
43. MALAN, D. H.: *A Study of Brief Psychotherapy.* Philadelphia: Lippincott, 1963.
44. HAVENS, L. L.: Clinical methods in psychiatry. *Int. J. Psychiat.*, 1972, 10, 7-28.

Hans H. Strupp

6

The Nature of the Therapeutic Influence and Its Basic Ingredients

by HANS H. STRUPP, Ph.D.

Although serious questions have been raised about the scientific status of psychotherapy, the search for the isolation of "necessary and sufficient" conditions has gone forward. Having struggled with this problem for a number of years, I wish to set forth, in brief outline, the substance of my current understanding of the problem. I will then comment on some implications of my position. I have tried to adhere closely to empirical observations, available from the clinical experience of all therapists. While somewhat different in emphasis, my views are consonant with the careful analysis of basic therapeutic processes provided by White (1).

BASIC INGREDIENTS OF THERAPEUTIC CHANGE

CONDITION 1. The therapist creates and maintains a helping relationship (patterned in significant respects after the parent-child relationship) characterized by respect, interest, understanding, tact, maturity, and a firm belief in his or her ability to help.

CONDITION 2. The foregoing conditions provide a power base from which the therapist influences the patient through one or more of the following:

a) suggestions (persuasion);
b) encouragement for openness of communication, self-scrutiny, and honesty (partly under Condition 1);
c) "interpretations" of "unconscious material," such as: self-defeating and harmful strategies in interpersonal relations, fantasies, distorted beliefs about reality, etc.;
d) setting an example of "maturity" and providing a model (partly under Condition 1);
e) manipulation of rewards.

CONDITION 3. Both preceding conditions are crucially dependent upon a client who has the capacity and willingness to profit from the experience.

These conditions may impress the reader as either too meager or too vague to be of significant value. However, as I will attempt to show, when properly developed, they seem to account adequately for the majority of phenomena in this domain.

Therapist's Attitude

There is no need to dwell on the common observation that all forms of psychotherapy (the reference throughout is primarily to the one-to-one relationship since it lends itself more readily to a discussion of the major issues, although similar principles apply to other forms) entail a *significant* human relationship. What makes a human relationship "significant" is exceedingly difficult to specify. For present purpose it is sufficient to note that it depends on the therapist and the client as well as the nature of their interaction. A therapist who is seriously deficient in the characteristics sketched in Condition 1 is not likely to facilitate a significant experience; conversely, no matter how much a therapist may have to offer, an inappropriate client will be unable to profit from it.

It seems that there is nothing esoteric or superhuman about the qualities needed by a good therapist: they are the attributes of a good parent and a decent human being, who has a fair degree of understanding of himself and his interpersonal relations so that his own problems do not interfere, who is reasonably warm and empathic, not unduly hostile or destructive, and who has the talent, dedication, and compassion to work cooperatively with others. Some aspects of this general attitude can probably be learned (through living, personal therapy, or both), but we may also be dealing with a native talent. In any case, the relative importance of these factors has not been worked out despite some beginnings (Holt and Luborsky, 2). It is my clinical impression that a cultured person who has gained a perspective on man and his place in the world seems preferable as a therapist, although he may not necessarily be more effective. In short, Condition 1 places greater emphasis on factors that facilitate the emergence of a relationship—it is not anything specific the therapist "does." However, as implied above, the therapist must avoid doing certain things (e.g., criticizing, "lecturing," and generally "getting in the way"). Indeed, a fair amount of what we teach our student therapists consists of maneuvers to be avoided!

In many forms of psychotherapy, notably the variety traditionally designated as "supportive," the therapist's healing attitude, as sketched above, provides the major leverage for therapeutic change. I agree with Rogers (3) that there is nothing unique about the "formal" psychotherapeutic setting and that any good human relationship can provide the leverage we are discussing here. I disagree with what I consider his overemphasis on genuineness, unconditional regard, congruence, etc., and his designating them as "necessary and sufficient" for the occurrence of therapeutic change in all clients. In my view, the proposition needs to be qualified in important respects which will be explored further in this chapter.

Therapeutic Relationship

As indicated, the therapist brings to bear a set of attitudes and values on the relationship he is creating with a client, and in many instances the nature of the psychotherapeutic influence is more or less completely encompassed by these attitudes and values. They are the "loving"—in the sense that Fromm (4) uses the term—aspects of psychotherapy and indeed a sine qua non for what is generally considered "therapeutic change." As already pointed out, psychotherapy shares these aspects with all good human relationships, and to the extent that it has nothing else to offer, it is little more than a professional friendship. To avoid misunderstanding, this statement needs clarification: the art (and to some extent the science) of this segment of psychotherapy consists in the proper handling of the therapeutic attitude. Specifically, Rogers' "therapeutic conditions" cannot be dispensed indiscriminately nor does therapeutic change bear a direct relationship to the quantity of the conditions being dispensed. They cannot be mechanically turned on and off like a faucet.

The art, which is to some extent teachable, consists of knowing when and how to communicate interest, respect, understanding, empathy, etc., and, perhaps even more important, when not to. Some people undoubtedly know these things intuitively and others can be trained. Still others, because of their own life history and personality makeup, cannot benefit from such training. In short, the therapist's response to the client's needs must be genuine, as Rogers correctly points out. However, the difference between a good and a "mechanical" therapist may be qualitative, not quantitative.

For a human relationship to become therapeutic it is essential that the client has the capacity to benefit from what the therapist, as a fellow human being, has to offer. While this formulation (Condition 3) appears to be self-evident, it has profound implications for the therapeutic enterprise.

All modern conceptions of psychotherapy are (not always explicitly) based on the supposition that the client possesses the capacity to profit from, and change as a result of, the forces operating in a "good" human relationship (Strupp, 5). This capacity of the client is deeply rooted in the early parent-child relationship, which is characterized by biological and psychological dependence of the immature organism on a strong and nurturing parent figure. To the extent that the memories of this early experience have a positive valence (which is fortunately true for most people), a subsequent human relationship has the potential of being therapeutic. Since many personal relationships derive their inherent gratifications, at least in part, from commonalities with the early parent-child relationship, it is possible to use such a relationship for the purpose of producing "corrections" in the deeply rooted substrate of man's need for dependency, succor, support, reassurance, etc. (MacAlpine, 6; Stone, 7). A significant part of Freud's contribution to the field of psychotherapy lies precisely in this realization, coupled with the development of techniques for the skillful management of the parent-child relationship as it manifests itself in the here-and-now of the therapeutic context.

For related reasons, Freud considered the "transference neuroses" the only proper field for psychoanalysis, and he excluded other "disease entities" which did not seem to fit this paradigm. The point to be made is that psychotherapy is potentially useful when the client has remained responsive to parental-type influences, and it is essentially futile where such receptivity has either never existed or has been severely frustrated—see Strupp (8) for a delineation of these situations. The "good" client appears to have a pervasive need to form a dependent (anaclitic) relationship with a nurturing adult (Andrews, 9), which also creates an exceedingly powerful base from which the client can be influenced (see below). Indeed, it may be laid down that, short of coercive measures, it is the only base from which a person's behavior can be significantly influenced. It was also one of Freud's profound insights that so-called neurotic individuals are particularly prone: (1) to remain entangled in parent-child relationships, (2) because of this entanglement to revive their "problems" with a nurturing parent-type figure (the therapist), and, (3) if the relationship is skillfully managed, to profit in a therapeutic sense from the revival of the early parent-child relationship. This, in substance, is the concept of the transference and its resolution. It also embodies Freud's definition of "neurosis."

The client's "neurotic suffering" may be seen as a yearning for the re-institution of a gratifying parent-child relationship, and his "motivation for therapeutic change" is a dim realization that, given proper circumstances, he wants to utilize this vehicle for working out his "problems." This realization, as clinicians know, presupposes a fair degree of intelligence, an ability to view one's feelings and behavior with a certain amount of objectivity (sometimes termed psychological-mindedness), a certain degree of maturity and willingness to undergo (or relive) painful experiences ("ego strength"), as well as time, money, and patience to go that route. For all of these reasons, a very large number of persons are unsuitable for what traditionally has been called intensive, long-term, reconstructive psychotherapy.

My purpose in raising these issues is not to discuss what is usually referred to as "psychoanalysis," but rather to highlight the conditions necessary for therapeutic change and to bring into relief the (severe) limitations of our techniques for such change, as implied in the formulations of Condition 3.

To state the matter another way, the combination of Conditions 1 and 3, which encompasses the vast amount of "supportive" psychotherapy (including prominently client-centered therapy, except insofar as it partakes of certain aspects of Condition 2, which are "officially" denied), links, for relatively brief encounters, a nurturing parent figure (therapist) with a receptive client (Chessick, 10). Therapy, then, becomes effective to the extent that such a relationship boosts the client's morale and hopes, allays his fears, assuages his guilt, encourages his tendency to cope (competence), and, in general, lifts his spirits. These are the "nonspecific effects" of psychotherapy (Frank, 11, 12), the effects attributed to "spontaneous remission" (Eysenck, 13, 14), and the "placebo effect" (Shapiro, 15, Calestro, 16). These effects are perfectly "respectable" and in many cases very real as well as lasting. However, they are hardly new to contemporary psychotherapy except insofar as we have achieved a better understanding of when certain ministrations work and when they fail, nor are they contemporaneously the exclusive domain of the trained psychotherapist.

Whether we want, in outcome research, to credit these effects as being "real" changes is not an empirical question; rather it is a matter of values and preference. In other words, if a large amount of psychotherapeutic change is attributable to the foregoing factors, we can choose to be impressed by it or shrug it off as commonplace (see Bergin, 17). While we have no convincing evidence at present that the techniques to be discussed under the heading of Condition 2 produce more impressive results than the foregoing combination, there is by now little question that in all forms of psychotherapy, including the various forms of behavior modification, the nonspecific factors play an exceedingly important part and, at the very least, powerfully undergird the operations under Condition 2. At the same time it is difficult to visualize a form of psychotherapy without the latter.

The Therapeutic Situation as a Power Base for Psychological Influence

The client's readiness and felt need for a parent-type relationship (even though the need may be vehemently denied), coupled with the "supplies" the therapist can provide, constitute the pivot upon which the psychotherapeutic relationship turns. As delineated so far, and if restricted to the interactions which have been described, psychotherapy provides no more (but also no less) than what a "good" relationship has always provided. Up to the point, the therapist essentially gratifies the client's wishes, notably those for dependency, support, understanding, and succor, which in many instances is all that is desired. What Freud's work, and that of his successors, has contributed is a far greater understanding of the conditions under which these ministrations are effective and, perhaps even more important, a careful explication of their grave limitations. It is quite clear that the beneficial effects of supportive psychotherapy, client-centered therapy, and the help provided by nonprofessional therapists can be very readily accommodated within such a framework.

It is less apparent that the therapist-client relationship constitutes an exceedingly powerful base for influencing the client's feelings, beliefs, and behavior (Strong and Matross, 18). Indeed, it may be asserted that when there exists a strong need in the client to reinstitute a parent-child relationship (transference readiness) and the therapist partially but effectively meets these needs, a matrix of virtually unequalled power has been created; it is within this matrix that the therapist's operations achieve their unique effectiveness. This is no more than a restatement of Freud's (19) trenchant observation that the patient's power of reason is much too weak to effect any changes, and that these come about solely through his attachment to the therapist. Consequently, when Conditions 1 and 3 are met, the various techniques listed under Condition 2 become powerful vehicles for effecting changes in the client. In this connection, I wish to make the following assertions:

(a) There is probably no therapeutic relationship in which one or more of the techniques mentioned under Condition 2 do not play a part. Similarly, I do not believe that a "pure" (nonmanipulative) psychotherapeutic relationship is ever possible. Whether in an "ideal" sense it is desirable is another matter which need not concern us here.

(b) Wittingly or unwittingly, all psychotherapists continually employ several of the techniques mentioned under Condition 2. In other words, the psychoanalytic position that psychotherapeutic change is due to unconscious rearrangements brought about solely or predominantly by "correct interpretations" is just as untenable as the client-centered position which contends that, ideally, none of the techniques under Condition 2 are to be used. Apart from being factually incorrect, neither position seems defensible on psychological grounds. In contrast, psychotherapists of all persuasions who are interested in producing or facilitating personality or behavior change in their clients employ a spectrum of psychological techniques—some crude, some exceedingly sophisticated—for bringing about such changes. Most of these techniques are in principle not very different from those which have been employed over the centuries by parents in raising their children. What dynamic psychology and learning theories have contributed during this century is a much clearer explication of the conditions under which these techniques exert their influence; the requirements for their effectiveness; the obstacles impeding their direct and uncritical application; and, not least important, an appreciation of the symbolic meanings which permeate man's feelings, attitudes, and interpersonal relations. Through recognition of these contingencies, it may be said that in a certain sense psychotherapy has become more effective.

The recognition that the parent-child relationship, with its characteristic dependency of a weak individual on a powerful nurturing adult, constitutes an exceedingly powerful context for mediating many kinds of learning, but particularly techniques and strategies in interpersonal relations, was of course one of Freud's fundamental insights. It was matched by his ingenious design of an analogous relationship between a therapist and a client which on the one hand takes full advantage of the power of the parent-child situation (made possible by the client's unresolved and frustrated yearning for such a relationship which constitutes his "illness") and, on the other, uses that same relationship for the purpose of inducing the client to outgrow his need for it. This framework, however, also spells the limitations of psychoanalytic psychotherapy. Since it is assumed that analytic therapy deals predominantly

with transference problems, that is, conflicts that are traceable to an interpersonal situation of the parent-child type, it follows that either (1) all
problems ever encountered in therapy have transference implications (an
improbable assumption which nevertheless seems to be widely held by practicing analysts) or (2) the therapist must exclude from "analysis" problems
which do not qualify under this rule. An extension of this position, which in
my opinion provides a frequent but shaky rationalization for interminable
treatment, is that while the transference implications of a given problem may
not be apparent at a particular point in therapy (because of an alleged
layering of defenses or similar unprovable constructions), they will become
salient, given sufficient time and work on the "analysis of defenses." Stated
somewhat differently, analytic therapy, to the extent that it eschews "non-
analytic" (other than interpretive) influencing techniques, disqualifies itself
from problems which cannot be transformed into an interpersonal conflict
between client and therapist in the here-and-now of the therapeutic situation.
Conversely, psychoanalytic psychotherapy operates on the powerful working
assumption that maladaptive feelings, beliefs, etc., can be effectively modified
in the context of an emotionally charged therapeutic relationship, provided
the painful affect associated with the original learning can be revived and
experienced in relation to the therapist or in a group. Most systems of
psychotherapy, including behavior therapy and experiential therapy, appear
to agree on this point.

In order to approach the problem of how the various techniques under
Condition 2 are fitted into the framework of psychotherapy of all types, it
will be instructive to examine the situation in analytic psychotherapy. A
parent-child relationship can have one of three possible outcomes:

(1) It is outgrown, which essentially means that it loses its fascination
for the growing child, who turns to other pursuits. To be sure, many of the
gratifications and satisfactions remain deeply imbedded in everyone's memory
and the early relationships provide a template for subsequent ones throughout
life, but in the ordinary course of events the child loses interest in problems
inherent in the "family romance." Parenthetically, I think it is fair to say
that Freud grossly overstated the importance of oedipal conflicts, at least as
a universal trauma. This is in no way to gainsay the crucial importance of
the early family situation for the lasting patterning of interpersonal relations,
the management and expression of feelings of aggression, competition, the
inculcation of beliefs and values, etc. In short, the "normal" solution consists
of gradually turning one's back on the halcyon days of early childhood and
infancy which pale in the light of other challenges.

(2) A hankering for such a relationship continues but is essentially denied.

The individual possessing a strong yearning of this kind, which interferes markedly with his adaptation as an adult, is designated as "neurotic" and is said to suffer from "unresolved transference problems."

(3) It is "analyzed." This process is analogous to (1) except that it is synthetically produced in therapy. In principle, the therapist subtly encourages the client to search for significant gratification in the therapeutic relationship, and when he vividly experiences these yearnings, the therapist interprets them as "infantile," thereby inducing the client to renounce or modify them. In this way, the therapist deliberately brings about a proper separation from the parents, helps the client "grow up" by forcing him to transform external controls (operating in the therapeutic situation) into internal controls, to tolerate frustrations and the delay of gratifications, and to accept more willingly at least major rules of conduct and values prevailing in the culture.

How does the therapist accomplish these feats? I submit that the therapist is effective to the extent that within the framework of the real or imagined parent-child relationship of therapy, as delineated by Conditions 1 and 3, he brings to bear the techniques outlined under Condition 2, of which the manipulation of rewards deserves particular mention. Scrutiny of the transactions occurring in the patient-therapist relationship discloses a subtle—and sometimes not so subtle—amalgam of the techniques which have been sketched. One example must suffice:

A client who, as part of his "symptomatology," complains of a phobia will sooner or later deal with the feelings, anxieties, and fantasies he experiences in the feared situation (Andrews, 9). Conditions 1 and 3 exist as essential prerequisites. Moreover, for a long time the therapist has encouraged openness of communication, self-scrutiny, honesty (2b); he has set an example of adult maturity by not belittling, criticizing, shaming, or judging the client; he has modeled fearless behavior in the presence of the client's anxieties, or has indicated in other ways that one need not be overcome or devastated by one's fears (2d); he has interpreted the meanings of the symptom by recourse to the client's fantasies, beliefs, and fantasied consequences (2c); he may have subtly suggested or implied that it is desirable to cope with a feared situation rather than to shrink from it, and that, in keeping with Western values, such coping connotes competence, maturity, and autonomy (2a); perhaps most important, and related to the foregoing, he has implied or suggested that the client's ability to master the feared situation will impress the therapist more than the avoidance reaction (2e) which, because of the existence of the parent-child relationship, provides a potent incentive to the client to go out and test reality.

Many situations in analytic therapy are far more complex than the preceding example, but they lend themselves to the same kind of analysis. The same contingencies will apply, *mutatis mutandis,* in client-centered or behavior therapy. In the latter form of therapy, the client's mastery of a phobia may be traceable to the therapist-patient relationship (in which the therapist has enormous ascendancy as a powerful healer), although "behavioral techniques" may augment the effects. But, in the end, the therapist encourages (forces?) the client to brave the feared situation *in vivo,* and the client will do so because his love for the therapist and the latter's approval are more important than the discomfort he anticipates or actually experiences. Of course, the client's new assertiveness may be reinforced by other significant people in his life or he himself may find it rewarding. Clearly, nothing succeeds like success, but also nothing defeats like failure.

IMPLICATIONS

The foregoing exposition has developed the thesis that therapeutic change is largely due to skilled management or manipulation (in the dictionary sense of "to manage or utilize skillfully") by the therapist, with the important proviso that the interventions occur in the framework of an emotionally charged affectional relationship. This formulation partly coincides with Freud's conception of the transference paradigm, with the notable exception that Freud rejected influencing techniques other than interpretations, extolling instead "the pure gold of psychoanalysis." In contrast, I have suggested that the full range of common influencing techniques is inevitably brought to bear upon any psychotherapeutic relationship, and that this indeed constitutes one of the defining characteristics of psychotherapy. Basically, these techniques are shared with education and other social influence processes.

While I have stressed the controlling aspects of psychotherapy, it is equally important to point out the seeming paradox that this control, when properly handled, provides the most unique vehicle for the development of self-identity, self-direction, autonomy, and independence. The implications of this proposition are implicitly understood by psychoanalytic therapists but are continually ignored or misapprehended by others. I will not restate these implications except to underscore that, while the analytic relationship provides for maximum control by the therapist, it also places extreme emphasis on the nonexploitative character of the relationship. That is, once the behavior of the client is brought under control by the therapist—or, perhaps more correctly, once the client relinquishes his faulty self-control to the therapist—the latter does not utilize this control for ulterior purposes but in a real sense "hands it back" to the client. The end result is that the client feels that the therapeutic gains are his own accomplishments, and to a significant degree they are. The problem of how external controls are transformed into internal controls is one of the most basic issues of psychotherapy as well as child rearing, and the two are indeed analogous in very important respects. Freud "located" the most important difference in the adult's "observing ego" which, through the "therapeutic alliance," facilitates the acquisition of insight, and because of the beckoning promise of therapeutic gains and surcease from suffering, undergoes the frustrations and privations.

The good parent is intent upon helping the child to develop his own talents and resources; he intuitively senses that as the child grows up the parent must gradually relinquish his emotional investment, supervision, and control; while the separation may at times be painful for both parties, the parent realizes that the goal of independence, maturity, and self-determination can be achieved only if the child is given the opportunity to explore, experiment, and, within limits, make his own mistakes. All of this becomes possible after the child has achieved self-control through discipline which initially had been imposed from without. Perhaps this is what the poet Robert Frost had in mind when he said, "Freedom moves easy in harness." It appears abundantly clear that analytic psychotherapy, or any form of psychotherapy which has as its objective the development of greater independence and maturity, traverses the same route and seeks to correct—through what Freud called an "after-education"—deficiencies or faulty learning which continue to plague the patient in adult life.

The discipline referred to above includes prominently control over one's behavior, feelings, and fantasies, but also over certain physiological functions. In the "psychosomatic" realm, for example, the patient may have acquired faulty controls over his breathing or digestive functions, which, like other "symptoms," express rejection or defiance of the external (parental) authority. In this as in other areas the job of psychotherapy is to deprive these symptoms of their interpersonal (neurotic, mischievous, controlling) function and to restore to the patient more adaptive, rational control. (Contrast this view with Miller's (20) view of "therapeutic learning," in which the interpersonal meaning of symptoms does not play a part.)

It should require no further demonstration that psychotherapy, as conceptualized here, resembles child-rearing in important respects, and makes use of the same psychological mechanisms, although in more refined and self-conscious form. Consequently, it has nothing to do with medical practice, and it is no more "treatment" than child-rearing is a form of therapy.

There is no such thing as "nonmanipulative" or "nondirective" psychotherapy if one is seriously interested in personality and behavior change, except insofar as a "good" relationship, in and of itself, exerts a palliative influence. Furthermore, the values of the therapist (and those of the culture he represents) permeate the therapeutic relationship.

To pursue at somewhat greater length the implications for psychoanalytic psychotherapy, it should be noted that this form of therapy is a sophisticated technology for persuading a person to change his feelings, attitudes, and behavior; to assume responsibility (control) for his impulses, feelings, and actions; and to conduct his life in accordance with a philosophy extolling such values as personal strength, rationality, reasonableness, moderation, and the "golden rule" in interpersonal relations. It accomplishes its aim by subtly but consistently "letting down" the patient, strengthening his ability to accept disappointments and disillusionments with greater equanimity, but rewarding him for his achievement with a stronger sense of self and less guilt. The successfully treated patient is sadder but wiser, and is more capable of (adult) enjoyment that does not produce guilt. At the same time, the interaction with the therapist, who has taken the stance of a reasonable, loving but firm authority, has—through implied disapproval—closed many avenues of infantile gratifications that the patient had unwittingly sought but that resulted in conflicts, "symptoms" and a profound sense of guilt.

This approach to therapeutic change, however, presupposes a person who potentially finds the foregoing philosophy congenial or who can potentially be persuaded to accept and live by it. Many people, as Freud already recognized and as has been elaborated by a large literature since, are either not properly "motivated" or for many other reasons "unsuitable." The personality of the successfully treated patient shows a strange mixture of docility and submission to higher authority (the analyst as a representative of society), as well as a rugged sense of independence and selfhood, coupled with a keen sense of limitations within himself, others, and life's circumstances.

It is difficult to say whether the "good life" proposed by psychoanalysis is one of freedom or conformity. In any case, it has become apparent that Western man, especially in America, has become greatly disenchanted with this model, which in many respects clearly embodies a Puritan ethic. The growth of the encounter movement and "humanistic psychology," not to mention the writings of Reich and Marcuse, certainly attests to the fact that many contemporaries believe that more "fun" can be derived from sensory experience than allowed by the Freudian doctrine. But even on its own terms, the goals potentially achievable within psychoanalysis are so beset with technical difficulties—partly encompassed by the problem of getting patients to accept the teachings mentioned above, and partly by the general difficulties of inducing anyone to change deeply engrained habits and beliefs—that radical change is a relatively rare occurrence. Thus, what psychoanalysis has also contributed is a profound understanding of the obstacles impeding any effort at therapeutic change—the difficulties of changing human feelings and behavior that have their roots in childhood, when the person was dependent and noticeably malleable and influenceable by the adults with whom he was involved in a powerful emotional relationship and who served as his models, inculcated in him their attitudes and values, and in numerous ways used his dependency to perform their educational function. In short, Freud made it abundantly clear that, in order to change a person in fundamental ways, it is necessary to involve him in an emotionally charged relationship and to utilize his dependency (strongly feared by all neurotic people) to influence him in desired directions. These directions are importantly determined by the culture and its values, and are in no sense absolute.

The crux of all forms of psychotherapy is the achievement of self-direction, autonomy—what in psychoanalysis is called "ego control." If it is true that "where id was, there shall ego be," we are faced with the fundamental problem of how a person becomes socialized, how he develops techniques for subordinating his impulsive striving to control from the outside, and subsequently to self-control. It might well be said that the paradigm is that of the domestic animal who becomes housebroken as a function of a congenital predisposition and human manipulations in which rewards and punishment prove decisive. The psychoanalytic credo states: if the growing organism can be brought to subordinate and adapt its asocial strivings to the social conditions, it can subsequently enjoy a sense of freedom. As has long been recognized, the so-called neurotic person is in conflict and suffers because he has not learned to modulate his impulses such that they can find partial expression and gratification. Instead, he has learned to oppose ("resist") the influence of the parental authority figures, and he plays a duplicitous game of seeking to give expression to his impulsive strivings, while at the same time denying to himself and others his secret goals. This inner rebelliousness powerfully fuels his guilt, perpetuates his inner warfare as well as his relationships with others, and contributes paradoxically to a sense of weakness and helplessness. What therapy provides is an opportunity to let these impulses appear in clear awareness in relation to an essentially nonthreatening adult (therapist)—the "transference." Depending on the therapist's attitudes towards these emerging strivings (approval, disapproval, and neutrality), the patient is then placed in a position of giving them a new, less "automatic" direction. In this process, too, the patient comes face to face with the residues of the early interpersonal conflicts, partly intensified by misunderstandings, actual trauma, but also by his own fantasies, which inaugurated his struggle against accepting the teachings of those in authority. The following alternatives are open to the patient in this quest: (1) he can reject the parental authority once and for all; (2) he can accept it and abandon his inner strivings that bring him into conflict with others and established authority; or (3) he can modify the internalized parental authority, as well as his strivings, and bring about a better modus vivendi both within himself and in relation to others. In successful therapy, the latter is generally embraced. It is this struggle that Freud conceptualized in ego-id-superego terms.

In sum, the battle fought in analytic therapy is between the individual's impulsiveness (self-will, narcissism) and the discipline-imposing outside world that demands a measure of conformity from all adult members of society. Freud showed conclusively that no one can have it both ways, unless he succeeds in molding his social milieu and the behavior of significant others to adapt to his inner needs. Most of us succeed more or less in this dual task, and the extent to which this solution presents a viable balance between inner needs and outer demands is a measure of our "mental health." The therapist's task is to help the patient work out such a viable solution—a solution that is maximally noncoercive, maximally responsive to the patient's own needs, and relatively tolerant of—but by no means oblivious to—the demands of reality and society. Thus, analytic therapy is an education for optimal personal freedom in the context of social living. At its best, it preaches neither conformity nor libertinism, but clearly recognizes that controls and restraints are essential. However, its preference is for rational rather than authority-imposed control. Freud, especially toward the end of his life, harbored strong ambivalence as to whether the foregoing solution is ever viable, lasting, or productive of a sense of productivity and happiness.

One of the major problems not adequately dealt with in the psycho-analytic theory of psychotherapy is the precise manner in which accretions to the person's intentionality come about; how it happens that an individual who has previously been "lived by" forces over which he has inadequate control gradually acquires strength, so that henceforth he can exert greater control over his life. It is clear that in every psychotherapy, regardless of orientation, the patient eventually must be brought to take a stand, to assume cognizance and responsibility for his impulses and his actions. Instead of construing himself as a passive object that is buffeted by forces over which he has no control, he must reach a point where he says: "I feel a particular way," "I deal with my feelings in a given manner," "I take action." Paradoxically, he achieves this control to the extent that he can surrender some of his willfulness and go-it-alone attitude to a stronger benevolent person, the therapist; he gains strength as he learns to trust his helper and, for crucial moments, can feel sufficiently secure to place his fate in the other person's hands. It appears that in order to develop a strong sense of self it is necessary first to be able to trust others and gradually to grow out of this dependency-trust instead of being jolted out of it. Therapy seeks to bring about a correction, and where it succeeds—through long-term "analysis," "focal therapy," or whatever—it produces the kind of growth and maturation that is the ideal outcome of psychotherapy. Unhappily, the magical combination of the "right" circumstances is as rare as is perfection anywhere else in this imperfect world; yet this is not to say that approximations are to be scorned.

ADDENDUM QUERIES

I

DR. BURTON: You place great stress upon the "readiness" of the client to become a client and refer such readiness back to parent-child history. Can you be more explicit as to the nature of the readiness to use the transference as a therapeutic mode?

DR. STRUPP: This is a very complex question that cannot be answered properly in a few words. However, this much can be said: In order for therapy to have some hope of success, the patient must have experienced at least some measure of a positive interpersonal relationship with an important figure of his childhood. Fortunately this is often true; but when it is not (e.g., in narcissistic characters), we face a serious uphill battle.

II

DR. BURTON: You imply that all therapies contain various admixtures of Conditions 1, 2, and 3 and that these are the effective factors in behavior change. Would you because of this dispense with doctrinaire schools of psychotherapy and label their methods as primarily I, primarily II, primarily III and thus eliminate the trappings of vested interests?

DR. STRUPP: Yes, labels have never impressed me as particularly valuable for the purpose of capturing what is *effective* in a particular form of therapy. As I develop in my chapter, what needs to be studied is the variables that produce change; and all forms of therapy share common ingredients, I believe.

III

DR. BURTON: You state in your chapter that adults who are still bound to their parents in certain ways are precisely those people who become analysands of psychoanalysts. Is this meant to be pejorative? What do you see as the optimal relationship of an adult to his parents—living or deceased?

DR. STRUPP: Neurotic patients, by definition, have unfinished business with their parents and/or significant figures of their childhood. What is important from the standpoint of therapy is not the attitudes, feelings, values, etc., of the parents as they are or even as they were, but the *internalized,* and typically unexamined, forces that are essential in the patient's *current* conflicts and character.

IV

DR. BURTON: Yours is a synthesizing approach to psychotherapy, and you describe the common elements in psychoanalysis, client-centered therapy, and behavioral modification. Can one be favored over the other? Or does one govern in certain forms of problem situations and not in others?

DR. STRUPP: The psychoanalytic viewpoint, in my judgment, has basically the most to offer, simply because it is far deeper and more comprehensive. I believe that while the other approaches may have something to offer under certain and often limited conditions they lack the all-important depth dimension. Still, there are common elements in all approaches.

V

DR. BURTON: Since you seem at best only mildly optimistic about psychoanalytic psychotherapy leading to that compromise of narcissism and social necessity involved in social being, can you think of alternate ways it can be attained as effectively and economically? Would you refer clients to the priests, historians, or educators in lieu?

DR. STRUPP: The analytic approach, if properly understood, has the greatest realism. I believe it is true that what can be achieved in therapy is often limited, i.e., the forces operating against significant therapeutic change are often tremendous. This must be realized and understood—it is not necessarily the fault of what we can offer therapeutically when we cannot accomplish more. Therapists are not magicians! The reality, here as elsewhere, reigns supreme.

REFERENCES

1. WHITE, R. W.: *Lives in Progress.* New York: Holt, Rinehart & Winston, 1966, p. 310.
2. HOLT, R. R., and LUBORSKY, L.: *Personality Patterns of Psychiatrists.* New York: Basic Books, 1958.
3. ROGERS, C. R.: The necessary and sufficient conditions of therapeutic personality change. *J. Consult. Psychol.,* 1957, 21, 95-103.
4. FROMM, E.: *Man for Himself.* New York: Rinehart, 1947.
5. STRUPP, H. H.: Psychotherapy. In Farnsworth, D. (Ed.), *Annual Review of Psychology,* Vol. XIII. Palo Alto: Annual Reviews, Inc., 1962, pp. 445-78.
6. MACALPINE, I.: The development of the transference. *Psychoan. Quart.* 1950, 19, 501-539.
7. STONE, L.: *The Psychoanalytic Situation.* New York: International Universities Press, 1961.
8. STRUPP, H. H.: On the technology of psychotherapy. *Arch. Gen. Psychiat.,* 1972, 26, 270-278.
9. ANDREWS, J. D. W.: Psychotherapy of phobias. *Psychol. Bull.,* 1966, 66, 455-480.
10. CHESSICK, R. D.: *How Psychotherapy Heals.* New York: Science House, 1969.
11. FRANK, J. D.: *Persuasion and Healing.* Baltimore: Johns Hopkins Press, 1961.
12. FRANK, J. D.: Therapeutic factors in psychotherapy. *Amer. J. Psychother.,* 1971, 25, 350-361.
13. EYSENCK, H. J.: The effects of psychotherapy. *J. Consult. Psychol.,* 1952, 16, 319-324.
14. EYSENCK, H. J.: *Behavior Therapy and Neuroses.* New York: Pergamon Press, 1960.
15. SHAPIRO, A. K.: Placebo effects in medicine, psychotherapy, and psychoanalysis. In Bergin, A. E., and Garfield, S. (Eds.), *Handbook of Psychotherapy and Behavior Change.* New York: Wiley, 1971, pp. 439-473.
16. CALESTRO, K.: Psychotherapy, faith healing, and suggestion, *Int. J. Psychiat.,* 1972, 10, 83-113.
17. BERGIN, A. E.: The evaluation of outcomes. In Bergin, A. E., and Garfield, S. L. (Eds.), *Handbook of Psychotherapy and Behavior Change.* New York: Wiley, 1971, pp. 217-270.
18. STRONG, S. R., and MATROSS, R. P.: Change process in counseling and psychotherapy. *Res. Bull. Univ. Minn.,* 1971, 12, 1-29.
19. FREUD, S.: Transference. *Introductory Lectures,* Vol. 16. London: Hogarth Press, 1963.
20. MILLER N. E.: Learning of visceral and glandular responses. *Science,* 1969, 163, 434-445.

Arthur Burton

7

Behavior Change Through Love and Suffering

by ARTHUR BURTON, Ph.D.

PART I

There is probably no one specific way behavior change takes place but rather a number of ways and contexts in which it is facilitated. But we continue to search for the therapeutic *gran via,* the one most efficient way to produce behavior change, in line with our pragmatic heritage and need for precision. We never specifically formulate what it is we set out to cure, and the general therapeutic experience is that patients most often leave with something different than what they came for.

The behaviorists have much less ambiguity than this in their treatment work because they more or less confine themselves to manifest molar symptomatology: an inability to comfortably attain the twentieth floor or similar

113

height to go to work; a fear of certain animals, which disturbs the man-pet relationship and constitutes an inherent symbolic disturbance as well; a need to be over-clean in situations which call for certain amounts of dirtiness; an orgasmic response to a nongenital stimulus, or a failure of orgasm or erection entirely, constituting an inferior form of sexual organization. But the patients who come to the therapist complaining of a loss of meaning in their lives, of emptiness and alienation, of generalized fear and inhibition, of depression—often accompanied by unruly or reduced somatic response—require a different order of behavior change than simple Pavlovian principles afford.

No one method of behavior change totally suffices across the board, and the need today is for the more versatile practitioner who is qualified in a number of methods. But we need as well to focus and synthesize the best and most useful in a large group of healing approaches rather than to continue our perpetual search for the Holy Grail of treatment, which probably does not exist as such anyway. The introduction of a "new" therapy to the public is often a quick way to fame, but it does nothing to answer the scientific question of what makes behavior change possible.

In this chapter we are not necessarily interested in describing a universal and all-encompassing treatment method which will give 90%-100% cures, and we look with some amusement and alarm at healers who claim just this. We are instead interested in understanding what it is in any and all treatment methods—both formal and informal—which permits patients to leave the consulting room with altered feelings and attitudes about themselves and their world and thereafter to act differently in a way more pleasing to themselves and to others. Psychotherapy is a "stirring-up" process, and all therapies disturb before they cure. The healing question then becomes: What disturbing factors in the dedicated healing relationship lead patients to view themselves differently and to act in revised fashion in the face of their fears and inhibitions?

In today's tendency toward the normalization of psychopathological behavior, as though such pathology were somehow ethically wrong, we overlook the fact that the neurosis of long standing is a variant form of existence or a way of being-in-the-world and not just a set of deviant symptomatic expressions.* There are, of course, transient neurotic and personality

---

* In this essay we will use the concept of the neurosis to include the character and personality disorders as well as all psychic disabilities which disable persons but leave their social reality intact. Even so, our arguments apply also to what we call the psychosis, for we see, rather than a simple dichotomization between a neurosis and psychosis, a continuum of need and behavior.

reactions to stimuli of all sorts which mostly heal themselves, but in this chapter we consider primarily the confirmed neurotic personality structure in which the defenses against life are fully incorporated as a life style and most often out of reach of conscious awareness or will. Such neurotics not only react neurotically, that is, with phobias, obsessions, compulsions, guilt, somatic responsiveness, and the like, but they believe in their inner recesses that they are not of this earth, that they are not like other people, and that they no longer have any essential home anywhere. Neuroticism is the biological penalty man pays for consciousness.

Neurotics are not only anxious—they are that, too—but their distinctive species problem is *dread*—a continuous form of super-anxiety which pervades existence and of which the blatant fears are only the tiny manifestations of a life no longer up to inner expectations or capable of giving basic satisfaction. The quantity of ordinary anxiety present as a measure of mental health no longer suffices as a gauge and is an outmoded and overused concept. Every person is anxious—the human condition is by definition anxiety—and we professionals tend to ignore the integrative and reinforcing aspects of anxiety. We have been overly impressed by a few laboratory experiments with infrahuman organisms in which anxiety has been shown to be paralytic. But in more natural states, say with chimpanzees, and certainly on the bright human social level, anxiety is the color or richness aspect of mental functioning, and its absence would make us all as interchangeable as loaves of bread.

It is dread rather than anxiety which is pathognomonic, for pervasive dread is the indicator *par excellence* that the existence of the neurotic has shifted from care and love and beauty to a constant and special vigilance which denudes it of energy and creative meaning. The most extreme example of this is schizophrenia, where patients are no longer self-involved in socialized living and yield it for an inner and more useful (to them) reality (1).

It is no happenstance that neurotics are so personally involved with barriers, screens, body parts, malfunctioning dynamisms, and subtle paranoid games which limit their social expression. This is perhaps best exemplified by hysteria, by the cloven body image, in which organs over- and underreact in an undying profusion, and where biological systems rarely operate as a unity, or give pleasure in sufficient quantum. All neurotics are by definition constipated or diarrheaic, or both, and have a soft failure of the oral, anal, and genital orifices. Emotionally violent events are kept off center stage to keep the world at bay, to avoid persistent dread, and they offer up a cafeteria of symptoms to provide an air of plausibility. The world sooner or later for them becomes a deforming, hostile place with insufficient love, brotherhood, and reassurance as compensation for the everpresent dread. The preservation of the psychic life is then very much in question. Neurotics there are constantly searching; what they seek is the spiritual reinstatement of Paradise Lost—of their place in the scheme of things, that is, some place to stand, which they presumably had as an infant or child.

Of course, as we shall see later, the neurotic personality stems from a special and unique family environment; as adults, neurotics cannot free themselves from the family contract they made long ago. They still continue to live in the family nucleus, even if they are physically removed from it. The transference is therefore nothing more nor less than an attempt to simultaneously reinstate them in and free them from the family romance, and it is this which provides the "negative mutuality" character of psycho-therapy. The Oedipal complex may lack the wide universality Freud claimed for it, but it is unquestionably part and parcel of every neurotic's makeup and must sooner or later receive attention in the treatment process. The families we have been describing can be designated as *viable* families: *intelligent, suffering, caring, ethical, sensual, romantic, fraternal,* and *achieving.* But this can be said as well of some families not of neurotic-creating scope. The essential difference in production seems to lie in the subtle quality of the family relationship, which not only gives a biased expression to the burgeoning Eros structure of the child, but to a Thanatotic clutching as well. All neurotics stand in a special relationship to death, are obsessively involved with it (both on symbolic and actual levels), and defensively lean toward Eros as a counterreaction to the pull of silent Thanatos. The neurotics' self-image is unconsciously that of the primal murderer. The nuclear family is for them the only cosmos available for the arena of love and murder, and little comes to have indigeneous meaning which is not balanced against the family philosophical schema. When latency and puberty finally come, neurotics lack the preparation upon which to hang their new and independent drives, cognitions, and feelings. They begin to dread their existence and become caught between historical and contemporary needs.

These families seem, in addition, to have more than their share of superego structure. They are above all moral or spiritual or feeling families in which Judeo-Christian verities and virtues are prominently placed even if not practiced in molar fashion. The idea of sin and redemption is prevalent, and the fear of failure of life's mission great. To fail in one's "family task" is a serious omission as well, and "good" or "bad" is a constant valuation in self and family obsession. They are in this way the modern prototype of the Eastern European Jew (and Hassid) who emigrated to America. Such families have a great or small demonology which they cope with in their daily life, and the demon is more often than not cast in the form of one of the family members; and the phenomenological family masochism—a source of great bewilderment to the tyro family therapist—is an unconscious attempt to mystify the demon and exorcise him. Jewish families, for example, are likely to be convinced of the dybbuk and live constantly with him. The family superego is Mosaic, that is, it brooks the golden calf of pleasure even less than does the individual superego of its members. Above all it impresses on its members that there is no fulfillment or survival outside of its own hegemony and boundary. The patient therefore learns not to attempt to problem-solve outside of the family circle. This helps explain why it is so difficult for the neurotic to start therapy to begin with or, even worse, for the family to apply for a family therapy approach. The therapist is the forlorn stranger, and they do not understand how he or she can possibly help.

The underprivileged, the poor, the deprived, and the physically handicapped are not the powerless ones of our society. The neurotic is the prime exemplar of the loss of Power. We live today in a social structure of personal power unknown to previous eons or to history. Power was formerly a collective, but today a single man (or a few men) can terminate or realign a good part of biological nature and of the structure of the civilized world. Personal power is manifested in the control of money, oil, political forms, mass media, nuclear energy, intellectual structures, sex, and race, and even in the manipulation of religious symbols. At no time in history has personal man felt so powerless and had such overwhelming power.* And he often fails to understand the source of his power, is bewildered by it, and lets it go by default. There is nothing extant like feeling totally without power—of being unable to determine one's fate—and of being at the mercy of unknown and malevolent forces. This is the general paranoia of the day.

Neurotics feeling their power loss in this way must compensate by imaginative construction, and they build an elaborate edifice—their castles in the air—and then live in them. By the time they make it to psychotherapy they have psychologically reversed their position of non-power and feel arrogantly superior, with of course inferiorities cropping out all over at odd moments. The coming to terms with neurotic feelings of power and powerlessness is an important part of any therapeutic approach and helps explain why treat-

---

* We once treated a neurotic who each week signed contracts with the military for rocket weaponry worth millions. But in his personal life he could not make and act on the simplest decisions involving love and agonized in a most frightful way over each of them until psychotherapy helped him. The discrepancy between military action involving the fate perhaps of millions and millions of people and the simple statement of "I love you" was startling, to say the least.

ment often seems to resemble an adversary procedure. At any rate, some are now busy exhorting people to be directly assertive, to sidestep the slow therapeutic confrontation, in recognition of the fact that the loss of power which a psychopathology brings no longer has the secondary (power) gain it used to have. And, as we shall see later, the truly powerful of the earth are the keepers of the madhouses and their modern derivatives, the psychiatrists, who are the only men in the world who can remove a President, mitigate a terrorist attack, arbitrate justice by insanity plea, rule on the termination of life, save "souls," and, in general, grant all kinds of hardship exemptions to the difficult business of living. Neurotics therefore properly come to the true social source of power to be healed while yet abjuring the power of their Fathers which got them into trouble to begin with.

Since neurotics basically want to live in the "Kingdom of Heaven" rather than in the "Kingdom of Man," it is surprising that they apply so rarely for help to the religious (therapist) or to religious institutions themselves. In fact, they are aware of Freud's intransigent atheism and come to us knowing that most often the analyst will be in the same mold: no worker of biblical miracles. This is by all means a paradox because their problem is, to begin with, as much a spiritual or S-factor one as it is an instinctual problem. Experience with intercurrent self-therapeutic forms reveals that the intense ambiance provided by a fellow sufferer—an alcoholic, an obese person, a drug addict, a schizophrenic, etc.—and perhaps by encounter groups of various kind makes a certain amount of behavior change possible by the suffering mood and atmosphere of the labeled group itself. It does not seem to matter much who leads it, who makes the interpretations, and who terminates it. The example of suffering, with the victory of suffering over fate, brings a certain spiritual or S-comfort (and inspiration) to the participants and induces them to use the conjoint suffering for behavior change. No one has been as surprised by the efficacy of this kind of behavior change as have psychoanalysts themselves. And yet in their own work they are the social symbol of empathic suffering brought to fruition. No one participates long in this form of healing process without that suffering communion which delegates a certain transformation power to the therapists and makes of them the kind of model described below. Psychotherapy is a moral and spiritual business as well as a scientific one.

The temporal nature of the neurosis has not been sufficiently appreciated and the backward-looking tendencies of psychoanalytic psychotherapy have obscured a part of the problem of behavior change. Frederick Perls, a long-time psychoanalyst himself, attempted to correct the deficiency by a gross reemphasis on the "present" in his Gestalt therapy formulations. The past is subsidized by the future in the neurotic and a part of the therapeutic task is to return the time parameters to a more proper balance. It remains an interesting question why neurotics live so much in the past, titillating themselves in this way with the nuances of evanescent pain and pleasure, rather than using the properties of the moment, often of considerable substance for them, to fulfill themselves. By keeping time frozen, by preventing the "present" and "future" from coming into a more proper juxtaposition, the Fates and the Furies are apparently stilled. The resistance to change is that one can always be worse off! In this sense the neurotic also, paradoxically, lives for the future—"When my analysis is completed"—almost as much as the religious who wait for a reincarnated life in the hereafter.

To find a proper balance between history, intercurrent actualization, and future promise is not easy for anyone; but for the neurotic it is almost impossible. There are wide swings of actualized pessimism and future-oriented hope, analogous to mania and depression, between the pull of the past and the pull of the future, so that a historical state of subduement and a futuristic-promising frenzy succeed each other during the treatment process. What therapy does that is so essential is to confine the neurotic to the *present,* to the interpersonal interchange of the hour, while ascribing to the agent of change, the transference, the important influences of historical alteration. While most therapists believe that transference is the important factor that leads to change, the truth is that in psychoanalytic psychotherapy one learns to live and problem-solve in the *now*—or at least to *feel, think,* and *be* in the *now* of the hour. Why have we consistently diminished this fact?

The resolution of the neurotic situation, as seen through the eyes of the therapist, resolves itself into three questions, all of which must sooner or later involve the patient in the struggle for change. They are: (1) "To be or not to be?"; (2) "What is the good life possible for me?"; and (3) "How much of self to yield in intimacy?" These will now be discussed in turn.

(1) All neuroses are questions of "to be or not to be," that is, the philosophical question of life which challenges the bedrock of existence, its meaning and value. The great majority of people in the world, for many reasons, never reach the point of asking such personal questions. Neurotics are therefore privileged in that they can subjectively challenge their existence, the immutability of their biology, and the controlling forces of the culture in which they are imbedded. Many therapists, Freud among them, believed the function of psychotherapy was to find a cultural/biological compromise that would make a less distressing existence possible. This is true but over-limiting; the wider conception of treatment is a self-examination of the motives and goals of existence and a rebellion against all the restraints to freedom. This

is the true sense of a psychotherapy called "uncovering" and led willy-nilly to the social activism of the sixties.

Now it might be said that it is perhaps unwise to tackle the existential parameters of life with all neurotic patients; that support, persuasion, and even placebo-effects tide the patients over so that their own reparative capacities reinstate them to wholeness without such an examination. The analogy is to medicine, where mothers are often told that their child will outgrow the disease they present. And it is certainly a basic canon of medicine that parsimony governs in every single treatment of record.

The problem here is that most such treatment forms are cross-sectional and expedient and do not consider the life history of the patient and the meaning it has for them. The symptoms are interpreted without regard to the motivational philosophy behind them, and treated merely as symptoms. The model is again the classical medical one, for the patient's philosophy of existence is considered irrelevant to, say, a staphylococcus infection. But we now are beginning to learn that health and disease as concepts are very much dependent upon will, motive, and a way of being-in-the-world. Under certain circumstances even death can supervene by a willful change of reparative threshold. What makes a staphylococcus infection into a life-endangering process is not only the absolute toxicity of the bacterium but its complex acceptance or rejection by the host, the person.

It then becomes a question of the nuclear personality situation of the patient, the so-called reflected human condition, and how frequently it should be worked-through in psychotherapy. Obviously, not all neurotic patients need to penetrate to the core of their existence to change discomfort. Indeed, this should be done with the greatest caution possible. The difficulty, however, is that by the time patients become identified and validated as patients, and come formally to us, they have a self-mandate to problem-solve the fundamental questions of their psyche. They can be put off by quick relief of symptoms; they do accept such relief, but they do not incorporate it into their personality with any residual permanence. They cannot in any sense be said to have been *fundamentally* helped.

Any psychotherapy which meets the definition of an analytic therapy must then, in at least the minimal majority of its patients, cope with the "to be or not to be" question. This must not be interpreted as the specific possibility of a suicide, but as a question of whether or not to continue to live in a chronic and deficient state of being. It is the central question of resistance to therapy, of the interference with those forces which foster freedom and growth and make people afraid to open the Pandora's box of the unconscious. We have too glibly assumed a self-preservation instinct; but on the psychic level there are many forms of nonpreservation, or partial preservation, or even death-equivalents which operate every single day. This is the phenomenology of crippling, its acceptance or rejection by the host, and any psychotherapy worth its salt must cope with partial death. Hope, that overlooked ingredient in every intercurrent treatment form, is simply the expectation that a solution will be found to the basic human (and neurotic) dilemma. Therapists hope this way as well or they would not be professional therapists for very long. The vicissitudes of psychoanalytic psychotherapy, or any other form of psychotherapy for that matter, are precisely those of helping the patients come to terms with their wish to both *be* and *not be.*

(2) It has become apparent in recent years that psychotherapy revolves centrally around moral and ethical issues. Behavior is most often inhibited not so much by fear as by the violation of some inner taboo or restriction. The patient is overconcerned in a Laocoon manner with "shoulds" and "oughts" and these represent duty, responsibility, and the "right thing to do" in his superego. Be that as it may, the question of "What is the good life for me?", "How shall I live and conduct myself?", "What shall be my standards of behavior?", are all central questions in neurotic functioning. This has led one investigator to postulate "admission of sin" and "restitution for damage done" as central concepts in his specific form of therapy (2). And it does appear that the more patients have in the way of material substance and aptitude—and it is usually a great deal—the less free they are to make use of it. The guilt is in proportion to the gifts.

Psychotherapy slowly but assuredly clarifies for the patient what his or her good life is or should be. In this process, money, sex, achievement, artistry, and all of the symbols and acts by which the good life is imaginatively judged come into therapy. Each such moral area of life becomes a battleground in therapy and the transference, the interpersonal therapeutic situation, and the acting-out and living-out away from the hour play their part in their resolution. The "good life" must first surmount the implications of "bad life," and the therapist as superego surrogate is expected to give permission for certain behaviors, or at least to help discriminate from among the possible choices. As we will see in Part II, therapists as models do some of this in a nonverbal way by the example they themselves set.

It is of course true that the product of a successful psychoanalytic psychotherapy comes close to reflecting the therapist as a person and this accounts for the fact that so many treated patients end up as therapists themselves, or at least in the health care professions. The "good life" becomes the healer archetype and the literate, sensate world is then stratified into two kinds of people: (1) healers, and (2) the people who are the object of their healing.

It would be possible now to give a disquisition on the beauties of psycho-therapy as a profession, as a field of caring and attainment, but this would be biased and out of place. We can make the reasonable claim, however, that putting oneself at the service of a suffering person, using one's intelligence and rationality fully, creating and recreating oneself in deep emotional en-counters, working at the borderlands of sensuality and pleasure, being simul-taneously scientific in the Freud/Jung tradition and artistically innovative at the growing edge, promoting personal freedom by structured change, and reaping, among others, special economic and social rewards, all point to a "good" life. We think so; most patients think so too.

(3) A point could be made that all neurosis is a form of narcissism. By this we mean that neurotic patients have the greatest difficulty yielding any part of themselves or their power to others. Their social estrangement is self-estrangement in that they want to keep everything and yet to yield it in love and agape. The adult need to yield in human relationships arouses infantile and childhood competitive counterneeds which interfere with the caring-for process. The neurotic thus characteristically fluctuates wildly be-tween bouts of outrageous generosity and the most anal-tightfistedness of record. There is almost a paranoid watchfulness to the neurotic narcissism in that submission to and defensiveness against intimacy assume the greatest urgency and have a deep aggression and surrender connected with them.

The struggle which is psychotherapy represents precisely that area of conflict in that the therapist demands a regularized intimacy with the patient. At first this is given as nothing more than a polite indifference, a quixotic and sometimes amused participation, then a diffused anger and hostility, turning finally to important affection and love beyond anything the neurotics have allowed themselves to experience. The ebb and flow of these positive and negative intimate feelings are the structure upon which newer cognitions and insights are permitted to do their work. The skill of being a therapist is in the promotion and management of such intimate feelings so that they ultimately lead to newer appreciations of self and world. If this is done well, the neurotic narcissism is recognized for its infantile character and ceases to become the battlefield of every more than casual relationship. But there is always sufficient self-centeredness left after any psychotherapy to motor achievement and attainment needs, and very few neurotics end up as Saint Francis anyway.

Before delineating, in Part II, what it is we think makes behavior change possible, we want to reiterate that the neurosis we treat is a way of being-in-the-world—a set of attitudes, tendencies, and dispositions making up a way of existing or perhaps a character structure—and that it has a history, a present functioning, and a future projection. We do not treat a neurosis or neurotic reaction but a neurotic person—and the person is always more important than the neurosis. This does not of course militate against reducing anxiety and conflict in any way we can and for any period of freedom-time possible. But we feel the secret of what makes behavior change possible lies where the change is more fundamental, deep-seated, and lasting. We are not interested in this essay in 15-minute states of self-actualization.

PART II

According to our conceptualization of behavior change as a regular form of treatment, it is brought about by five sets of change-influences which we descriptively label: (1) "The Therapist As Model"; (2) "The Transference"; (3) "Hope And Persuasion"; (4) "Archetypal Continuity"; and (5) "The S-Factor." These are discussed in turn below, but first coupled with some general observations on behavior change in society.

What basically motivates peoples to change, to overcome the stasis of personal defensive security, is *crisis*. Crisis can be defined as the psychological dilemma produced when neither choice-option open is satisfactory; by behavior requiring a social responsibility not sought or even thought possible; and by stimuli which challenge the fantasy security constructions of years' standing. Anxiety is unequivocally an accompaniment of crisis, and if not quickly resolved leads to panic and despair-formation in their most chronic aspects. Patients then feel there is no choice or solution at all open to them. The following are all presenting crises which resulted in people coming to psychoanalytic psychotherapy and to the consideration of behavior change for themselves.

1. The possibility of impending death.
2. The loss of a loved mate.
3. The loss of a life career.
4. The loss of wealth.
5. Sexual impotence.
6. The death of a mother.
7. Jail and incarceration.
8. Persistent anorexia.
9. Persistent insomnia.
10. Unremitting pain.
11. Depression and autism.

Crisis situations of this kind do not necessarily mean losing one's life and can often go on for years unresolved, but they invariably result in a reduction of self-concept.

The conceptualized ego-power was formerly vested in what has now been lost; or one feels one is about to lose, say, one's mother or one's money, and one cannot conceive of an existence without her or it. Crisis is the stuff of which mania/depression are made and the meaning of one's life then presents itself as a duebill.

Thus all neurotics have by definition lost something powerful by their crisis and seek to recover it in the psychotherapeutic relationship. It is their covert mission, whatever their presenting symptoms, to replace the lost object, or lost power function, and thus be secure again in the old way.

With the loss or power disturbance, reparative functions automatically take over in the personality much before therapy is even a distant possibility. The ego-disturbance is self-evaluated in its full dimension in respect to the particular life in question and adaptations made as best one can.

It so happens that if the psyche has been peculiarly sensitized to the area of power loss, if there is a history of early trauma with regard to it, the adaptations cannot be easily made, or they are inadequately or incompletely made and persistent nagging and anxiety follow. Now, we do not mean to imply that every neurosis is a situational power loss, but there is always a *felt* loss of power, a loss of meaning, and an inability to function. After a self-healing struggle which may last for years, the person is, so to speak, now prepared to become a patient, and seeks only the proper auspices for such dedication of self.

Even so, self-reparation mostly failing, neurotics look to the various institutional healing agencies of society for relief. Closest to hand, most familiar to them, and least expensive, is the family physician. This failing, there are the minister, the professor, the scientologist, the friend, the astrologer, and others. If sufficient relief is afforded by such institutional helpers, then the problem may be resolved at this level or held in a static state. It should be here noted that such help may involve as well biochemistry, faith, psychodynamics, agape, scientific knowledge, placebo, the godhead, the cosmos, mysticism, etc., as well as the personality of the institutional helper. Help for neurotics at this level is sometimes more effective than we have allowed ourselves to perceive, for in our practice we see only its failures. But we know as well that vast numbers of people fail to solve their neurotic problems in this way and do apply for psychoanalytic psychotherapy or similar forms of technical healing procedures. They have for reasons unknown been unable to change their behavior, or to allow anyone to help them change, below the level of the formal therapeutic encounter which psychoanalytic psycho-therapy represents. Their crisis deepens by now and seems more than ever insoluble. They may even become secondarily depressed and autistic, and there is added to this the crisis-conflict about applying for psychotherapy, sharing their dilemma with a stranger, and becoming involved in a process they have no basic confidence in. And, paradoxically, the greater the resistance to coming to the healer, the better the chances of behavior change resulting, and the more certain that the person will eventually have to come for such help.

Considerable damage, in our estimation, has been done by well-meaning Crisis Clinics and paraprofessional helpers through untimely attempts to resolve the crisis which untowardly drain off the *dynamics of becoming a patient*. It is like lancing a boil before the pus is ready to come out. Timing is everything in the therapeutic process and it is maximally functional when it carries the crisis forward and uses feelings and tensions to fuel needed changes and alterations in the personality. Help is only semi-skilled when it resolves the tensions before the personality can incorporate the meaning of the crisis into the ego.

The search for a professional therapist, one who can provide an unconscious salvation-analogue, is a deep, intense, and serious one. While panic may be present because of psychic crisis, the patient's conscious and unconscious shrewdness in the appraisal of the therapist-to-be is not abridged. There is an objective and economic reason why so much of psychotherapy in the world consists of merely a single interview.

The appraising psyche of patients seeks a prediction as to their fate with this particular healer and with his or her specific methodological approach. The first meeting, the prospecting interview, is about as shrewd a bit of horsetrading as, say, buying a new automobile. One patient said in describing her successful treatment, and after failure with two earlier therapists, "I felt as if you had a gun at my temple in the first hour." Here the conscious, preconscious, and unconscious decisions are made to continue therapy or not to come back, and just how much to "give" to the therapist if the patient does return. The appraisal-prognosis is made in part on the pull of the five factors now discussed, and which we see as the psychodynamic basis of any behavior change that comes about from this form of relationship.

1. *The Therapist As Model*

It is obvious that the prospecting patient not only seeks a credible thera-peutic helper, but a specific historical kind of helper as well. As we will see in the section on transference, such helpers must have familial symbolic or reinstatement value, or they will not do. But Strupp (3), we feel, exaggerates the part parental role models and transference projections play in treatment. The intercurrent relationship between patient and therapist, as involved people, has its own modeling rationale and specific therapeutic healing importance, and it is a *real* laboratory in which problem solving is done.

What is it then that patients search for in addition to those functions which have reminiscence value of their parents for them? Aside from such rational (and conscious) sought-after factors as therapist talent, graciousness, and availability, patients seek someone mirroring their own image, their own form of pathology, or at least someone who can relate to their suffering and deprived outlook at the moment. Patients and analysands in private practice are a highly select group, but so are the people who do the healing. There is a social sorting-out process which makes special forms of congeniality (and hostility) engage each other in the therapeutic arena; and they complement each other as needs. Without this unconscious sharing of personal and historical circumstances, most psychoanalytic psychotherapy would not get off the ground. Projecting this event ahead, the termination of treatment is the gradual—and sometimes sudden—dissolution of this unconscious-awareness bond drawing the two participants originally together. So strong and urgent is this choice factor—its counterpart is the overwhelming love of a (nontherapist) person—that patients in long-term therapy say that "therapy is their life" during the process.

It must by now be patent that only by drawing all cathected energies on to the therapeutic situation can it be employed to resolve fundamental character issues. Before going into the therapist model itself, we would like to ask what are the traits and capacities which patients bring to the therapeutic task, what are the reasons we accept them, and how do they aid in the sought-for behavior solutions? What is that state of readiness and availability of becoming a psychoanalytic psychotherapeutic patient?

A. *Intelligence.* Psychotherapy is a highly verbal and cognitive process and proceeds by way of language, signs, and symbols. Patients have most often had some college work, or could have gone had they wanted to, and bring considerable achievement with them to the task. They are prepared to honor information from authoritative and knowledgable sources, to rationalize it, and to incorporate it into their apperceptive mass. It is interesting to observe how the patient in therapy comes to assume the vocabulary, syntax, and grammar of psychotherapy as the analytic process proceeds. While many recent attempts have been made to constitute a less verbal psychotherapy, to give greater recognition to body language, psychotherapy remains very much a resource for the intelligent, informed person, and the outcome of treatment is invariably an even more informed, cultured, and intelligent person.

It is an interesting observation that where the patient has intelligence superior to that of the therapist, the psychotherapy proceeds uneasily, and many times does not go well. The making of a therapeutic interpretation is not only an emotional response of note but a cognitive and intelligent act of moment. All of us tend with some guilt to discount what an intellectual task psychotherapy is. Herman Hesse's bead game is the proper parable of the place of intellect in the psychotherapeutic process. The need for an M.D. or Ph.D. to practice psychotherapy is not so much related to the needs of the treatment situation as it is a manifest indication that the general intelligence requirement of the therapist is being met. Patients like to see therapists who write books because they feel this qualifies their therapist intellectually as well. While psychotherapy with the mentally retarded is feasible, it is intellectually unsatisfying to both participants (4). The patient, to become a patient of analytic therapists, must have beyond-average intelligence, to couple with a similarly beyond-average intelligence of the healer. One may marry a dullard, and one often does, but a dullard would be unacceptable as a therapist!

B. *Dynamic Involvement.* There are those people, the vast majority in the world, who couldn't care less about psychology/psychoanalysis; and there are those people who live and die by it. There may be an analogy here to the attitude some people have toward astrology, religious miracles, gambling-runs, drugs, and certain similar belief-phenomena. The faith-healing practice of evangelical ministers seems to bring forth in their patrons the image of them as a surrogate all-seeing, uniquely powerful, and ultra-benevolent Father. And the godhead is the model. Our patients, on the other hand, are committed to a faith in psychodynamics, and the symbol of Freud/Jung serves as the equivalent Father principle. In their own way, Freud/Jung have a power equal to the godhead for some people in the world.

Psychotherapy is charismatic—some therapies involve more charisma and some less—but faith dynamics, whatever they are, project upon the healer-agent the "other-power" to provide relief, instill euphoria, and generally make things better. If one is then psychodynamically minded, the psycho-therapeutic process makes sense as a primary means to a personal salvation, often called "cure," and its obvious weaknesses and deficiencies as process are disregarded, as they are in the religious arena. Almost without exception, the family background of the patient reveals an aptitude for verbalizing pain and conflict, for cognitive and intellectual attempts at restructuring things, and for a dependency on strength. The patient merely carries these family tendencies forward. Pastoral, marital, industrial and allied counselors all recognize the prevalent psychodynamic-going tendency in our society, and often surrender religious, personnel, and marital techniques for psychodynamic ones. The sensitivity training movement, an industrial development, is a case in point.

The aptitude for psychodynamic insight is thus a special form of readiness for psychotherapy, almost a mandate for it in a sense, and involves unconscious deposits or mental residues of long standing which must be disgorged because of the way in which they invade consciousness. The psychotic person has this encroachment in baldest relief; but we subtly discourage psychotherapy with psychotics for historical reasons, many due to Freud's personal feelings. The "psychotic break" is not a break at all, but a precipitous and violent disgorgement of mental contents, where a graduated and integrated release of them is no longer possible. Even the strongest of dams can give way. The psychotic patient, we might thus say, is at the apogee of psychodynamic readiness, but with smallest hope of therapeutic interpretation. At any rate, consciousness must put some kind of order into its unconscious discontents or founder upon itself. Psychoanalytic psychotherapy offers it a way. That all of this is not just poppycock is demonstrated by the methodological and thematic adoption in modern literature and drama of the dream, symbol, and free-association modes; by the pervasive adoption of Freudian concepts about the nature of culture and man; by the influence of anthropology, sociology, and the behavioral sciences generally in the United States; and by the fact that the commercial media now use Freud/Jung covertly to sell products in large quantities.

C. *Ego-Strength*. It takes considerable ego-strength to complete a long-term psychoanalytic psychotherapy, and neurotics are in their own way tough and persistent characters. It is commonly overlooked that while they are wrestling with their demons, like Jacob with the Angel, and appearing totally helpless, they operate banks, create new products, teach in universities, produce movies and television programs, and do a million or more creative things valued by society. Neurotics are in a certain sense the necessary but painful fulcrum of society.

The kind of ego-strength required to enter and see a psychotherapy through is different from, say, hoisting a 200-pound barbell, driving a sports car at Le Mans, or being a warrior in Viet Nam. It differs in quality because there is no public recognition for the attainment reached, no Medal of Honor is awarded for neurotic resolution, and the resistance to be overcome, the enemy, is always an internal one. Many men face death with a form of euphoria, with a basic trust in their luck or fate; but in psychotherapy there can be no such luck, and one's fate is everlastingly obscured at any particular moment of therapeutic impact. It is therefore not surprising that patients prefer to externalize their conflicts rather than subjectivize them in treatment form.

Critical honesty is the most terrible weapon of all. Satire reveals this, and when directed at the self by the self, it can be very sadistic indeed. Psychotherapy demands not only such honesty, but an invested faith in a mortal stranger, and in an unknown and often despised process as well. This process might well direct honesty toward the patient as a surgeon uses a scalpel. Participation in it calls for the ability to suspend belief in one's own evolved system, in personal history, and to become involved in still another system. And the patient is by now quite anti-system. The business of therapy never comes easy, and only the relatively few in the world really make it completely.

D. *Willingness.* A surprising number of people who have the requisite intelligence, the psychodynamic-mindedness, and the necessary ego-strength are unwilling to enter psychoanalytic psychotherapy. They are either embarrassed by the process, find it comical, or are ultra fearful of its devilish and reducing aspects. This was true of Rainer Maria Rilke, Henry Luce, Richard Nixon, F. Scott Fitzgerald, and a host of others. Some even become therapists or crypto-therapists to avoid the healing process. We are indeed suspicious of any therapist who has not been personally analyzed and who avoids analysis over a professional lifetime. Like the alcoholic and drug addict, with Alcoholics Anonymous and Synanon respectively, it takes a suffering personality base of a high order to provide the "will" for the analytic process over a long haul. This "willingness" factor is something we seriously attempt to gauge before accepting a patient for treatment. If the applicant is still functioning on a safety-raft basis, and desires perhaps only to move to a larger raft, or perhaps seeks only to have it anchored closer to the pier, the prognosis for long-term analytic resolution is unfavorable.

The "willingness" to undergo psychotherapy, as described here, also involves the willingness to pay for it, to give the time to it, and to interpret it to relatives and others in a sympathetic way when it is challenged. The continued role of patient/analysand is a loaded one and both desirable and undesirable in American society. In certain fashionable circles, as for example Beverly Hills, not to have been on the couch makes one an outsider at most cocktail parties. Yet to be in psychotherapy is chafing and demeaning in another sense, and we all shrink from infantile-style dependencies in this macho world of ours. Screen writers, motion picture producers, and similar creative people are heavy personal users of psychoanalysis, and it is revealing to study the way they portray the analyst. Such portrayals range from the Freud/Jung model to the avant-garde Esalen-type encounter leader to a semi-comic healing symbol of upper middle-class society. But in most instances, the depiction of therapists fails to present their dynamic identity, their fundamental interest in people, or the benevolent aspects of the analytic work itself. The typical therapist in the American cinema is a modern-day capitalistic Mesmer at work on a more or less helpless social victim.

The will factor is obscure and complex and cannot be satisfactorily evaluated by the appearance of persons for treatment or by their statement that they now are ready for such treatment. Precisely the contrary may be the case. Szasz is certainly correct when he claims that most people who become patients are constrained to do so in one way or another.

The only true guide, such as it is, for measuring openness to treatment is an empirical test coupled with the intuition that a "suffering readiness" exists for it. Something similar is seen in marital choice where the decision to marry may be delayed for years, then made quickly in a single day on what appears to be specious grounds, and the marriage endures for a lifetime as a kind of permanent bond as though it were imprinted. The "no-marriage" becomes "yes-marriage," and is held positively with the original negative fervor.

E. *Time, Money, and Patience.* Even where willingness, intelligence, ego-strength, and psychodynamic-mindedness are present, there is a fifth and pragmatic motivational aspect that is required before behavior change can occur through psychoanalytic therapy. This is the broader ability of the patient to enter a contractual relationship which stipulates a certain process cost, the method of payment, and an investment of substantial time. It is also necessary to suspend the need to see change immediately.

Patients regularly assess what they give in time, money, and energy against what they receive. This is no different from any other service contract. But since they are not buying as tangible a service as a car repair, they do not have the usual means of evaluating the results. There is today a growing suspiciousness of therapists—perhaps of all service professionals—and patients are less and less willing to offer carte blanche in this way. They are also quicker to seek legal remedies for malpractice. The general information level about psychoanalysis/psychotherapy is now so high that a great deal of the mysterium and awe of the process has vanished. Only the charisma of the therapist more or less remains untarnished and is being offered in increased dosages as compensation for failing magic.

Now that we have outlined the patient's contributions to the healing model, we will proceed to what the therapist brings to the task as model, recalling in so doing that a highly attractive match-up is required for the process to work. While the quotation below describes the background of Jewish emigrants to the United States, it seems to say something about the makeup of American psychotherapists, many of whom come from this ethnic and Eastern group.

> A rich and complicated ethic, a readiness to live for ideals beyond the clamor of self, a sense of plebeian fraternity, an ability to forge a community of moral order even while remaining subject to a society of social disorder, and a persuasion that human existence is a deeply serious matter for which all of us are finally accountable (5).

The psychotherapist, as the modern provenance of mental health, of joy and sorrow, is encapsulated in the drives of such a people. It is what sets therapists, often without awareness, to dedicate themselves to others less psychologically fortunate, and they can in this way continue as well to problem-solve their own history and coordinates (6). But to best describe the psychotherapist as model, the following schema has been adopted.

(a) Moral Person
(b) Rational Person
(c) Creative Person
(d) Literate Person
(e) Concerned Person
(f) Powerful Person
(g) Sexual Person

(a) *Moral Person.* There is today a loss of moral and ethical values in society. The eternal verities by which we guided our lives have been uprooted, have become at times comic, and the uprooting has disturbed the foundations upon which our personality rests. For the first time man has the absolute ability to destroy himself on a mass scale and he has difficulty distinguishing ordinary from absolute aggression. The increase in violent crimes reflects the loss of moral standards and the denigration of life itself. But it reveals as well the uncertainty of aggression. While it is on the one hand more difficult for the State to legally execute a condemned murderer, people die easily and indiscriminately in terrorist bombings, on the highways, and in hunting accidents.

In all of this social disorder the therapists stand untouched in their belief in the order and meaning of society. They relate the violence to love and clarify the unconscious roots of the aggressive instincts by which man wishes to destroy himself. They do not give in to pervasive despair and feel confident that man will find a corrective solution to his nature and his being. Indeed, in a world rapidly cast adrift from moral and ethical moorings, psychology has never been so well established as a social entity, which is to be contrasted with theology, education, law, medicine, and similar fields.

It must be understood that patients require such moral order and certainty to guide them through their growth, for otherwise they would become lost in a vast nihilism. Therapy is the basic moral reinforcement that beauty, justice, and freedom will triumph, and that the therapist knows the way to reaffirming them. While mental healers are often parodied as playing with dirt and misery, they are actually the ongoing basis of all that is moral and ethical.

(b) *Rational Person.* Rationality and intellectuality are demeaned capacities in the 20th century, and the social failure of Western science—organized rationality—has added to the burden. Reason has had a checkered past. Hegel's search for the logical absolute, for the beauty of the mental process, is now in sad retreat. The intellectual prescience of Marx has been corrupted to the military communist state, and Marxian workers are no closer to an egalitarian society than were workers when Marx wrote his texts. Idealism is now considered romantic nonsense by a cynical world.

But we therapists are not really so gloomy. Man's intelligence, his focal consciousness, and his ability to love stem from his unmatched biological evolvement. Intellect cannot be faulted if it goes unused or misused. Freud/Jung were if nothing else rationalists who put their brilliant intelligence to the problem of man's psyche. And it is only by intelligence that we will problem-solve the exigencies of socialized living.

Psychotherapy is a great intellectual achievement, even though we ascribe to emotion the behavior change which takes place. Such ascription is often made theoretically after the fact of healing since we really do not know how it occurs. And we are reluctant to present ourselves to the world as intellectuals since intellect has never been a popular commodity in America. But we do our best to attract the bright and intelligent patient, even rejecting those not so qualified, or become quickly bored with the others who do not challenge our intellectual fantasies and constructions. We transpose id to symbol to make the treatment process more imaginative and intellectual. Our "interpretations" are the intellectual monads which shape the patient's new gestalt of self, but they give us the greatest satisfaction as well. It is all a rational enterprise which attracts primarily those people who want to and need to and can be rational.

(c) *Creative Person.* The new humanistic need is to be creative. That is, every literate, organized, and thinking individual needs regularly to re-arrange his or her perceptions into new and more meaningful forms as a constant process. We are all our own artists and we seek to construct the truths central to our existent being. The mass uniformity of intercurrent identity, of being precisely like everyone else, is anxiety-producing and must be countered by creative efforts to uncover the core of self through artistry.

To patients in their creative distress, it appears as though the therapists are the model of the truly creative person. They help shape lives, originate new psychic ideas and discoveries, influence literature, drama, and dance, and are the repository of the arcane mysteries of more than 2000 years of mystical human transformation. They bridge science and art by icon and symbol and coordinate them by mathematics to attain the deepest statistical understanding. But most of all they are the Neo-Cerberus—the guardian of the Unconscious—whose toll must be paid before the journey may be made underground to new creative vistas. It is a fact that psychoanalytic psycho-therapy makes less creative people more creative. Because of this they are rewarded by promotions, Ph.D. degrees, published books, motion pictures, and other signs of their growing creativity. To be healed is to again become creative.

(d) *Literate Person.* There is an immense chasm between the literate and illiterate person. The difference between one who reads *The New York Times Book Review* regularly and one who does not read at all is almost the dif-ference between Renaissance and aboriginal man. Examination of the life-styles and values of these two forms of existence reveals a basic abstract and concrete division in ways of expressing the world. Few plumbers seek psycho-analytic psychotherapy; but we are on the other hand loaded with writers and professors. Why is this so? Psychotherapy, as Freud created it, was never cast as a living-out experience; it was always meant to be a symbolic resolu-tion of mental forces. That is, the essence of behavior change is a revised psychological experience, and the molar behavior which often follows it is only secondary. This is precisely what the behaviorists confuse in their equa-tion of behavior and contentment. The assumption behind psychoanalysis was that once the mind restructured itself the appropriate molar behavior would follow close behind. It was therefore not thought necessary to pay too much attention to the motor aspects of behavior, and the monads of the analytic psyche became wishes, images, impulses, feelings, and similar mental constructs. Instrumental acts themselves during certain phases of the treat-ment were felt to be resistances. Thus patients can think of punching their analyst, and this is frequently considered appropriate mental content; but to do it *in actuality* would cause the treatment to stop. Imaginal content is highly approved of regardless of its primitive nature, but acting out impulses counters the entire philosophy of psychoanalysis.

Literate people do not act out feelings and impulses in the same way as do the nonliterate; they tend to use images and symbols as vehicles for their feelings of love and aggression. Their novels are their lives, and while their heroes may get into actional difficulties, and usually do, it is by the use of images, symbols, and metaphors that the life story is evolved and finally completed.* We seek (and obtain) literate people for our healing work, and we are happiest with them. This is, we believe, part of the strange passivity of the analytic form of healing dialogue. The treatment of children is by necessity active and preliterate, as it is with highly disturbed patients. But the behaviorists notwithstanding, patients obviously require a highly literate person to help them write their "novel" and thereby bring their message to the world.

(e) *Concerned Person.* In a society which no longer cares, and certainly does not care deeply for its deviants, the therapist remains the one person who really cares about the atypical, the gauche, the awkward, and the crippled. All systems of healing, and this includes the behavior therapies, give a central position to the healer. And some, like that of Carl Rogers, make the "positive regard" of the healer the cornerstone of behavior change. Whatever the true state of the healer's regard for the patient, it is clear that therapists offer what Heidegger called *Care,* and they devote their professional life to extending *Care* to those who can use it.

It is difficult to get anyone today to listen to one's problems even though "crisis telephone lines" have proliferated. Patients have often found it necessary to write books to get someone to listen to them and others have perhaps had similarly to murder to get a hearing. But going to a therapist assures one of undivided and undisturbed attention, and an empathic one at that. It is many ways better than going to the priest, who seems ordinarily to rise up above routine consultation only at birth and death, and is anyway somewhat uneasy with mental disease. The value of the audience itself which the therapeutic hour makes possible must not be diminished as a force in behavior change. More important yet is the example of a caring person, the therapist, who is concerned—concerned about the loss of joy—when others no longer care and make the patient out a low-grade nuisance.

The Christian concept of "love thy neighbor" applies to the healing enclave, and the concerned therapeutic model is designed to help patients also become concerned and involved. They are induced to leave autism and

---

* A good recent example is John Fowles, *The Ebony Tower,* New American Library, 1974.

paranoia behind and to test the interpersonal encounter on a new basis. Demonstrated humanism in treatment is the means by which the alchemical transformation takes place.

(f) *Powerful Person.* It is questionable whether patients would long endure in psychoanalytic psychotherapy if they experienced the therapist as a weak and helpless person. The shock would be of the same order as that of pubescents when for the first time they see their adored fathers in a realistic and limited social light. It is necessary to the goals of treatment for the therapist to be seen as powerful, and it is fortunate that therapists are anyway a socially powerful group. One of the difficulties of having sexual relationships with a patient, beyond the ethics of it, is the loss of treatment power which is inherent in the intimacy. But, obversely, should healers begin to feel superpowerful and to abuse their power by innovation and in other ways, then difficulties begin to arise in the treatment.

Powerful people attract, and they attract most specifically the weak and dependent. Power is a vacuum which draws to it the vassals and instruments necessary to carry out the mandates of power. In this instance personal power is used for opening the world of others whose existence is coarcted. Patients in treatment first borrow their therapist' power, make a part of it theirs, and then go on to create their own. Not a single healed case of record was not more powerful at the end of our treatment than before. Indeed, so powerful do patients usually become that they eventually engage and ultimately defeat the therapist. This defeat is precisely their cure.

(g) *Sexual Person.* The sexual (and pleasurable) aspects of psychoanalytic psychotherapy are not frequently referred to as aspects of treatment. But sensuality, the id, is the inevitable subject matter before the house in our work. The dialogue itself is between persons who are covertly attracted to each other, are most often of complementary sex, and whose attraction comes eventually to be labeled "positive," and even by the term "love." Therapists foster emotional arousal, in an affectional framework, with the awareness that its step-brother, hostility, is just around the corner and needs to be worked through. There is a heightened feeling of affection in therapy which is not objectively justified by the properties of the situation or even by the people involved. This has its historical infantile aspects, but both participants seem pleased to be transported in this way by their feelings and seek the titillation.

If the treatment problem were merely sexual, then neurotic patients could be cured by going to sexual libertarians or to prostitutes and they would not come to us. The resolution of their sexual conflicts would be directly actional through intercourse. Much group work makes available such sexual benefits as a side issue. But the resolution of sexual conflict with a therapist is a much more complex, even more dangerous, but more certain path to solution. It is necessary for patients to closely approach the incest chasm, to test their love against its taboos, and to experience its imaginal magnificence as did Oedipus Rex. It does not therefore suffice for patients to love just anyone, for they have to love precisely that person whom they are not permitted to love. This is what comes to happen in psychotherapy.

On a realistic level, and in Western culture, we represent a high point of social attractiveness to the patient—creativity, wealth, power, youth, knowledge, charisma, travel, etc.—and some of them become our camp followers similar to those attracted to boxers, race drivers, rock bands, and religious revivalists. The therapist becomes the sexual symbol of a defeated sensual development which promises greater release than ever thought possible. The patient even dreams about it! We thus uneasily place our sexuality at the disposal of such patients—without, however, being sexual. But there should be no misunderstanding about it. No transference is worth the paper it is written on if it does not carry some form of sexual freight. The saving grace is, as O. Spurgeon English puts it, that we marry our wives and not our patients. Such distinction is the difference between love as a concept of treatment and love as the center of a family. And never do the twain meet.

Now that we have delineated the therapist as model, the second factor, that of transference, can be discussed.

2.   The Transference

The great discovery of modern psychiatry is the fact of transference. All therapists are aware that when they formally undertake to bring about a behavior change they are not alone with the patient, for the ghosts of the patient's past are very much present. It is the covert mission of patients to reinstate/relive certain historical experiences in their lives which they never fully experienced or solved to their satisfaction. This is their search-quest and they cannot yield it permanently. Therapy puts them back into the ancient family arena and gives them another chance at it.

None of us ever completely lose the image of our childhood, and it is a residual need that we preserve the image as long as possible. In sensitized people, say neurotics, this is a mandate, for neurotics feel that they have left their more important self somewhere in childhood and that they cannot be an adult without recovering it. They grope perpetually in the limbo for it and will not live without it.

Our patients appear at our door with a transference readiness, even select their therapists with such unconscious mission, and then proceed to transform the hard realities of the healer into the historical family person they loved or hated. The transference is an uneasy thing with us because so much of it is unreality, and so much unearned. It can switch from love to hate in an instant. But it is a felt "honest" reality of the patient, which is the phenomenological difference between the healer and the to-be-healed, and only when it has this personal numinosity can the treatment be truly effective.

Obviously, love and hate are the emotional vehicles of growth and development. The child is prepped for love and hate in marriage, work, social relationships, and in many other ways. This is what parenting is all about. But Freud limited man too much when he confined the family romance to only sex and pleasure. There is certainly an Oedipal attraction between parents and offspring, and we even believe it is a more or less universal phenomenon. But what is perhaps more important is that father/mother become the central existential fact for the child—the humanistic model of being—and life fails without it. In the Warsaw ghetto some Jews introjected their Nazi captors and behaved like Nazis toward other Jews. Children, similarly, introject the father/mother, and under unhappy circumstances never are able completely to relinquish the powerful introjection; they spend their lives fighting it or capitulating.

Psychotherapy begins with the unwritten premise that treatment will not be enduring. The best relationship stops at the moment it begins, and every hour is tested against "how much longer?" The family romance may be forever, but psychotherapy makes it finite. It stops the introject.

Observations of young children reveal how controlling parents truly are, how they foster dependency in a thousand and one ways, and how they resent the growing independence of their children. Much effort is expended by the parent in forming *my* child as *my* child, that is, like *me*. Rebellion, which is becoming unlike the introjected parent, is a source of great contention and conflict. A diffuse resentment by the child begins to color familial love, ambivalence rears its ugly head, and the violent and adoring mix of feelings must ultimately be brought to therapy. Two loving enemies then agree to meet and resolve their feeling on a new and modern battleground.

But transference is more than what happens in a therapeutic relationship. We believe, for example, that transference is an important element in the selection and retention of a mate, in the worker's relationship to a supervisor, in the intimate constitution of a friendship, in collective attitudes toward the social entity, and in feelings toward the maimed, the destitute, and others. Transference is a highly emotional life flux. While it has a specific phenomenology and predictability in the therapeutic situation, outside of it, it ebbs and flows like the tides of the sea. It is also the fundamental aspect of "falling in and out of love," now the preoccupation of modern man.

There is now a tendency to demean the transference in Gestalt therapy, encounter and sensitivity training groups, transactional analysis, behavioral modification, various body approaches, and the like. But these modes of therapy close their eyes to the transferential effects of the person of the therapists in favor of their methodology. It is felt to be more scientific and more respectable to vest the healing power in a set of operations rather than in the person of the healer. But all such variegated treatment methods are revealing themselves as having equal curative effects, so that we are willy-nilly left with the differences (and similarities) of the healing personalities involved. The point is that the transference is a powerfully established tool, now validated for a century, and our healing would be even less effective than it is without acknowledging its effects. There is, we suppose, some residual guilt in standing in for a parent when directness and confrontation are the vogue. Therapists as well have unresolved feelings about their own parents.

We recognize the power of the transference, are grateful for it, and utilize it where we can for behavior change. We do not interpret it as still another neurosis, the so-called transference neurosis, and we do not analyze it as a formal set of propositions. But we know that if a transference is not at all possible, then psychoanalytic psychotherapy will probably not proceed very far, and the patient is best referred to other modes of behavior change.

3. Persuasive Healing Forces

There are a host of quiet healing forces which congeal around the thera-peutic situation but which are obscured by it. These are ages-old change influences and are part and parcel of all therapeutic enterprises through history. We consider in this section such concepts as *persuasion, suggestion, faith, placebo-effects,* and *hope.* These are in a sense distasteful aspects of psychotherapy since they lack elegance, are scientifically obscure, and are considered contaminated by popular use and misuse through the ages. They nevertheless help bring about behavior change and are very much a part of every therapeutic situation.

(a) *Persuasion.* There is an element of persuasion in every attempt to minister. The healing ambiance is one which persuades, and which claims: "We know the way. If you follow us, we will bring you change and joy." While this does not in the modern therapist have the staged dramatic persona of the shaman, it is yet sufficiently staged and dramatic for its purpose, as

Goffman has demonstrated. And therapists add to the natural healing persuasion of the situation by a special reserve, by upstaging their mysterium, by instrumentation, by books, by ancillary personnel, etc. Indeed, everything is done to make it difficult for the patients to say that they will not be helped, or that they have not been helped. The greater the repute of the therapist, the greater the persuasive effects. It is almost impossible, for example, to go to the Mayo or Ochsner Clinic and then make the public statement that one has not been helped at all.

In psychoanalytic psychotherapy, by the time patients come for treatment, they are already half persuaded that they will change. One has, for example, only to offer a mild hypnotic trance to such a "pre-sold" patient to see how quickly the complaining symptoms are reduced. The same thing can be done by merely saying to patients that they will get better and insisting that they do. Our principal patients, neurotic personalities, are highly suggestible and persuadable people. Patients subtly recognize the persuasive situation and want to be persuaded into change. They look earnestly for prestige figures who can coerce them into health while yet denying the power of authority.

Charisma and persuasion are closely related. Charismatic healers persuade by a vast, quiet confidence, by a special insistence, by an appeal to both emotion and logic, by magic, and by claiming to be the best of all that is known and practiced in their art. The will to believe takes over, and there is a surrender of critical faculties and ego-forces for a higher good. The best therapists are aware of their persuasive abilities, employ it not as a direct force but as a framework for working through, and make it a part of the certainty of their professional ego. Frank has noted that behavioral therapists use persuasion and suggestion to highly refined degrees (7).

(b) *Suggestion.* Tape recordings reveal that more suggestion and suggestive reinforcement is used in psychoanalytic psychotherapy than we have heretofore known. This is somewhat different from operant conditioning, where the intent to influence is more direct. The therapist's "third ear" not only has a "timetable" for the evolvement of the patients but an image as well as to what they should be like at any specific moment. We use quiet suggestion to steer our patients through this timetable, to keep them on course, and to shield them from the various interferences to the major goals of treatment. We may at times even make direct suggestions, or make demands on the patient. Indeed, the entire course of a therapy can be described by the suggestive healing parameters involved. At termination of treatment and as proof of it, the suggestive bag has been used up, for patients will no longer accept the suggestions they eagerly seized upon earlier in therapy.

There are, of course, forms of therapy which center themselves directly around suggestion. Hypnotherapy and assertion training are two examples. The results, insofar as we know, seem to be neither better nor worse with certain kinds of patients than other forms of therapy. But our point is that one does not need to make suggestion the central focus of any treatment since it is present in every form of treatment anyway and its importance in behavior change is for us only peripheral.

(c) *Hope.* Neurotics as a group are more or less hope-less people and have notoriously poor morale. Psychotherapy is an attempt to reinstate morale in them. Hope is a projection of present into future, with a more salubrious outcome expected and, whether warranted or not, changes the human predicament as intercurrently experienced. The truly hopeless—those condemned to death—cannot basically participate in behavior change.

The therapeutic situation is by nature one of hope. Every new patient is approached by the healer with an optimism warranted not only by past successful outcomes but by an indigenous hopefulness not so objectively sustainable. Psychotherapists are at any rate hopeful people who see the brighter side of human relationships and refuse to become depressed by the human condition. They offer the patient optimism in the face of long-standing self and family pessimism or, more properly, they refuse to participate in the self's defeat of self.

Patients in every longer-term treatment attempt to get the therapist to share their depression, sometimes even to make them crazy, to abide with them in their inner world of gloom, and to concur in their belief that they are hopeless. But we have never met a patient, not even a regressed hospitalized schizophrenic, whom we didn't feel hopeful about in some way, and our distaste of the mental hospital is that it has been, for the most part, "the place of little hope."

Whether or not the titred hope is rationally based or has merely fantasy aspects is not at the beginning a material question. The opening phases of psychotherapy call for some subtle guarantees of outlandish hope, and we know that even patients with diagnosed terminal cancer sometimes remit their disease. As scientists we do not find any prognosis 100% certain, and a possibility of some viable improvement is always present in any state of being as long as life is present. The function of a psychotherapy is to use this outside possibility of improvement as motivation to change, and then to bring such hope to fulfillment, if at all possible, in a realistic way.

(d) *Faith.* Faith has been usurped over the centuries by priests and theologians as a dynamic uniquely their own. But it is very much a part of behavior change as we find it in psychoanalytic psychotherapy. The entire philosophical underpinning of healing seems to be a kind of primordial or holistic fath that it will work. Those who live by the idea of psychoanalysis are helped by psychoanalysis; those who lack such faith in psychoanalysis are not often helped by it. And it is the same with any form of behavior change extant.

The charismatic minister "heals" the sick because the patients' faith in the godhead, and in the minister as God's agent, does integrate them, at least for the moment, and they really feel better and more effective. In our thera- peutic work, we demand a similar faith and most often receive it, for other- wise the realities of the scientific therapeutic situation would not always justify our optimism. The faith in Freud/Jung as symbols, in the free-associa- tive mental process, in the encounter with the healer, assists the patients in healing themselves, that is, in fulfilling their faith. Without such faith, they are indeed in desperate circumstances. With it they can for the moment, and as a model of broader possibilities, step outside of their neurosis, offer themselves up to a new vista of self, and have the belief of change. Maintain- ing therapeutic faith then becomes an important part of the entire therapeutic process, and it is reinforced by the visible gains made hour by hour backed by the viable forces of the transference. When therapeutic faith is no longer present, the psychotherapy loses its potency, and patients begin to look elsewhere for a place to deposit their faith. They then enter the termination phase insofar as our work is concerned.

(e) *Placebo-Effect*. Many studies have demonstrated the aptitude for change by use of inert chemical ingredients masquerading as curative potions. In controlled studies tightly designed, the placebo was often as effective as the medicament given on a blind basis. This is a disturbing phenomenon to scientists and unexplained as yet.

It does not seem to us farfetched to extend chemical placebo-effects to persons. Thus we feel that therapists can have placebo-effects on their pa- tients. While therapists are not taken internally, their introject is very much metaphorically ingested. In the psychotherapy of schizophrenia, for example, we often find that just being-with the therapist is healing in its own right. And sometimes it appears to us that just *being-with* the therapist for a *substantial number of hours* is what cures regardless of anything that is done. Is this placebo-effect?

The placebo must in some way galvanize and/or organize patients to im- prove their circumstances because they believe that they have been given a "magic bullet," or equally powerful weapon, against their demon/distress, and believe further that they are not permitted to disregard the magic. They cannot allow it not to work, and must give up their complaints to actualize the magic. The therapist thus delivers the promise of the placebo by force of will, by a focal consciousness, and by a reassignment of energy. In some similar way, the person of the therapist comes to stand for the "magic" of transformation, and "instant" cure is now a matter of record. Placebo-effects help explain the curious fact that all therapeutic systems tend to heal equally, and that all healing persons of whatever training do heal somewhat. Faith and hope and persuasion and suggestion are doing their quiet work in placebo form.

4. *Archetypal Continuity*

The study of culture reveals that nothing symbolic is ever lost and only the forms of expression change. We speak here of what Jung called archetypes, or those universal symbols which form, express, and integrate human energy. In the neurotic there is a discontinuity or break in archetypal structure which the dream and fantasy attempt to restitute. We can classify these archetypal discontinuities for discussion purposes as relating to the *body*, to the *psyche*, and to the *cosmos*.

Much has been written about the reaction of neurotics to their bodies (8). The point is that there is a biological continuity in all species, and it is necessary for the members to accept their organic nature to feel whole or intact. Neurotics are divorced from organic nature and find no joy or meaning, for example, in the beauty of a lake, mountain, or sea. The sun and moon do not seem to exist for them other than as simple external regularities by which they live. They are in a sense disembodied and denatured people, while yet very much exploiting and abusing their bodies, and being poetic about nature. Neurotics do not themselves perceive their bodies as human, as part of themselves, and in their deeper recesses consider themselves disembodied spirits rather than constituent flesh and blood. Obviously, if the body is not present, it cannot feel sensate sexuality and pleasure.

Psychoanalytic psychotherapy helps make the body, the body image, more palpable. It first of all reassures patients that their bodies are there; it then allows a comparison of their bodies with the visible body of the therapist. And finally it makes it possible for the bodies to meet, even to touch. But most of all what it does is return biological continuity to the patients and give them renewed membership in the somatic club. Thus it is not unusual for most patients during treatment to enroll in judo, tai chi, karate, boxing, massage, or other body contact training. They are rediscovering the archetype of the body.

Little remains to be said here about the *psyche* of the neurotic. Again, there is a feeling of a gap or discontinuity in the neurotic's psyche, of a mind that does not belong, and which cannot function. The patients fear their psyche, their unconscious part of self, their creative powers, and will not join their (demonic) psyche to anything—certainly not to other people. This is one reason they keep so free-floating and unattached.

To be human and actualized requires that the unconscious contain all of the archetypes necessary for existence: that they be manifested, experienced, and integrated into the mainstream of life. Communion with others is based upon that feeling of universality which the archetypes make possible. They are as well the basis of the state of calmness, of belongingness, and of life meaning. This is what we call the *cosmic* aspect of the archetypes.

The primary task of psychoanalytic psychotherapy is the freeing of buried symbols, the energy they contain, and recasting them for more efficient human interaction. An example of this is the mandala, which sooner or later appears in every patient's dreams and creative work. The mandala, as we know, is the most ancient representation of the self in geometric form. But the transforming symbol may just as well be an apple, a library, a piece of bread.

At any rate, the Jungian archetypes of animus-anima, Great Mother, sun and moon, Wise Old Man, and many others are the metaforms around which the energy and content of the therapeutic hours revolve. They are what get clarified, interpreted, and transformed. Their reinstated continuity is what heals in the final sense.

5. *The S-Factor*

Psychotherapy is today a part of what Mishima calls the disease of objectivity—the attempt of Western science to stamp man and nature in the mold of 20th century physics (9). Admittedly, the physics of Mach and Einstein is the model of all creative science, *qua* science, and the discovery of the nature of the atom which followed is unrivaled in the history of man. But the outcome of this physical discovery has been a pervasive social pessimism, especially in such scientists as Einstein, Szilard, Rabi, Oppenheimer, Bronowski, and others who made it possible. The appearance of the "final" destructive weapon, the final solution to aggression, the possibility of an unleashing of massive quanta of unbridled energy, leaves civilized man at the mercy of primitive and unregenerated hostile minds.

Science is at any rate more than physics, more than constituent matter; and mind, psyche, and spirit can no longer be relegated to a mysticism categorization and left outside of the purview of science. The former authority and awe of science are now damaged, and very few university students accept

scientific method as the way to truth or to the good life. Science has become instead the backdrop of political institutions, of industrial process, often
with tremendously damaging effects on man and society. Above all, it has
lacked a superego, an ethic, to guide its great creations, and to put them to
socially constructive use. The ascent of man (of Bronowski's) can perhaps
be better rephrased, as "the descent of man."

In psychoanalysis, Freud's attempt to produce an objective science modeled
on his first love, neurophysiology, has failed; but it was necessary to make
the attempt. Even so, he was accused of being a non-scientist then, and was
never admitted to academic respectability at the University of Vienna. It
seems therefore ironic that we should now demur from what we consider an
over-determined Freudian biological view of man.

The deep therapeutic encounter forces us to a different realization about
the *human* role of science, and this is particularly true for the wild exuberance
of the psychotic mind. Such patients teach us that they cannot be healed
by a biological methodology alone, and that they require certain metapsy-
chological constructs to understand their psychotic state of being and to help
change it. We call this the S-Factor. The term "soul," which is perhaps most
appropriate to such a metapsychology, is repellent to us as scientists if for
no other reason than 2000 years of Judeo-Christian theology has abused the
word. What we mean by it comes closest to what jazz or rock musicians call
soul. It is not even acceptable to us to call our phenomenon "spirit," or say
that it is "spiritual," for again it seems to us that these terms have been
corrupted by vested religious interests. We are therefore content at this time
with the appellation S-Factor, without relating "S" specifically to spirit or
soul as we know it from theologians.

The following fragment about the work of C. G. Jung is perhaps a useful
introduction to the S-Factor.

> Again, a doctor with a practice in a remote mountain district of Switzer-
> land asked Jung to see a simple girl of the hills who he thought was
> going insane. Jung saw her and realised at once that she had neither
> the intelligence nor the need for a sophisticated and intellectually de-
> manding analytical treatment. He talked to her quietly in his study and
> came to the conclusion that all she suffered from was the fact that her
> community, in a sudden enthusiasm for what was thought to be modern
> and progressive, had poured scorn on all the simple beliefs, ideas, cus-
> toms, and interests which were natural to her. Her own natural state,
> her first, as it were, primitive self, had lost such honour with herself
> and others that her heart wilted because of a lack of incentive in the
> kind of prospect life held out for her.
> Accordingly, he got her to talk to him at length about all the things

she had enjoyed and loved as a child. As she talked, almost at once he saw a flicker of interest glow in what had appeared to be burnt-out ashes of herself. He found himself so excited by this quickening of spirit of a despised self that he joined in the singing of her nursery songs and her renderings of simple mountain ballads. He even danced with her in his library and at times took her on his knee and rocked her in his arms, undeterred by any thought of how ridiculous if not preposterous would be the picture of him in the eyes of orthodox medical and psychiatric practitioners when told of what he described with a great laugh to me as "such goings on."

At the end of a few days the girl was fully restored to a state of honour with herself and he sent her off in high spirits to her home. She never again regressed. Indeed, the result appeared so miraculous that the learned doctor in the mountains wrote to Jung and asked him how it had been achieved. Jung wrote back to the effect that "I did nothing much. I listened to her fairy tales, danced with her a little, sang with her a little, took her on my knee a little, and the job was done."

But the doctor was never persuaded, Jung told me, that his leg was not being pulled, although the girl stayed what the world termed "cured" (10).

Every patient in psychotherapy must be treated as a one-of-a-kind metaphor and not as a set of biological or social systems. Only by understanding, embracing, and transcending the metaphoric life of the patient can he or she be led to behavior change. No psychotherapists of record apply their learned methods exactly as stated in classic textbooks, as their teachers taught them, or even as they might claim that they are applying them. If they do not in some way deviate from objectivity and appeal to the metaphor of the patient, they ultimately lose that patient or stop short of the patient's goal. So they improvise. They fill in the gap between their *method* and the *in vivo* person by the S-Factor.

This was the essential difference as well between Freud and Jung as healers. Freud quietly insisted that his patients fit his theoretical formulations, and said in justification that this was the only way they could be healed. Jung never took the announced Freudian neurotic etiology so seriously, and he diminished theory for the phenomenological transaction with the patient. Freud was ever the observing scientist and his patients were never free of his microscope. Jung lived his psychoanalysis and did not seek intellectual confirmation for scientific hypotheses at any cost. He sought his data rather in ancient and scholarly texts, as did the progenitive Scholastics. Jung was thus holistic and gestaltist, while Freud was descriptive, categorizing, and generalizing. One sought scientific laws; the other, to experience suffering humanity.

It was of course ordained that Jung would come to the S-Factor, and not only because he stemmed from a line of ministers. His early work with chronic schizophrenics at Burgholzli taught him that a psychotherapy could never be a formalized or mechanized thing, and that the examination of the unconscious called rather for an improvisational and artistic approach than a systematic one. Each schizophrenic patient has a code, and that code has, so to speak, to be broken. It could not then, and cannot now, be broken by a cool, aloof, objective therapeutic stance, Only by the deepest communicable and archetypal resonance of the healer with the patient can it be done. Such resonance others have labeled "soul" or "spirit" because it transcends the sensate and carries the bearer to higher states of being. The S-Factor we would therefore define (in psychotherapy) as those transcending influences which heal, which change things, but which go beyond defined stimulus-response relationships. It is the essence of man meeting the essence of man on the highest level of communication, one which is not yet clear to us.

The hiatal relationship between spirit and matter is the great philosophical question of the day. The problem can no longer be avoided. The world within, the ontic nature of being, the place of the imagination, etc., can no longer be explained on the basis of a biochemistry, and matter and "S" meet somewhere inside every person and have important behavioral effects. The world without, the world of objects, is more straightforward, more explainable, conforms to scientific possibility; but in that space between inner and outer, the vessel, as Perry calls it, is the difference between a philosophy and a science.

Consciousness is the stuff of psychotherapy. But so little is known of consciousness that 100 years of psychoanalysis has only begun to touch the fringe areas of repression and resistance. Consciousness in our sense is a feeling of being a part of things, of an awareness of the purpose and goals of existence, of being fundamentally related to all men, and to the cosmos itself. When consciousness is restricted or coarcted, the person falls into dis-ease.

In our concern with healing methodologies, we have misplaced the person for the method; we have failed to understand the unconscious in the way Jung thought necessary. The appearance of primal scream therapies, of "psychotic blowouts," etc., is recognition of the fact that we have missed something fundamental in our therapies which only the most primitive forms of statement and expression can now reinstate.

There is an S-Factor experience in every long-term treatment situation. Psychotherapy is not just a place where the shit of mankind is deposited. It has a positive or S-Experience aspect as well. It is Rogers' positive regard carried to its most logical evolvement. Love, agape, care and concern do not completely describe it. It is better stated by the poetic encounters of Dante and Beatrice, Laura and Petrarch, Héloise and Abelard, etc. It is so powerful and moving a force that it is what life is all about—at that particular moment. And self-preservation itself yields to it. It is Maslow's peaked peak experience, and it is surrounded by awe and reverence and beauty. It is not only "sensate," but transforming, transcending, and transporting as well. It is language with unspoken syntax and instant identification and introjection. It is verification and validation of being human with a new set of ground rules. It manifests itself in those special states which govern at birth and death.

In religion, the S-Factor is personified by Christ, Buddha, Mohammed, Vishna, and others. All spiritual or S-feelings are related to the functions of such deities. The personified deity counters the devil, keeps him at bay, and sets standards for grace and salvation. But such personifications are not necessary to modern psychology, can even be harmful in the search for truth, and often leave patients no better off in their worship. The emphasis for us is best placed on the S-experience itself rather than on the personifications. We must therefore allow ourselves to scientifically examine "S" in the same way as we are now doing with parapsychology and hypnosis.

The S-Factor is the residual of all those factors which are instrumental in behavior change and which have been described above. It is scientifically non-describable at this time, and is known principally by its effects. This does not, however, make it not so. The S-Factor is the nonorganic aspect of the psyche, of its growth and change, and luck, fate, odds, and synchronicity are small parts of it. Metapsychologically it is transcendent communication, massive openness, Maslow's peaked peak experience, the point beyond love, the deepest form of introjection, and a cosmic feeling of unity, identity, and peace. Such feeling states are present sooner or later in every psychoanalytic psychotherapy and are related to the outcome.

There is some evidence that the S-Factor is feminine and that the incandescent meeting of the feminine and masculine, the animus and anima, provides for the S-experience. Historically, the "S" was contained in the divine priestess who sought truth by deep intoxicated communication with the depths of her soul and then related it to world events, the masculine. Certainly the S-Factor is a part of the collective unconscious in that it is the function of the unconscious to bind the organic and the psychic into a single mode. In that flux, the instincts are temporarily suspended and the creative cathexis vastly magnified. This provides a glow, a numinosity, an ambiance, a set of feelings, an aura of hope and transcendence which is "S." The S-Factor must then be considered a part of the collective unconscious from which all humanity stems. It defeats and goes beyond mere sensation, and psychoanalytic psychotherapy is a matter of "S" as well as of learning. Not much more can safely be said about "S" except the conviction that just as modeling, transference, hope, suggestion, faith, and persuasion have now been found to be important aspects of behavior change, so is the ineffable S-Factor. It is a spirit of change which leads to change on a basis above and beyond what we know of the causality of learned events in human existence.

PART III

In concluding this essay on the nature of behavior change it is necessary to consider the broader question of "behavior change for what purpose." People do not change character readily, and most of them never change at all. For change to take place, as departures from basic and set personality patterns, there must be an overriding motive to change. Adjustment, self-preservation, reduction of anxiety, etc., no longer adequately describe the circumstances of modern life and the way behavior change occurs.

It seems apparent to some of us that the idea of repression as the *bête noire* of mental functioning is now an overdone thing. Expression (of impulses) is the order of the day and the libido flows in great quantities in nearly everbody. Hysteria has abated, repression lessened but still people complain of malfunction and unhappiness. Indeed, the dissatisfaction with life, in the face of affluence and impulse-satisfaction, has never been so great. In many instances, psychotherapy even involves making provision for a few repressions rather than their dissolution.

Anxiety as a measure of psychic disablement can in the same way no longer be employed as defining psychopathology. It can no longer be a goal to leave a person free of anxiety, for it is the motor, the basis for object cathexis, and the quality of his or her life. Anxiety was never the psychic crippler Freud thought it to be. Since we can no longer accept Freud's sexual etiology of the neurosis either, the anxiety surrounding sex, the *deus ex machina* of neurotic inhibition, falls of its own weight. To reduce anxiety is no great feat; to instill meaning and purpose to existence around that anxiety is a considerable achievement. Behavior change to be more than pedestrian must somehow involve the core of the patient. We treat the person, not the anxiety.

It seems that infancy and childhood as the genesis of adult psychopathology, as the developmental time and place of neurotic occurrence, and as formulated by the classical Freudians, has receded. We no longer look to developmental traumas for the answers to adult behavior. This is not to say that the experiences of childhood have no effects, but to point up the modern finding that in adult resolution they can be set on the sideline more than we had ever thought possible. It is as though adults change their behavior, leaving their childhood situation an island, but an island which no longer troubles them in the old way. Childhood trauma has often become epiphenomenal.

Personal history has become devalued along with most other devaluations, and increased importance is being placed upon the interpersonal situation in the here and now. Patients solve not their history but their intercurrent problematic situation. And so it is that will, faith, hope, morale, and similar concepts play a greater part in treatment than we had ever thought possible.

In the history of psychiatry the collective aspects of the psyche have been slighted. Group therapeutic approaches were until recently merely a holding or finishing action for patients in individual dialogues. Jung received a great deal of abuse for his ideas on the collective unconscious. But our experience now is that behavior change under collective influence is highly viable. It often succeeds where psychoanalytic psychotherapy fails. Intrapsychic introspection, if resistant, seems often to come to a good outcome when its labors are placed in a collective setting. The principle of privacy of conflict resolution must now be amended to include a kind of group disclosure when the group disclosed to has a certain suffering or stigmated affinity.

In all of this, insufficient attention has been given to self-healing on the part of the organism, to the time-limited nature of the various psychic problems, and to the "burning out" of conflicts with age. Just as crime seems to be a disturbance of youth and early adulthood, so do neuroses (and psychoses) seem age-connected in this way. Biological and psychic rhythms, the timing of major mental crises, their periodicity and valuations, are only beginning to be understood. The question therefore of how many people spontaneously heal themselves, or outgrow their conflicts, or no longer find their conflicts useful, is a material one. Some of the cure which occurs through these factors is attributed to the work of psychotherapy, but just how much is a matter of dispute. Eysenck would have us believe that psychotherapy has little or no effect on behavior change.

The categorical (imperative) designations by which psychiatric diagnoses were heretofore made now apply only loosely at best. That is to say, the presence of anxiety, phobia, depression, obsession, compulsion, perversion, paranoia, autism, splitting, and similar symptomatic criteria do not add up to a disease. The clue to this shift is to be found in the modern novel. The novelistic "heroes" of Faulkner, Shaw, Bellow, Updike, Hemingway, Steinbeck, Jones, Mailer, and others, all have one or more of these stigmata, but they are nowhere considered psychiatric cases. Indeed, these behavior patterns are offered not specifically as character assets but as unique personality patterns which confer distinction on the particular "hero" and give him tortured strength. The way he goes about using his disability becomes the texture of the plot, his life, and it is not intended for the hero to be a mental case. This permits readers to identify with the stigmata of the hero without considering themselves a case as well.

The old and comforting diagnostic structures by which people were hospitalized, or were offered psychoanalytic psychotherapy as a mandatory need, now turn out not to have been a guide at all. They were something culture, through its representatives, urged upon people. Even the old reliable criterion of "psychotic break" no longer applies in the same way, for the reintegration of reality testing now occurs so quickly—a day or two—that one cannot truly call it a break at all. In the absence of a manifest hallucination, it is no easy task today to evaluate the workings of a mind and to categorize it as neurotic or psychotic. And what shall constitute our normality is still way beyond reach. People just are, and their situation is not categorical but phenomenal. What to cure becomes ever more risky.

The manifest anxiety of our patients is very little in the direction of Eros, but considerably in the shape of Thanatos today. Not the joining of love, but the separation of death is the important symbolic event of a current life. Freud began to sense this as he himself got older, and as he became more and more disenchanted with Eros as *the* instinct. But no psychotherapy we know of is as yet oriented toward the anxiety and despair of death or of the death equivalents in life. We act as though pleasure and repression were still the problem, and we continue to help people to change in the direction of a psychic cultural lag. We then justify it as of the patient's own choosing.

We thus have the transitional drama of a healing form, psychotherapy, offering not only a myriad of techniques for bringing about behavior change but a highly labile and shifting philosophical and cultural base for any change which might be undertaken. Some of us settle for less; some, for more. Some are satisfied to cast patients in their own image; but others, only in the ideal of that image. The results of psychotherapy are therefore a vast unevenness of theory, of technique, and of final product. It takes a great faith today not only to be a patient but to be a healer.

In Freud's triadic theory of personality—the ego, id, and superego—the superego is the manifest stepchild. Libraries have been written about the ego and the id; but not much really has been said about the superego. It appears that the next phase of psychoanalytic development will be in the elaboration and the extension of the superego. But it will be a dilated concept which will include the goals, values, feelings, spirit, and meanings of persons as constituted in their superego formation. The superego does not merely set standards for the ego but defines the existential possibilities and parameters by which the ego thrives. The superego is in a sense the ancient repository of all that is social in man, but includes as well his spirit, religious ideas, and morality. The new concept will incorporate Jung's collective unconscious, but will place it in a better relationship to the ego and the id than he did. Man and his therapy can be expected to become more spiritual and religious.

If we then at this final point again raise the question of the purpose of behavior change, it can now be stated that its purpose is to make man more fully man. Man actualizes not only his instincts, but his spirit and the symbols which have had universal meaning for all men through eons of history. It is only in this way that he can feel whole, relate himself to nature, and feel belongingness with all men. This is certainly the higher purpose of behavior change and it is what psychoanalytic psychotherapy strives for. Whether or not it attains it is still an open question.

REFERENCES

1. BURTON, A., et al.: *Schizophrenia as a Life Style.* New York: Springer, 1974.
2. MOWRER, O. H.: *The New Group Therapy.* New York: Van Nostrand, 1964.
3. STRUPP, H. J.: This volume.
4. BURTON, A.: Psychotherapy with the mentally retarded. *Am. J. Ment. Def.,* 1954, 58, 486-489.
5. HOWE, I.: Immigrant Jewish families in New York. The end of the world of our fathers. *New York Magazine,* 1975, 8, No. 41, p. 76.
6. BURTON, A.: *The Patient and the Therapist.* Sacramento: Hamilton Psyche Press, 1975.
7. FRANK, J. D.: This volume.
8. LOWEN, A.: *Bioenergetics.* New York: Coward, McCann and Geoghegan, 1975.
9. MISHIMA, Y.: *The Temple of Dawn.* (Trans. by E. D. Saunders and C. S. Seigle). New York: Pocket Books, 1975.
10. VAN DER POST, L.: *Jung and the Story of Our Time.* New York: Pantheon Books, 1975, pp. 57-58.

John Warkentin and Elizabeth Valerius

8

Seasons in the Affairs of Men

by JOHN WARKENTIN, M.D., PH.D., and
ELIZABETH VALERIUS, PH.D.

There is a season for everything,
a time for giving birth,
and a time for dying.

A time for planting;
a time for uprooting what has been planted.
A time for searching;
a time for losing;
a time for keeping;
a time for throwing away.
A time for keeping silent;
a time for speaking;
a time for loving;
a time for hating.
A time for knocking down;
a time for building.

A time for healing.

(Ecclesiastes, Chapt. 3)

152

These observations by an ancient writer express our own thoughts about the rhythms of life. The work on this chapter is an exciting season of unfolding and becoming for us. We are writing this at our Retreat Center in the Blue Ridge Mountains. Repeatedly we turn from the typewriter to look across the ancient hills. Far from the bustle of our Peachtree Road office in Atlanta we gaze with wonder at the movements and moods of the natural world around us. We note the seasonal changes in the trees, the plants, and the animals who are our friends here. These changes in nature remind us of the changes we see in people, of the seasons of living. Shakespeare spoke of these using another analogy: "There is a tide in the affairs of men, which taken at the flood leads on to fortune. . . . We must take the current when it serves or lose our ventures" (*Julius Caesar*, IV, 3.).

How can we know our life calendar, so that we might take advantage of our personal rhythms? We cannot predict them, we recognize only vaguely from whence they come, and we have no assurance how they will affect us. They happen. We suppose that we are endowed with an inner-directedness to continue becoming ourselves in our life-time-space. We also assume that we have a limited predetermined amount of energy with which to accomplish the particular mission of a season. This means a change from one condition or phase to another, a process in which energy is created and utilized. How can we best conserve it and convert it into a renewed living of which our heart and wisdom approve?

The season for personality change is not always with us. Of that we are certain. To what degree are we passive pawns on the personal battlegrounds of life? How much can we determine the flow of our rhythms? Are the changes intrinsic in our seeds and early childhood so that we live the emerging manifestations of our sleeping potentials? The answers seem unknowable.

We do know that when we are deeply stirred we may parlay this energy into a redirecting of life. How can we recognize a time when we shall risk uprooting our accustomed life script? Shall we now throw away the security of familiar habits? If so, can we do it alone or should we seek an Other who will serve in catalyzing our movement? How can a professional therapist help? The remainder of this chapter will consider these issues.

The authors are professional psychotherapists and will discuss personality change as they have experienced it in their own lives and in many years of clinical experience. Psychotherapy offers a testing ground where persons may explore their readiness to change themselves. There one can discover whether one is yet at a season of sufficient desperation and determination. One may wish to postpone the effort. Perhaps one will try oneself out further with friends and other warm people who will support one in one's journey, and they may even help one to recognize a good time for a special effort with a professional therapist.

There are three ingredients which combine to form the agent of change: (1) the patient's awareness that the season of opportunity has arrived and that he or she wants the participation of a collaborator; (2) a therapist committed to participate as an instrument in the patient's effort; (3) a developing "fortunate collaboration" between the partners. These three factors constitute the essentials for the *nuclear process* of the change experience, the significant intrapersonal and interpersonal happening.

The contributions of patients are the first prerequisite to the nuclear process. Patients bring all the wealth of their prior life experiences, knowledge, and humanity. They will recognize some seasons and milestones of years past, such as being a rebellious teenager in the process of becoming their own person. Now with the therapist they can explore the depth of their distress and their desperation to change themselves further. The patient's commitment to risk the pursuit of a new adult identity is often a large question mark for both partners in the enterprise. Such commitment involves a deliberate decision to pay the cost in anxiety and struggle, plus an unconscious drive to continue becoming. The forsaking of one's childhood identity, which one got second-hand from one's parents, means that one will also forsake the security of their platitudes.

A good example of positive contributions by the patient was a young man just out of college and beginning a vocational career. He had recognized his shyness as resulting from low self-esteem, had been expecting for some years to see a therapist eventually, and was now anxious regarding his new start in life. He had read some books about psychotherapy and said, "I'm ready to give it all I've got." It was a satisfying experience for both partners.

The young man in this example had committed himself to a re-examination and awareness of his inner person, had chosen to overcome his shyness, and had decided to move in the direction of greater self-esteem before he ever saw the therapist. The remaining task was to implement his further movement. With fear and trembling he acknowledged that he could not pull himself up by his own bootstraps. He was willing to risk the precarious exposure of self to an Other (which is often a stumbling block to prideful patients). It required several recommitments during his therapy journey to maintain movement in his chosen direction.

In contrast to the example above, a person may come for a visit with the therapist without any commitment, in order to ask, "How can I grow in capacity without professional help? To have therapy is such a confession of being a failure in life!" We gladly accept this kind of inquiry. We explain that life is like a dance where it takes two to tango, that people find personal meaning and definition in relation to an Other. We may add that the experience of developing a new Self is like a pregnancy leading to rebirth, and that people cannot give new birth to themselves in isolation any more than a real baby can. The therapist's gentle approach can enable the inquiring persons to reorient themselves and eventually make a commitment to engage in a serious psychotherapy effort.

The commitment of the therapist is the second prerequisite in the nuclear process of personal change. We have much to offer. Our most significant contribution is the sum total of our person, the evidences of our life style, the distilled essence of our experiences, the impact of our attitudinal presence. The therapist's entire being is committed in the service of the patient's effort. Our whole character is present and to some degree perceptible to the patient. As therapists we have struggled in our own personal therapy to achieve an inner security which helps us to go with our patients in their times of stress and uncertainty. Whether the patients consciously recognize our various personal qualities or not, these have an impact on them and dominate the climate of the office experience. Our personal modeling will always speak louder than our words.

An example was an experience with a middle-aged divorced woman who came for therapy during a suicidal period of stress. She was overflowing with anger, which she soon focused on the person of the therapist, one of the authors. After many tense, angry interviews she came to a week of joyful peacefulness. The therapist asked, "What in the world made this change in you?" She thoughtfully considered the question and said, "It wasn't anything you said, I think it was just your attitude."

A different example of therapist modeling was experienced by a young couple in the midst of a marital struggle. They felt that the therapist was discouraging their marriage, so they discontinued. A year later they learned that he had then been going through his own divorce struggle. They felt relieved with this understanding and made a new effort with another therapist. (It would have been easier and perhaps more helpful if the first therapist had informed the couple of his own marital stress.)

The degree of self-revelation which therapists permit themselves depends on their overall professional orientation. Therapists differ greatly in this matter, from the extreme of being a blank screen to the opposite extreme of no holds barred in the emotional and physical relating. The orientation of the authors is *Experiential Psychotherapy*. This term does not designate a theoretical system or school of therapy. Our approach arises from practical experiences during years of clinical practice where we learned that we are more lively and useful when we participate with a disciplined sharing of ourselves. We always remember that the concerns of the patient constitute the primary focus of interaction; yet we may also intrude a personal concern which involves us so greatly that we cannot ignore it during the interview. For example, when one of the authors experienced a death in the family, he informed his patients that he was struggling with his personal sadness.

Our usual practice as Experiential Therapists is a thoughtful, direct participating in our patients' experience. We try to think and feel what they present. We react with questions for clarification, extensions, and possible alternative views. We encourage patients to ask us personal questions, and we answer these honestly or else respond that we do not want to answer, but wish that the patient would continue asking. In one case where the therapist refused to answer a question the patient looked relieved and said, "Now I can ask you anything." Patients realize our interest in their here-and-now experience with us and they gradually learn to interact increasingly in the present tense.

The specific details of how we make ourselves available to the patient will set the stage for our entire interaction. The preliminary telephone arrangements for the first interview can influence the relationship. For example, one of us returned the initial phone call to a new patient in the evening after a long day; he was tired and slightly confused. The patient did not understand this and for many subsequent interviews persisted in thinking of the therapist as not very bright.

The quality of the waiting room and of the interview office help to set the tone of communication and are reflections of our way of life. The feelings and thoughts of the two strangers in their first few minutes together will echo and re-echo through further interviews. Our manner can serve to ease or to accentuate the apprehension of the new patient. With a positive initial experience, the impact on both people can be almost magical. In fact, it is difficult to overemphasize the significance of this initial encounter. By the end of the first interview the patient may leave with increased courage to explore his or her unknown self, having had an initial experience of being understood and respected.

The experience with Deborah illustrated such a positive beginning. She was a shy, naive woman in her thirties who had recently received her first serious marital proposal. She was conflicted over the close attachment to her mother and a concern that marriage would seriously hinder her religious life. With great anxiety she came to a woman therapist, one of the authors, who liked her and expressed genuine respect for her religious concerns. In trusting response, Deborah gave herself wholeheartedly to a reassessment of her life, including many questions about her sexuality. The feeling between the partners readily became very intimate. In ending, the therapist even gave some suggestions about make-up and more attractive ways to dress. Deborah was leaving Georgia, and this allowed for only ten interviews and two group sessions. In this brief experience she became less secretive, began to see her desirability as a marital partner, and decided to marry despite the fact that her mother would not come to the wedding. In a letter to the therapist about a year later, Deborah reported that she was enjoying a good marriage.

We are repeatedly surprised at the capacity of patients to utilize very brief contacts. A dramatic case was that of a young man who spent the day in our waiting room periodically asking for a brief interview. The therapist finally saw him for five minutes between appointments. The "patient" was worried that he might be homosexual; the therapist said that even if this were so, it was a normal phase in development. We never even learned his name, but received three notes subsequently to say, "Thanks," that he was doing all right, signed, "Your 5-minute Patient."

In the two preceding clinical vignettes the therapist's skill in interviewing was a significant factor in the outcome. When patients come to a professional catalyst in their life movement, they are entitled to expect more effective help than they might get from a good friend, more facilitation of communication in a shorter time. The skilled therapist promotes economy in the patient's developmental movement. Techniques as such produce no change, but they help set the stage on which patient and therapist can interact. Mature therapists do not use tricks like a detective to get confessions out of reluctant patients. They exercise their expertise in bridging the emotional distance between themselves and their patients.

A basic technique is the honest relating of the therapist with patients. This does not mean that we must say everything we think or feel, but we must not misrepresent ourselves. Sometimes young therapists, in their effort to be honest, let their hostilities hang out to the exclusion of their affection. One form of covert hostility with difficult new patients is to confront them with conclusions arising from their history. The authors find that patients rarely need to be confronted, especially in early interviews. They are likely to feel unworthy enough in their patient status. A helpful substitute for confrontation has been for us to share briefly something of our own growth struggles. Eventually we can arrive together with our patients at insights which would have been painful in earlier interviews.

Getting a detailed life history from patients without unduly offending them is a skill which we continue learning. Good will is not enough. In addition to the factual data, we need to learn the social and emotional history of the patient. This requires the facile availability of questions to ask which will help the patient to communicate.

For example, a college senior was referred by his professor. He came in rather surly, saying that he did not see any reason for this. The therapist noted his downcast expression and asked, "Have you been discouraged lately?" The patient said, "Yes, I feel like sleeping a lot but I'm still making my grades. I'm perfectly all right." The therapist said that he accepted the patient's annoyance, but wondered, "What do you think about as you are going to sleep?" The patient said, "I just want to sleep a long time." The therapist asked, "Would it feel nice to sleep for days and days, or even forever?" The patient brightened up and said, "Yes, that would be nice." The therapist asked other questions such as: "How does it feel when you are alone?" "When do you like yourself best?" "When was a good time in your life?" "Do your dreams ever worry you?" "What kinds of things excite you?" "What was your favorite childhood fairy tale?" "Do you have a close friend now?" "Could I possibly be like a friend to you for a while?" The young man acknowledged that he often had suicidal thoughts. He came for a number of interviews and made a new beginning in his life.

In asking about the antecedents of the patients' lives, their traumas, hiatuses in experience, and developmental phases, we have learned to avoid "why" questions. Instead we ask, in regard to a given experience, "Can you see any steps which led up to that?" "How did you feel about that?" "How do you think about it now?" "Are there people whom you have never forgiven for the trouble they caused you?" "What can we do about your unlived life?"

The trained therapist can encourage a patient whose thoughts are blocked. There are times when the course of wisdom is silence, and times when the therapist should speak. If patients become anxious about their silence, a gentle response might be, "Would you like to sit some more with your blocking until you get an idea about what you are avoiding?" If the patient remains frozen, we may suggest, "Whatever you are blocking will probably still be there. Would you like me to ask you some questions?" In this way we exercise our initiative in promoting the continuing excitement of the interaction. Before an interview with a relatively nonverbal patient we may glance at pages of questions we have collected so that we might refresh our memory with useful ideas of what to ask.

The measure of any therapist's skill is seen in his or her dealing with difficult patients: the rebellious teenager who was forced in by a court; a patient with psychosomatic illness whose internist gave up on him; the deeply angry married woman who concentrates on blaming her partner; the successful businessman whose family accuses him of being a poor father and husband. These are examples of patients who demand more than ordinary initiative from us.

The authors accept the challenge of difficult or negativistic patients. We directly invite them to return for further interviews so that we might go beyond a difficult beginning. We are likely to think of such patients between appointments, and perhaps discuss them briefly with a colleague in order to get helpful suggestions and also to know that we are not alone in our professional effort. Simultaneously we humbly acknowledge to ourselves that our skills may not suffice for a given patient and that we may not be the best therapist for that person. When our contribution to the nuclear process is clearly insufficient, we acknowledge that we need help and invite a consultant into the interview with the patient. The technique of in-therapy consultation was devised in 1945 by members of our group at the Atlanta Psychiatric Clinic. Consulting with each other has been a great encouragement through the years as well as an in-service learning experience. The consultant usually comes in "cold" without prior briefing; the therapist reviews the patient's history for ten or fifteen minutes, and then takes notes for the remainder of the time while the consultant conducts the interview. Such a consultant should be a respected colleague who will try to understand where the patient is and who will also evaluate the therapist's participation and the quality of the relationship. Many times during such a three-way meeting with a consultant, both therapist and patient have developed new insights into their process with each other. After the interview the consultant explains his or her observations to the therapist, who can then report these to the patient at their next meeting. Repeatedly a consultant has relieved an impasse in therapy or facilitated a process which was in slow motion.

Personality development and subsequent behavioral change in the adult are so fraught with obstacles that therapists need all the skills they can learn. There are many useful techniques, such as attention to body language, physical contact as this may be appropriate, tape recordings and playback to the patient, and role-playing.

A final technique for consideration is group therapy with patients from our office practice. The group participants get a multiple feedback which is far beyond that which they can get from the therapist alone. Since the authors practice in adjacent offices, they both refer patients to the same groups. In this way our patients are related to two therapists. Our closed groups meet every two weeks for a two-and-a-half-hour period. The authors alternate in meeting with them as leaders, so that each of us meets the group once a month. This arrangement enables and encourages the group to have its own intra-group process to which the leader is always a participant visitor. This alternation of group leadership has stimulated more creative group initiative by our patients than other techniques which we have tried in the past. Additionally, we cultivate a Tuesday night open group for all our present and past patients. This is a weekly opportunity for a person to come and see us without appointment, for an ex-patient to return with a progress report, or for a fearful new patient to experience our way of working with groups.

Our many techniques are designed to promote the nuclear process and to link the patient with us or with members in a therapy group. The patients come with much inner knowledge of which they are not aware, and a significant part of formal psychotherapy for them is training in the use of language and symbols by which to share themselves in an intimate relationship. This also provides the patients with a conscious conceptual framework, a communicable structure into which they can fit their learnings. Patients find security and satisfaction in their new facility to express their insights with others. They are enabled to compare their adult attitudes and values with the restraints of their childhood platitudes, i.e., the rules for living which were appropriate to them as children.

A brief example was a single young lady, age twenty-nine, who was referred because she repeatedly got into conflict at her work. She described herself as a very sincere, conscientious person, and explained her difficulty as follows: "I always thought that people should be strictly honest, and I just tell them when I don't like something, but they do not appreciate honesty." The therapist helped her to become less painfully outspoken and to recognize that "what she always thought" must have come out of her early years and was not appropriate to her adult status. She continued in therapy in order to learn more satisfying ways of sharing herself.

A kind, caring therapist becomes heir to a multitude of secrets shared by patients. Along with one's formal training, this wealth of privileged information constitutes the ultimate in learning about human nature. For example, we know about mutuality of feelings in face-to-face relationships. So when a patient asks, "How do you feel about me?" we can respond, "The feeling climate here is probably similar for both of us; how do you feel toward me right now?" Whatever the patient says, we can then state our own inner experience.

The therapist's knowledge was decisive with a couple who had been married for ten years and spoke of divorce, stating, "We no longer love each other." They had lost their honeymoon feeling some two or three years previously. The therapist was able to explain the "ten-year-syndrome" of being no longer in love, and that the couple now had an opportunity for a new contract in their relationship. At this season of life they could cultivate a more durable and satisfying experience together than ever before, sexually and otherwise. An alternative possibility would be for them to separate, find new partners for falling in love, and eventually arrive at another ten-year syndrome. This couple thoughtfully chose to promote their investment in each other's lives.

We learned about the time-limited transference phenomenon of being in love from a fifty-year-old divorced woman who reported that she had fallen in love every ten years since age twenty. She asked, "Is this all I can expect of life? How do people love each other for more than ten years?" The therapist complimented her on the insight about her life seasons, and they discussed how she might cultivate a more durable affectionate relationship.

As in our social living, we recognize seasons or phases in the office experience with a patient. The early interviews may constitute a honeymoon phase of positive transference. By acknowledging this joyful relating as temporary, we prepare for a later phase of possible negative transference. This kind of forewarning helps patients to accept the phasic quality of all human relating, and particularly with us, so that they will not terminate prematurely. As the partners continue with each other, they can cultivate nontransference interactions so that their final ending is founded more on realities than on fantasies.

Further valuable information for patients to know is that there may be times during their therapy when they will be quite paranoid. Paranoia or "therapeutic psychosis" is often a hallmark of change in patients, when they are "shedding the old skin" and feel very vulnerable. A warning to this effect may be sufficient to keep patients from making their suspiciousness known and getting into social or occupational difficulties during such a time.

Of the many other facts of life which we can share with our patients we mention only one more: the "Unconscious" of Freud and the "It" of Groddeck. Many life experiences become less mysterious to patients if they will accept their nonconscious functioning, such as mood changes without reason or strange accidents or dreams.

Our knowledge, understanding, and acceptance of human nature with its phases from birth until death constitutes the basis for our faith in persons, so that we can offer the priceless hope of new becoming to patients. Our knowledge enables us to be less hesitant to involve ourselves and wiser in structuring the limitations of the therapeutic relationship. However, with any new patient we must ask ourselves the initial question, "Do I want to involve myself with this person? Is this patient one in whom I will invest a part of my energy? Can I anticipate sincerely respecting this patient's life

effort?" If so, after some preliminary interviews, we can then commit ourselves to be deeply involved. Such a commitment may require firm self-
discipline, especially if the patient persists in a negativistic attitude. With
some patients we may go for many interviews just relying on our belief that
the more two people become acquainted the more affection they will have
for each other.

We can energize the interaction with our enthusiasm, make it a matter of
dreary indifference, or sink it with our hopelessness about the patient. How
we relate to a patient is to some degree a reflection of personal identification.
Our capacity to identify with others depends on a flexibility far beyond the
usual natural endowment. The preparation for a readiness to see in ourselves
evidences of all the human hang-ups results from our own experience as
patients in psychotherapy. We have become convinced that the therapists
who are likely to offer most to their patients are those who have had extensive
experience as patients themselves.

In the developing intimacy of the relationship both patient and therapist
gradually lose some of their objectivity. It is incumbent on us to recognize
evidences of the transference and countertransference involvements. We are
responsible for keeping the focus on the patient's movement and to continue
differentiating between the patient's transference and reality (nontransference) relating. Professional functioning requires that we repeatedly evaluate
the evidences of countertransference in ourselves. When colleagues are available for discussion, they are valuable assistants in this process. The ideal procedure is to invite a consultant into the interview (as noted above). We are
aware that transference factors operate to some degree in all intimate human
relationships. Our special task is to cultivate a maximum awareness of these
otherwise hidden influences in our office relating.

We have discussed briefly what the patient brings to the therapeutic relationship, and we have discussed at length what the therapist brings. This
discrepancy in emphasis reflects our understanding that therapists present
themselves as experts in the ways that growth is possible, while patients are
relative novices looking for a skilled assistant. We believe that success or
failure in the dynamics of therapy depends primarily on the person of the
therapist. As we now deal with the third component required for the nuclear
process of change, the fortunate collaboration of the two partners, we will
continue to emphasize the therapist's knowledge and capacity to facilitate
their interaction.

Whether the flowing together of patient and therapist participation develops in a fortunate way will depend on their mutual sincere effort *plus* an uncertain factor which we postulate as the *"C-Factor"* or *"Collaborative Factor."* This C-Factor comes to our awareness in unexpected ways in office relating with patients. We define the C-Factor as similar to the slang expression "vibrations." It is a distinctive emotional reaction between two persons in a way that we sense even though we cannot discover a logical perceptual basis. It is a phenomenon of special connectedness, an intangible special bond which may give us a weird feeling of strangeness or even of uncanny uneasiness. On other occasions we are inspired with wonder at the inexplicable kinship of spirits with certain patients. We think of it as a baffling confluence of esoteric unrecognized attitudes in us and in the patient.

In reviewing many case histories we have noted that this mysterious C-Factor was absent with some patients. With many other patients it has been present as a positive validation of the office interaction. With a third group of patients we have experienced the C-Factor as a special emotional resonance despite the patient's apparent dislike of us or even gross criticism and objection to the relationship. We have never sensed this puzzling factor as present in an indifferent way.

In earlier professional years both of us distrusted these odd subjective experiences, assuming that they must be unresolved countertransference reactions which we should not be having. We also wondered whether we were insufficiently controlling our intuitive feelings. In recent years we have become less fearful of the obscure realities beyond reason. Our inability to understand the specific origins of the collaborative factor no longer prevents us from recognizing it within ourselves and perhaps sharing our awareness of it with patients as this may be appropriate. We are now more often aware of this factor and take it seriously. Even in very brief therapies, we feel more secure in ending the relationship with a patient when we have some sense of this preintellectual bond.

Strangely enough we have never experienced this special connectedness as sexual in nature. We think of it as a primitive experience in which our heritage from all our prior years and that of the patient match in an unpredictable way. We experience it as a mutual sharing with the patient and a sense of knowing each other which exceeds reasonable expectations.

We sense the C-Factor especially with patients who are openly emotionally hungry. A case in point was a middle-aged couple who came for help with their inactive marriage. After the first interview the therapist thought of them as highly sophisticated impossibles; he also had severe hunger pangs so that he had milk and crackers before he continued with the next appointment. The patients were very polite, soft-spoken people and only his hunger after every interview notified the therapist that the C-Factor was operating in the relationship. He asked a colleague about his strange hunger. The colleague responded, "They are negativistic hungry people and are exhausting your blood sugar." Months later the manifestations of the collaborative factor switched from negative to positive and then the therapist no longer had hunger pangs after interviews. Simultaneously he and the patients developed a profoundly affectionate relationship.

We question to what degree the C-Factor is either available or dormant in persons, and how much it enters into all human interactions. We have learned with patients that it can be present in our initial contact with either a positive or negative valence. If present initially, this experience of unexpected synergy may cause uneasiness in both partners so that the next interview is very cautions. We call this the "Second Interview Phenomenon." Our more usual experience is that the C-Factor becomes apparent gradually over a period of time until we finally notice and acknowledge it.

One important observation regarding the fortunate collaboration with patients is that we have experienced our rare significant moments only with those where the C-Factor was present. These are moments which we cannot plan. They are brief times of a minute or less in which we experience a peaceful intensity. They are usually nonverbal. Such moments always seem as though they are happening to us and to the patient at a time when we are free from problem solving or other deliberate efforts and are simply in communion with each other. We believe that these moments signify a core experience in the office relationship following which both partners may find a new freedom of relating to each other.

Another nonrational phenomenon in the close collaboration with patients is extrasensory perception (E.S.P.). This also is an unpredictable happening. "We are such stuff as dreams are made on." To illustrate, one of the authors received an emergency phone call early one morning some years ago that his mother had had a near-fatal heart attack in a distant city. He made plane reservations for that afternoon. He kept his first appointment with a woman patient who was profoundly involved in her therapy. She arrived quite disturbed and reported she had dreamt that morning that the therapist's mother was very sick and he would be leaving to be with her. He told her that her dream was factually correct and thanked her with much feeling for participating in his life. By acknowledging this unexplainable phenomenon to her he was confirming the profound relatedness between them. Supposing the therapist had kept his professional distance, not acknowledging the facts and offering to analyze the patient's dream?! We wonder how much adventure we forgo by ignoring such nonrational experiences.

The foregoing discussions have emphasized the unpredictability of patient-therapist synchrony in their effort together. There is no amount of training or experience which can assure the therapist that the collaborative factor will be operative with any given patient since that is a nonrational aspect of the relationship. For this reason we have suggested to some new patients that they go therapist-shopping when there seemed to be a question about the compatibility with us. This has worked out favorably for patients, and in those instances when they came back to us they had usually clarified their sense of purpose and commitment. In this process we have felt more specifically selected as therapists than with a referral based only on reputation.

We have described the three essential ingredients of the nuclear process of change: the patient's determination, the therapist's commitment, and the fortunate collaboration between them. An example of how this process operates is the case of Grody. He was a young man who had been abruptly dismissed by his first therapist after months of therapy because he had fallen in love for the first time in his life—with his male therapist.

Grody had grown up in an austere religious home where neither parent touched him physically after he was six years old. He got through high school and into college, where he flunked out. At the age of twenty-six he was still a sexual virgin and was actively suicidal in his loneliness. He was working in a filling station, and it was his boss who had referred him to psychotherapy. After this ended unhappily, his boss referred him to another male therapist, one of the authors. Grody's initial question was, "Am I hopelessly homosexual?" The second therapist complimented Grody for his capacity to love at all. After some preliminary interviews they made an agreement to work together until such a time as they would both agree to an ending with each other.

The second therapist accepted Grody's initial hostile and suspicious manner, and explained that paranoia during therapy is one of the hallmarks of a maturing adult. He also helped Grody to realize that he must have gotten significant support in his first therapy effort or else he could not have developed so much warm feeling, and that some therapists are fearful of this. Grody learned that, because of the parent-child quality in psychotherapy, falling in love with a therapist is different from the feeling which leads a young couple to the altar. (Later the therapist explained the concept of transference.) In the early months Grody often spoke of being confused; the therapist suggested that this could be due to the differences between the two therapists as well as to the relinquishing of a familiar life-style.

For a time Grody lived homosexually. Despite much anxiety and occasional panic states he never missed an appointment. Gradually the partners developed increasing affection, while also continuing the educational endeavor such as helping Grody to understand his history in terms of psychosexual development. Grody finally became secure enough with his therapist to say, "I wish I could have had a grandfather like you." He also dared to ask, "Have you ever been a homosexual?" The therapist happily answered that his best experiences had been his loving relationships with men and women. There were also other moments of intense togetherness. The therapist facilitated the interaction by refraining from confrontations until late in the therapy when Grody asked for help in recognizing his defensiveness. Grody began by coming once a week, later spaced this out to every two weeks, and after about three years was coming once a month. By this time he had discontinued his overt homosexuality, was risking himself in dates with women, and was depressed only for brief periods. He seemed engaged in a gradual ending process, so the therapist asked, "How long should we plan on our ending process?" Grody cheerfully replied, "Well, John, how about a year?"

We easily recognize in Grody's first therapy experience how the uncommitted therapist made the nuclear process impossible. The fact that Grody fell in love with him means to the authors that a fortunate collaboration was possible but was aborted by that therapist.

Grody came to the second therapist with a desperation to find a happier way to live or else to kill himself. From the first interview this therapist recognized evidences of the C-Factor and had a feeling of being kindred spirits with Grody. This therapist accepted the designation of "grandfather" and committed himself to work with Grody until they might arrive at a mutual ending. Thus the partners had the ideal stage setting for their undertaking.

There was a religious quality in the experience with Grody. As he became less depressed, the excitement and tension of the office relating increased and Grody was asking some of the great questions: "Who am I?" "Where am I trying to go?" "What do I really want out of life?" "What are the priorities in my value system?" "Am I being moved by forces beyond my control?" These questions, which allow no complete answer, also concerned the therapist. He and Grody agreed in their belief that the unknowable inner core of a person has the greatest creative or destructive potential and that we are surrounded by powerful influences which transcend our understanding. We also believed that these forces were blessing our welfare with each other.

In our work with many different people we are impressed by the variety of their histories and goals. We are constantly challenged to participate in the idiosyncratic effort of various persons. We also recognize a general sequence or pattern in the change effort, somewhat as follows: (1) a growing awareness of the Self in detail and new insights; (2) approval or disapproval of the personal qualities which are being discovered; (3) finding possible directions among which to choose; (4) the decision to pursue a chosen new direction; (5) the step-by-step implementing of movement along the chosen path.

Not infrequently in our office experience the patient may try to short-circuit the normal slow process of growth. A clinical example was a compulsive young man complaining of premature ejaculation. After a few interviews he recognized that he was a perfectionist in his sexual expectations as well as otherwise. He promptly asked, "Now, what can I do about my perfectionism?" The therapist recognized the prematurity of the question and asked, "Do you mean that you want to stop doing excellent work?" The patient looked puzzled and said, "Of course not, but 'perfectionist' sounds like a dirty word, shouldn't I stop that?" The patient had clearly arrived at the first of five steps in his developmental process and was trying to bypass thoughtful consideration in his readiness to "do something." Insight was not sufficient to bring about personality change.

A very different example of how people come to us was that of a couple in their sixties who sought therapeutic help at the insistence of their grown children, who objected to the marital bickering. They came six times. They were too rigid to do much exploring of their personal structures, so the therapist participated in their discussion of the realities in their disagreements. They bypassed any new insights, and the therapist merely emphasized their choices of how they could compromise with each other. The therapist's secret agenda was to help this couple to become more tender with each other, while he discussed with them specific details of their daily interaction. They happily developed a new courtship with each other, and it was the therapist's assumption that their unconscious purpose had been the same as his own unstated agenda.

The above couple experienced a healing of symptoms. The therapist also saw them initiating growth in their maturity. We need not make a distinction between healing and growth since all psychological development partakes of the same process, that of becoming something more. Whenever patients achieve relief from emotional symptoms they are also involved in a further outgrowing of their childhood identity and remnants of inadequacy.

A third example in regard to the nuclear process demonstrates how it can fail. Jack and Gloria had both grown up as spoiled only-children. After five years of marriage they consulted a therapist before divorcing to make sure that they had "tried everything." Jack had fantasies of male partners, and Gloria kept thinking of a new home and a new marriage. They both told the therapist that their goal was a comfortable, happy life. The therapist, meanwhile, persisted in his assumption that their deeper purpose was to grow up some more, but no collaboration developed. After three years of tedious interviews the therapist finally believed them. Jack and Gloria wanted to be "just comfortable." It was an unhappy ending.

We are continuing to learn how to listen carefully to the stated goals of patients and to note the presence or absence of the collaborative factor. Beverly had been recently divorced and sought therapy because she was still very upset and was more afraid than ever before of going insane. She also admitted a wish for psychosis, saying that she fantasied being happily crazy in a locked ward. The therapist felt a warm kinship with her. After a number of interviews, she arrived unexpectedly with a suitcase in hand asking to be locked up. She was admitted to a hospital seclusion room where she tore off her clothes and danced around in psychotic fashion. The therapist saw her in daily interviews for two weeks, at which time she was suddenly again sober and asked to be discharged from the hospital. This was arranged. She continued with a number of outpatient interviews and the relationship came to a satisfactory ending. In retrospect, we wonder what might have happened to Beverly if the therapist had not accepted her stated purpose of going crazy.

Emotional regression is essential in the nuclear process of some patients because they have no other access to the powerful emotional remnants of childhood. Intellectual recognition of early traumas does not suffice. A degree of re-experiencing may be necessary for the patient, and this requires parental protectiveness by the therapist. The "warm breast" of a parental therapist provides the necessary security for the patient's regression. In this process we must remind ourselves periodically that the patient may have had a lifetime of criticism and may be supersensitive to any negative comment from us. Simple honest statements of appreciation by us at those times when we feel special warmth for the patient are important for both partners in order to reinforce our experience with each other.

Sometimes patients identify the emotional age level of their regression with such statements as, "I feel like a real baby and want to feel your hands on me." Or they may exclaim, "I just feel like saying 'No! No! No!' to you." Or, "Would you rock me on your lap?" Or, "I'd like some milk."

Affectionate physical touching in developmental relationships comes quite naturally. As therapists we rarely initiate physical contact other than a warm handshake. We respond to the patient's initiative according to our felt experience at the moment. Usually such physical gestures as holding hands with a patient, touching our feet together, or hugging at the end of the interview seem appropriate in acknowledging the warmth of the relationship. However, there are also discordant experiences. One patient asked to sit on her therapist's lap at a time when the relationship seemed largely hostile, and he answered, "I do not feel with you in that right now." A particularly incompatible experience would be any erotic genital touching between patient and therapist; we consider such behavior a hindrance to fortunate collaboration of the partners.

When the therapeutic relationship is that of parent to child for a time, both partners may be tempted to persist in this "dream." But then patients are likely to introduce various moves toward increasing independence. They may question the therapist's dictums, and gradually enter a full-fledged argumentative rebellion complete with offers to discontinue treatment. The therapist must not misunderstand such behavior as being merely a negative transference. It may be the exuberant expression of the patient's self-appreciation and what we call "Therapeutic Adolescence." During this time the therapist's ego can benefit by discussion with a colleague so that he or she does not become inappropriately defensive at this stage of the nuclear process.

A reassuring process in the collaboration with long-term patients is the gradual development of adult-to-adult relating. We call this a "Therapeutic Friendship" which validates the worth of both partners. However, we limit extra-therapy relating with patients so that we might remain focused on their therapeutic goals. Whether we develop a regular friendship after the ending of therapy depends on all the usual considerations which operate in the forming of friendships.

Concluding the nuclear process is as significant for the lives of patients' as was the beginning. The onset and the ending are natural complements of each other, counterparts which bracket a significant episode in their life span. As therapists we are responsible for helping patients recognize the experience which they have had with us, lest they forget it like other dreamlike experiences and subsequently disown it. The disengaging of the partners in a nuclear process of conscious and unconscious interaction ideally includes a thoughtful retrospective sharing of their remembrances. We remember that our patients came to us with a referral to new life; in ending we must now again refer them to a further new life effort with significant others.

In psychotherapy all is well if it ends well. We consider ourselves to have served patients successfully if they have initiated new movement or change in their living. Sometimes the "operation" seems to be a failure but the patient may be a success. To illustrate, Cynthia was a young career woman referred because of her depression. During her childhood and teenage years her father had abused her so that she was very fearful and resentful of men. However, she was compliant and even obsequious during the early interviews with the male therapist. Following a honeymoon experience in therapy she gradually became openly hostile. After further months of significant struggle she surprised her therapist by announcing, "This is my last time; you have taken my money under false pretenses of helping me and I hate you!" She used the rest of the hour to berate him in an abusive monologue. He felt hurt and defeated. A few years later he saw her name in his schedule. Cynthia came in obviously happy to see him again and reported many improvements in her life since her therapy. The therapist commented, "I am so glad we can meet on happier terms than the last time." Her surprised response was, "I don't remember any unhappiness!" She had planned this one interview to report her personal successes and to thank the therapist for his help. He thought of it as the ending of her negative transference with him and an ending with her father whom she formerly hated. Had Cynthia not returned, the therapist would have thought of her as one of his major failures.

There are many types of failures in therapy, the most common of which is lack of perceptible change in the patient. One kind of failure is specifically related to the thesis of the authors that all three nuclear ingredients are essential for a successful outcome. We have worked with patients who seemed fully devoted to the therapy effort and to whom we felt fully committed as well, but somehow the "collaborative factor" simply never developed. We consider the resulting outcome to be a "No-Fault Failure." This is our term for the unsatisfactory ending of a therapy which never quite began. Years ago we refused to recognize such an incompatibility. We would struggle through many interviews, assuming that we would eventually develop a fortunate collaboration. Our practice now is to acknowledge the unusual difficulty, and we may have a consultant come into an interview. Sometimes he or she helps us to begin a significant interaction. If this does not occur, we explain to the patients that we started with two necessary ingredients, their determination and our commitment, but we are not achieving the third ingredient: a meaningful involvement. Neither of us needs to apologize. We suggest that this kind of "no-fault failure to relate" can occur in any human relationship and that the patient should seek a more compatible therapist.

We have described the beginning, middle, and ending of the nuclear process of change as we experience it in our office practice. It is our assumption that the process we have described also operates in other contexts. We recognize that people have matured through the ages of human history without benefit of a psychotherapist and weekly interviews. We give credence to nonprofessional growth experiences, whatever the circumstances may be. We also believe that the dynamic process is similar in all adult personality change: A human being who is desperate to change finds an Other as a supporting ally, and their participation with each other is an almost magical collaboration. A fortunate person may find a succession of such significant Others. We have designated these maturing experiences as the "Social Extended Process of Change."

In our consideration of the extended process of change we describe only the function of the "Social Therapist." He or she can be a significant person to the patient prior to professional psychotherapy, perhaps during, and again following the formal effort with a therapist.

We define a social therapist as a parental person who may be a friend, a lover, or an affectionate teacher who respectfully supports the one who is in the process of becoming something more. In our own histories and those of patients we have recognized supportive persons who have conveyed the message, "You are worthwhile and I like you." Such messages of approval have led us and many others to promote a relentless inner drive to grow and grow and grow! The soliciting of a professional therapist in this process is actually a temporary expedient, an opportunity available to middle-class people who can afford the luxury of a therapeutic facilitator who has been trained with special skills. Repeatedly we find that the referring person was a social therapist who knew when to suggest that a professional therapist was indicated. We have learned to ask patients regarding such antecedent therapists.

The history of Virginia is a good illustration. She was eighteen years old when she met her Berlitz German teacher, Anna. They liked each other and became friends. Virginia was repeatedly invited for exciting weekend swimming and other occasions with Anna's family, who warmly accepted Virginia and helped her to feel important. (Later Virginia married a man who spoke German.) In the struggle of subsequent years she comforted herself with memories of Anna, who was a significant social therapist and probably not aware of her importance. Virginia went through college and entered graduate school. There she was befriended by a professor who recommended professional psychotherapy. We call him the "Referring Social Therapist."

Just as there are "many roads leading to Rome," so there are many influences in people's lives which lead to an eventual adult healing and growth effort. These benevolent vectors which point the way to a possible new birth in an adult may include the modeling of original parents who continued maturing, the appreciative affection of loving friends, the enthusiasm of teachers who found pleasure in the learning of their students, pastors who ministered to the psyche as well as the soul, and social and professional therapists. We cannot be certain which of these life-supporting persons were most crucial. As professional psychotherapists we try to define our function at it may serve patients in the season when they come to us.

SUMMARY

All growth is seasonal, and this includes the growth of Man. His special prerogative is to influence the time and circumstance of his personal seasons. Our concern as therapists is to help people make the most of their periodic opportunities. Patients come to us with distress in their living. We assume that their underlying quest is for more than symptom relief and that they are seeking an increased capacity to meet the stresses of life. We conceptualize a "Nuclear Process" as the agent of change. This process evolves from the confluence of three essential factors: the contributions by the patient, those by the therapist, and an open warm relating between them.

The ideal patients bring their pain, desperation, and determination to change.

The ideal therapists bring a candor born of their own experience as a patient, a skill and wisdom learned in their training and living, plus a willingness to commit themselves as instruments in the patients' effort.

The ideal relating is a movement toward increasing intimacy between patient and therapist. It depends on their bilateral sincere efforts plus an uncertain factor which we call the "C-Factor" or "Collaborative Factor." This factor is a distinctive emotional reaction between the partners, an intangible bond, a joining of spirits. (When this factor is unavailable the therapeutic outcome is likely to be unsatisfactory and we speak of it as "No-Fault Failure.") With the achieving of a fortunate collaboration, the partners may experience brief times of harmonious communion which transcend words and reason, moments which we do not analyze but simply acknowledge.

The clinical sequence of the unfolding nuclear process goes through similar phases with all patients. Patients gradually become more aware of the details of their identity, evaluate what they consider desirable in themselves, choose a further life direction, decide to pay the cost of pursuing it, and proceed with a step-by-step implementing of their change. The goals, results, and ending of therapy remain idiosyncratic for each patient. For example, he or she may end successfully in any phase of therapy provided both partners agree. As therapists we consider ourselves to have been useful to patients when they are engaging in a new journey in living.

Our emphasis on collaboration and mutual sharing with the patient we call "Experiential Psychotherapy." This is not a theoretical system, but designates our approach to disciplined participation in the patient's therapy. We treasure the privilege of these professional experiences and especially the occasional significant moments of involvement.

ADDENDUM QUERIES

I

DR. BURTON: The concept of a *social therapist* is a novel one for it bridges friendship and healing which were formerly believed to be antinomous. Can you elaborate in some greater detail as to what a social therapist is—as compared to a friend—and what the qualities are in a person which contribute to this capacity?

DRS. WARKENTIN AND VALERIUS: The wide scope of beneficent human influence includes many types of relationships such as between friends, physician and patient, pastor and parishioner, and also parent and child. The social therapist is a nonprofessional parental friend who relates warmly to a receptive friend. In all of these types of relationships there are specific subtle differences in orientation. Social therapists are characterized by their offer of affection without asking for rewards in kind, a controlled empathizing tolerance, and a noncompetitive participation in the life of the younger or dependent friend. Typically the receptive friend is likely to provide the excitement or adventure while the parental friend provides the stability. Both are rewarded—the social therapists by confirmation of their maturity and personal worth, and the receiving friends by the further unfolding of their life.

Neither the social therapist nor the friend are likely to identify themselves in these terms. They may recognize the parental modeling of the one and the dependent identifying of the other but still think of it as a regular friendship. In a usual friendship the entire purpose is to enjoy each other and anticipate lifelong affection. By contrast, the social therapist and the friend are likely to come to an ending as the receiving friend gradually matures and seeks peers while the other finds new challenges.

II

DR. BURTON: There is a small implication from your chapter that therapists must be in some way *saintlike* in their regard for their clients, or at

least have an ultrapositive regard for them. How do you face or respond
to the *demonic* side of the client which inevitably manifests itself as the
therapy proceeds?

DRS. WARKENTIN AND VALERIUS: The tone which Dr. Burton
picked up could be our appreciation of all human nature as a good thing.
We believe that there are no superficial people, although we see people who
insist on behaving superficially. We hope that our patients will help us to
respect them in the way they present themselves. We are not living a life
of sainthood, and positive regard for others does not always come easily
to us. We do often find people interesting and easy to like, so that we may
anticipate an affectionate association as we get to know each other. There
are also some patients who come to us with the problem that they antagonize
others, and they may include us in their antagonizing. With them we repeatedly remind ourselves to treat them as we might want to be treated if
we were in their situation. Such a patient occasionally will say, "It feels
like there is a demon inside of me who pushes me to be nasty." Our task
requires that we oppose the patients' provocations without rejecting them.
Our strength for this endeavor grew out of an awareness of a demon within
ourselves. Valerius experiences a feeling of excessive panic at times in response to a minor rejection or even with no apparent provocation; Warkentin
suddenly gets depressed at times for no evident reason, as if a bad spirit
had invaded him. To the degree that we have been able to counter the
tormenting forces or passions within us we are then enabled to confront such
a spirit in the patient. When this effort has succeeded, our patients have
been very grateful and on occasion have attributed saintly qualities to us.
An interesting experience in this connection occurred when we married—each
of us had patients who wished for us a more worthy partner.

On rare occasions we have faced a new patient who felt to us like an
evil person, motivated by a powerful unclean spirit. When a consultant could
not help us to move beyond this impression, we have recommended that the
patient seek another therapist.

We have not recognized in our practice the emergence of a demonic side
of the patient as therapy proceeds, other than the usual negative transference
or a teenagelike rebellion. Dr. Burton has now alerted us to the possible late
surfacing of a demonic quality.

III

DR. BURTON: The concept of *fortunate collaboration* is an interesting
one. I have sometimes felt that such fortunate collaboration was a program-

med or fated thing, and that it either worked or didn't work, for reasons beyond any properties of the intercurrent dialogue. Do you think this is a matter of transference, of affectional feelings, a solid determination to be different, or some other unknown variable?

DRS. WARKENTIN AND VALERIUS: Our experience is consonant with that of Dr. Burton, that the presence or absence of the "C-Factor" seems like a matter of fate. We consider this collaborative factor as resulting largely from unknown variables beyond our understanding of transference. Nevertheless, we consider the C-Factor to be an essential component of the nuclear process in psychotherapy.

IV

DR. BURTON: Do you ever find it *necessary to use suggestion and persuasion?* Or even to demand or threaten as a more assertive approach to problem behavior? Some therapists believe that clients give up their old ways only when they desire the approval of the therapist, whom they deeply care for, more than the "satisfaction" which their symptoms provide.

DRS. WARKENTIN AND VALERIUS: We try to be aware of the power vested in us by patients, and we are cautious lest we mislead them with unwise comments. Our life style and the charisma ascribed to us by patients make us significant models to them. Our presence, manner, and unspoken attitudes convey messages which are worth a thousand words. We also spell out our opinions regarding the patient's living and our relationship with each other, depending upon the degree of relatedness. We give suggestions regarding helpful ways to use our interview time, mention books and movies which might help the patient, and make specific recommendations as these seem appropriate. Our underlying conviction is that the built-in drive of patients to actualize their personal potential always takes precedence over any opinions of the therapist. Patients remain the absolute arbiters of how they will live.

Forceful demands or even threats by the therapist are hindrances in psychotherapy. Such assertiveness would have to be based on the therapist's assumption that he or she knows what is best for the patient, and we disagree with such an assumption.

V

DR. BURTON: You make the allusive statement that the best psychotherapy has *a religious quality* about it. I would tend to concur with this.

Can you state with greater clarity what is religious or spiritual about psychotherapy?

DRS. WARKENTIN AND VALERIUS: The religions of Man reflect his desire to feel at home in an unknowable universe and with daily experiences of mysterious origin. Man's use of symbols, analogies, myths, and images of unseen forces constitute his giving in to living with the incomprehensible. We consider to be sacred those experiences in which we can find no logical or sensory origins. We cannot even understand why we dearly love an Other. Consequently we make allowance for unknown powers which pervade and surround us and employ the language of symbols or rituals to communicate our metaphysical experiences.

The C-Factor in psychotherapy may be considered to be a religious concept, a symbol of uncanny forces which we cannot control but acknowledge respectfully. Our best therapy experiences are those where the patient and we accept the presence of obscure forces, while also seeking logical insights which contribute to our understanding of therapeutic movement. In this way we interact simultaneously on two levels, the nonrational and the rational, trusting that the outcome will be benevolent.

VI

DR. BURTON: Failures in therapy have usually been attributed to inadequate motivation or lack of cooperation on the part of the patient. A few psychotherapists have blamed themselves for poor outcomes. How can you escape the responsibility of the patient or therapist by speaking of *"no-fault failure?"*

DRS. WARKENTIN AND VALERIUS: The patient and therapist are both fully accountable for their individual participation in the therapeutic endeavor. Either one of them can stop the process by refusal to continue. The third essential component of the nuclear process is not available to direct deliberate control by the partners. They may both approach their task with good will and sincere effort and yet fail to achieve a fortunate collaboration. If so, they are facing an incompatibility beyond their control for which they cannot be held responsible. If the patients or therapists were to blame themselves for this no-fault failure, it could not be a learning experience, how to do better the next time, but would constitute an inappropriate discouragement to them.

Albert Ellis

9

A Rational-Emotive Approach to Behavioral Change

by ALBERT ELLIS, Ph.D.

What makes behavioral change possible in or outside of the therapeutic process? No necessary or sufficient condition, as far as I can see. Carl R. Rogers wrote a famous paper on "The necessary and sufficient conditions of therapeutic personality change" in 1957; and I invalidated all of his hypotheses in a rebuttal (Ellis, 1, 2). Let me even more strongly, in the present updating of my views, review his and others' contentions about personality change and show why none of the conditions that they set turn out sufficient or necessary.

After doing this, I shall go on to indicate some of the more important, and in some ways almost crucial, elements in basic personality change; and I shall conclude this chapter by showing how rational-emotive therapy (RET) concentrates on and facilitates these more crucial elements. But first let me say a few words about behavior change itself. Theoretically, it consists of any modification of human behavior—including temporary and more permanent, light and profound, one-sided and more encompassing, inelegant and elegant. All such kinds and degrees of change probably have importance, but I shall concentrate in this chapter mainly on what we may call basic personality change. I define this as a profound and enduring alteration in people's thinking, emoting, and behaving. In terms of psychotherapy, those who make such a basic change not only experience an amelioration or removal of some disturbed symptom—such as a specific obsession, compulsion, phobia, or fear of inadequacy—but they also have a different outlook on themselves, others, and the surrounding world; they tend to cope better with a variety of personal and social problems; and they remain relatively unupsettable when confronted with a new set of troublesome conditions.

I do not exactly refer here to what I sometimes call the "elegant" solution to therapeutic problems. For I have an ideal, which I have seen few of my own (and, so far, none of anyone else's) clients achieve which I call "unupsettability." Those who reach this ideal first achieve minimal anxiety, depression, hostility, and feelings of worthlessness; and then, after therapy ends, they keep working on themselves and improving their emotional state, so that no matter what happens to them in their later lives, they practically never make themselves seriously disturbed about it. Including cancer, war, and famine? Yes, including all these and similar "catastrophes." When anything like this occurs, they allow themselves to feel appropriately sad, mournful, annoyed, and highly critical (at times) of their own behavior. But they do not *awfulize, whine,* or grandiosely *command* about virtually anything. Hence, they have *really* undergone an elegant and profound personality change!

The kind of basic modification I shall discuss in this chapter will remain on a less ideal level. I shall acknowledge that people have changed significantly and basically when they have reached the more modest state mentioned two paragraphs above: when they have rid themselves of their presenting symptoms or at least experience them much less often and drastically, and when they show evidence of coping with life's hassles, including their own recurrent upsets when these occur, and of significantly lessening their previous neurotic inhibitions and overreactions to almost any new set of troublesome conditions that might occur in the future.

Does this kind of unideal but still profound personality change actually occur in many individuals? Yes, I think it does. But I can discover no necessary and sufficient conditions for bringing it about. Let me briefly review some of the assumed conditions which Rogers and others have posited in this connection and show why they all ring false.

1. For basic personality change to occur, Rogers (3) contends, two people, notably a therapist and client, must have psychological contact. On the contrary! I have personally known, and virtually all of us have heard about, individuals who changed virtually their whole lives when (a) they had an unusual experience, such as almost dying, and came out of it nicely; (b) they listened to a lecture or sermon, sometimes recorded, by a person with whom they never had any personal contact whatever; (c) they read an article or book which they found profoundly moving or instructive; or (d) they saw a film, TV show, or other form of "entertainment." In my own case, I have hopefully affected hundreds of clients by my psychological contact with them. But I also have evidence that my writings and recordings—particularly my books *Sex Without Guilt* and *A New Guide to Rational Living*—have helped thousands of others, including some who had years of hospitalization for serious psychotic states, enormously change their ways of thinking, acting, and feeling. Rogers may well argue that an individual's having unusual life experiences or reading a book will not most *effectively* cure him or her. Probably not. But his implication that such nonrelationship methods *never* work obviously lacks validity.

2. Rogers contends that for basic personality change to occur clients have to experience a state of incongruence and feel vulnerable or anxious. Wrong! Many largely congruent and unanxious individuals change themselves significantly—usually for the better but sometimes for the worse!—by life experiences or reading. As I and other therapists have pointed out, some of the more congruent and less disturbed individuals benefit *most* by therapy—especially by various kinds of group therapy, including encounter groups. And, conversely, some of the most anxious and incongruent individuals benefit least, and even experience traumatization, as a result of psychotherapy.

3. Rogers holds that "the therapist should be, within the confines of this relationship, a congruent, genuine, integrated person. It means that within the relationship he is freely and deeply himself, with his actual experience accurately represented by his awareness of himself. It is the opposite of presenting a facade, either knowingly or unknowingly." I quite go along with Rogers here—if he wants to say that under most conditions (but not all) congruence in the therapist proves a highly desirable, though hardly necessary, condition for basic personality change. I think that all of us know clients of highly disturbed and *in*congruent therapists who seemed to get considerable help from these therapists. And I, for one, have seen disturbed people who apparently worsened because they just could not or would not accept what I considered the marvelous honesty, congruence, and integration on the part of their psychologists or psychiatrists.

4. Rogers next lists as a necessary condition for personality change the therapist's experiencing unconditional positive regard for the client—by which he means "a caring for the client, but not in a possessive way or in such a way as simply to satisfy the therapist's own needs." Again, Rogers turns a desideratum into a necessity! Unconditional positive regard, or what we call in RET unconditional acceptance of the client by the therapist, usually has salutary effects. But I have at least occasionally seen clients of highly exploitative, manipulative, and even condemning therapists considerably helped. We can easily say that such clients received help in spite of and not because of their therapists' uncaring attitudes. Perhaps so. But the fact that they did improve in therapy and solidly believe that they did so because of their therapists' attitudes tends to negate Rogers' view that basic personality change *requires* a therapist's unconditional positive regard.

5. Rogers claims that personality change invariably follows from the therapist's "experiencing an accurate, empathic understanding of the client's awareness of his own experience. To sense the client's private world as if it were your own, but without ever losing the 'as if' quality—this is empathy, and this seems essential to therapy." It does? Empathy, as Rogers defines it, seems excellent. When a therapist *understands* and *feels with* the client's emotions, sees this client's behavior from his or her *own* frame of reference, and does not literally feel personally disturbed as the client does or believe in the irrationalities of the client, that proves quite helpful. But *necessary?* Clearly, no.

I know several therapists, and an even greater number of my own clients, who don't really empathize with or feel with people's private worlds, and who rather dogmatically and arbitrarily try to indoctrinate these others with more "rational" or more "practical" philosophies of life. Oddly enough, they sometimes succeed, and help these others considerably. Similarly, some notable bigots, such as Savonarola and Hitler, have had minimal empathy with others and nevertheless helped these others make profound personality changes, some of which we could argue with and some of which proved constructive. So even if Rogers can show, as he quite possibly can, that empathizing with another's private world *usually* helps this other therapeutically, can he really show that empathy constitutes a sufficient or necessary condition of personality change?

6. Rogers contends that the client must perceive, "to a minimal degree, the acceptance and empathy which the therapist experiences for him." *Must?* —or *had better?* As I pointed out in my original paper disproving Rogers' theses, I have on several occasions seen evidence contradicting this hypothesis. Thus, I have seen paranoid clients who insisted that I did not empathize

with them at all but who, as I kept showing them the irrationality of their attitudes and actions, including their anger toward me, finally began to accept *my* frame of reference and to make significant personality changes. In some instances, I may well have shown little empathy for such clients (though, of course, I *thought* I did); and in other cases the clients *later* admitted that I had acted empathically, although at first they did not acknowledge this. But as long as I understood their basic irrational ideas and helped them give these up, my degree of empathizing with their feelings or their acknowledging that I did so seemed to relate relatively little to some of the personality changes they made.

7. Theorists like myself (Ellis, 4, 5, 6; Ellis and Harper, 7), George Kelly (8), and Victor Raimy (9) tend to say that philosophic or cognitive change remains a prerequisite to basic personality change. Naturally, I think they have a valid point! But in all honesty, I have to admit that *some* profound changes occur seemingly without any conscious or even unconscious cerebration. If anything, people sometimes change their thoughts or attitudes *after* they make certain behavioral or emotive alterations. Suppose, for example, you have a phobia against riding in cars but you get placed in a situation where you simply have to use them several times a day—you have to go to work or school or visit your love partner, and no other means of transportation seems available. So you take hundreds of auto rides, at first feeling most uncomfortable during all of them, but finally you get "used" or "conditioned" to them and feel comfortable. You never knowingly convince yourself that riding in cars doesn't feel "awful" but merely uncomfortable and you don't do any other cognitive work to get over your phobia; still, you not only lose it but after awhile really like riding in cars and feel highly disappointed when you have to use other means of transportation.

We could say, of course, that you "unconsciously" convinced yourself of the "unawfulness" of cars; that you somehow got to "see" that riding in them didn't include the dangers you previously imagined; and that you now "think," "believe," or "know" that they have more advantages than disadvantages. Therefore, we could conclude, your therapeutic change has taken place for highly cognitive reasons.

Perhaps so. But although most people, under similar conditions, consciously and clearly *see* that they have merely imagined "dangers" about car riding and that, now that they have chanced it many times, these dangers no longer exist, others never quite see this and still make significant advances in giving up their phobias. I would therefore, in spite of my own personal biases in favor of the cognitive aspects of behavioral or emotive change, tend to conclude that you may require some degree of "insight" or "philosophic" restructuring for the most *elegant* form of personality alteration, but that such rethinking hardly seems necessary for *any* kind of basic change.

8. Many behaviorists would tend to argue that fundamental metamorphosis won't occur in humans unless they *practice* new patterns of thinking, emoting, and behaving over a reasonable period of time. For the most part, I would tend to agree. But not entirely! As noted above, some people have quickly turned themselves on to some philosopher or religionist and have almost immediately changed their behavior in radical ways. True, they kept practicing the new behavior *after* the turn-on occurred, and we cannot accurately say, therefore, that *no* practice took place as they changed themselves. But where other individuals have to laboriously practice new thinking and behaving for a long period of time before they begin to feel comfortable with it, and they then automatically *maintain* their new behaviors, these instantly turned-on people seem to act radically differently from the start and also *feel good in* their new roles. Assiduous practice, then, seems a highly desirable and important element in most basic personality change. But not in all!

9. Some therapists, such as those in Gestalt therapy, hold that powerful awareness of one's present here-and-now feelings constitutes a necessary condition for basic personality change (Perls, 10). Clearly, no evidence sustaining this viewpoint exists. Innumerable clients seem to have made highly significant changes in their behavior as a result of undergoing psychoanalytic sessions, where they dwelled almost exclusively on their past instead of present feelings; and innumerable other clients have benefited significantly from focusing, with their therapists, on present rather than past conditions but almost entirely staying with their present thoughts and behaviors rather than with their feelings (Adler, 11; Wolpe, 12). Awareness-centered therapists may well contend, if they wish, that here-and-now apprehension (and/or expression) of feelings comprises a better or more elegant path to personality change, but they can hardly prove that *only* this path to significant alteration of behavior exists.

10. Both psychoanalysts (Freud, 13) and abreactive therapists (Reich, 14; Janov, 15) often hold that basic personality change depends on people fully understanding some of the "traumatic" events of their early childhood and emotionally expressing and working through these early traumas. Again, lots of evidence exists that myriads of individuals change themselves appreciably when either (a) they have no particular knowledge of or insight into their past "traumas" or (b) they understand their past histories but never experience any intense abreactive feelings connected with the severe "pains" they underwent in their early years. Thus, people obviously at times make deep-seated personality changes while undergoing behavior therapy, rational-

emotive therapy, Gestalt therapy, and various other kinds of treatment procedures which ignore insight into or abreactions about past "traumas."

From the foregoing analysis, I think we can agree that all kinds of thinking, emoting, and behavioral procedures seem to accompany, and at times appear causally connected with, basic personality change. But not one of them, by itself, invariably leads to such change, entitling it to be labeled a "sufficient" cause of that change. And not a single one of them proves utterly necessary to significant personality modification. Having disposed, therefore, of the myth of any necessary or sufficient conditions for therapeutic change, let me spend the rest of this chapter considering some of the more important conditions that *usually* or *frequently* seem to abet modification of human behavior.

The Concept of the Possibility of Change

People definitely change even when they don't believe that they can. A woman, for example, joins one of my therapy groups because she wants to work on her compulsive overeating; but at the same time that she thinks she can change that symptom, she stoutly believes that she cannot act unshyly and extravertedly. Although at first she seldom speaks up in group, and then only about her own problems, after she has come to ten sessions she turns into the most open and most talkative group member, and begins to act uninhibitedly and comfortably in outside social groups as well. So she thinks at first that she can't change in her group interactions with others; but she obviously can—and does!

Even she, however, came to therapy because she thought that she could experience *some* kind of alteration of her behavior. So do the great majority of people who participate in therapy or in other change-facilitating experiences. They assume that they can learn to play tennis, improve their public speaking, relate more intimately to others, or overcome their anxieties. When they believe they can't, and enter therapy for other reasons—such as feeling forced to do so in a hospital or prison setting—they feel much less motivated to learn new ways of behaving and they usually do so to a lesser degree.

Behavioral change, then, partly and significantly depends on the realization that one can learn new ways. Without that realization, an enormous degree of resistance and inertia tends to occur. With near fatal results!

The Desire to Change

Most disturbed individuals have a reasonably strong desire to change, and those who come to therapy especially do. But not always! I have seen adolescents by the dozen who have managed to get into serious trouble at school, at home, or in their social life, and who show little desire to change, and none to get therapeutic help. I have also seen spouses, dragged into marriage counseling sessions by their mates, who think that they have no serious problems, that only their mates do, and that reasonably good conditions exist in their obviously low-level marriages. Some of these reluctant clients really believe, albeit defensively, that they behave very well. Others acknowledge their vulnerability, but very frankly have no intention of *working* at changing it. Still others fully admit that they have very serious problems—but insist that they have had them so long and so deeply that they just "naturally" act the way they do, have no ability to change their ways, and must therefore accept their doom.

Perversely, I have helped some of these D.C.'s (difficult customers). Sometimes I show them that they clearly keep screwing up and getting into difficulties and that they'd damned better, for their own sake and not for mine or their parents' or spouses' sakes, change. Sometimes I prove to them that they only can rid themselves of their anxiety, depression, and self-downing by concerted work; and that however hard that work may prove, they will really experience *more* work and pain if they don't undertake it. Sometimes I convince them that they have great difficulty in giving up their disturbances but that they definitely *can* do so—especially if they stop idiotically telling themselves that they can't!

So "hopeless" and "unmotivated" clients can importantly change. But a strong desire to do so still helps! Not merely a New Year's resolution to change—for we know just about how ineffective that can prove. But a powerful wish to behave differently, *plus* the determination to work one's ass off to back up that wish, seems one of the prime factors in personality modification. Or any other kind of human change!

Willingness to Work at Change

Continuing the ideas posited in the last two sentences: what I call Insight No. 3, in *Reason and Emotion in Psychotherapy* (2), constitutes perhaps the most important element in personality change for most people most of the time. Insight No. 1 consists of the recognition that your disturbed behavior has important "causal" antecedents—not merely in your past history (which may have relative unimportance) but in your present thinking. You feel upset, at point C, your emotional Consequence, after you have had an Activating experience, at point A, not "because" of A but largely because of B, the Belief system that you hold *about* what has occurred at A. Recognizing this and fully acknowledging that *you* make *yourself* disturbed, at C, with *your* Beliefs, constitute a very important "insight."

Insight No. 2 consists of the acknowledgment that you keep sustaining or carrying on your Beliefs, at point B, no matter how or with whose help you originated them. Even when someone, such as your parents, helped indoctrinate you with these Beliefs, you *choose* to keep believing them today; and you *therefore* keep upsetting yourself with them. Another very important insight!

Insight No. 3—ah, here we have the rub!—consists of the insight that insight alone will not normally work. *Knowing* that you directly cause your own emotional Consequences and that you keep doing so today, no matter who or what encouraged you to do so in the past, will rarely help you change very much—unless you willingly *work and practice* to give up your present cognitions, emotions, and behaviors. For, as a human, you *habituate* yourself to acting in certain disturbed ways, and only a continual and prolonged amount of dishabituation will usually get you *habituated* to easily and "automatically" behaving differently. Tough—but true!

Your willingness—nay, eagerness—to *work* at changing yourself, then, remains the issue. You can resolve forever. Promise yourself almost anything. Vow to do all kinds of things. No matter. Unless the determination to work and practice against the old behavior and for the new modes of living truly exists, forget it. You probably won't change very much in the first place; nor, if you do, stay changed in the second place. To your *desire* to modify your disruptive behavior, therefore, you'd better add a few other factors: determination to work; forced (often much against the "grain"!) action; unwhinyness about your discomfort while you keep changing; and practice, practice, practice at giving up the old and establishing the new behaviors!

Note particularly, in this respect, the propensity to make changes in themselves of many notably deluded individuals. They adopt a quite "crazy" creed—such as the devout belief that their particular religious leader has divine qualities or that the end of the world will occur soon, and they therefore *enthusiastically* adopt some form of discipline, such as praying several hours a day, that they normally would never carry out. Their enthusiasm and determination help them get so habituated to this discipline that they "naturally" and "easily" perform it; they then correctly see that they *can* control themselves enormously (where previously they felt sure that they could not); they view themselves and the world much differently; and they turn into teetotalers instead of drunks, or compulsive workers rather than hippie-like drug addicts. Seemingly, therefore, even a delusion-motivated enthusiasm and determination to change can significantly help. Better you do so for saner reasons! But determination to *work* at self-modification remains a key issue.

Understanding of What Blocks Change

Assuming that you desire strongly to change, you know that you can, and yet you *don't* determinedly follow up your "willingness" and "insight" with concerted action, you probably have one or more strong blocks to changing. You can conceive of these, if you wish, in all kinds of terms: such as, as most psychoanalysts would assume, that you "really" don't want to change; that you rebel against doing so in order to do in your parents; that you have a powerful unconscious conflict, such as an Oedipal conflict, which blocks you from changing, etc. Perhaps so, but I, after practicing psychoanalysis for several years, remain highly sceptical.

You can, however, have *some* conscious or unconscious reasons for desiring to better your "personality" and actually not doing so. Some of the main reasons I find in this connection include these:

1. You devoutly believe (at point B, your Belief system) that you *must* do well and *have* to receive the approval of others for doing well. You cling so strongly and persistently to these self-defeating beliefs that you (logically) engage in various kinds of self-sabotaging behaviors and you (logically) resist giving them up. For instance, you make yourself exceptionally anxious about succeeding at your job or career because you dogmatically believe that you absolutely *must* do so to prove your worth as a human. As long as you cling to this silly belief, you will almost inevitably make yourself anxious—for how can you *guarantee* that you will keep succeeding? Moreover, if you resolve to work at changing that belief, you will probably insist that you *must* succeed at *that* endeavor—and will make yourself anxious about doing so! Again, you may give yourself RET "homework" assignments of taking risks in forging ahead at work—and then you will demand that you *have to* do those assignments well, and probably won't try to do them. Or you will make yourself anxious by insisting that (a) you *must* please your therapist; (b) you've *got to* act rationally; (c) you *should* persist at working at therapy all the time, etc., etc. In one way or another, your *must*urbation about giving up your anxiety will turn into a "Catch 22" that prevents you from actually working at giving it up!

2. You can prevent yourself from working at personality change by believing (again, at point B) that others *must* treat you well. Thus, in regard to your job, you may insist that your boss and fellow employees *have to* treat you kindly and fairly; that your mate *has got to* appreciate how hard you

work to get ahead; that various people *ought* to help you get a better job; and so on. And if you go for therapy, you can command that your therapist *must* specially favor and like you; that he or she *must* charge you practically nothing; that he or she *has to* make you change. Any or all these ideas may prevent you from working at changing your ways.

3. You can sabotage the work of modifying your personality and behavior by demanding that conditions of life prove easy or easier. You can produce low frustration tolerance and inertia on your job by insisting that your parents have more money; that economic conditions turn out better; that your superiors die or leave their jobs, to help you get a better position; that certain rules and regulations for your getting ahead on your job get suspended, etc. Then again, if you do go for therapy to help yourself over these self-defeating attitudes, you can insist that easy and magical solutions exist for your changing yourself; that therapy not take time or money; that you do not do the therapeutic homework but only attend to what goes on during the actual therapy session.

If you fully understand these kinds of ideological blocks to your working at changing yourself, know that you create the blocks in your own head and have the ability to uncreate them, and show willingness to work at giving them up, you will probably help yourself considerably to change. You may change yourself without any such understanding; but you well may not!

A Clear-cut Understanding of the Major Elements in Change

You can significantly change yourself without clearly understanding the major elements in change—as when you merely recognize, even vaguely, that getting over a fear of public speaking involves forcing yourself to keep making speeches; and you do so without also recognizing that you had better concomitantly work at modifying your attitudes and emotions about public speaking. I think I largely did this myself many years ago, when I felt exceptionally self-conscious about giving talks in public, forced myself to give many of them in a short period of time, and *then* largely changed my attitude about the "horror" of giving a poor talk or of having the audience laugh at me. I *now* see the important cognitive and emotive elements that I unconsciously altered in regard to making public talks, but I only had vague awareness of these elements at the time I got over my phobia of speaking.

Preferably, you had better fully know that basic personality change involves cognitive, emotive, *and* behavioral components. Today, if I had a public-speaking phobia, I would still force myself to give many talks in a row—as I did during my twentieth year. But I would *also* work very hard at giving up the belief that I *must* impress others with my speaking and that my life would turn into *holy horror* if I did not. And I would *furthermore* work at giving up several concomitant feelings of shame—such as, my shame of revealing myself to close friends, or turning in a poor essay in school, or dressing unmodishly at a social gathering.

Let me again underscore! No matter how severe my fear of public speaking, I may well overcome it by having (a) an understanding of one major mode of therapeutic change (e.g., in vivo desensitization) or by having (b) *no* understanding of therapeutic change but by accidentally forcing myself to do the right thing for the wrong reasons—e.g., forcing myself to speak in public because I want to retain a certain job rather than doing so in order to overcome my phobia. But the more I understand *how* to rid myself of my anxiety, the more efficient and persistent I will probably behave in regard to eliminating it. So, as usual, this kind of understanding gives me a highly desirable, though hardly necessary or sufficient, handle on changing myself.

Other Desiderata for Change

Do I need anything else to help myself effect a basic personality change? No, not *need;* but *could use to advantage.* Lots of things! In order to change myself significantly and permanently, I could well have these kinds of things: (1) unusually good intelligence and a high level of energy; (2) a sceptical, nondogmatic attitude toward life and toward the teachings of others; (3) a favorable human environment, including significant people who do not damn me for my errors and who keep encouraging me to achieve my potential for growth; (4) a favorable socioeconomic environment, which provides me with sufficient food, clothing, shelter, education, career opportunities, freedom of movement, toleration of my individuality, etc.; (5) a wise, accepting, active-directive therapist, who keeps showing me how I upset myself and what I can specifically do to anti-awfulize and pigheadedly refuse to keep upsetting myself; (6) specific training in the logico-empirical, scientific method and its application to personal as well as to general problems.

I don't present this as an exhaustive list, and feel sure that I have omitted significant desiderata from it. But it will do for a start! Let me say in conclusion: Basic personality change seems to have no single or multiple requisites. But it preferably involves many different conditions—including a person's having a clear-cut concept of the possibility of change, a strong desire to modify his or her behavior, a willingness to work at and practice changing, a lucid understanding of the common cognitive-emotional blocks to change, an understanding of the major elements in altering human behavior, and the existence of several favorable hereditary, environmental, and therapeutic factors. The more these factors exist and the more you understand and feel determined to use them, the more profound and lasting changes you will probably make in yourself. For you, as a human, partly—and never fully—control your own destiny. If you *will!*

ADDENDUM QUERIES

I

DR. BURTON: You state in your chapter that there are no "necessary and sufficient" conditions to bring about personality or behavior change and take Carl Rogers to task for explicating precisely such "necessary and sufficient conditions" found in his own therapy procedures. Do you therefore conceive of psychotherapy and behavior change as a kind of immediate improvisation by certain healing personalities, with all the necessary tools required available, much as a journeyman plumber might have and might pull out of his bag? And does this imply that if such "necessary and sufficient" conditions are never forthcoming friends, fellow sufferers, or paraprofessionals, educators, ministers, etc., do as well as professionals in the healing enterprise?

DR. ELLIS: A good question! My answer: partly yes and partly no. On the one hand, I do not see psychotherapy as more of an art than a science. Quite the converse! I think that a trained therapist had better, first, have a good *theory* of psychotherapy—realize, for example, that people largely get disturbed (or, better, disturb themselves) in certain statistically prevalent ways—especially, by devoutly believing in absolute *shoulds, oughts,* and *musts* and by accepting or inventing antiempirical views of the universe. Once the therapist sees personality disturbability and change within a fairly accurate theoretical framework, he or she can *then* assess individual clients in terms of *their* variations on various major themes of emotional dysfunctioning and *their* personal tendencies to cling to and refuse to surrender various of their self-defeating behaviors.

Having made this kind of assessment, the therapist goes into his bag of tricks (something like the journeyman or full-fledged plumber does) and selects the presumably most useful tools—including, usually, some form of cognitive restructuring which he or she *teaches* the client, and various kinds of behavioral homework assignments and emotive procedures to back up and confirm these new teachings. The therapist's effectiveness will therefore partly depend on (1) theoretical outlook, (2) good therapeutic guesses, (3) native skill in making guesses and implementing them with effective techniques, (4) artistry in teaching, persuasion, ways of relating to clients, etc., (5) availability of a good many potentially useful therapy procedures, (6) persistence at assessment of clients and applying selectively chosen ways of helping them with their emotional problems, etc.

Your analogy between an effective therapist and an effective journeyman plumber, Dr. Burton, therefore makes a great deal of sense. But since humans have more complex ways of behaving and misbehaving than, say, toilets, and since helping them "fix" themselves has a large number of possible variations, a qualified therapist normally requires much more training, skill, artistry, and knowledge than a qualified plumber. Eventually, as knowledge of basic personality structure and therapeutic procedures accumulates, a greater possibility may well exist of a paraprofessional therapist's understanding the basic causes of *many* or *most* human disturbances, and having the ability to catalyze basic personality change in a *good many* disturbed individuals. But at the present time so many lapses in therapeutic knowledge and skills exist that paraprofessionals, under supervision of more highly trained therapists, can probably achieve only limited gains with selected kinds of clients.

Similarly with friends, fellow sufferers, educators, ministers, and other potential helpers. *Some* of them, because of their basic understanding of human disturbance and what they can do to help disturbed individuals, can probably do much better with many sufferers than can *many* professional therapists. But these special sub-professional helpers constitute a small minority and as yet we had better not endow them with more ability than they actually possess.

Your term "immediate improvisation by certain healing personalities" seems a good one to me and, as the state of the psychotherapeutic art and science progresses, probably takes on even sounder meaning. Once a therapist has a good amount of training, skill, artistry, and knowledge of a large body of therapeutic "tricks," I think that he or she can largely resort to "immediate improvisation" in regard to which of these "tricks" to use and how to employ them. But remember that improvisation itself includes many (often hidden) artistic and scientific elements. It does not consist of pure guesswork or "intuition"!

II

DR. BURTON: Your disagreements with Sigmund Freud are of course well known through your various lectures and writings, but I have never heard you comment much on C. G. Jung's, Wilhelm Reich's, and Alfred Adler's contributions. Yet I believe you have been very much influenced by these three men. Is this correct?

DR. ELLIS: Yes, and it is correct that I have learned from the work of Freud, particularly his concept (often neglected by his followers) that human disturbability seems to flow from an innate, biological tendency of people to think irrationally and behave self-defeatingly, and by his concept of the defense system—which, again, largely seems innately predisposed in humans, and only very partially the result of their "conditioning" by their parents and others.

Actually, I have written quite a bit about the work of Alfred Adler, most of whose theory of personality and personality change I agree with; and, in fact, I hold membership in the American Society of Adlerian Psychology. My book, *Humanistic Psychotherapy: The Rational-Emotive Approach* (5), contains a chapter entitled, "Reason and Emotion in the Psychology of Adler." Let me quote from the final paragraphs of this chapter:

> Adler's latter-day formulations regarding private intelligence and common sense reasoning distinctly improve upon his earlier overemphasis on the inferiority-grandiosity model of human behavior. RET, enriched by Adlerian thought, has gone forward, providing an improved model of psychotherapeutic understanding and practice.
> There are essentially three different views of the origins of human emotions and how they can be changed. The first view is that of the behaviorists and of the Freudians: namely, that emotional reactions are primarily caused by external stimuli, events, or experiences—either in the individual's past or present life. The second view is that of the anti-intellectualists, many of whom are now represented in the modern encounter group and sensory awareness movement: namely, that emotions are sacrosanct unto themselves and essentially spring from themselves. The third view is that of the stoics and the phenomenologists: namely, that emotions are the result of human evaluations, appraisals, interpretations, and cognitions. Adler was largely in this third camp. He unequivocally stated:
>
> > No experience is a cause of success or failure. We do not suffer from the shock of our experiences—the so-called *trauma*—but we make out of them just what suits our purposes. We are *self-determined* by the meaning we give to our experiences; and there is probably something of a mistake always involved when we take particular experiences as the basis for our future life. Meanings are not determined by situations, but we determine ourselves by the meanings we give to situations.*

---

* *What Life Should Mean to You*, New York, Basic Books, 1932; New York, Capricorn, 1958, p. 14.

This seems to me to be an essentially rational and sensible view of human emoting and experiencing. It is the main view, moreover, which profoundly and distinctly shows what humans can do to change their disordered and inappropriate emotionalizing.

Although Adler at times was not too clear about how, in detail, people's self-defeating emotional reactions can be modified, he was very definite about the general method of changing them: namely, education. He above all other modern therapists pioneered in advancing the concept that psychotherapy is education and that education would better be psychotherapeutic.

As for Carl Jung, I have not spoken or written about his work very much, largely because he himself wrote, in his book, *The Practice of Psychotherapy* (New York, Pantheon, 1954), that his technique consisted of a combination of Freudian and Adlerian methods. I also have always personally found his interpretations of dreams and other "unconscious" processes quite mystical-minded, overgeneralized, and unscientific—and even worse, if possible, than the Freudian sex symbolism overgeneralizations. But I do think that he, along with Adler, clearly saw the human propensity for self-actualization and individuation, and I have used, sometimes without due credit, some of his concepts of creativity and self-fulfillment. On the other hand, although I feel that he, as much as anyone in the field of psychotherapy, clearly understood the innate tendency of humans to create irrationalities, I think that he pessimistically gave in, in a way, to this tendency and thought that as therapists we have to go along with it rather than vigorously and rigorously teach clients to combat it. Where I consider religiosity and dogmatism perhaps the main philosophic source of emotional disturbance, he actually encouraged these tendencies to some extent and often seemed to recommend that his clients go to church!

I find Wilhelm Reich another complex and highly self-contradictory theorist. On the one hand, he wrote a fine book entitled *The Sexual Revolution* (New York, Farrar, Straus, and Giroux, 1968), quite advanced for its day (I think its original German edition appeared in the 1940's); but on the other hand, he wrote *The Function of the Orgasm* (New York, New American Library, 1970), one of the worst pieces of tripe on sex ever penned. He clearly saw that physical and sexual blockings *occasionally* or *sometimes* lead to emotional blockings; and, in a typical psychotic manner, he profoundly and dogmatically concluded that *all* emotional problems stem from physical inhibitions in general and (going crazily beyond Freud) sex inhibitions in particular. Ironically, though I have gained a reputation as one of the leading exponents of sexual liberation in the world, I remain heartily opposed to practically all Reich's supersexual views of disturbance; and I think that he and his various followers—such as Elsworth Baker, Alexander Lowen, Will Schutz, and Fritz Perls—do much more therapeutic harm than good in their obsession with bodily processes. Just about none of the neo-Reichians, moreover, adequately distinguish between appropriate negative emotions—such as concern, disappointment, and annoyance—when unpleasant events occur in one's life and the *in*appropriate emotions—such as anxiety, depression, and hostility—which one foolishly creates by whining about these events and about one's appropriate negative feelings. Wilhelm Reich may well have had elements of genius in his theorizing; but his severe paranoid thinking not only loused up his personal life and helped drive him to an early grave, but also got inextricably intertwined into much of his theorizing and practice.

III

DR. BURTON: You speak about "elegant solutions to therapeutic problems" as if they were paradisiacal and unobtainable. Do you settle for less with your clients or hold out for more—even against their resistance? How far, professionally speaking, can a therapist go in helping clients change and in changing the culture in which they are imbedded?

DR. ELLIS: I hold out as long as feasible, though not as long as possible, for the elegant solution. I strive, with virtually every client, to help him or her bring about a basic or thoroughgoing change in his or her philosophy and behavior, and to maintain that change after therapy ends. But if I see that the client simply will not go this far, I "settle" for the most elegant solution feasible. Even when clients "resist," I try to push them toward more elegant solutions. But if I and they fail, we fail. Tough! I do not denigrate them or myself for failing; and I accept, and gracefully lump, this relatively grim reality.

I think that therapists can go very far in trying to help clients change, and can persist for a fairly long time in this regard and use every technique they can creatively adapt and employ. I find that many of my highly recalcitrant clients do, as long as I do not make myself impatient or condemning about their resistance, finally make remarkable changes in themselves. But many only change moderately—or far less than I would personally like to see them change. Again: tough!

In regard to society, I think that a therapist can certainly try to help change the culture in which both he or she and the client remain imbedded. I try to do this myself in several ways: (1) by helping clients to change; (2) by helping clients to work with their friends, relatives, and associates, to help *them* change, too; (3) by writing a great deal of material that I hope will abet social as well as individual change; (4) by working with certain organizations, such as the American Civil Liberties Union, the American Humanist Association, and the Association for Humanistic Psychology, which overtly strive for political and social change.

I don't think that a therapist *has to* try to help change the culture or to work for general social as well as individual client change. But I do think it highly preferable if he or she does!

IV

DR. BURTON: You highlight an important and often overlooked phenomenon: that behavior change under religious, philosophic, or similar auspices can occur very quickly and last a long time. This even happens in psychotherapy where healing is afforded by a person's simply calling for an appointment and never going any further. Would you comment further on this increasing form of behavior change in our society.

DR. ELLIS: Another good question! I quite agree that people can and do motivate themselves to change by making a therapeutic appointment, later canceling it, and never going any further with formal therapy. I think that under these conditions they think over their problems, see them differently, make some new philosophic conclusions regarding them, and consequently change. This would tend to support my thesis that we usually upset ourselves and definitely have the power to unupset ourselves again if we modify certain key cognitions.

I believe that significant personality change has always occurred more as a result of people's informal experiences and contacts, including their experiences with books and lectures, than it has as a result of formal psychotherapy; and I expect this phenomenon to continue. Quite probably, less disturbed individuals benefit the most from informal "therapy" while more disturbed ones require formal treatment. But I have also known many individuals in the "psychotic" category who changed significantly after reading—and sometimes rereading and rereading—a self-help or "inspirational" book. We have rarely, as psychological researchers, studied this fascinating phenomenon; and I believe that we had better study it more intensively.

I also feel that, especially during the last decade, many more Americans than ever before who normally would go for formal psychotherapy have started to patronize various philosophical and religious systems, including Scientology, Erhard Seminars Training, Arica, Silva Mind Control, Transcendental Meditation, Yoga and Science of Mind, which claim that they do not have links with therapy and whose main practitioners have no professional training; and I predict that, unfortunately, this trend will continue. I personally view all these systems as forms of psychotherapy—and, usually, misleading, unscientific, and potentially dangerous forms of therapy at that. Should practitioners of such "therapies" meet educational and training standards now required of formal therapists? Especially when they do more than write or lecture, and in addition employ exercises normally used in therapy groups? I would say Yes. But how we would actually arrange this almost boggles the mind!

V

DR. BURTON: The desire to change, the possibility of change, and the willingness to work at change loom large in your schema. But such desire and working attempts are also found in enduring clients who never leave therapy and never change to any great extent. What really is the desire to change on a more fundamental or dynamic level? Can you elaborate this here?

DR. ELLIS: I have rarely seen a long-term client who had the desire to change, accepted the possibility of change, had the willingness to work at change, and who kept seeing a *competent* therapist who did not change significantly. In fact, I have seen many such clients make great changes in themselves in spite of the fact of their seeing what I would personally call highly incompetent therapists. And to me—though of course I have my own prejudices!—a therapist remains incompetent whenever he or she does not give the client highly specific, active, checked-upon homework assignments. When the therapist does give such assignments, particularly those that require activity on the part of the clients that counterattacks their basic phobias, obsessions, compulsions, hostilities, and depressions, and when the clients literally work at doing these assignments, they virtually always, in my experience, significantly change themselves.

In other words: the desire to change, on a more fundamental or dynamic level, invariably includes actually *working* at effectuating such change *no matter how painful that work or the interim discomfort may prove.* As Harold Greenwald points out in *Direct Decision Therapy* (New York: Jason Aronson, 1975), a true decision to do something includes the *action* to back up that decision. What I call the "desire" to change or the "willingness" to work at change includes concerted and often prolonged action to back up that desire or willingness. I would guess that virtually every "client" who has a decent piano or tennis teacher and who does the homework assigned by that teacher significantly changes his or her way of playing the piano or tennis. A few exceptions to this rule would include neurologically or physically deficient individuals who have no real ability to play the piano or tennis. Damned few! I would hypothesize that the same holds true of psychotherapy: almost all, though of course not absolutely all, seriously and moderately disturbed individuals have a good deal of capacity for significant personality change; and when this great majority go for psychotherapy with a competent therapist and actively engage in the homework assignments given by this therapist, they do make significant personality changes in themselves. The basic ingredient, therefore, in the desire to change that results in actual personality modification: *action* to back that desire!

REFERENCES

1. ELLIS, A.: Requisite conditions for basic personality change. *J. Consult. Psychol.*, 1959, 23, 538-540.
2. ELLIS, A.: *Reason and Emotion in Psychotherapy.* New York: Lyle Stuart, 1962.
3. ROGERS, C. R.: The necessary and sufficient conditions of therapeutic personality change. *J. Consult. Psychol.*, 1975, 21, 459-461.
4. ELLIS, A.: *Growth Through Reason.* Palo Alto: Science and Behavior Books, 1973.
5. ELLIS, A.: *Humanistic Psychotherapy: The Rational Emotive Approach.* New York: Julian Press and McGraw-Hill Paperbacks, 1974.
6. ELLIS, A.: *How to Live With a "Neurotic."* Rev. ed. New York: Crown Publishers, 1975.
7. ELLIS, A., and HARPER, R. A.: *A New Guide to Rational Living.* Englewood Cliffs: Prentice Hall; and Hollywood: Wilshire Books, 1975.
8. KELLY, G.: *The Psychology of Personal Constructs.* New York: Norton, 1955.
9. RAIMY, V.: *Misunderstandings of the Self.* San Francisco: Jossey-Bass, 1975.
10. PERLS, F.: *Gestalt Therapy Verbatim.* Lafayette, Calif: Real People Press, 1969.
11. ADLER, A.: *Understanding Human Nature.* New York: Fawcett World, 1974.
12. WOLPE, J.: *Psychotherapy of Reciprocal Inhibition.* Stanford: Stanford U. Press, 1958.
13. FREUD, S.: *Collected Papers.* New York: Collier Books, 1963.
14. REICH, W.: *Character Analysis.* Enl. ed. New York: Farrar, Straus and Giroux, 1974.
15. JANOV, A.: *The Primal Scream.* New York: Delta Books, 1970.

Victor Raimy

10

Changing Misconceptions as the Therapeutic Task

by VICTOR RAIMY, Ph.D.

The evolutionary development of man has recently been estimated by various anthropologists to have occupied a time span of from four million to perhaps fourteen million years. During this enormous period of time there is every reason to believe that man acquired conceptual capacities which usually control and guide his behavior. In the not too distant past when man's sojourn on this planet was thought to be a mere hundred thousand or so years, the proposition that human behavior is conceptually controlled was reasonably suspect. Our new time perspective, however, makes such a proposition increasingly plausible, particularly if we add to the evolutionary changes in conceptual development the enormous indoctrination in conceptual control imposed during the socialization process even by primitive societies. Emphasis upon conceptual control does not, by any means, imply that the biological drives and their associated passions have been eliminated, or even reduced in strength. Nor does this point of view imply that human beings are always guided by accurate reasoning. Rather, conceptual controls are viewed as channeling and organizing man's drives, his interpersonal relations, and his interactions with nature to a much greater extent than had been previously imagined.

This new perspective on man makes more understandable and acceptable the two-hundred-year-old contention that "morbid ideas" are the root of neurotic or otherwise maladjusted behavior. The early hypnotists of the last century saw their therapeutic task as the elimination of faulty ideas from the mind. The awesome power of morbid ideas was described by Janet in 1899 when he wrote, "The idea, like a virus, develops in a corner of the personality inaccessible to the subject, works subconsciously, and brings about all disorders of hysteria and mental disease" (cited by Ellenberger, 1). Obscured by different vocabularies and buried in complex theories of psychopathology and psychotherapy, the elimination of faulty ideas, under one or another label, still remains one of the central themes of many psychotherapies.

This cognitive conception of what makes behavior change possible can be summarized in the terms of the misconception hypothesis: "If those ideas or conceptions of a client or patient which are relevant to his psychological problems can be changed in the direction of greater accuracy where his reality is concerned, his maladjustments are likely to be eliminated" (Raimy, 2).

We are asserting, therefore, that the basic task of the psychotherapist lies in helping the individuals under treatment to bring about changes in the misconceptions which control their neurotic or otherwise maladaptive behavior. In short, what makes behavior change possible is the change in unrealistic conceptions. Such a point of view provides a two-way street, in that maladjusted behavior is seen as the product of the learning of faulty conceptions, while the transition from maladjusted to adjusted behavior results from the correction of the relevant misconceptions.

The process within the patient which brings about changes in misconceptions is here referred to as *cognitive review*. Even though we know little about it, we can assume that it is the same process which occurs in the forming and changing of concepts, since misconceptions are simply faulty conceptions. The principles of cognitive review can be stated most simply as follows: For individuals to change a concept of any kind, they must ordinarily be afforded opportunities to examine and reexamine all available evidence that is relevant to the concept. Complex misconceptions in psychotherapy rarely yield to a single or even several examinations of the pertinent evidence, hence the need for repeated review.

For purposes of contrast, we can compare the misconception hypothesis with three other common hypotheses that also attempt to designate the essential changes which must occur in the patient before readjustment occurs. Although the misconception hypothesis has a long history, the expression-of-emotion hypothesis has been its ancient rival. This latter hypothesis is largely responsible for the designation of psychological disturbances as "emotional" disorders. A more recent addition, largely inspired by Freud, is the redistribution-of-energy hypothesis which depends upon the notion of psychic energies and their distribution as determining the degree of adjustment of the individual. The most recent addition comes from the behavior therapists who advocate the behavior-change hypothesis, according to which therapists need only be concerned with observable behaviors rather than cognitions, emotions, or psychic energies.

Cognitive review is as commonly encountered in everyday life as in therapy. Most of the time we are only vaguely aware that we are engaged in such a process when we ruminate about problems we are facing. Over and over again we may examine all facets of a problem, until eventually we see a better solution or discard the problem as unsolvable, at least for the time being. The same process occurs in therapy, although most therapists refer to it under different labels, such as working through, or the need for more time, or the requirement of patience on the part of the therapist. Behavior therapists have developed systematic procedures for cognitive review, particularly when they repeatedly present the same or similar stimulus patterns to their clients, as in systematic desensitization or in implosive therapy.

The review process is not coldly mechanical and appropriate only for highly intellectual, scholarly, scientific, or judicial purposes. These are extreme instances in which systematic efforts are made, usually without complete success, to exclude affective elements. Cognitive review must include consideration of the cognitive aspects of affective responses. There is no intention of slighting the role of affect or emotion in this cognitive approach. Rather than viewing emotions as the primary target of therapeutic intervention, emotions are viewed as the product of faulty conceptions. If the relevant misconceptions can be changed, then emotions and feelings will also undergo change. There are still further roles played by affect in the present cognitive approach. Emotional responses themselves include cognitive data which often influence the self-concept and produce misconceptions. Characteristic patterns of affect may often identify individuals to themselves, as when one asserts, "I am a hot-tempered person." That particular individual may be less tempestuous in his reactions than the average person, but as long as he believes the assertion, he is likely to act upon it. Affect is also important within therapy, as inappropriate affect is likely to be an indicator of significant misconceptions.

Must a therapist be present for cognitive review to be effective? Not necessarily—although talking things over with another person may be helpful in a number of ways. Communicating problems to another person requires some organization of the problem, which is not required in solitary thinking. The necessary use of language sharpens the content presented. The troubled person is also likely to adopt a more objective attitude toward his difficulties in the presence of another. Finally, the listener may make truly helpful comments by pointing out errors, indicating relationships within the content which have escaped attention, and suggesting alternative concepts which may not have been available to the individual. Since all of these matters, except the content supplied by the listener, are also available to the solitary thinker, there seems to be no inherent need for another person during cognitive review. If we conclude from reports of its failure that solitary cognitive review is relatively useless, we ignore a most important aspect of the issue: that most personal problems of most people are solved by solitary cognitive review. Successful instances are not ordinarily reported to therapists.

There is still a second question to be answered: Why is cognitive review not always effective? There are several plausible answers.

1. Avoidance reactions may supervene to prevent consideration of either the misconceptions responsible for the maladjustment or consideration of important evidence which maintains the misconceptions. Many explanations have been suggested in attempts to account for such avoidance. Perhaps the best known is the psychoanalytic notion that repression occurs to block all mental access to content related to supposedly fearful or shameful experiences of the individual. In addition to repression, other defense mechanisms such as denial or projection may also account for avoidance reactions. More novel suggestions have been made, such as Frank's proposal that maladjusted individuals often engage in self-fulfilling prophecies whereby they unintentionally reinforce some of their worst fears about themselves, particularly when they behave in such peculiar fashions that they receive negative feedback from others. Still other explanations can be found in the behaviorist's assumption that avoidance reactions are conditioned and therefore outside the control of the individual. In any case, avoidance reactions may impede even intensive cognitive review so that pivotal misconceptions may be kept from reappraisal unless psychotherapy procedures are utilized.

2. Naive introspection may also fail to reveal pivotal misconceptions be-

cause of psychological "sets" which simply mislead individuals as they engage in cognitive review of their problems. If one believes, for example, that most of one's problems are due to sexual difficulties, one acquires a set to ignore those misconceptions which are not sexually related. Such sets, of course, can also be viewed as misconceptions which hinder the examination of un-related misconceptions. Another example can be found in the phobic reaction. Although phobics tend to have a distorted concept of the fearful object or situation, the pivotal misconception does not concern the feared object but rather the phobics' faulty belief that, if they permit themselves to remain in the presence of the feared object, they will be precipitated uncontrollably into intense panic and possible collapse.

3. One's own misconceptions are frequently much more difficult to re-cognize as faulty beliefs than are those of other individuals. Reality-testing of one's own beliefs, particularly those about the self, is likely to be a murky procedure in which even the defining of one's long-held beliefs may encounter obstacles such as their being embedded in rarely verbalized conceptions, or the individual's unwillingness to disturb a semi-satisfactory self-concept. The Buddhists have recognized this problem in reality-testing with their aphorism about "the eye which sees but cannot see itself." A provocative sidelight on this issue has been commented on by many group therapists. Neurotics or even psychotics who completely lack insight into their own mistakes in thinking or self-evaluation can frequently display acute insight into the mistakes of other persons.

4. Learned avoidance reactions may not yield to repeated cognitive review without some kind of systematic intervention, such as extinction or counter-conditioning. This claim, however, must be examined carefully; for if some conditioned-avoidance reactions yield to cognitive review, there is reason to suspect that most or all of them would also yield to cognitive review if we knew how to establish the proper conditions. The question becomes an em-pirical one which requires more evidence than is now available. As a practical matter, there is no reason why therapists should not utilize extinction or counterconditioning if their attempts to employ only cognitive review fail. However, it should also be recognized that neither extinction nor counter-conditioning procedures are free of cognitive influences. The automatic or mechanical nature of conditioning and extinction procedures has been rudely questioned in recent years as the influence of cognitive factors has regularly been demonstrated in laboratory investigations of the conditioning process. Resorting to systematic desensitization, or other behavioral techniques, may simply be resorting to specialized cognitive procedures for changing mis-conceptions.

5. Patients may fail to verbalize their misconceptions and the supporting evidence with sufficient precision, thus failing to make the relevant misconceptions salient. They may also fail to alter their style of self-examination, thus remaining trapped in their own vicious circles.

Illustrative Cases

Although the principle of cognitive review may sound complex when it is described, the following short case of Freud's (Breuer and Freud, 3) illustrates how simple it may be in actual practice, once the therapist or patient discovers and focuses upon the relevant misconceptions. Freud reported his findings on this case in 1895.

While on a hiking trip, Freud was approached by the 18-year-old Katharina, who told him that she had seen his name and medical title in the visitor's book of the small inn run by her mother. She asked his help, saying, "The truth is, my nerves are bad. I went to see a doctor in L........ about them and he gave me something for them; but I'm not well yet." Her two-year illness had begun with vomiting, later supplanted by shortness of breath, pressures on the eyes and chest, feelings of dizziness, choking sensations, and a hammering in the head.

Recognizing her symptoms as anxiety attacks, Freud guessed a sexual etiology, and suggested to Katharina that the attacks first began when she had seen or heard something that greatly embarrassed her. The girl readily agreed, stating that two years earlier she had unexpectedly observed her father having sexual relations with their servant girl. Further questioning revealed that the father had attempted intercourse with Katharina when she was 14 and also 15 years old. She had not told her mother about the incestuous attempts, but she had told her about the servant. When the wife confronted her husband with the daughter's story, he was enraged and blamed Katharina for the subsequent divorce. He also threatened "to do something" to her. After the brief interview, in which she evidently perceived the psychological explanation for her symptoms, Katharina became, in Freud's words, "like someone transformed. The sulky unhappy face had grown lively, her eyes were bright, she was lightened and exalted."

Freud's explanation of Katharina's anxiety attacks was based on his early hypothesis that any exposure to sex in "virginal individuals" during their "presexual period" produces anxiety. In Katharina, he claimed, the anxiety produced by her father's attempted seduction, plus her observation of him in bed with the servant, "isolated" the group of sexual memories from her ego, thereby producing her symptoms. Freud's talking with her, he thought, brought about "an associative connection between this separated group of memories and the ego." Freud later abandoned this early description of cognitive review in favor of another theory, based upon expression of affect. We can, however, examine his therapy in this case as an example of cognitive review which changed some of Katharina's misconceptions.

We must begin with her major misconception that she suffered from a physical illness due to her nerves. This mistaken idea was strengthened by her visit to the doctor in L........, who had reinforced the misconception by giving her medicine for her nerves. She still adhered to the misconception when she approached Freud. Instead of questioning Katharina about her physical symptoms, Freud asked her about the psychological events which preceded their development. There is no evidence in Freud's account that the girl had seen a relationship between her symptoms and her observations of her father's sexual behavior. But Freud's question about those observations implied to Katharina that Dr. Freud was telling her that her symptoms were related not to her nerves but to the frightening experiences with her father. When the girl was able to perceive the relation between her anxiety symptoms and those frightening events, the misconception was eliminated and the symptoms apparently vanished. The evidence she obtained during this review was sufficient to convince her that she did not suffer from a physical illness.

Katharina probably had a second misconception: that her sexual responsiveness to her father, although suppressed, was actually fear. This misconception can only be inferred, but it probably kept her from examining (reviewing) too closely her own role in her father's attempted seduction. We are indebted to Freud for recognizing by 1905, when he published *Three Essays on the Theory of Sexuality,* that sexual attempts on children often result in their sexual arousal, which may then evoke considerable guilt. At the time of the Katharina report, however, Freud attributed all of her anxiety to the trauma produced in a virgin by "the mere suspicion of sexual relations." Thus, both Katharina and her therapist suffered from the same misconception.

Freud took almost a decade to correct his misconception, as evidenced by his 1905 book on sexuality, but Katharina required a much shorter period of time to correct hers. It would appear that the girl recognized her sexual responsiveness to her father when Freud asked her at the end of the interview, "What part of his body was it that you felt that night?" He described her response: "But she gave me no more definite answer. She smiled in an embarrassed way, as though she had been found out." That it took longer for Freud than Katharina to dissipate the misconception about sexual responsiveness in young females can probably be attributed to the girl's having more corrective evidence available than he did at the time.

The following example (one of my own cases) illustrates not only the use of cognitive review of a misconception but also the problem faced by the therapist when the patient presents a number of possibly crucial misconceptions at the same time. In emergency situations, the therapist faces the dilemma of choosing one misconception to serve as the focus of immediate treatment. When there is no emergency, the therapist often gains by allowing the patient to select the topic of most interest, thereby saving the therapist from having to make a decision for which he has insufficient knowledge. Sometimes, however, the therapist must intervene as quickly as possible, either to save the patient from fruitless self-explorations or to resolve an immediate crisis. The following illustration relates to the latter problem.

A 38-year-old chemist was recovering from a depression precipitated by an extremely unhappy love affair. After three hospitalizations, he was beginning to resume his normal activities. Unexpectedly, he was thrust into an encounter with the woman whose loss had had much to do with his initial depression. Considerably shaken by the encounter, he made an emergency appointment for the following day. When he appeared, he was obviously agitated despite his apparent superficial control, and soon he began to sob. The gist of his disconnected, spasmodic efforts to talk centered around the resurgence of his great feeling of loss when he saw the woman, interlarded with fears about being thrust back into depression and into another hospitalization, "which I can't possibly go through again; the only thing is suicide."

On several previous occasions I had warned him that, as he gradually recovered, he might misinterpret strong emotional reactions of a normal nature as the return of the feared depression. We had discussed these warnings, and he had seemed to understand them. On the day of the emergency, however, he had only a hazy recollection of them. He was convinced that his relapse was entirely due to the emotional impact of the unexpected encounter on a "sick mind." Rather than concentrating on his reawakened feelings of enormous loss, I decided to work directly on his expressed fear of needing further hospitalization, which he associated with being "on the verge of insanity" (during his longest hospitalization he had been told by a resident that he was suffering from psychosis).

For almost an hour, we discussed his confusion over his current emotional reactions and the experiences he recalled during the depths of his depression while in the hospital. Similarities and differences between the two sets of events were analyzed to help him perceive his mistake in thinking that he was doomed to repeat the depression. After another hour he left the office in a much better frame of mind. On the following day, despite considerable exhaustion, he was able to return to work and carry on his activities.

Although I had pointed out in our earlier discussions that a strong emotion during recovery might unnecessarily precipitate his fear of another depression, my assumption that I had thereby prevented such a fear was incorrect. A statement he made at the beginning of the emergency interview alerted me to the possible need to work on his fear rather than his feeling of loss. In an aside while sobbing, he said, "I guess I'm more afraid of becoming insane than I thought. I originally denied to you that I had any such fear."

This case illustrates the need for repeated cognitive review of misconceptions which have many sources of evidence to support them. The necessity for repeated review of deeply embedded misconceptions constitutes much of the work of psychotherapy. This necessity is particularly important in dealing with the common fear of becoming psychotic, which I have elsewhere referred to (Raimy, 4) as *phrenophobia*. This fear or faulty belief, which sometimes amounts to a conviction, may dominate much neurotic and, paradoxically, much psychotic behavior. In both neurotic and psychotic fears of this nature, the concern is directed towards the illogical but stereotyped belief that psychotic individuals may lose forever not only all control of themselves but also their personal identity. Phrenophobia is also surprisingly common in moderately and severely depressed patients, who often explain some of their suicidal tendencies as a result of their abhorrence of "becoming insane for the rest of my life."

In working with patients who suffer from phrenophobia, I am continually impressed with its tenacity. By now I have learned that a patient's apparent insight into it as a misconception is usually accompanied with reservations which are difficult to root out, because they often depend upon vague but crucial feelings of disruption and disorganization. Because such feelings are strongly associated by laymen with psychosis, they have difficulty in accepting the fact that anxiety may produce these same sensations in a nonpsychotic individual; hence the need for repeated review, usually accompanied by information from the therapist about the ravages of anxiety, which the patient cannot be expected to know.

Repeated Cognitive Review in Various Psychotherapies

Most, if not all, approaches to therapy utilize the principle of repeated cognitive review, either explicitly in theory or implicitly in practice. So widespread is the tendency of experienced therapists to help patients review their misconceptions repeatedly, on either a systematic or a nonsystematic basis, that sufficient warrant exists to establish it as a general principle of psychotherapy. In the practice of psychoanalysis, for instance, the patient's task in *working through* clearly involves cognitive review of misconceptions. Fenichel (5) defines working through as "a chronic process which shows the patient again and again the same conflicts and his usual way of reacting to them, but from new angles and in new connections." In a 1914 paper, Freud (6) describes the process of working through as "the part of the work that effects the greatest changes in the patient and that distinguishes analytic treatment from every kind of suggestive treatment." Such working through, in Freud's view, will occur in the course of treatment when the patient is ready; the analyst therefore should "let things take their course, a course which cannot be avoided or hastened." Menninger (7) refers to the product of working through as ridding patients of their misconceptions (although Menninger uses the term illusions): "For it is an empirical fact that the same general type of material and the same general type of resistance reappears in the analysis time after time, to the considerable dismay of the young analyst, who feels that, having accepted everything (that is, the analyst's interpretations), the patient has relinquished his insight for the same old illusions." Fromm-Reichmann (8) comes to a similar conclusion: "Any understanding, any new piece of awareness which has been gained by interpretive clarification, has to be reconquered and tested time and again in new connections and contacts with other interlocking experiences, which may or may not have to be subsequently approached interpretively in their own right. That is the process to which psychoanalysts refer when speaking of the necessity of repeatedly 'working through'."

Fromm-Reichmann illustrates the complexity of the interlocking experiences, which must be repeatedly reviewed in working through, with the case of a female patient who evidently had the misconception that she had to be *both* submissive and superior in her love relationships. The woman had had four unhappy love affairs. The analyst discovered that the patient displayed both hero worship and submissiveness, combined with an attitude of superiority toward all significant persons in her life. The analyst showed the patient how this pattern operated in her relationships with her parents, her four lovers, and her analyst, as well as in her "dissociated" childhood experiences. Despite these explanations, the patient failed to integrate the understanding until it had been repeatedly worked through in the transference situation with the analyst.

The great importance of working through is also recognized in brief analytic psychotherapy, although Alexander and French (9), for example, stress the advisability of avoiding the working through of infantile experiences. Instead, they advocate the working through of current problems and the transference relationship. In accordance with their principle of flexibility, Alexander and French also appear more likely than classical analysts to take a direct hand in encouraging repeated reviews of the same theme by the patient, rather than waiting for nature to take its course. They even advocate ending interviews with a clearly defined problem on which the patient is expected to do "homework" before the next interview.

In summary, psychoanalysts are well aware of the significance of repeated review, although they may explain its effectiveness in somewhat different terminology. There is also a difference in opinion among analysts as to how active the therapist should be, both in directing the process of working through and in selecting problems which should be the focus of the patient's attention.

The Viennese psychiatrist Victor Frankl (10) developed a technique called *paradoxical intention* as part of his more general treatment approach called logotherapy. In paradoxical intention, the therapist repeatedly urges patients to produce consciously those symptoms which they fear the most, such as collapsing or losing other forms of control; this technique allegedly produces "a reversal of the patient's attitude toward his symptom" (p. 163). Frankl believes that the technique is most effective with phobias and obsessive-compulsive symptoms. One woman, for example, with a 24-year history of severe claustrophobia, was cured in five months; during that period, she was instructed to attempt to pass out and to become as fearful as possible whenever she was in enclosed places. Repeated review appears to be an integral part of paradoxical intention, although some simpler cases seem to yield in one treatment session.

The principle of repeated cognitive review is quite apparent in the verbatim reports of Gestalt therapy, although I have been unable to locate any explicit statements concerning it. In reading reports of Fritz Perls's therapy, I have been struck by the frequency with which he repeatedly instructed his patients to act out their "feelings" about one of their misconceptions in a variety of ways. He not only asked for repeated display, but he returned to the same theme time and again until the patients said they had changed, or until Perls decided that no change was possible in that session. Unlike the analysts who expect that patients will return of their own accord to the same misconceptions, Perls quite directly took charge and taught patients how to talk about and act out their reactions to the theme which Perls identified.

The following example is my analysis of one episode (lasting 20 or 30 minutes) in the case of Liz, who was treated by Perls before an audience in one of his Dreamwork Seminars (Perls, 11). When asked for a dream, Liz said only, "I dream of tarantulas and spiders crawling on me. And it's pretty consistent." Because Perls believed that every item in a reported dream represents some aspect of the dreamer, he immediately asked her how it would feel to be a spider. Her response indicated that she perceived a spider as something which covers up someone who is "inanimate" and unaggressive. Further questioning by Perls indicated that Liz consciously described herself as being inanimate, unaggressive, having only two legs, and lacking in color. Following more instructions, she played her revealed self talking to a spider, during which it turned out that she could not view herself as important because she was not perfect. Here she provided Perls with one of his favorite themes (or, in my terms, misconceptions): "I can only be important if I am perfect."

For the remainder of this episode, Perls had Liz repeatedly review her misconception that she could not be important if she was not perfect. He had her approach it from many angles and with many techniques while trying to convince her that she was wrong. I have been able to detect 26 sorties in his prolonged attack on this one misconception: (1) After telling Liz to conduct a dialogue between herself and the spider, Perls criticized her dutiful statement that it is mentally healthy to "feel self-important and worthy" (deriding a complaint intellectualization). (2) He instructed her to play the role of a spider who wishes to be beautiful (exploring the patient's conception of a spider). (3) He instructed her to give reasons why the spider is important (further exploration of the meaning of *spider*). (4) He had the spider compliment Liz (exploring Liz's conception of herself). (5) He announced to the audience that Liz unnecessarily lacked self-confidence (enlisting group support for his attack upon Liz's misconception). (6) He again instructed the spider to give Liz appreciation (exploring Liz's reaction to the group's agreement that she had a misconception about herself). (7) He accused Liz of suffering from "the curse of perfectionism" (labeling the misconception in negative terms). (8) He explored her willingness to change her misconception. (9) He rewarded a positive self-reference made by Liz. (10) He presented verbal evidence of her misconception. (11) He explained how misconceptions are maintained. (12) He pointed out that impossibly high standards produce self-devaluation. (13) He publicly derided her perfectionism. (14) He emphasized that her perfectionism inhibited her enjoyment. (15) He tried to get Liz to reject her perfectionism publicly. (16) He explored the historical source of the misconception. (17) He explored the historical influence of the misconception. (18) He publicly derided perfectionism and its history. (19) He tried to get Liz to shake off undesirable associations. (20) He tried to evoke uninhibited reactions in Liz. (21) He tried to get Liz to reject her perfectionism publicly. (22) Recognizing her unwillingness to change, he suggested private consultations and again emphasized the desirability of changing her misconception. (23) He elicited support from the audience for his point of view about the undesirability of perfectionism. (24) He pointed out the negative consequences of the misconception. (25) He again pointed out the negative consequences of the misconception. (26) He personalized the negative consequences of the misconception. These 26 sorties illustrate the many ways in which at least one Gestalt therapist repeatedly helped his patient to review her misconception as he attempted to explore and change it.

The originator of implosive therapy, T. G. Stampfl, regards it as a procedure whereby an anxiety response to an ordinarily harmless aversive stimulus is extinguished when the response is repeated without reinforcement. In Stampfl's (12) procedure, the therapist repeatedly gives vivid verbal descriptions of the aversive situation, which the client imagines as thoroughly as possible. The therapist attempts to produce as much peak anxiety in the patient as he can; relaxation is never induced. Since the aversive stimulus is essentially harmless, and since the patient's anxiety is therefore clearly unrealistic and uncalled for, Stampfl's procedure can be considered a review of a misconception. The repetition principle is followed methodically until extinction (or cognitive reorganization) occurs. Although Stampfl reports that implosive therapy may be effective for a circumscribed emotional reaction in only one session, many more 90-minute sessions are ordinarily required. Repeated review is, therefore, likely to occur over a considerable period of time. In addition, Stampfl customarily requires "homework" of his clients as a routine aspect of treatment. At the end of each session, the clients are instructed to implode themselves, using the same scenes that have been presented to them by the therapist during the treatment session. Such instructions, when carried out, further assure repeated review of the misconception.

The behavior therapists are most systematic of all in arranging the necessary conditions for repeated cognitive review. In their rationale, changes in behavior are the product of a learning or conditioning process. Repeated presentation of a stimulus situation, in order to evoke a desired response or to extinguish an undesired response, is the customary procedure employed in conditioning paradigms. Although behavior therapists are unlikely to agree that *cognitive* review of a misconception is an essential part of their treatment, their procedures ensure that cognitive review must take place repeatedly. Their patients and clients are provided with a precise understanding of the problem being treated; that is, more specifically than in other treatment approaches, the patients are told *what* they are being treated for, *what* is wrong with their behavior, and *what* are the criteria for improvement.

The best known of the behavioral techniques, Wolpe's (13) systematic desensitization, ensures repeated review of patients' misconceptions about the harmfulness of the phobic object and the inappropriateness of their own reactions to it. Systematic and repeated review of these misconceptions occurs throughout treatment as the patients, previously trained in relaxation, imagine themselves coming into contact with the feared object. Other writers, particularly Bandura (14), Wilkins (15), and Locke (16), have also commented on the heavy reliance in Wolpe's methods upon the cognitive processes which occur in repeated review.

There has been a growing tendency within the behavior-therapy movement to make use of the client's cognitive capabilities. These efforts have not yet developed into formal treatment approaches, but they are frequently reported as being successful adjuncts to treatment. Among the earliest treatment adjuncts which appear to depend for the most part on cognitive principles is the technique of *assertiveness training,* which has been interpreted by Salter (17) as "excitatory" and by Wolpe (18) as an inhibitor of anxiety. In assertiveness training, patients are explicitly taught (through role playing or through performing tasks of graded difficulty) how to assert their own rights as human beings. Logical arguments are directed against the irrationality of the patients' submissiveness, and the advantages of assertiveness are advanced in such phrases as, "You are making a mistake in not asserting yourself; if you follow the procedures you are being taught, you can expect improvement in your problems." Repeated review—induced by explanation and assisted by the self-demonstrations inherent in role playing and homework assignment—seems to be the most parsimonious explanation of the success of training in assertiveness. It is essentially a coaching procedure. Confirmation of this explanation has been reported by McFall and Twentyman (19), who concluded after four experiments that behavior rehearsal and coaching are the significant ingredients in assertion training; "symbolic modeling added little to the effects of rehearsal alone or rehearsal plus coaching."

Peterson and London (20) report success in three treatment sessions with a three-year-old child who had difficulty with bowel training. The treatment consisted in stroking the child's forehead while he was reclining, and monotonously repeating to him that he would feel "real good" when he moved his bowels. In an earlier era such a procedure would have been interpreted as suggestion; and, in fact, the writers originally had attempted to use hypnosis without success. Peterson and London, however, interpret their success in a fashion that readily squares with cognitive review of a misconception: "To the extent that a therapist can show a patient that the latter's previous cognitions were inaccurate and that more correct explanations are possible, just to that extent will the patient modify his behavior" (p. 294).

A form of role playing termed *behavior rehearsal* (Lazarus, 21) is used by many therapists to help patients review repeatedly their faulty conceptions of themselves in troublesome situations. The therapist partially controls the patient's successes and failures as he or she acts out a variety of scenes with the patient in which the roles may be frequently reversed.

In a procedure called *covert sensitization or aversive imagery,* an imaginary event with an aversive consequence is presented to the client, who is at the time imagining or in the presence of the undesirable activity which is to be suppressed. This procedure contrasts with traditional aversion therapy, in which an external aversive stimulus, such as an electric shock, is administered when the client is thinking about or actively engaged in the undesirable activity. Cautela (22), who introduced the term covert sensitization, believes that cues associated with the imagined noxious stimulation, such as the imagined nausea and vomiting described to the alcoholic patient, become discriminatory stimuli for avoidance behavior. Rachman and Teasdale (23) regard aversive imagery as "the most promising alternative to the traditional aversion therapies." Moreover, according to Rachman (24), "Covert sensitization and aversive imagery are techniques which emphasize the effects of cognitive manipulations on behavior." He goes on to cite evidence that cognitive factors can influence autonomic changes "in a remarkable manner." In the same vein, Murray and Jacobson (25) discuss the multiple cognitive factors which can be discerned in traditional aversion therapies. In their view, the effects of aversion therapy may be due in large part to "changes in the individual's beliefs about himself, especially his ability to control his behavior." Certainly, the techniques of covert sensitization and aversion therapy provide much opportunity for repeated cognitive review. Cautela, for example, not only provides imaginal practice during the treatment sessions but also recommends additional practice by a patient at home after each session.

Facilitating Cognitive Review in Psychotherapy

In the preceding section we have seen that various psychotherapies provide many formal techniques for facilitating repeated cognitive review of patients' misconceptions. These techniques are usually integral parts of a particular therapeutic approach, but there is also much borrowing back and forth among the various therapies. In some therapies, moreover, there is an explicit claim that the particular technique which identifies that therapy is either the only way or the most effective way to achieve improved behavior change. Unfortunately for those who hope that they have found the one and only true path to success in psychological treatment, there seem to be innumerable pathways to achieving change in misconceptions and in their associated maladjusted behaviors. Individuals in any kind of treatment, for example, often review spontaneously some of the significant experiences of their preceding therapeutic sessions. This well-known phenomenon is encapsulated in the frequently heard aphorism that progress in treatment takes place between sessions rather than during the therapy hours themselves. A more realistic point of view is that significant change is likely to occur whenever clients seriously consider and reconsider their misconceptions, either in or out of therapy. Insight, which is defined here as recognition that one suffers from one or more specific misconceptions, is so intimately a product of one's own cognition that it does not depend solely upon stimulation by a therapist anymore than one's dreams depend upon stimulation by a therapist.

Nonetheless, just as we know that discussions that occur in therapy can influence a patient's subsequent dreams to some extent, we also know that interpretations, suggestions, or instructions provided by the therapist can influence the kinds of thinking the patient engages in during the therapeutic hour as well as afterwards. One of the fruits of this common knowledge is the frequent assignment of "homework" to patients. Such homework may consist of instructions to engage in actual activities during which the patients can often demonstrate to themselves that they are capable of engaging in more adjusted behavior, or it may consist of suggestions to think about certain "problems" between sessions. Although homework assignments are often thought to be a recent contribution by behavior therapists, homework as such was recommended by Alexander and French (26) 30 years ago, and undoubtedly can be traced back into history. Penance imposed by a priest following confession represents an ancient institutionalized version of the use of homework to bring about cognitive changes.

For several years I have been practicing a very informal kind of homework assignment which compensates to some extent and with some patients for the short period of time I can spend with them. I became irritated with the scanty notes I took after therapy sessions, partly because note-taking is an onerous task for me, and partly because I recognized that my notes never seemed to fulfill any real function in the treatment itself. Although I usually remembered most of the significant interview material, the patients frequently showed serene innocence about matters we had discussed thoroughly. On impulse, I decided to write out in longhand an occasional sentence which either described a major misconception revealed during the interview or which raised a question about a suspected misconception. These were written on separate three-by-five slips of paper while the misconception was being discussed, and then handed to the patient without comment. A number of individuals have referred to them as "your prescriptions," but in actuality they rarely take the form of prescriptions for desirable behavior. Instead, they are written attempts to describe as specifically, concretely, and graphically as possible what appear to be one or more major misconceptions harbored by the patient.

Here is only one example of this very simple technique designed to increase the chances that patients will mull over some of their important misconceptions. A 35-year-old school teacher revealed his considerable dependence upon others in many different contexts in several successive interviews. While discussing this tendency which frequently got him into difficulties, I became impressed with his despairing reiteration of, "I guess I really do depend on others too much," as though he were simply recognizing an irreversible character defect in himself. Trying to avoid falling into the moralistic trap, I handed him a slip of paper on which I had written, "Must I ask others for help all the time? Can I do these things myself?" He asked what he was supposed to do with the slip, to which I answered, "Whatever you want. It's yours to keep or throw away." In the next interview he confessed that he had started to throw it away after leaving the previous session, but then decided to tape it to the wall next to his mirror. During the interview, he proceeded to discuss his dependent behavior in a much more insightful fashion without any of the moralizing in which he had taken refuge during previous sessions.

I hand out these slips fairly often without giving instructions for their use as some persons become either intimidated, thinking they have to perform intellectually for our next session, or irritated because they do not want to work between sessions. My rationale is that they will remember and at least occasionally consult the written slip if it is meaningful to them, but will ignore it if it is tangential to their immediate problems. Most of the slips are usually referred to in subsequent interviews. One patient who was given three slips while he was openly psychotic, discussed them at great length while recovering from his psychosis, and then brought them out of his wallet to discuss two years later when he was again admitted to the hospital for another psychotic episode.

The techniques discussed in this section are not only intended to insure the repeated review of significant misconceptions but also to offset the *teacher's fallacy* which often impedes and sometimes disrupts the course of therapy. Teachers often believe falsely that their students must have grasped the clear-cut explanations given during a lecture. Similarly, therapists are often misled into believing that once they have grasped significant misconceptions in their patients' thinking following intensive discussion during the therapy hour, the patients also must have gained and retained the same clear understanding and subsequent insight. Menninger (27), while discussing the process of working through in psychoanalysis, also commented on the teacher's fallacy when he described the dismay of the young analyst who finds that even after extensive discussion patients often retain "the same old illusions."

During the therapy hour itself there are innumerable opportunities for helping patients to review over and over again the misconceptions from which they suffer. Many of the more formal techniques espoused by various therapeutic approaches have already been discussed in the preceding section. As a result of my own need to devise simple techniques to encourage patients to engage in repeated consideration of their misconceptions, I have been using since 1971 a procedure termed *Repeated Review*. Since then, I have used it with more than 65 cases of avoidance reactions, about half of them patients in long-term therapy, the other half with students who came only for treatment of isolated disturbances. Five graduate students have also used it successfully. One of them, M. G. Smith (28), employed it on a group of test-anxious undergraduates. The experimental group reduced their fear of test-taking quite markedly when compared with the control group.

Once the specific avoidance reaction has been isolated, I ask clients to close their eyes and imagine themselves in a concrete situation where they must interact in some fashion with what they fear or avoid. They are also asked to "describe what happens and tell me how you feel." They proceed at their own pace with little interference from the therapist unless they introduce conditions which would nullify the imaginary interaction. No training in relaxation is given, nor are the imaginary scenes hierarchically graded in terms of estimated threat. If a particular scene appears to be too threatening, the therapist can alter it instantly by changing or deleting some of the details. The clients or patients are requested to open their eyes at the conclusion of each recital. If the avoidance reaction has not been satisfactorily dissipated in imagination, they are asked to repeat the task until the imagined avoidance disappears.

To illustrate, a man in his mid-twenties who had been hospitalized for severe anxiety and a depression of several years declared that he would be unable to meet his ex-wife for fear that he would lose control of himself by striking her. Despite his objection that she no longer meant anything to him, he was asked to imagine that he met her on the street. Reluctantly, he described the meeting and discovered to his surprise that when she asked him what he had been doing he replied and then asked what she had been doing. After two repetitions consuming about fifteen minutes, in each of which he carried on an imaginary conversation with her, he reported that he walked away from the encounter feeling "very good about myself." At the next interview he reported that he believed that many of his conflicts about women had disappeared, and he no longer felt angry with his ex-wife.

The technique has worked successfully with misconceptions or irrational fears of taking tests, viewing one's nude and obese body, speaking in public, talking with one's friends after a mental breakdown, taking an extended trip, and encountering small animals or spiders. The technique contains elements of many other approaches to therapy. Contemplating imaginary scenes is found in systematic desensitization and implosive therapy. Describing one's feelings and carrying on imaginary conversations is found in Gestalt therapy and various forms of role playing. Encouraging clients to work out their own solutions to problems is characteristic of client-centered therapy. In fact, the technique seems to be a variant of most forms of therapy, but as a technique it is surprisingly simple. Its main element is the repetition in imagination of the individuals' interactions with the object of their misconception. The repetition facilitates the individuals' review of the evidence which supports their misconceptions.

The following reactions are consistently seen in hospitalized patients and in college students when the technique is employed. There is usually some preliminary skirmishing in which the individuals deny that they are able to imagine the situation. Humor is often displayed during these denials. Facial grimacing in the early part of the recital is usually very prominent. Some somatization of the affective reactions often occurs, as when there are complaints that "My stomach is hurting or upset" or "I'm beginning to develop a headache." The second recital of a specific scene is likely to be far more detailed than the first. This is in accord with the principle that as perceived threat diminishes, the perceptual field broadens and therefore more details are added.

The following brief case of Pete is presented only as an illustration of the procedure. This 48-year-old truck driver was hospitalized at his own request for treatment of arm and shoulder pains which prevented him from working and led to his decision to sell his truck. Because he was also mildly depressed, had little self-confidence, and had suffered a blackout period while driving his truck, he was transferred to a psychiatric ward. No physical disabilities were discovered except for mild arthritis.

During several hours of history taking and general orientation for the therapist, it was discovered that Pete's primary problem seemed to reside in his complete avoidance of anyone but his immediate family. He feared that he had cracked up and was greatly ashamed about a feud which he had carried on with a government agency. His symptoms had persisted for about six weeks before I saw him. He complained of being reduced to watching television outside the hospital, since he could not force himself to visit friends. Previously he had been a very sociable person who greatly enjoyed the company of other men; at one time he had owned a bar.

Since Pete had mentioned one of his former supervisors, Bill, with whom he had been friendly for several years but had not dared to visit for six weeks, I asked him to close his eyes and imagine that he was paying a social call on Bill during his next weekend pass. At first he protested that it was impossible; that he had tried to visit Bill several times but had never reached his house. Finally he agreed to try, and closed his eyes while grimacing. As expected, Pete's first reaction was again an avoidance response: he described reaching Bill's house only to find a car parked in front of it; he returned home because he was certain that Bill had visitors. I then assured him that there were no visitors there. Pete started his second attempt by saying that he was taking his wife with him on the visit because her presence would take some of the "spotlight" away from him. This time he managed to ring the bell and entered the house with his wife. Bill greeted him in his usual fashion but "looked carefully at me to see how crazy I am." Pete was so uncomfortable that he left after only a few minutes, feeling very tense. On the third try, Pete again took his wife with him and managed to stay about half an hour; this time Bill did not seem very suspicious of his mental status. Since our time was up, the three scenes having taken about 40 minutes, I suggested that he try visiting Bill over the weekend, but Pete shook his head doubtfully.

When I saw him again, on Tuesday of the following week, Pete talked about other things until, looking pleased, he said that he had visited Bill two days ago without his wife. He said that he was quite tense at first but that Bill had treated him as always and he had had a good time. He had not only talked the whole afternoon with Bill, but Bill's brother, whom Pete barely knew, was there for an hour during his visit. After having demonstrated to himself that he could engage in his usual social activities, Pete visited other friends the following day, attended to some business matters in downtown offices, and asked for his discharge before the week was out.

Repeated Review is not a complete therapy in itself, but examination of many forms of psychotherapy will reveal that clients and patients spend much of their time in treatment discussing many of the same problems over and over. In the technique of Repeated Review, the therapist has an opportunity to focus the individual's attention on a particular problem and then to repeat the cognitive review until a different, more satisfactory solution is reached. Neither the limits of the technique nor the extent to which it can be used to facilitate therapy is known at the present time.

There is still another technique, related to Repeated Review, which I have found useful not only in helping individuals to review their misconceptions, but also to discover them. I have termed the technique *Reencountering* because it provides patients with opportunities to examine in their imagination their relationships with significant persons in their life, and to evaluate many of the influences of these persons upon their own personality. The basic aspect of reencountering consists of having the patients talk out loud to an imaginary significant person who is sitting in the therapy session with us. The patients are instructed to imagine that the person, living or dead, to whom they are talking is sitting quietly and will say nothing in return. The patients are also told that they should not worry if they become emotional, repeat themselves, or become confused or temporarily mute while telling the imagined person how "you feel about him." Where living significant persons are concerned, an additional instruction is necessary. Many patients will immediately suspect that they are being conned into rehearsing conversations which the therapist expects them to carry out when they again meet the person in reality. In order to help the patients to talk as freely as possible to the imaginary person, they are told emphatically that whatever they say or do to or with the real significant person is up to them—they need feel no fear that they are being rehearsed for their next meeting with that person.

The technique of carrying on a conversation with an imagined person or with a personification of a part of the self is probably at least as old as the practice of prayer. In more recent times, Jung (29) included it as part of his technique of *active imagination*. Much more recently, the Gestalt therapists have employed certain variations of the same technique, which they refer to as the "empty chair."

For the sake of simplicity, I usually limit the instructions for the process of reencountering to having the patients tell the imagined significant person how they feel about him or her, but I make no effort to interfere with the patients' recital once they begin to comply with the task. Recitals can last for any length of time from one minute to thirty. They are repeated whenever it is deemed necessary and until the problem with that imagined person is resolved either during the reencountering or in the lengthy discussions which often follow even very brief recitals. Considerable emotion is often elicited in both males and females. Reencounters with parents who have been dead for even 10 or 15 years often reveal misconceptions which grew out of much earlier relationships but which still dominate many of the patients' current personal affairs. In some respects, reencountering can be viewed as a process for speeding up the consideration of transference material which may often be revealed so subtly in ordinary interviews that the therapist is unaware of it or its significance. In this context, of course, transference reactions are viewed as misconceptions the patient has about the therapist based upon his distorted perceptions influenced by earlier significant persons.

CONCLUSION

Psychotherapists have devised a truly astonishing number of apparently distinct procedures for helping human beings with their personal and social ills. Most, if not all, encourage repeated cognitive review of misconceptions. The low pressure, nondirective procedures of analysts and client-centered therapists contrast sharply with the insistent, directive procedures of the behavior therapists. There is little reason now to believe that any one procedure in therapy is more effective than others in the long run, although some may be more efficient for particular kinds of problems. The similar effectiveness of very different treatment procedures for similar problems is one of the abiding mysteries of psychotherapy.

As outlined above, the misconception hypothesis is an attempt to dispel some of this mystery which has haunted psychotherapists for several decades. The mystery seems to demand for its solution a conception of the control of human behavior which permits multiple, disparate, and even contradictory therapeutic procedures to have similar effects.

One might use the analogy of the primitive from the Australian outback when he first observes automobiles being driven by different occupants. First he sees an adult male leisurely driving with one finger on the wheel while talking with the other occupants of the car. On the basis of his observations, the aborigine concludes that an automobile must be guided by one finger of a relaxed male who is discussing matters with his assistants. But then the aborigine sees another car in which a female driver is hunched forward, clutching the wheel with both hands, and studiously ignoring the other passengers in the car.

At this point, the aborigine's observations logically lead him to conclude that driving a car depends upon the presence of an adult, male or female, who may be relaxed or tense, using one finger or both hands. The great power of the car as evidenced by its high speed obviously requires the ministrations of a powerful adult of either sex plus one or more assistants. Then, to his surprise, the aborigine observes another car driven by a four-foot-ten-inch girl who has no assistants and is listening intently to a radio while she jitters from side to side and chews gum in time to the music. At this point he may well decide not to try to solve the mystery unless, of course, he notices that the only important factor in guiding a car is the direction in which the steering wheel is turned, regardless of the age or sex of the person behind the wheel, or the presence or absence of other occupants.

In this analogy, the steering wheel represents the conceptions which individuals, patients or otherwise, have about themselves and their worlds. No matter how these conceptions are influenced, by solitary ruminations, by individual therapy, by group therapy, by reading, or by religious exhortations, it is the change in conceptions which alters the behavior of the individual. Metaphorically, the steering wheel can be lovingly caressed, tapped sharply, gripped evenly, or remain untouched for short periods, and still the car responds to its steering mechanism.

This analogy permits even further parallels to the control of behavior by conceptions and misconceptions. For example, the steering wheel may become useless because there is a defect in the coupling and no guidance is possible. So in human beings, physiological dysfunction may inhibit all behavior as well as conceptions. For a more important parallel to therapy, however, one can suppose that the car's guidance system must be explained by the aborigine. One could hardly fault him if he concludes that as long as there is a wheel on the driver's side, the car is steerable. What he fails to recognize, of course, is that the steering wheel is only the observable part of the steering mechanism, and that various mechanical couplings are essential for successful guidance. In many respects, this is a clear parallel to the conceptual control of behavior.

For the conceptions and misconceptions which therapists observe (along with their patients) are, like the steering wheel of the car, only the clearly observable and graspable parts of the human guidance system. The conceptions may be obscured and may at times lack clarity and definition, but since therapists and their patients spend their whole lives trying to clarify and grasp vague conceptions, their lot in therapy is but little different from other aspects of living. Moreover, since even vague conceptions and misconceptions are observable and understandable, they are of enormous importance in therapy even though they are not the whole of human psychology.

Departing from the analogy, we must point out what everyone knows. Conceptions and misconceptions are learned; they are also influenced by other internal immediate events such as moods, feelings, and emotions; there is an underlying physiology which can blot out or distort cognition; and there is always an external situation which may exert strong distorting pressures on many of the less stable conceptions. Nonetheless, as long as misconceptions can be altered by any method of therapy, there is good reason to believe that disruptive behaviors can be modified or eliminated.

ADDENDUM QUERIES

I

DR. BURTON: The return of the cognitive to center stage, as detailed in your chapter, is an interesting and important development in psychotherapy. Is this a reaction to the emphasis in the last century on "emotion" and "energy" as causes of maladjustment? Or does it spring from the interest in cognition long apparent in developmental psychology and experimental psychology?

DR. RAIMY: Over the past half-century the thinking of psychotherapists has been largely constrained by the dictums imposed upon psychology by the behaviorists and those imposed upon psychiatry by the psychoanalysts. Breaking out of intellectual molds imposed by one's training and discipline is always a difficult and hazardous task. The monolithic edifices of classical behaviorism and psychoanalysis both began to crumble in the 1950's, so that much more freedom was possible for variant points of view in both psychology and psychiatry. Long repressed urges to explore nonbehavioral and non-analytic approaches to understanding human beings burst forth in a rash of new therapies and of broadly based investigations in both experimental and developmental psychology. The interest in cognition is only one of the many new departures in thinking which arose when the older constraints were lifted.

Much of the interest in cognition among psychotherapists can certainly be attributed to the fact that the developmental and experimental psychologists broadened the concept of cognition and rescued it from the doldrums in which it had lain for decades when cognition was viewed as only a constricted, systematic, coldly intellectual process which influenced human behavior largely in artificial settings such as mathematics, legal proceedings, and formal logic. Both classical behaviorists and psychoanalysts not only viewed conscious "thinking"—the commonsense definition of cognition—as superficial and epiphenomenal, but they also believed that the basic events in human behaving and experiencing occurred unconsciously and mechanically.

Within the field of psychotherapy itself, however, the cognitive tradition has never been dead. Despite the dominance of psychoanalysis, the cognitive approach of Alfred Adler always remained mildly respectable and even flourished obscurely and often unrecognized in writings of the neo-Freudians such as Karen Horney and Harry Stack Sullivan. The avowedly cognitive approach of George A. Kelly in his 1955 psychology of personal constructs was followed in the'60's by two other independent cognitive approaches when Jerome Frank wrote about the need to change "assumptive worlds" and Albert Ellis wrote about rational-emotive therapy. These are only highlights, of course, as there are many other influences which the historian of psychology will eventually detail.

II

DR. BURTON: As you describe it in your chapter, cognitive review is something that happens in the client to bring about personality change. You have also shown that most, if not all, therapies provide opportunities for repeated cognitive review by the client. What, however, can the therapist do to promote cognitive review other than providing opportunities for it?

DR. RAIMY: To me there seem to be four general methods which have been in widespread use by therapists (and also by teachers, friends, and people in general) that are aimed at facilitating cognitive review. These are age-old procedures that we are all familiar with and that have been adopted and adapted by therapists of many different persuasions. The four methods can be referred to as explanation, self-examination, self-demonstration, and vicariation or modeling.

Explanation is simply the therapist's attempt to provide clients directly with information designed to change a misconception. In explanation, the therapist feeds in information which the clients can add to whatever information they already have for review purposes. In self-examination, the therapist maneuvers the clients into examining by themselves their misconceptions and related material with relatively little help or interference from the therapist. Free association is one example of self-examination, while the client-centered approach is another. In self-demonstration, the therapist maneuvers the clients into situations where the clients can observe themselves in action. Hopefully, such self-demonstrations will show the clients that they are capable of behaving or experiencing more constructively than they had thought. Having clients perform homework related to the discussion going on in their therapy or placing clients in a group would be examples of self-demonstration. The fourth method, vicariation or modeling, is a procedure whereby the therapist directly demonstrates improved behavior to the clients in order to stimulate them into imitating the improvements. All four of these methods are essentially procedures for helping clients to review their misconceptions cognitively.

III

DR. BURTON: In the past the inhibitions placed in the way of efficient cognitive review in psychotherapy have seemed insurmountable, and you describe them most cogently. Do you feel that such barriers no longer apply, or perhaps only to a negligible degree?

DR. RAIMY: I suspect that the barriers to efficient cognitive review are simply part of the complexity of the mind and that they will always be with us. In the past most therapists have believed that they were struggling to overcome the handicaps to adjustment imposed by ungovernable emotions, impounded emotions, unconscious impulses, or mechanically conditioned responses. Now as it becomes more feasible and respectable to consider that the handicaps to adjustment are primarily the misconceptions which neurotics and others have learned about themselves and their relationships to their significant others, therapists will devise increasingly efficient methods for zeroing in on the relevant misconceptions. As long as the problem of therapists as they saw it was only incidentally concerned with misconceptions, little effort was expended upon how to locate and to change or eliminate misconceptions. The specification of a problem usually facilitates the development of methods for its solution.

IV

DR. BURTON: The use of "written slips" and what you call *Repeated Review,* as you describe them in your chapter, seem to be devices for impelling the client to deal with certain misconceptions as defined by the therapist. Do you feel that such approaches utilize persuasion and suggestion, the *forces majeures* of the therapist, to insure that the misconceptions as viewed by the therapist are seriously considered? Is there a danger that the client's real misconceptions might be obscured and lost when suggestion and persuasion are used in this fashion?

DR. RAIMY: I suspect that you are touching here upon one of the major dilemmas faced by all therapists, including psychoanalysts and behavior modifiers. How active can the therapist become without obscuring problems in the client because of the therapist's own ideology or misconceptions about the client. This is a hazard which I have written about more fully in the first chapter of my book *Misunderstandings of the Self*. I am sure that the danger you mention is very real, as I have often encountered it in my own work with clients.

Nonetheless, I believe that the other horn of the dilemma—remaining completely inactive and following only the client's leads—is also dangerous in the sense that it may unnecessarily prolong therapy without much benefit to the client. The solution to this dilemma that I have chosen is to employ written slips and Repeated Review as very tentative procedures. If they help, fine; if they fail, little is lost.

That is why I have been so interested in developing cognitive review techniques which fit smoothly and easily into the therapeutic interview without disrupting the client or the overall process of therapy. The written slips, for example, may take thirty seconds to write out in longhand, and they always immediately follow the discussion of the misconception. They are handed to the clients with little or no comment except that they should do with them as they see fit. In Repeated Review, the utter simplicity of the procedure, as well as its brevity, if the clients so decide, does little to distract the clients from what they have been discussing or what they have already specified as a handicapping avoidance reaction. Asking clients to close their eyes and to imagine that they are in the kind of concrete situation which they just stated produces avoidance, fear, or hostility may produce further avoidance: but I have as yet failed to encounter a client who thinks we are disrupting therapy. Even experienced therapists with whom I have used the technique regard it as a natural, albeit novel, kind of therapeutic procedure. When it fails to help, it can be quickly discarded without hindering whatever discussion has been underway.

As for the danger of those *forces majeures* which you mention, suggestion and persuasion, I have a somewhat different point of view. One of the most important clinical skills in my opinion is the facility of the therapist in maneuvering a client into the kind of therapy which the therapist regards as appropriate for that client. I use the term *maneuvering*, or open explanation by the therapist of what he wants the client to do, in contradistinction to *manipulating*, which is usually defined as employing deception to influence others. Maneuvering must occur in all forms of psychological treatment. Client-centered therapists as well as psychoanalysts engage in considerable maneuvering to train their clients to become good subjects for the client-centered approach or for psychoanalysis. Other therapists use other maneuvers. Suggestion was originally defined as "an unknown psychological force," to explain what happens in hypnosis; that definition still seems applicable despite the reams that have been written about it. Persuasion, at least as employed by the great Swiss therapist Paul Dubois, whose cognitive theory resembled but preceded Adler's, was defined by him much as I have defined maneuvering, and not as it is defined in pep courses for salesmen.

V

DR. BURTON: Are you optimistic or pessimistic about the direction that behavior change has taken? You began with a client-centered orientation and now have grown in the direction of an eclectic, cognitive psychology. As a long-time observer, what do you see as the outcome of the many current trends in psychotherapy and behavior change?

DR. RAIMY: I'm afraid that you give me more credit for growth than I deserve. In a very real sense, where psychotherapy is concerned I have been in the same old rut since my first year as a graduate student when I mostly talked, but also did some writing, about the self-concept. Two years later, when Carl Rogers came to Ohio State, I was enthused about the opportunity to investigate self-concept theory (such as it was) in the context of client-centered therapy in which the therapist tries to keep from influencing the client's self-references. My interest has always lain in trying to figure out how to change "relevant" aspects of the self-concept, and I have never believed that the client-centered approach is the only suitable vehicle for bringing about such changes. For many years, however, I could not refine self-concept theory sufficiently to use it as a concrete, specific method in dealing with psychological disturbances.

Finally, when I returned to psychotherapy about 1960 after doing many other things, I began to see that perhaps the self-concept is made up of the convictions, beliefs, and notions that people have about themselves and their relationships to their worlds. I began to speculate that perhaps faulty convictions and beliefs might be the major hindrances to readjustment, thus leading to the misconception hypothesis.

My current eclecticism, as you put it, is only an eclecticism where methods or techniques are concerned. I suspect I am rigidly glued to the proposition that behavior is controlled and guided (not determined) by cognitions, and that the central task of therapy is to discover and change the faulty cognitions that are relevant to the psychological problems under treatment. As I view the most important relevant misconceptions as being primarily concerned with the self, I am still talking about the self-concept, but in a much more concrete, specific fashion. I fail to see, however, how there can be any one most efficient or effective method for bringing about changes in misconceptions which, after all, are just beliefs or concepts. As I indicated above, ideas or concepts have traditionally been changed in normals as well as in abnormals by explaining things to them, by helping them to examine their own ideas, by helping them to engage in behavior where they can demonstrate to themselves that their beliefs are faulty, and by showing them in actuality that their beliefs are false. Thus eclecticism of method in psychotherapy seems to me to be a reasonable recognition that misconceptions can be changed in many different fashions, so that psychotherapists must recognize that they live in a pluralistic world of method.

As for current trends, I have been only hopeful and delighted since psychotherapy broke out of the straitjackets imposed by the "schools" which flourished until the 1950's. Those schools undoubtedly contributed the enthusiasm and the competitive urge to drive therapists to develop their thinking and their techniques, but also imposed limited horizons which clamped their proponents into rigid molds. Today, psychotherapists can publicly say almost anything, no matter how outrageous, and many of us do, without being excommunicated.

REFERENCES

1. ELLENBERGER, H. E.: *The Discovery of the Unconscious*. New York: Basic Books, 1970.
2. RAIMY, V.: *Misunderstandings of the Self: Cognitive Psychotherapy and the Misconception Hypothesis*. San Francisco: Jossey-Bass, 1975.
3. BREUER, J., and FREUD, S.: *Studies on Hysteria*. New York: Basic Books, 1957. Originally published in 1895.
4. *Op. cit.*, 2.
5. FENICHEL, O.: *The Psychoanalytic Theory of Neurosis*. New York: Norton, 1945.
6. FREUD, S.: Further Recommendations in the Technique of Psychoanalysis: Recollection, Repetition, and Working Through (1914). In *Collected Papers*, Vol. 2. London: Hogarth Press, 1950.
7. MENNINGER, K.: *Theory of Psychoanalytic Technique*. New York: Basic Books, 1958.
8. FROMM-REICHMANN, F.: *Principles of Intensive Psychotherapy*. Chicago: U. of Chicago Press, 1950.
9. ALEXANDER, F., and FRENCH, T. M.: *Psychoanalytic Therapy*. New York: Ronald Press, 1946.
10. FRANKL, V.: *Psychotherapy and Existentialism*. New York: Simon and Schuster, 1967.
11. PERLS, F. S.: *Gestalt Therapy Verbatim*. Lafayette, Calif.: Real People Press, 1969.

12. STAMPFL, T. G.: Implosive Therapy: An Emphasis on Covert Stimulation. In Levis, D. J. (Ed.), *Learning Approaches to Therapeutic Behavior Change.* Chicago: Aldine-Atherton, 1970.
13. WOLPE, J.: *The Practice of Behavior Therapy.* New York: Pergamon Press, 1969.
14. BANDURA, A.: *Principles of Behavior Modification.* New York: Holt, Rinehart & Winston, 1969.
15. WILKINS, W.: Desensitization: Social and cognitive factors underlying the effectiveness of Wolpe's procedure. *Psychol. Bull.,* 1971, 76, 311-317.
16. LOCKE, E. A.: Is 'behavior therapy' behavioristic? *Psychol. Bull,* 1971, 76, 318-327.
17. SALTER, A.: *Conditioned Reflex Therapy.* New York: Farrar Straus, 1949.
18. *Op. cit.,* 13.
19. McFALL, R. M., and TWENTYMAN, C. T.: Four experiments on the relative contributions of rehearsal, modeling, and coaching to assertion training. *J. Abn. Psychol.,* 1973, 81, 199-218.
20. PETERSON, D. R., and LONDON, P.: A Role for Cognition in the Behavioral Treatment of a Child's Elimination Disturbance. In Ullman, L. P. and Krasner, L. (Eds.), *Case Studies in Behavior Modification.* New York: Holt, 1965.
21. LAZARUS, A. A.: Behavior rehearsal versus nondirective therapy versus advice in effecting behavior change. *J. Behavior Res. & Ther.,* 1966, 4, 209-212.
22. CAUTELA, J. R.: Treatment of compulsive behavior by covert sensitization. *Psychol. Record,* 1966, 16, 33-41.
23. RACHMAN, S., and TEASDALE, J. D.: Aversion Therapy: An Appraisal. In Franks, C. M. (Ed.), *Behavior Therapy: Appraisal and Status.* New York: McGraw-Hill, 1969.
24. RACHMAN, S.: The role of muscular relaxation in desensitization therapy. *Behavior Res. & Ther.,* 1968, 6, 159-166.
25. MURRAY, E. J., and JACOBSON, L. I.: The Nature of Learning in Traditional and Behavioral Psychotherapy. In Bergin, A. E. and Garfield, S. L. (Eds.), *Handbook of Psychotherapy and Behavior Change.* New York: Wiley, 1971.
26. *Op. cit.,* 9.
27. *Op. cit.,* 7.
28. SMITH, M. G.: *Cognitive Rehearsal: A Systematic Investigation of a Psychotherapeutic Innovation.* Unpublished doctoral dissertation, University of Colorado, 1974.
29. JUNG, C. G.: The Transcendental Function (1916). *Collected Works,* Vol. 8. Princeton: Princeton U. Press, 1960.

Ivan Boszormenyi-Nagy

11

Behavioral Change Through Family Change

by IVAN BOSZORMENYI-NAGY, M.D.

Traditionally, the goal of psychotherapy, or therapy in general, originates from the wish to eliminate illness. Physical health is then defined "objectively" from the vantage point of one individual: the absence of processes or outcomes detrimental to the biological welfare of the organism, or, conversely, the optimum potential functional state of the given organism at the given age. Psychopathology, defined as one form of illness, fits into this individual (medical or psychological) model. Consequently, the traditional goal definitions of psychotherapy were confined to changes aimed at the improved functional health, i.e., diminished symptomatology, unhappiness, or psychopathology of one individual.

The perspective of the family therapist is so radically different from the perspective of the individual therapist that it requires a careful definition of what the concept of change connotes in one case and in the other. The

227

field of family therapy is concerned not merely with a new technique but with a new understanding of the causes and meaning of human behavior on a variety of levels. Although this point has been made repeatedly in the literature, it has been often stated that family therapy lacks consistent ideological cohesiveness.

Family therapy approaches are often perceived as being essentially "discontinuous" in their departure from the individual basis of psychological description and understanding. The main characteristic of "systems puristic" family therapy approaches is often criticized as impersonally manipulative, in relative disregard for any individual family member's discrete psychological needs. The fact remains, however, that no mature therapist can ignore human concern, empathy, and consideration of other persons' needs, which constitute vital elements of close relationships. In reality, relationship theory underlying family therapy should broaden rather than invalidate individual personality theory.

The psychological or individual framework should not be rejected or replaced but, if transcended, included. Each family member's individual health aspirations become components of the therapeutic contract. Psychodynamic knowledge about motivational conflicts, projection, self-destructive tendencies, etc., continue to be vitally useful areas of knowledge for the relational or family therapist. However, each person's "outside reality" is not relegated to a nondynamic random sequence of impersonal facts but is seen as the dynamic interlocking of all relating partners' needs. One person's dynamic need configurations constitute part of the other's outside reality and vice versa. Furthermore, the understructure of the "external reality" of each family member includes suprapersonal regulatory dynamic forces.

Another area in which spelling out the premises of dialectic intergenerational family therapy leads to a useful distinction is the relevance of human values for behavior change. The great social ethical issue of all times is the balance between egalitarian, democratic concern for everybody's welfare as contrasted with the Nietzschean world of conquest by the powerful, rugged individualism, subjection of the weak or disadvantaged and, ultimately, genocide. The egalitarian concept of everyone's right to the pursuit of optimal physical and emotional health is founded on social justice and equitability. It is based on the premise that one person's health interests are coterminous with those of any other person. Thus, while it is in the interest of A's life goals that, for example, his coronary attacks be prevented from recurring, it is assumed that this goal does not infringe on B's aspirations for a healthfully effective life of his own. To carry it one step further, if A is B's slave (or useful resource person), it becomes B's selfish goal to keep A optimally healthful and effective.

As we make the transition from the notion of "health" to that of "desirable change," the importance of ethical value issues becomes increasingly obvious. What is desirable, for instance, from the vantage point of the exploiter is usually not desirable from the viewpoint of the exploited one. It is a common observation that, inadvertently, people can have a neurotic investment in the self-defeating "symptomatology" of their spouse or child. A mother's security may collapse at the point when her school-phobic son returns to school, and she may request psychiatric hospitalization for herself. What then is the desirable goal from the vantage points of (a) the mother's therapist, (b) the son's therapist, or (c) the family therapist respectively? Furthermore, beyond the complexities of adversary positions, is it possible to integrate them into a mutually satisfactory shared therapeutic strategy?

The widespread notion that psychic (behavioral) function and human values should be considered in separation from one another is untenable, false, and "pathogenic"—both individually and socially. The criteria of both malfunction and desirable change have inevitable value connotations. To ignore or deny these connotations would lead to further confusion and mystification of the public in an era of already existing value confusion. Our age has experienced frightening examples of large-scale political change-makers whose seductively phrased ethical premises turned out to be consistent with genocide and absolute subjugation of the justice and freedom of millions. Effective electronic mass indoctrination of children and adults into either a valueless or a destructive value orientation can produce amorphous or directional destructiveness respectively between the members of one social group or toward outsiders. The view of family therapists is inevitably affected by their observation of striking examples of both selfless devotion and callous exploitation.

I realize that a broader than behavioral concept of change is liable to exact a considerable cost on the part of the therapist. A simple behavioral concept of change appears to provide a safer basis for therapeutic contract; all your patient wants is to lose weight and you are the one to teach him or her how to achieve this goal. Such a deceptively simple model does away with all notions of human conflict, destructiveness, exploitation, selfishness, and even resistance to treatment.

By contrast, therapy defined as a thoroughgoing evaluation of the life goals of patients, aimed at helping them to reexamine their accounts and to find liberation through balanced interpersonal fairness, sounds threatening to many people—as if concern with deeper "ethical" issues implies too costly an intrusion into a patient's life.

Yet, obviously, as soon as we consider the welfare of more than one human life, we enter the field of competition, interlocking complementary and non-complementary needs, hunger for trust and confidence, concern and loyalty, disappointment, exploitation of the other one's trust, betrayal of confidence, revenge, forgiveness, guilt over disloyalty, insensitivity to guilt of harming others, etc. If we simplistically assume that each family member struggles to influence the other in the direction of "desirable behavior," the question still arises: from whose vantage point should the therapist determine the desirability of behavior? Human life is thus inseparable from its relational ethical context.*

I strongly advise therapists to be interested in whole human lives, not just in behavioral modification. The essential goals of any therapist as behavior modifier and of the one to be modified by him or her lie, of course, beyond the technical realm of simply "how to do it." There is diversity between the goals of the two individuals and also between the various levels of aspirations within each individual. As a rather shockingly awakening example of unidimensionally therapist-defined goals of behavior change, I have seen occasions of successful "reinforcement" by therapists of the patients' independence, autonomy and self-actualization in disregard for the built-in, "abnormal" over-devotedness of the patients to their families of origin. In a number of cases, admirably successful "separation" was followed by suicide or even suicide-murder. The escalating guilt over filial disloyalty was not dealt with, and it backfired.

In essence, this chapter challenges the nondialectical concept of the individual as a self-contained goal for self-actualization. (See also Boszormenyi-Nagy and Spark, 1.) Attempts will be made to expand the realm of dynamic depth psychology into an existentially/ethically grounded theory of relationships. The relevance of such relational dynamics will be examined here as a basis for psychotherapy in general and for family therapy in particular. Finally, it will be suggested that family therapy and its relational conceptual understructure offer a far-reaching leverage for the coordinative strategy of all types of psychotherapy, for strategies of prevention, and for a relational definition of the model of "healthy" behavior. Accordingly, individual-based

---

* The term "ethical" is not used here to designate any particular religio-cultural code of behavioral prescriptions. Instead it connotes an intrinsic dynamic property of human relationship according to which each party to the relationship is inherently accountable to the other for the existential impact they mutually exert on one another.

therapeutic strategies will have to be coordinated with the comprehensive relational understanding suggested here.

The Dialectical Aspects of Relationship Theory

One of the characteristics of twentieth century thought is its departure from an orientation toward fixed, thing-like entities as the discrete elements of its world view. The replacement of the assumption of absolute facts by a consideration of the process-like vicissitudes of relative determinants represents a shift toward an increasingly dialectical view of reality. Even if direct evidence of a causal link between Hegel's early 19th century dialectical philosophy and the dawn of non-Newtonian physics is questionable, Einstein's theory of relativity is logically consistent with the dialectical world view. Furthermore, the relational humanism of Martin Buber (2), introduces the dialectic view of man as being unthinkable without his being party to a dialogue with another.

On the other hand, the conceptual revolution of the 20th century has hardly reached the everyday philosophy of contemporary Western man and his social institutions. The elaborations of modern psychological theories have continued to confirm the view of the individual as a self-contained universe. Selfish disregard for the interests and needs of others has been elevated from vice to scientific object and political myth, the latter disguised as unconditional liberty. Resistance to the conceptual challenge posed by a dialectical view of understanding goes, hand-in-hand, with resistance to the recognition of the importance of a reexamination of ethical priorities.

Returning to the therapeutically significant question of what constitutes "desirable change," therapists have to consider the long-range "cost" of current function vis-à-vis their own or their patients' notions about desirable change. By recognizing that human function is deeply determined and substantially programmed by invisible interpersonal accountabilities and family loyalties (Boszormenyi-Nagy and Spark, 1), therapists have to learn to critically reevaluate the dominant myth of our Western civilization. They will find that the dynamic understructure of close relationships is at variance with the idealized images of both the absolute autonomy of the fully grown-up adult and the individual's total separation from the family of origin. They will also find it necessary to redefine the relational significance of both standard assumptions about human life aspirations: (a) heterosexual gratification as the ultimate basis of marriage and (b) simple criteria of power and success as need-satisfaction. Concurrently, the practitioners' own life-long investment in the values of their cultural myths will have to be examined as possible causes of their resistance to recognizing the structuring significance of deep-dynamic relational ledgers. Furthermore, some of the therapists' genuine conflicts in their own close relationships will have to be confronted and integrated into a balanced multilateral view of relational goals.

The relationship between individual and relational (family) therapy strategies raises the question of indications. Usually, the question is posed in the form of assuming that the family approach should define a special basis for indication. This is based on the unspoken premise that individual-based therapy is the generally applicable or baseline form of psychotherapy and, therefore, that the relationally-based approach needs a special justification. Yet, conversely, we have postulated that the broadening of understanding, humanistic concern and therapeutic contract with all persons prospectively affected by the intervention is *never* contraindicated.

In accordance with our thesis the question should be reversed, based on the premise that what is always indicated is a broad-based, combined—i.e., relationally *plus* individually grounded—understanding of dynamic processes. Thereafter, the question needs to be asked: What are the *risks* of a narrowly defined *individual-based* therapeutic strategy? More specifically, the cause should be shown why the extended understanding and increased leverage for change, implicit in the relational approach, should be ignored. It may be accurate to say that the only contraindication to a broader understanding and concern lies in the available therapist's own personal limitations for facing the existential/ethical issues involved in close human relationships.

Of course, it should be the right of all therapists to choose the limits of their own approach, and to function within their own recognized preferences and competence. This is all that can honestly be expected of them. No one should be obligated to perform professional work which will cause depression, lost sleep, or psychosomatic illness. Nor would it be fair to expose clients to techniques inadequately mastered by a therapist. Even if surgery is the treatment of choice for appendicitis, it would not be fair to put the knife in the hands of a well-meaning dilettante, self-proclaimed surgeon, regardless of how pressing the symptoms of the patient may appear.

From Individual to Relational Concepts of Change

Individual concepts of "desirable change" as the goal of therapy originate from the traditional medical framework of health and illness. Health is a one-dimensional construct; it is the ideal antithesis of illness. Illness in a physical sense is a fault in the machinery of the body: it interferes with effective function and longevity. All individual concepts of physical or mental health therefore relate to effectiveness, power, success, and enjoyment of effectiveness. Their ethical premise is that man is committed to his own good in an isolation from the goal of others.

Such otherwise radically different therapeutic approaches as psychoanalysis and classical behavioral therapy still converge in their individual-defined goal of the desirable change: health, effective function, and freedom from symptoms. Although their definitions of need-configurations clearly differentiate the two theories, both are basically confined to a need-satisfaction or pleasure-principle type of goal. Both classical psychoanalysis and classical behavioral therapy aim their change-inducing strategies at the success and psychological satisfaction of one individual. Both approaches confine the formation of the therapeutic contract to one symptomatic individual and the therapist. Changes in the patient's close relatives are considered incidental and assumed to be automatically advantageous to those others. Both approaches would refer the treatment of coincidentally occurring symptoms in a relative to what should become separate, *de novo* treatment contracts.

First, the notion of discrete individual personality change, allegedly occurring outside the context of relational change, requires investigation. Since long-term relationships obviously require a mutuality of need satisfactions, the restriction of clinical contractual interest to the need-satisfactions of one person amounts to an advocacy for the advantages of ignorance. It is as if the denial of the interlocking mutuality of human need satisfactions would result in a "clearer," more manageable task.

Yet it is obvious that as people become more effective in the pursuit of their need-satisfaction, to the same extent they become more capable of making others the objects of their needs for security, dependence, trust, stimulation, etc. Consequently, any change in the capacity of one person to use the other as a need-satisfying object naturally affects the balance of need-satisfactions the other can achieve for him- or herself. Relationally-based dynamic understanding and therapeutic strategy are therefore clearly based on the premise that man is committed to the good of his relationship system.

It is logical to assume that in order to maintain a fair balance, as one's capacity for need-satisfaction increases, one's concern for the other's needs should also grow. Unless one is capable of including such concern for the mutuality of one's relationships, one is likely to fail in all of one's long-term attachments. Thus, the systemic dynamic principle of multipersonal change coincides with the attitude of ethical openness to concern, caring, and trust as interlocking dynamic determinants of relationships. In long-term, close (e.g., parent-child) relationships, it is inconceivable that the fate of the other's needs could remain completely indifferent to the self. Emotional investment, of course, can take both positive and negative forms. Sacrificial devotion and passionate anger are both based on intensive involvement.

At this point it is important to recall that the concept of ethics underlying our further explorations is by no means synonymous with any particular system of moral regulation. On the contrary, the broad humanistic base of a genuinely relational ethic will inevitably challenge and test the priority schemes of particular traditional moral codes. In my view, dogmatic concepts of good or bad will have to be replaced by the dialectical notion of the consideration of both sides of any relationship. The relational solution is a classical Hegelian one: out of a simultaneous synthetic consideration of the two antithetical sides of any relationship, the conflict between reciprocal need gratification efforts has to be transcended and resolved into an equilibrium of fairness, tolerance, concern, trust, and reliability—mutually needed for the survival of the relationship.

The implications of the dynamic significance of such an ethical point of view are hard to overestimate; yet its adoption as therapeutic rationale exacts considerable emotional cost from most therapists. It requires that the therapist set the traditional Western efficiency, power, and reward orientations to values at a critical distance. Moreover, it is only human to resist the adoption of the ethical balance point of view, since its acceptance calls for increased accountability, a seeming cost-increase in relationships. Furthermore, the criticism has often been raised whether an ethical point of view will rigidly impose the therapist's own moral code upon the family. Of course, nothing is further from the truth. On the contrary. On closer examination, the customary, "value-free" professional orientation can turn out to be rigidly value-based.

The allegedly value-neutral therapist can be deeply committed to the desirability of "separation" from previous, especially seemingly unsatisfactory, relationships. Often, in supporting the ideal of separation, the professional can lose sight of the personal interests of all parties involved. Predictably, the majority of contemporary therapists would almost automatically endorse what they perceive as adversary interests of a young family member against the "possessive" influence of the parent, for example, by unconditionally supporting the notion of "separation" of young adults. By contrast, dialectical relational therapists will tend to reduce the seeming adversary positions of close relatives into a mutuality of genuine interests. They have learned that both parent and child would pay with significant lasting guilt for an ultimate "victory" of one over the other. Furthermore, by a simultaneous consideration of the mutuality of fairness from both sides, therapists become liberated from their own rigidly biased side-taking position and are ultimately rewarded by an increased satisfaction in their professional work.

Even if some of these basic resistances can be overcome, a considerable complexity of levels has to be understood before the dialectical ethical principle can be translated into pragmatic, strategic thinking. On this level of sophistication, the simple notions of reward and pain as motivators could hardly explain the complexity of close, existentially interlocking relationships. For example, the seeming beneficiary of unilateral generosity becomes, on a deeper level, through accruing indebtedness to the partner a helpless captive of a sense of irrepayable obligation, indebtedness, and worthless selfishness. The self-denying giver becomes the ultimate taker in every long-term, close relationship.

> A 27-year-old man was diagnosed as having an incurable illness. He was faced with the prospect of losing both his life and the young woman he was planning to marry within a year. However, his fiancee did not desert him. Despite all advice from her family, the young woman persisted in the relationship and went through the wedding as planned. Moreover, she did so in the face of warnings from several of her husband's physicians that not only was his prognosis for life very guarded but in case of survival he would lose his male fertility.
>
> As it turned out, the young man survived the operation and did indeed became infertile. From the vantage point of his own needs, first and foremost, he had to face the threat to his own life and the continued fears of recurrence of his illness for years after the operation. Needless to say, his wife's uncommon integrity and devotion helped him in his struggles with anxiety. Thus, from his point of view the marriage was a highly need-satisfying relationship; he became the beneficiary of his wife's noble integrity. Considered from the wife's vantage point, the relationship could be regarded as sacrifical, unilaterally unsatisfying, or even self-defeating. Although her husband could not be blamed for his illness, for the subsequent atmosphere of anxiety, or for his ultimate infertility, all three circumstances tended to deprive his wife. Yet the young woman disclaimed credit for any unusual act of integrity and stated that she had simply acted on her great love for her fiance.
>
> Therapeutic exploration some twenty years later revealed that the husband did not feel that he was obligated to his wife. The prevalent explanation in his mind was that, in the main, he had been preoccupied with the threat to his life which he had gradually overcome through the years. Thus he saw himself unfairly victimized by fate rather than as the cause of his wife's unhappiness. He was not aware of his wife's being frustrated because she could not bear her own child. His wife had kept reassuring him by asserting that she had never wanted a natural child and that she was perfectly satisfied with having a child through adoption.
>
> Upon further investigation, it turned out that the wife's attitudes to

all of her relationships and to the world as a whole were based on sacrifical devotion and self-denial. The question could then be raised: Is her unselfishness itself a form of selfishness? Was her choice of mate essentially a need-gratifying one? Does the beneficiary of her unconditional devotion have to become the carrier of a sense of accountability, guilt, intrinsic selfishness, even inferiority? Furthermore, is it possible that the husband pays part of the accumulating cost of the wife's martyr-like, over-devoted attitude vis-à-vis all of her relationships?

A technical illustration of the relational dialectical point of view results in the practice of inducing children to reveal the secrets of their families. While the measure can lead to a desirable change on a communication-transactional level, it may turn out to be costly for the child in terms of betraying filial loyalty. As a matter of fact, the more the therapist tries to side with the child against the parents and the more he or she counts on the child's cooperative contribution to the therapeutic strategy, the more likely is the child to be entrapped in filial disloyalty.

The foregoing has direct practical implications for the individual approach to psychotherapy. The traditional individual contract for psychotherapy follows from the medical model of illness and health; it disregards the unplanned consequences of the intervention for persons whose lives are closely interlocked with that of the "patient." This is consistent with the traditional medical notion of the therapeutic contract being between the doctor and the patient for the benefit of the patient. Procedures that emphasize the individual-based privacy, confidentiality, and legal accountability of such contract all tend to imply its exclusiveness and possibly its adversary character vis-à-vis the claims and interests of all other persons.

Only occasionally has the literature on traditional individual based therapeutic procedures considered the importance of the potential conflicts between professional and familial *loyalties*. When considered, it usually surfaces in the form of strategies designed for the obstructionistic or otherwise resistant attitudes of the relatives whose behavior could otherwise hamper the treatment goals. In the relational or family therapy context, patient-relative and patient-therapist loyalty conflicts have to emerge as dynamic leverages of the greatest practical significance (Boszormenyi-Nagy, 3).

Recent insights into the nature of the dynamics of close and especially intergenerational (parent-child), relationships have emphasized mutual accountability and invisible loyalties as crucial motivational determinants (Boszormenyi-Nagy and Spark, 1). Detailed demonstration of the relevance of such invisible interpersonal mechanisms to behavioral change will have to become the object of further careful study. It can be envisaged that the demonstration of such hidden relational mechanisms will meet difficulties similar to those encountered in past efforts aimed at the documentation and proof of the existence of unconscious "Freudian" mechanisms as determinants of visible human behavior. The ubiquitous psychic defensive tendencies of avoidance, denial, reversal into the opposite, etc., on the part of each participant individual will make the demonstration of such invisible relational determinants even more difficult. As in the case of searching for "scientific" evidence for unconscious psychological determinants, it is impossible to prove the connection between invisible relational "ledgers" of accountability and overt behavior except through the therapeutic effectiveness of strategies based on the knowledge of such underlying dynamic motivational forces.

There is no space to develop here the full theory of deep relational structures as manifested through the "merit ledger" and "intergenerational legacy." However, it is of the utmost importance to stress that the essence of these mechanisms is *not psychological*. Loyalty to personal and familial legacies is not merely a question of each family member's superego psychology. The existential structure of the legacy is a primary given which preceded the psychological adaptation of the offspring and, in fact, of subsequent, not-yet-born generations. The circumstances, for instance, in which the mother's relatives were wiped out in concentration camps, or in which three or four preceding siblings died of physical illnesses, or in which a mentally retarded sibling was born have their existential structure independently of anybody's psychological processes. Conversely, such existential structural determinants affect each individual family member's psychic organization as specific, structured outside realities, i.e., external expectations. The varying ways in which all family members share responsibility vis-à-vis the fulfillment of their legacies create the vicissitudes which make such reality a dynamic determinative force.

A more detailed knowledge of the depth structure of family relationships would picture each family member as partner to an oscillating balance sheet of inputs and withdrawals. The nature of the balances is a three-dimensional one. For example, at the same time that the "delinquent" adolescent withdraws from the family's shared accounts, he or she can be repaying heavily on another level as being the last one to leave the home. Sacrifice of one's own success and psychosomatic health may amount to alternating "currencies" by which invisible "pathological" repayment can be made.

The Relational Outlook and Premises for Change "Techniques"

The relational outlook to therapy and change has to take two major considerations into account. First, the contract between the therapist and the patient or the family has to be broadened to a point of view of "multi-directional partiality" and empathy. Second, the therapeutic task, i.e., the realm of phenomena to be changed, has to be broadened to include a fuller understanding of the deep existential grounding of close relationships.

As mentioned earlier in this chapter, the individual definition of psychotherapeutic contract is predicated on the therapist's offering to the patient both expert technical performance and a deep alliance, both to the exclusion of the interests of the members of the patient's family. As described elsewhere in detail (Boszormenyi-Nagy and Spark, 1), the overcoming of such benevolent professional bias and partiality is the most decisive step in becoming a family therapist. The term "multidirectional partiality" was coined to capture the essence of this therapeutic stance.

In addition to overcoming the natural limitations of the basic individual definition of the therapeutic contract, most psychotherapists have to learn to transcend their intrinsic bias for siding with the child against the parents. In choosing their profession, most psychotherapists are influenced by their emotional commitment to the cause of the suffering, "emotionally disturbed" individual. At the core of their empathy with the suffering child-self of any prospective client lies the memory of the therapists' own suffering. In their marginally conscious desire to share the "techniques" of mastery of their own childhood suffering, most psychotherapists implicitly scapegoat the patient's family of origin. In assigning the role of causation of detrimental developmental influences to the patient's parents, and in nobly fighting the cause of the patient's liberation, therapists may easily overlook their own hidden psychic benefit, derived from the intrinsic exoneration of their own parents at the expense of the patient's family of origin. An act of invisible loyalty to one's ambivalently protected parents is a frequently overlooked major dynamic cause of deep existential conflict in therapists themselves, too.

In order to comprehend all major relevant dimensions of both change and resistance to change, therapists have to transcend not only the behavioral but also the psychological limitations of their conceptual armamentarium. In considering behavior change, it is essential to define the premises of that which does change or fails to change. While overfocusing on the need for visible behavioral change, therapists may lose sight of the reasons for malfunction.

Behavior changes deemed desirable from the change-agent's viewpoint can be induced by threats, rewards, suggestions, and hypnosis. Such change may attest to the power and the skill of the professional, without necessarily reflecting the patient's motivational aims. In order for the behavioral change to become a part of the spontaneous self of the patient, it has to become syntonic with, or at least neutral to, the spontaneous motivational tendencies of the patient. If behavior change and basic motivations are in conflict, the change will eventually be rejected like an incompatible surgical transplant. Experienced intergenerational therapists have learned to balance the conflicting motivational aspects, each on its respective dynamic level, so that their therapeutic impact will have spontaneous endorsement on the part of all or most family members, and a chance to endure.

> A couple in their mid-twenties came to the office for help with their marital problems. Although he has better than average intelligence, the husband holds a rather undemanding job. Drug addiction of several years' duration has made his job security even more tenuous. At home he spends most of the time sleeping, and sexual contact between the spouses has dwindled to near nothing. The husband freely admits that he is not doing his share of household chores. Both spouses recognize that although they would like to have children, they are far from capable of planning a family.
>
> The husband is the only son of possessively anxious parents, who have the habit of dropping in on the young couple, unannounced, many times during the week. He has been unable to say "no" to his parents' intrusive initiatives. His parents also insist on paying many of his expenses while they completely refuse to accept anything he or his wife offers to them in return. In the continuous argument between the spouses, each seems to be defending his or her own family of origin. It seems that the husband has been tied closely to his parents by a never-repayable, shapeless, total obligation. In an attempt to avoid facing both his failure of adult assertion and his guilt over escalating indebtedness to his "devoted and helpful" parents, the husband has inflicted an unfair burden of unilateral adult responsibility upon his wife. His own irresponsibility and absenteeism as a husband are the chief means whereby he "parentifies" her.
>
> For several months the couple attended a couples' group program. The emphasis there was on giving tasks, utilization of paradoxical injunctions and improvement of communications. Yet, in the long run, nothing changed as a result of this effort. In my view, lack of significant change in such cases is often associated with lack of therapeutic consideration of the relevant relational understructures. The ethical-existential roots of this couple's marital problems have been deeply anchored in the nuclear family context of the husband, coupled with the collusive pattern of marital transactions contributed by a wife who has undeniable martyr-like inclinations. Simple inducement of a "more mature" behavior on the part of the spouses could lead into further imbalance, intensifying the husband's sense of guilt over filial disloyalty in the face of his "pathological" overloyal relationship with his parents. The question for the therapist then is not to choose whether to work behaviorally or in terms of a deep relational strategy, but in what way a therapeutic

Figure 1

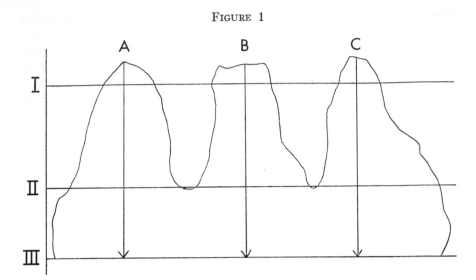

strategy can be designed to liberate this young couple from both the symptoms of marital failure and the destructive legacy of overcommitment to their respective families of origin.

In order to design their therapeutic strategies, dialectical relational therapists need a comprehensive evaluation of the balance of the relational determinants exemplified in the foregoing clinical vignette. This would include the dimensions of the husband's individual psychopathology marital evaluation, evaluation of the husband's relationship to his family of origin, assessment of spouse-team collaboration regarding relationships with both families of origin, the evaluation of the intergenerational legacies of obligation in each family of origin, and the assessment of the prospective parenting team relationship of the spouses if children are ever to be born to this nuclear family. In order to indicate the interlocking complexities of relational dimensions to be considered, figure 1 is presented.

The peaks A, B, and C represent three closely related individuals, for example, grandparent, parent, and child. By analogy they can be considered to represent three icebergs, each showing one-tenth of its mass above the symbolical water level, represented by the line between Zones I and II. If the navigator's vision could be extended to cover all of Zone II, he still could not tell whether he is dealing with three separate icebergs or three peaks of a single huge iceblock. Conversely, the observer who could only have information about Zone III, could not tell whether the peak consists of 1, 2, 3, or more separate entities. He would be dealing with one apparently continuous ice-slab.

The figure symbolizes the three essential levels of relational dynamics and therapy:

Zone I is the realm of visible behavior and overt inter-individual interaction. Most pertinent functions are conscious in the interacting individuals, though not necessarily so. This is the realm in which the outside observer can notice both malfunction and its change to improved function. Easily recallable or observable shared knowledge or customs are also located in this realm. Customs and habits characteristic of a certain religious or ethnic background, if manifestly practiced, are also located in Zone 1.

Zone II comprises the covert, although not necessarily unconscious, part of inter-individual interactions or transactions between closely related persons. A shared secret may be conscious for the participants but not visible to the outsider. The vertical arrows within each peak designate the dimension of intrapersonal surface versus depth. This is a psychological dimension: inside the individual there is a realm of consciousness and, on the opposite, a realm of continually decreasing consciousness to the point where dynamic psychological exchanges are distinctly unconscious. However, Zone II contains not only individual psychological characteristics and attitudes but systemic properties of person-to-person relationships. Genuine dialogue between two individuals can build up trust in each and a relational atmosphere of trustworthiness and balance of justice between the two of them. The existence of concern connects the needs of both: it is in my interests to consider your needs, if I want to stay in close relationship with you. The resulting systemic ledger of give-and-take determines the fluctuating balance of inter-individual obligations, and is distinctly different from the psychological responses of each individual to the state of their relationship. Guilt may or may not be registered in each individual, though not necessarily in proportion to the extent of the factual imbalance in the pattern of give-and-take between them.

Essentially, *Zone III* is the realm of the deep understructure of close relationships. Whereas each individual represented by a peak is positioned at a certain location relative to the understructure, none of them determines the relationship of the other two individuals to the common understructure, which is determined, so to speak, by fate or by the special destiny of their birth. The importance of Zone III is relatively negligible in casual peer relationships but crucial in existentially interlocking—e.g., intergenerational—relationships.

Dimensions of the Dynamic Understructure of Relationships

It is important to indicate five major dynamic dimensions, though space does not permit a full elaboration of a theory of deep relational understructures.

(A) Legacy. This dimension could be called the transgenerational call for existential obligations. The basic existential/ethical obligations derive from the generative, enabling significance of parent-child relationships. For example, regardless of whether the parent enjoyed or regretted becoming a parent, the child's existence is irrevocably owed to the parent. Particular burdens that the parent had to carry—exceptional fears of childbirth, damage to the mother's body, for example—contribute to additional primary ethical claims of the parent on the child. Both family ancestry and religio-ethnic background can assume the appearance of creditors toward new members who are the recipients of life and of patterns of survival. However, the ethical demand characteristic of the legacy has to be clearly differentiated from the transmission of patterns through transgenerational learning. The outcome of (B) and (D) feeds into the legacy of the next generations.

(B) Existential Vicissitudes. Not every family has to survive under excessive degrees of extenuating circumstances. Yet, in certain families most members were wiped out by the holocaust. In other families several consecutive generations lost their mothers at an early age. Early death of several siblings or the birth of a brain-damaged sibling can constitute rapid escalation of overweighted legacies which calls for an existential rebalancing of the unfair destiny of the family and its members.

(C) The Ledger. The mutually quantitative, balance-like nature of the fluctuations of give-and-take in human relationships can best be described in terms analogous to those of financial transactions. Not only are there ledgers to be balanced between members regarding fair equitability of give-and-take, but each member can be perceived as a potential debtor vis-à-vis the legacy of the family. The measure of mutual indebtedness is not given by the criteria of an outside, "objective" justice, but has meaning only between persons in relationship. Nonetheless its reality exists, and can be uncovered only through a multilateral consideration of merits from all the vantage points of all participants. Most of the time the fluctuation of positive or negative balances on the ledger is not conscious in the minds of family members. The ledger becomes significant at points at which stagnant, fixed imbalance develops, usually reinforced by denial and avoidance. An especially damaging imbalance can be created in children by the parents' non-receiving attitudes,

which can make the child's obligation toward the parents unrepayable, amorphously global and all-encompassing.

(D) Acts of Collusive Commitment. Concerted actions on the part of all family members, both in response to expectations of the legacy and in fair consideration of each other's interests, contribute to the survival and further elaboration of the deep understructure of relationships. An illustration of such action is the collusive postponement of mourning (Boszormenyi-Nagy, 4). In this act every participant is a contributor to the collusive act and also a seeming beneficiary of the shared intention to spare everybody from pain. Such acts naturally contribute to the "invisible establishment" (see under E) of a stagnant, inadequately balanced "overencumbered" relationship system. Consequently, all family members become obligated to share the detriment arising out of the resultant pathogenic, stagnant imbalance of relationships.

(E) Invisible Establishment. The invisible establishment is based on a quasi-political set of rules of operation, which are the resulting reified products of the total build-up of the loyalty expectations of a family. Its nature is inert, static, and possibly stagnant. The invisible establishment has no primary ethical claim; its dynamic characteristic is activated whenever it opposes attempts at free individuation or acts of disloyalty to the family. It places the individual in a passive recipient or accepting role unless the individual member appears to be disloyally assertive. The invisible establishment prescribes specific rules of operation; for example, in the case of collusive postponement of mourning, it may expect certain specific behaviors and prohibit others. Members may consistently avoid certain important subjects of discussion, aiding each other also in the perpetration of a conspiracy against clarity, meaning, and individuation. In my view, Stierlin's (5) important concept of parent-induced "delegation" represents dynamic processes belonging mainly to this category.

The foregoing brief description of depth relational structures only indicates the complexities of invisible dynamic configurations which constitute the context of psychopathology and therapeutic strategy. It shows also the important limitations of the conceptual frameworks of both individual (psychological) dynamic theory and transactional-interactional systemic formulations. If we are to arrive at a broad-based theory of therapy and behavioral change, both thought models have to be considered and integrated.

That a specific relational mechanism of existential vicissitudes or destiny of family events is able to program long-range determinants of behavioral patterns was outlined in a recent exploration of the family background of Hitler (Boszormenyi-Nagy, 6).

The Relational Definitions of Change-Inducement Strategies

The criteria of therapeutic change are usually considered from the vantage points of either subjective psychological experience or observable individual behavior. Although both of these dimensions of change are important for family therapists, they learn in the course of their work that the most significant leverages both for behavioral change and for resistance to behavioral change lie in the dynamics of close relationships. Consequently, our definition of change also has to be a relational one, its smallest unit being balance between at least two people, rather than the psychology of any given individual.

The majority of contemporary psychotherapists probably would tend to overlook the dialectical implications of the risk of encouraging filial disloyalty while endorsing a young adult person's "individuation" or "separation." Even if such therapists are able to avoid the pitfall of "countertransference acting out" based on their own unrecognized conflicts about filial loyalty, many a young adult's "pathological" over-devotion needs a sophisticated relational approach for behavioral changes to prevail. Traditional uncovering individual therapy usually reveals that patients are ambivalently tied to their (introjected) parents through hidden and disowned ambivalent attitudes. Subsequently, it is a common therapeutic expectation that patients own up to their ambivalent feelings, try to understand the roots of these feelings, accept them, and become adjusted to at least a partial separation from the family of origin. As a result of such "insight" into and "working through" needed separation, it is hoped that the patients' overt behavior will obtain the best chance for a lasting change. From our vantage point, however, even while visible progress is being made toward functional autonomy, it should be examined to see if it is confined to the patients' acceptance of their negative filial attitudes as the end-point of therapeutic relational goals. If so, the patients are likely to end up with an increase of conscious or unconscious guilt over disloyalty, even though they may learn that their loyalty is excessive and pathologically reinforced. Guilt over existential disloyalty is capable of undermining patients' behavioral gains and, in the long run, it can lead to self-destructive "backlash" motivations.

Transactionally based, "puristic" family therapy approaches can also suffer from a lack of dialectical relational sophistication. Transactionally oriented family therapists frequently emphasize the "here-and-now" significance of what appears to be an inter-member competition for *power*. They suggest that the more clinically experienced therapists are, the more accurately they can perceive and describe the manipulative communicational-behavioral binds.

Subsequently, therapists are advised to design "paradoxical" or other behavioral techniques for unscrambling the power arrangement and, hopefully, for liberating the victimized family members from the tight holds of such power schemes. It is apparent that the traditional individual approach and the transactional, power-oriented "systemic" family approach have much in common, in that they both disregard the loyalty-based invisible understructures of relationships.

The dialectical relational outlook provides an extension of the understanding of the change-inducing implications of one of Freud's great discoveries: the phenomenon of *transference*. Traditional psychoanalytic theory appropriately assumes that a primary, quasi-familial investment of the person of the therapist on the part of the patient is a requirement for thoroughgoing therapeutic change. Much of psychoanalytic literature unnecessarily confines the therapeutic significance of this important relational event to the therapist-patient relationship. As a matter of fact, in their clinical practice, many experienced analysts, especially child therapists, give practical recognition to the fact that the intensification of the therapist-patient relationship occurs in a live dynamic equilibrium with the patient's commitments to other close relationships.

Of particular practical significance are the loyalty implications of the transference phenomenon for change, regardless of whether they are considered in individual or in family therapy (Boszormenyi-Nagy, 3). In short, it can be assumed that the symptom or pathological behavior can be partially determined by the patient's loyalty to the family of origin. Naturally, the more destructive and self-destructive the symptom is, the more paradoxical this reasoning seems to be. Paradoxically, also, at the point when therapeutic success leads to the motivational reorientation of patients, reinforced by the transference wish to please the substitute parent-like figure through progress towards health, autonomy, and growth, they also become intrinsically disloyal to the "pathogenic" expectations of their own families. The more positive the transference, the greater the risk of filial disloyalty. This consideration has far-reaching strategic implications (Boszormenyi-Nagy and Spark, 1). It necessitates techniques which restructure the therapeutic goals and avenues in such a manner that patients will not have to incur significant disloyalty as the price of change toward a healthier function.

Naturally, family therapists have to deal with the collective convergence of parallel dynamic configurations anchored in all members of the families they are treating. Given the specifics of a certain familial legacy, they may expect a certain amount of "pathological" behavior. In addition, in order to minimize inter-member controversy and suffering, family members owe each other loyalty of collusive mutual commitment. Family therapists have to acquire sensitivity to the intergenerational and inter-member ledgers of merits and obligations. Through life experience of their own and through their professional experience they have to learn the principal ways in which family members can actively rebalance merit ledgers so that they are not left with the helpless feeling of pessimism, despair, and inactivity. Conversely, they have to learn about patterns which reinforce captive indebtedness and lock members into irreversible exploitation. Naturally, the cost of imbalance is both existential and psychological, and the two factors have to be considered in separation. For example, if it is discovered that a wife has a hereditary illness, possibly a malignant one, it becomes a complex question to determine whether she is more the victim or more the one who, though unintentionally, inflicts both damage and pain on her husband and children. The existential balance of such situations does not result from the feelings, thoughts, wishes, and other psychological characteristics of these individuals. On the contrary, their feeling reactions and thoughts are secondary to the basic existential/ethical configuration. Aware only of having been unfairly victimized by destiny, the hereditarily ill wife may overlook the fact that, nonetheless, she has become indebted to her husband for staying by her, never bringing up the subject, handling all the exigencies, and remaining sexually loyal to her.

If therapists who want to induce "desirable behavioral change" lack a sensitivity to the underlying deep issues, they will at best manage to patch up the condition temporarily while remaining ignorant of deep-rooted ethical issues. For instance, a therapist might want to have the essential creditor make further concessions to the seeming creditor. The foregoing example illustrates the relevance of deep existential structures to the question of enduring change, and the limitation of simple interactional or transactional definitions of change often used even by sensitive and complexly humane therapists: ". . . families must change their ways of functioning so they will not nurture harmful modes of interaction and perpetuate ineffective or damaging models of behavior from one generation to the next" (Satir, Stachowiak, and Taschman, 7, p. 11).

An even more important practical consideration follows from the recognition of the connection between the notions of existential/ethical ledger and behavior change. Doubtlessly, valuable effort has been spent on developing simple behavioral reinforcement-based models of the management of close relationships. Readers of these contributions can benefit from the wisdom of behavioral "techniques" which can lead to smoother function and mutual inducement of more gratifying behavior. However, insofar as such behavioral models of intervention are limited to the individual-anchored notions of need gratification and power, such techniques may encourage the active avoidance of the ethical/existential meaning of relational action. Moreover, while learning techniques for the smooth inducement of "desirable behavior"on the part of, for example, the child may aid the latter's useful socialization, it may also lead to symbiotic, lifelong enslavement of the child. The subsequent short-term rewards and penalties do not account for the total "cost" of any change of behavior. The following "Skinnerian" citation should illustrate the foregoing point: "Much seemingly complex human behavior can be understood in terms of a person's efforts to maximize rewards and to minimize pain" (Patterson, 8, p. 9). If the parent's "emotional cost of living" is reduced at the expense of a consecutive long-range cost increase for the child, the apparent behavioral improvement formula is more antitherapeutic than therapeutic.

According to classical psychoanalytic theory, therapeutic effort should ultimately be aimed at changing the patient's pattern of defenses. Once that is accomplished, the actual change of manifest behavior requires minimal or no therapeutic guidance. Parallel reasoning could be applied to the relational theory of therapeutic "mechanisms." Accordingly, the attitude of responsibly facing the ledger is the step most intensively defended against by family members. Progress toward a decreasingly resistant facing of the ethical/existential implications of a relationship amounts to facing the costs of responsibility, accountability, and guilt over unfair exploitativeness of relationships. Once the family members can afford to confront the balance of their accountabilities, their inner satisfaction over the evolving, more genuine, relatedness will be the "rewarding" determinant of their visible behavioral change.

What Buber defined as the genuine "I-Thou dialogue" (Friedman, 9) is implicit in the systemic notion of the ledger of merits and of balances of give-and-take. A simple additive summation of all family members' needs would not ever lead to the dialectical concept of the ethical/existential ledger. It could only lead to power competition and coalition models of understanding. Only through the dialectic of the genuine mutuality of needs, of A's concern about B's needs, can we arrive at the concept of the ethical existential ledger, according to which no concerned relative can gain by the "success" of exploitative mastery over the other members of the family.

It is essential for the family therapist to develop a multilateral or multidirectional view of partiality in order to overcome a common bias shared by all traditional individual psychotherapies, i.e., finding the thing or person that is "wrong." The culprits assumed to have such pathogenic influences are numerous. *Developmental* theories stress the detrimental characteristics that can lead to faulty development: critical periods for imprinting, early deprivation, parental inadequacies, lack of object constancy, among others. Another group of pathogenic circumstances may be defined as *medical* limitations: brain damage, hereditary conditions, defective intelligence, and metabolic diseases. A third category of detrimental causative circumstances is designated as the realm of *intrapsychic,* usually unconscious, conflict. The proper correction of this condition usually is conceived in terms of long-term classical individual therapy or psychoanalysis aided by transference toward the therapist, with the resulting insight and gradual rearrangement of behavior. A fourth category of "wrongs" is ascribed to the notion of *faulty learning.* Accordingly, in the course of their early or current life experience, patients have acquired nonadaptational, nonrewarding, and noneffective ways of coping with life situations. The habit of having learned wrong patterns is supposed to prevent the individual from a self-correction of the error, as it were, and from adopting new ways of coping. Systematic attempts at reconditioning would be the procedure of choice according to this therapeutic orientation.

In contrast with goals aimed at changing pathology in individual family members, the basic strategies of relational therapy are aimed at the utilization of available relational *resources.* *Personal availability* of the other person is naturally the baseline of relational resources. The early loss of one's parents or spouse amounts to a drastic loss of primary resources. The so-called "empty nest" syndrome refers to the difficulty of parents at the time when their children have left the home. On the other hand, death and permanent separation of any kind usually bring out the hidden resources which have resided in the otherwise ambivalently accepted relationship with the lost one. The relatively fortunate configuration of the familial *legacy* constitutes a resource in comparison with the detrimental legacy of another family. The availability of the degree of *reason* and *rationality* in certain families is a great resource aiding the development of the personalities of the children, in contrast with families in which impulsive, chaotic, bizarrely motivated interaction is the rule. The extent of *accountability* prevailing in a given family determines the degree of one of the most important relational resources available. In certain families, members know that, despite a seeming distance, they can count on one another in case of a genuine need. In other families, accountability pertains to fairness in the handling of business matters, to the exclusion of concern for the personal emotional needs of other members. One of the most significant relational resources, of course, is the availability of basic trust, i.e., an *atmosphere of trustworthiness.* As family members get used to seeing one another as trustworthy, children acquire the building material for the fundamental stage of personality development: basic trust (Erikson, 10). The degree of *courage* for initiative, honesty, commitment to relationships and to action characterizes certain families and constitutes a major relational resource for the offspring.

The concept of *relational stagnation* (Boszormenyi-Nagy and Spark, 1, Chapter 5) leads to the consideration of forms of negative resources in relationship systems. Relational stagnation connotes much more than fixed repetitious patterns of behavior. Its essence lies in a fixed imbalance in the ethical/existential ledger of relationships, connected with an enduring avoidance of facing the imbalance. For a variety of reasons, the natural self-correcting relational processes of families do not seem to work either intergenerationally or between members of the same generation.

Space does not permit the description of the main manifestations of relational stagnation. Basic unrelatedness, symbiotic clinging, undifferentiated ego mass (Bowen, 11), negative loyalty (Boszormenyi-Nagy and Spark, 1) are some of its more frequently found forms.

Guidelines for Intervention

A brief summarization of the principles of the therapeutic rationale of dialectical intergenerational family therapy and its application to relationally-based individual therapy helps to clarify the question of family-based behavioral change. A more complete outline of the rationale of this therapeutic approach is found in *Invisible Loyalties* (Boszormenyi-Nagy and Spark, 1). Since the essence of the approach is anchored in the depth dynamic of relationships, its practice requires more than "technical competence." The persistently active, guiding attitude of this type of therapy cannot be sustained without the therapist having a deep-going conviction about the validity of the fundamental premises of the approach. A capacity for facing and dealing with the ethical aspects of human relationships can only be acquired at the cost of the therapist's willingness to apply the same premises to the exploration of his or her own relationships. Such personally worked-through conviction is a requirement for the successful application of dialectical relational therapy. As Wynne (12) has pointed out, the personal competence of the therapist is a major part of the indicational criteria for the undertaking of family therapy.

Implicitly, the therapist's insistence on relationally based or family therapy by itself constitutes an extension of concern for the multilaterality of the family members' need-configurations. The offering of such simultaneous concern for the conflicting needs and interests of all family members is founded on the therapist's capacity for a corresponding humanistic ethical stance rather than on particular indicational criteria of a given family. This is an extremely significant, often overlooked point. The therapist's offer of simultaneous concern for the balance of fairness in relationships is thus *a priori* and not dependent on diagnostic criteria, the family's awareness of shared problems, or the particularities of feelings and hidden motivations in family members. The essential definition of family or relational therapy lies, therefore, in the therapist's capacity for transcending the ethical limitations of the traditional individual psychotherapeutic contract.

The foregoing basic rule of relational therapy is anchored in the principle of *conjunction*. Accordingly, regardless of the outside criteria of interactional behavior, the therapist should assume that close relationships are the greatest potential resource for trust, security, and personal fulfillment. In fact, the more a relationship is presented in negative terms, or even its very existence denied, the more likely it is that the basic assets of close relationships are not being utilized. According to such relational dialectic principle, the overtly or ambivalently angry son's attitudes toward his family of origin should be explored not only from the point of view of the psychological roots of his anger, but also from the perspective of his underlying concern for his family, Like the passionately angry rejected lover, the frustrated family member has an underlying core of concern, wish for love, and desire for giving. By the same principle, the therapist should point out to the childishly fighting, divorcing parents that their children are the major parties affected by their decision. The principle of conjunction implies that the therapist should have no fear of alienating the parents by directing attention to their children. In other words, the assumption that the fundamental interests of parents could be genuinely adversary to those of their children is always false. The widespread professional notion that adolescents or young adults have to be helped to "separate" and "cut" their relationships with their families of origin as the price of their capacity for peer involvements, for the establishment of their proper social life, and for their eventual new nuclear family is unfounded but consistent with the cultural ideology of the last two centuries of Western civilization, according to which individuals should be helped to untangle themselves from all power schemes of manipulatively controlling authorities—kings, bishops, lords, fathers, teachers, presidents, and policemen are automatically suspect. This political attitude is then associated with the valid discovery of behavioral science that children are usually most critically victimized by their own families of origin. It is to be expected that by allying themselves with their patients, therapists tend to form an implicit alliance against the patients' families of origin.

It is easy, for instance, to see patients as the deprived, inhibited, wounded children of their families of origin, who need someone to parent them so that they can grow up into more wholesome human beings. Taking the option of such unidirectional professional partiality would be automatically adversary to the alternative option: siding with the patients' parents as potentially deprived and injured children in their own families of origin. The advantage of the intergenerational approach is that it encourages the therapists to put themselves in the role of their patients' children and, by the same logic, to look critically at their patients, from the vantage point of the patients' parents. Through such a dialectically balanced multi-intergenerational position of siding with the parent and child side of each relationship, the adversary point of view dissolves into a new synthesis. The application of the conjunctive principle helps to discover the leverages of hidden resources contained in intergenerational relationships and provides the maximum psychotherapeutic leverage available.

Although the leverage of intergenerational dynamics leads to the most advantageous elicitation of information ("history") about the family, the main therapeutic goal is not knowledge or insight but a responsible, active attitude of facing the ledger of merits and obligations. Therapists have to train themselves to make the transition from a primarily psychological orientation to one of recognizing ethical balances. This is made difficult by the family members' tendency toward denying the ethical/existential ledger and by the weightiness of the implications of the ethical ledger, when confronted.

> An attractive young woman underwent severe strain and a transitory guilt-laden depression following the death of her father, who was suffering from cancer. An uncommonly painful scene took place at the father's burial at which time the family, including the mother, openly blamed this daughter for ingratitude and disloyalty. The accusation was based on the fact that the young woman did not remain with her dying father during his last five weeks of terminal illness, while he was hospitalized. However, further exploration revealed that the only family member who had given thorough nursing care to the ailing father was this daughter. She performed the duty as if it were both for herself and for her mother, who could not stand the stress of these months. Only at the point when she felt physically and emotionally depleted did she arrange for her father's hospitalization and her own return to the city where her fiancé was living. The young woman refrained from becoming a counter-accuser of her mother by not using her good ground as a bludgeon, and was thus able to utilize this leverage for a constructive reexamination of the life-long distance which existed in her relationship with her mother.

Relationally enlightened therapists need a combination of courage, commitment to fairness, skill, and compassion as they approach the dramatic situations in which, for example, a mother's hidden complicity in a father-daughter incest has to be examined. Similarly, standing up for the right of an adopted child to learn about and meet with his or her natural parent requires significant courage and conviction on the part of therapists. The underlying deep ethical balances on the interpersonal ledger constitute the premises and regulate the prospects of lasting individual or transactional behavioral change. Being able to therapeutically utilize this deep dimension of relationships, rather than merely follow the "technical" rule of "seeing family members together," is the real criterion of family-based therapy. Naturally, there are special conditions for which it is almost mandatory to actually deal with more than one family member—for example, if one member has suicidal inclinations.

In their concern about liberating all family members from the relational ties of "captivity," therapists are faced with several types of binds. They have to design their strategies in the knowledge of the nature of the familial legacy, the expectations of the invisible establishment of the family, the true state of the merit ledger between the members, and the characteristics of each member's internalized ledger (superego). This can only be accomplished if the therapists are able to assume the attitude of multidirectional partiality. Much harm has been done in the past by therapeutic attitudes that lead to labeling mothers or grandmothers as detrimental influences only in need of exclusion. The multidirectionally partial therapist has to be sensitive to the alternate aspect of any family member's being either on the overdrawn or the overpaid side of the merit account of relationships.

Dialectical intergenerational therapy requires a fundamentally active orientation. Unceasingly, regardless of the state of the ledger in which a particular individual finds himself or herself the therapist should seek and encourage active, courageous strategies rather than passive contemplation, commiseration, or mere insight into feelings.

A mother of two teenage children was seen in an exploratory interview. She had spent a number of years in psychiatric hospitals for periodic depressions with greatly regressive symptomatology. She had two unsuccessful marriages and was living in marked social isolation. The exploration of the merit ledger of her family of origin revealed that she has been used primarily as the parentified child in a family in which the parents' continuous, hopelessly unresolvable conflict placed the children in a "split loyalty" situation. This term indicates a situation in which children are repeatedly being recruited to side with one parent against the other and vice versa. Consequently, they can never be loyal to both parents at the same time. In such families not only are the conditions for the development of basic trust missing but the "legacy" of the helplessness of the parents' marriage places the children in a structural expectation of automatic "parentification" (Boszormenyi-Nagy and Spark,1). For example, as an adolescent girl, this daughter was the first person, including mother, to whom father had revealed his decision to get a divorce. Her comment eloquently described her situation during the subsequent years: "I'd be home and I'd be hearing things about my father, and I'd go down to my father, and I'd be hearing things about my mother."

The legacy of such a split loyalty situation burdens the child with an unresolvable, heavy expectation and it can cripple one of the offspring—to the extent of serious suicide attempts in the foregoing case. According to the conjunctive principle of therapeutic strategy, such a person should be encouraged to find an active attitude of exploring the relational roots and origins of her parents' basic humanity, rather than "cutting" off her relationship with her family of origin. Such encouragement is contrary to the usual professional attitude. However, the ultimate relational economy of the conjunctive strategy can actually reduce the number of serious suicide attempts made by relationally trapped individuals. This is consistent with the general clinical experience that the more individuals are "cornered" in their basic life aspirations, the more necessary it is to regard their symptoms in the context of the depth aspects of their personality and their close relationships.

The required attitude of multidirectional partiality can be just as taxing on therapists as on the family members. The therapists have to be able to absorb the cost of their own abrogation of the scapegoating of the patients' parents. Moreover, resisting the hidden "psychic economic gain" of scapegoating the patients' rather than their own parents presents a challenge to the balances in the therapists' own familial merit ledger. In summary, the essence of the relational (family) approach is not a conjoint "technique" that excludes communicational, behavior modification, game analytical, or individual-based psychological techniques. The relational approach presumes a deep respect for all relevant factors rather than opting for "short-cuts."

A regard for the complexities of the interlocking ethical reciprocities must be a common denominator of most family therapists' professional choice, even though there are variations in the capacity to spell out their premises in sufficiently dialectical terms.

Concerning the therapeutic impact of the relational approach, change is not the ultimate criterion. In accordance with the conjunctive therapeutic principle of its strategies, dialectical intergenerational therapy utilizes the leverage of unused relational resources. The goal includes—but does not require—desirable change. At a minimum the baseline of the goal spectrum is a situation in which the therapist avoids an artificial disjunctive intrusion —one that could jeopardize relational resources.

In essence, the ethical/existential, conjunctive ideology of dialectical intergenerational therapy raises the ethical question of basic therapeutic goal: change in whose interest? In accordance with the thesis that no family member's cost of relational accountability should be diminished at the expense of increased costs to any other member, it becomes evident that the desirability of change has to be evaluated from every member's vantage point. This includes the deceased parents, the family "legacy," and, even more significantly from a preventive perspective, the yet unborn child. Thus, dialectical intergenerational therapy emerges as an implicit strategy for the future, with its ultimate value residing in prevention—the most desirable "change" imaginable.

ADDENDUM QUERIES

I

DR. BURTON: All psychotherapeutic approaches which follow Freud are more or less dependent upon an unyielding devotion to or love of the patients and their irrationalities—at least in point of some limited time parameter, which is the course of treatment. The patients challenge to determine the limits of such trust, and will yield their therapy and growth if dissatisfied with the results of their challenge. How, therefore, do family therapy approaches satisfy this requisite of patient-therapist belongingness in more than a pro forma or theoretical way? Is there not a danger that no one will gain from therapy?

DR. BOSZORMENYI-NAGY: Perhaps my answer somewhat restructures the premises of your question. I respond to your question mainly in terms of its challenge to my extension of the therapeutic contract from one patient to all relating family members.

If the individual therapeutic contract and its consecutive "love-affair" (transference-countertransference) necessitates that therapists actively disregard the welfare of all those affected by their intervention, its very definition is not only arbitrary but deceptive. Therapy cannot itself create or invalidate existential/ethical interdependence, births, parenting, filial gratitudes, and ingratitude. The latter are, instead, constituents of the ethical/existential ledger created by the genetic interlocking between the generations.

Subsequently, the options of parental abandonment, infanticide, cruel filial ingratitude and parenticide are costly but permissible ones. They may cause psychological maladjustment, psychosomatic illness, alienation, and large-scale social disintegration.

It is paradoxical to talk about the "danger" of extending genuine concern to all those affected by therapeutic intervention. In reality, there is much more danger in accepting an individual or even marital definition of therapeutic contract, and base its success entirely on the welfare of the contracting adults. Their children, absent and under-represented, often tend to be the ones who pay the highest cost. According to the basic principles of intergenerational family therapy (see also *Invisible Loyalties*, 1), children have to be considered as the main contractors of therapeutic work affecting their parents. In the long run, divorce often means an exciting and liberating, though disappointing, game for the adult participants. For the children, their parents' divorce may mean the end of the trustworthiness of their world.

In summary, the "danger" of the extension of the strict individual therapeutic contract exists only for those who expect an exploitative unilateral gain from therapy.

II

DR. BURTON: Your chapter seems to reify the family in an almost Old Testament way. By this I mean that the Judaic Covenant with Yaweh seems to come through as a sacrosanct family covenant which is tampered with only at great peril. Yet family breakups and divorce occur in the millions, new interpersonal arrangements are made, and the world goes on. Are there then specially sensitized or delegated families who may or may not be representative of the rank and file?

DR. BOSZORMENYI-NAGY: I would like to stress the distinction between reification and the existence of invisible, denied, underlying dynamic forces. I would like to emphasize also the interhuman rather than religious connotation of obligation ledgers. Human history shows that religious notions of obligation to the Godhead can be used to bypass and avoid interhuman accountability. Adherence to reciprocity of fairness is, in my view, the opposite of authoritarianism.

Even if the notion of accountability sounds old-fashioned or boring, in the long run nobody can benefit from denial of interhuman accountability. Usually, such denial is the foundation of the multitudinous manifestations of "relational stagnation" (*Invisible Loyalties*, 1). The large number of divorces is a perfect example of the fatal strength of invisible loyalty obligations, amounting to unwitting testimony to overtly and consciously denied, invisible filial loyalty.

III

DR. BURTON: Your emphasis on the ethical and existential aspects of psychotherapy is refreshing since most healers prefer to disregard these dimensions of their work. But the question arises as to whether your emphasis on family intactness and equilibrium is not itself a value, and one which goes counter to modern developmental trends. Is successful psychotherapy that which maintains the dimensions of the family—its substance—and permits society to continue, or is the treatment successful when perhaps one or two family members make a brilliant or original contribution to mankind. Whose values are being served?

DR. BOSZORMENYI-NAGY: Relational accountability is indeed an ethical issue which should take high priority if society is to prevail. Yet its underlying dynamic relational premise—a reciprocal balance of fairness—is not only a value. In terms of the classical Freudian dimensions of ego, id, superego, and external reality, it can be ascribed to the realm of dynamic relational reality. What in the classical theory was conceived as a relatively nondynamic "external reality" of the person consists relationally of the highly dynamic id, ego and, superego configurations of persons he or she is closely related with.

It is true that a mutual consideration of one another's welfare is to some degree contrary to the modern ethos of Western civilization, ever since the early 19th century utilitarians tried to equate the ethical issues of right and wrong with the sensual issues of pleasure and pain. The limits of such thinking begin to show in what appears to be the threatened disintegration of our civilization. Reciprocal human accountability has often been abandoned in the aristocratic belief that brilliant individual contributions can justify the exploitation of others. From the winner's point of view, slaveholding, genocide, and pollution of the other nation's river are excusable. Selective disregard for the others has often been justified in the name of an allegedly sympathetic Godhead, sacrosanctity of racial or religious superiority, etc. In families, the mentally retarded, the helpless child, or the aged can be exploited in the name of utilitarian necessity. I maintain that the best guarantee against overtly or covertly exploitative ideologies lies in the principle of reciprocal fairness and concern.

IV

DR. BURTON: It is not clear from your chapter whether you are giving up the pleasure principle for some family ego principle. Does personal pleasure (id) come only when the family is requited? Or is it that for our patients pleasure comes basically through the family or with family permission?

DR. BOSZORMENYI-NAGY: The notion of pleasure or of pleasure principle is a typically individual one. These concepts belong to a different systemic realm than the relational concepts of reciprocity, justice, fairness, ledger, etc. If pleasure means an overall long-range satisfaction with one's life, it has to transcend the notions of "id," as Freud himself recognized when he alleged that his reality principle is identical with a long-range, economical pleasure principle. More specifically, as individuals liberate themselves from an unnecessary amount of stagnant, invisible, unrequited obligations, they are bound to obtain more satisfaction from their personal lives.

V

DR. BURTON: Would you comment on children (and families) raised in kibbutzim, which several independent observers have recently claimed as perhaps a new mode of family or mental health? Are such children (and families) indeed less neurotic than those in the United States?

DR. BOSZORMENYI-NAGY: The high emphasis of our civilization on the desirability of the nuclear family pattern of living certainly does not increase the available resources badly needed by young parents. Careful attention has to be given to all possibilities which reconstitute supporting structures around the modern nuclear family. The kibbutz experiment is one of many which try to remodel the social support systems around the nuclear family. With appropriate modifications accounting for cultural and historic specifics, the kibbutz and similar social undertakings are worth exploring in terms of their possible contribution to strengthening the integrity of social relationships throughout the "civilized" world.

REFERENCES

1. BOSZORMENYI-NAGY, I., and SPARK, G.: *Invisible Loyalties: Reciprocity in Intergenerational Family Therapy.* New York: Hoeber-Harper, 1973.
2. BUBER, M.: *I and Thou.* New York: Charles Scribner's Sons, 1958.
3. BOSZORMENYI-NAGY, I.: Loyalty implications of the transference model in psychotherapy. *Arch. Gen. Psychiat.*, 1972, 27, 374-380.

258   WHAT MAKES BEHAVIOR CHANGE POSSIBLE?

4. BOSZORMENYI-NAGY, I.: The Concept of Change in Conjoint Family Therapy. In Friedman, A. S., et al. *Psychotherapy for the Whole Family.* New York: Springer, 1965, pp. 305-319.
5. STIERLIN, H.: *Separating Parents and Adolescents.* New York: Quadrangle, 1974.
6. BOSZORMENYI-NAGY, I.: Comments on Helm Stierlin's "Hitler as the bound delegate of his mother." *Hist. of Childhood Quart.* (in press).
7. SATIR, V., STACHOWIAK, I., and TASCHMAN, H. A.: *Helping Families to Change.* New York: Jason Aronson, 1975.
8. PATTERSON, G. R.: *Families. Application of Social Learning to Family Life.* Champaign: Research Press, 1975.
9. FRIEDMAN, M. S.: *Martin Buber: The Life of Dialogue.* New York: Harper & Bros., 1960.
10. ERIKSON, E. H.: Identity and the life cycle. *Psychol. Issues,* 1959, 1, 1.
11. BOWEN, M.: Family Therapy with Schizophrenia in the Hospital and in Private Practice. In Boszormenyi-Nagy, I., and Framo, J. L. (Eds.), *Intensive Family Therapy.* New York: Hoeber-Harper, 1965.
12. WYNNE, L. C.: Some Indications and Counterindications for Exploratory Family Therapy. In Boszormenyi-Nagy, I., and Framo, J. L. (Eds.), *Intensive Family Therapy.* New York: Hoeber-Harper, 1965.

Erving Polster   *Miriam Polster*

12

Therapy Without Resistance: Gestalt Therapy

by ERVING POLSTER, Ph.D., and
MIRIAM POLSTER, Ph.D.

We are living in an age of amplification. Movie blood is redder than life's blood, LSD trips have outdone the wildest of Hieronymus Bosch's fantasies, electronicized sound dwarfs conversation, hyped-up terror captures moviegoers and a beer commercial advises us that we only go round once, so go for the gusto. Our culture is inundated in sensation-mongering.

Understandably so because these exaggerations make us attend to what is otherwise overlooked. They reverberate from a valid need to recover lost experiences of sensations and feelings and the accompanying respect for personal awareness.

The so-called third force in psychotherapy was spawned by these concerns. Its contribution to a new level of personal awareness in our culture is considerable and long overdue. Nevertheless, the consequences of the long period of stunted awareness which preceded the recent psychotherapeutic developments are evident in indiscriminate and poorly integrated behaviors which have made caricatures of some of these techniques. The grim beating of pillows, for one example, is an attempt to sensitize awareness of aggression and anger. What is frequently overlooked, however necessary these forced marches may sometimes be, is that there is *also* a more organic way into the sensate experience. Amplification of experience emerges organically when one pays attention to what is *already* happening. One of the great recognitions of gestalt therapy is that attending to one's own personal experience from moment to moment mobilizes the individual into a growth of sensation and an urgency for personal expression. As this momentum gathers greater amplitude from each moment to the next, it impels the person to say or do what he must. This progression leads to closure; to the completion of a unit of experience. With closure comes a sense of clarity, as well an absorption in fresh developments without the preoccupation which unfinished situations call forth.

In working towards behavioral change, therefore, there are two paradoxical (1) principles to follow. The first is: *What is, is.* The second is: *One thing follows another.* Instead of trying to *make* things happen, the psychotherapist following these precepts must focus on what is actually and presently happening. The present moment offers an infinite range of possibilities which may interest the therapist; the patient's beguiling voice, dramatic story, contradictory statements, perspiration, glazed eyes, flaccid posture, unfounded optimism, ad infinitum. The therapist's own attitude, imagery, sensations, etc. are also fair game. From this range the therapist chooses a focus. When the therapist is absorbed with what is current, and brings the patient's attention to current experience, a resuscitative process is started which brings liveliness to very simple events. A therapeutic fairy tale will illustrate. A man complains that he is unable to enjoy himself at picnics. He feels neurotic and dull. While he is talking his face is screwed up in a painful expression. The therapist suggests that the patient attend to his face. He is surprised, when he focuses on his face, to notice a tension there. As he stays with this sensation he begins to feel warmth developing in the tense area and he experiences a slight movement. It is an involuntary grimace, he says. As he concentrates on the grimace his tightness grows, revealing a pain. When the therapist suggests that he make a sound that would fit his particular sense of tension and movement, he screws his face up and grunts several times. When asked what that sound feels like, he says it feels like he has to take a shit but can't quite get it out. He feels weird about this fantasy but also feels some relief from the tension. Also, he likes making the sound but is embarrassed and blushes as he speaks. "Suppose," says the therapist, "that you just make the sound, temporarily setting aside any meaning it may have for you." He goes into the sound again and this time his hands begin to move slightly as though in rhythm with the sound. Asked to notice how his hands are joining in, he now says, in surprise, that they are giving a beat to the sound and he then begins to snap his fingers. Soon, laughing, he says this is incredible fun. He goes into lively song. Finally he is overcome by hilarity, falls to the floor saying this is more fun than shitting. Furthermore, he can do it publicly. He is aware of absorbed internal excitement and is also aware of being carefree, no concern about either shitting or any other mistake which free expression might lead him into.

This fairy tale took seriously the simple events that were happening. The process of moving from each event to the next had natural amplification powers and moved on to climax and closure. In the stalemate between the fear of shitting and having fun, new ingredients were recognized which changed the chemistry of the struggle. Such ingredients, in this instance, tension on his face, grunting, snapping his fingers, song, etc. always change the chemistry of a situation so as to form a new configuration. *What is, is. One thing follows another.*

BEYOND RESISTANCE

Fairy tales are not reality, of course, and some of you may object that there is a complex set of forces, usually including resistance, which interferes with such easy resolution. This concept of resistance has, of course, had a useful history. Through it contradictory motivations inhibiting behavior and feeling have been recognized. People do interrupt behavior and feelings which *seem* to be in their best interest. People *should,* after all, enjoy themselves at picnics. They should succeed at work, cry when sad, play with their children, have orgasms when sexually engaged, etc. When it is obvious to us and to themselves that they should be doing these things but are not, we look for resistance. Ideally then, the resistance would be obliterated, leaving the individual free to be the person he or she could or should be.

The troublesome implication is that resistance is, first, alien to the individual's best interests and second, like a germ, its removal would permit healthy function. Psychological leeching of the unhealthy organism does not work, however, because what is called resistance is, after all, the individual's own behavior, not a foreign body. It is through re-incorporation of the alienated energy bound up in this behavior that the individual achieves more full functioning.

Reformulating the concept of resistance along these lines requires an altogether open mind about the priorities in people's feelings and behavior. Not assuming the person is behaving wrongly, resisting, leads us to stay with each expression of the person, as it arises, moving always with the actual experience, innocently witnessing the unfolding of fresh drama.

There are several basic difficulties in encompassing such an attitude and it is hardly likely that any therapist would wholly succeed. Some of the difficulties are:

1. It is only natural for people to look ahead in any process and to set goals for themselves. This is true, of course, for both therapist and patient. If not for the inspiration of personal goals there would be no therapy in the first place. People want to get better in specific ways. The task of the therapist is to be able to bracket off these goals so as to function in terms of present experience—even though at heart wanting the patient to give up alcoholism, improve relationships with people, find good work, say goodbye to dead parents, etc. The difficulty of coordinating goals with immediate process is not unique to psychotherapy. A home-run hitter in baseball will tell you he cannot focus on hitting a home-run. He must attend to the ball and to his own stroke. Great novelists do not foreclose their own surprise at how their characters develop. Psychotherapists also must tune in and remain faithful to what matters in the unfolding situation.

2. In the age of the psychological detective, the uncovering of the hidden has been magnetically attractive. Most of us are fascinated by following clues until we find a hidden ingredient. The temptations of psychotherapeutic detection are supported by fact that we often *can* discover that which has already been there. Mother bakes a pie. Child hopes it is a pecan pie. It is covered, though. Child lifts the cover and sees a pecan pie. The excitement irradiates the child. It is a new delight. But the pie *was* already there. Only the discovery is new.

For these reasons it is difficult to transcend the magnetism of the uncovering phenomenon and to replace it with the creativity phenomenon. The creativity phenomenon is the development of that which has never existed before. It is more like what mother experiences when she bakes the pecan pie. Though she may have had a lifetime of experiences with pecan pies, this new one never existed before and her pleasure, if she is not already jaded, comes from the process of the creation and freshness of experiencing an altogether new pie. So also in therapy do we discover that which is created anew. We discovered in the earlier illustration that the person unable to have fun at picnics did something which was initially reminiscent of shitting. We were not oriented toward uncovering the "origi-

nal" and now anachronistic trauma about shitting. Instead we were oriented
to follow the sequence of experiences which culminated unpredictably in
lively song. There are also, of course, uncovering aspects in the experience
and those who prefer viewing it from that perspective are not "wrong." We
just prefer to follow the freshly unfolding process itself rather than to view
the process as uncovering something previously obscured. We would rather
bake a pie than look for one.

3. The psychotherapist must exercise considerable connoisseurship in distinguishing between what is happening in the present moment and what is
distractingly preoccupying. The distinction is a subtle one; rules about what
is a present experience will only clutter up one's good sense. The very act
which appears to be a preoccupation, when focused on, may turn into present
occupation. For example, the woman who looks around the room when
talking seems preoccupied rather than presently engaged. When the therapist suggests that she notice how her eyes wander and that she say what she
sees (rather than telling her she is resisting), what may be revealed is inordinate curiosity, which, when acknowledged and accepted, results in lively
visual experience. So, although the original inclination of the therapist may
be to consider looking around the room as irrelevant to the current process,
a mere deflection, the fact may well be that looking around the room is
basic and talking to the therapist would have been a deflection. The basic
propellant to change is the acceptance, even accentuation, of existing experience, believing that such full acknowledgment will in itself propel the individual into an unpredictable progression of experience.

4. Though it is true that simple experience teaches, it is also true that
people have an inherent reflex to assign meaning to the events in their
lives. This meaning gives dimension, support, and context to events. Without
the context which meaning provides, events are torn out of their natural
settings, empty and discontinuous, as with the labile manic whose pressured
liveliness accelerates into forced moments, each unrelated to the previous
moment, springing in frantic isolation from any personal context. He walks
on air, like the cartoon characters who, when they notice they have been
walking off the edge of a cliff, suddenly fall.

According to the gestalt theory of figure/ground relationship, there is an
inherent integration of experience (figure) and meaning (ground). When
this integrative function is impaired it may be necessary to formulate a
verbal context for the immediate experience so that the harvest of the experience may find a place within the daily existence of the individual. To
recognize the relevance of a current experience to other experiences in one's

life gives coherence and continuity which are crucial to a sense of security and general well-being.

The proportions of experience and meaning vary from person to person. Some well-integrated individuals could not articulate the meaning of certain events in their lives even though the unity between figure and ground is, for them, quite sound; others could articulate it well. Sometimes insistence on meaning upstages experience and interrupts the pure flow of involvement. On the other hand, sometimes the experience can be desultory and futile because there is no development of the sense of fit into personal context which would provide ownership and dependability. The therapist's artistry must take this into account when establishing the direction and the emphasis of work at any given moment.

COMPOSITION

When a therapy views expression as creative rather than resistive, how does the consequent internal struggle between two equally respected parts of the individual move toward closure? No need of the individual exists alone; its counterpart also exists. The combination is only rarely peacefully achieved.

The gestalt concern with polarities addresses itself to this internal struggle. Each faction in this struggle wants to dominate, but each is also subordinate to the individual's struggle for internal unity. The course of these internal struggles is varied; where two parts of the person seem incompatible with each other there may be out-and-out ambivalence, or one side may be submerged in deference to the other. The subdued part may appear ineffectual or it may work underground, frequently in disrepute, sabotaging the dominant faction but making life uneasy at best, and panic-stricken at worst. Frequently the struggle is frozen in anachronistic concerns or in personal horror stories about the consequences of allowing full expression of one or the other of the competing forces. To bring the interaction up to date, the warring parts must confront each other, the struggle must be expressed and articulated. The neighborhood tough guy may, for example, also have a soft side which once plagued his existence. Showing his soft side may actually have got him into trouble, or he may have internalized the standards of his childhood scene and so views his periodic moments of softness as threats to his own self-esteem. So, in the interest of survival, as he sees it, he covers over and subdues his soft responsiveness. He got the message of toughness-über-alles early and forgot what he reflexively wiped out of existence.

The therapist must be alert to the surfacing of polarities because, although they are sometimes obvious, they are often discerned only through sensitive attention. A moist quality appears around the tough guy's eyes when he is talking brusquely about his mother being exploited by her employers or his father beating her up. There may be only a flicker across his eyes, a swelling in his lips, or a relaxation of his wrist. At first the disowned soft side would be easy to disregard; he has been doing it so long. Even if the person is willing to engage the two parts of himself in dialogue, there would at first be a poor quality of interaction, including mutual disregard, scorn, low energy involvement and a sense of the futility of any interactions; what could they have to say to each other? The therapist, however, enters his observations and brings to the patient's awareness the chronic discounting and stand-off. The patient is intrigued and some vitality enters into the dialogue. The two disputants address each other more vigorously, each insisting on recognition for what it contributes to the totality of the individual's experience. Gradually the acknowledgement comes, that each does something to define the person in full dimension; rather than being a one-dimensional stereotype of a tough guy, he can be a compassionate tough guy, a tender but outspoken professional, etc. He is free to invent for himself all the possible permutations of being tough *and* soft. When this happens, he is whole and more open than before to doing what had once seemed unlikely and troublesome.

CONTACT BOUNDARY

Bringing alienated parts of an individual back into contact with each other is a natural extension of the fundamental gestalt principle that contact creates change. We are all bounded in our existence by the sense of what is ourselves and what is not ourselves. We are also bounded by the need to make discriminations between these two, always imperfect but indispensable. Perls (2) said, "Wherever and whenever a boundary comes into existence, it is felt both as contact and as isolation."

As always, paradox befuddles the soul. Where the discriminations between self and other become most difficult to make, the individual runs the highest risk of either isolation from the world or such union that swallows him up, wasting his identity by living the will of another.

Since contact is to people as chemistry is to the relationship of physical elements in the universe, we must conclude that "through contact one does not have to *try* to change: change simply occurs" (3). The philosophical equivalent of our chemical interaction is the Hegelian view that each thesis gives birth to its own antithesis and contact between these two entities results in a new creation, a synthesis. We see human contact, also, resulting in mergers between that which is ourselves and that which is not ourselves.

We are, therefore, immensely affected by our environment and we must sustain a sense of ourselves while at the same time remaining open to these infinite influences. We are continually confronted with the artful choice between assimilation and rejection of what we encounter. As Perls, Hefferline, and Goodman (4) said:

> . . . fundamentally, an organism lives in its environment by maintaining its differences and more importantly by assimilating the environment to its differences; and it is at the boundary that dangers are rejected, obstacles are overcome and the assimilable is selected and appropriated. Now (that) which is selected and assimilated is always novel; the organism persists by assimilating the novel, by change and growth. For instance, food, as Aristotle used to say, is what is 'unlike' that can become 'like'; and in the process of assimilation the organism is in turn changed. Primarily, contact is the awareness of, and behavior toward, the assimilable novelties; and the rejection of the unassimilable novelty.

The rejection of that which is not assimilable saves us from becoming what we don't want to become, from relinquishing individual identity. There are limits, however, to a person's freedom to stave off what he or she is steeped in. Non-smokers would have to hold their breath to keep out the noxious fumes of smoke-filled rooms. Accordingly, it is important for the individual to select or create environments which will make healthy assimilation or rejection most likely without exacting too great a toll. The therapeutic environment, be it the one-to-one relationship of individual therapy, the therapy group, or the therapeutic community, must offer improved possibilities for making good-quality contact. This may be accomplished in therapy through five pivotal elements: (1) Creation of a new interactive climate, (2) Personhood of the therapist, (3) The expansion of I-boundaries, (4) Sharpening of contact functions, and (5) The development of experiments.

(1) New interactive climate

People coming into a therapeutic situation quickly discover it is a very different world from the one they are accustomed to. First of all, it is a relatively self-contained unit of people with little seepage into the everyday world. This reduces, though of course it does not eliminate, the specter of catastrophic consequences. People are less likely to be shot, adjudicated, ostracized, flunked, ridiculed, or otherwise pilloried as a result of their actions or words. The general expectation is one of ultimate acceptance even during painful interludes when acceptance may be in doubt. Only rarely is a person working on a problem not seen from a respectful perspective by at least some of the group. People are not crowded by the complex, contradictory requirements of the world out there. The climate is usually one of live and let live; there is a subtle optimism that the puerile, the confusing, the disgusting, the frightening, etc., will soon turn the corner and become vibrant, touching, revealing of inner beauty, and restorative. Consequently, there is less need to interrupt people. When one believes that what is happening will turn out well, even though presently painful or problematical, acceptance becomes easier. Each individual may discover a new extent of psychological space within which to function. Crowding of one's psychological space supports prematurity or delay because these alien requirements impinge on the individual's range of possibilities.

The new community is, of course, not Eden. People do get angry with each other, misunderstand each other, trick each other, walk out on each other, and shower a whole range of kindred brimstone on their co-sufferers. Usually these mutual tortures are more readily recognized and dealt with because of the basic exploratory climate, the extended time opportunities and the presence of a therapist who is commissioned to watch the store.

(2) Personhood of the therapist

In a therapy where contact is seen as a major organ of personality, the personhood of the therapist is given central importance in the creation of behavioral change. Most excellent therapists we have known have been exciting people. They are readily radiant and absorbed. They encompass wide areas of personal experience. They can be tough or tender. They can be serious or funny. They change fast, according to the stimulations they receive. They are incisive in their perceptions, clear and simple in their articulations and courageous in assimilating new experience and in facing the dragons of the mind. If patients spend considerable intimate time with such a presence, some of it will frequently rub off on them. Patients absorb a new way of perceiving, articulating, considering. They learn to seek new perspectives. They recognize alternatives to whatever is happening. They engage in a new partnership of feeling. They experience someone who knows how to accept, frustrate, arouse. They meet surprise and adventure. Hopefully, they imbibe a respect for what it is like to be a human being.

In the face of such an awesome pattern of characteristics, the reader may well ask whether humility is also included. Fortunately it is not indispensable that the therapist be such a marvel as we might all wish he or she were. What is more crucial than the specificity of desirable characteristics is the unavoidable fact that, social designations aside, the therapist is, after all,

a human being. As one, he or she affects one. Once when we were referring a
parent to a therapist for his fourteen-year-old son, we asked the father
whether he would like his son to be influenced by this particular man. That
is not a bad question for any person to ask about a therapist. It is plain that
the therapist's personhood ranks high along with technique and knowledge
as a determinant of therapeutic direction. A kind person will affect people
through his or her kindness, a demanding person through his or her demand-
ingness, a person interested in power through this interest, a politically interested person through this orientation. Clearly many of the therapist's
characteristics or interests evident elsewhere might not enter into the therapy
session. What is important, however, is that the therapist not be required to
hide these characteristics or interests when they do organically appear in
order not to unduly influence the patient. On the contrary, the therapist's
influence is indispensable and unavoidable, and if the exercise of it risks
putting inappropriate trips on the patient this only reminds us that there is
no guarantee of a good job. Permitting the influence to appear does not free
the therapist of the transcendent requirement for exercising an artistry which
unites his or her own personhood respectfully with the authentic personal
needs of the patient.

(3) Expansion of the I-boundary

People's I-boundaries include the range of contact experiences which their
identity will allow. They will make only those contacts which do not exces-
sively threaten their sense that they are still themselves. It is therefore important that they learn to experience aspects of themselves which they had
formerly obliterated so that as unpredictable stimulations arise they will
not be unduly threatened by their reappearance. The prude endangered by
forgotten sexuality, the macho man terrorized by his impotence, the chronically supportive person engulfed by disquieting rage, have all narrowed their
I-boundaries and refused to accept certain alienated parts of themselves. The
whining person, the saboteur, the leech, the ogre, may all be exiles from
awareness calling for their right to be heard. Malaise ensues because the risk
of reappearances of these characteristics causes unbearable disturbances for
the individual's self-image. When unacceptable characteristics can be reas-
similated and given a voice, individuals may discover themselves to be quite
different in actuality from what they feared they might become if they listened
to these alienated parts of themselves. Their sense of self expands, encompassing new possibilities in behavior and feeling, setting contemporary limits based
on present experience, not past trauma.

Fixity of behavior and feeling always limits the world in which people may live nourishingly. Since there are limits to their control over the world and its confrontations, the more flexible people's acceptance of themselves is, the more securely they can live in a changing world. When their own worst fears about themselves are altered and they begin to assimilate the validity of these formerly alien characteristics, the possibilities for improved contact are increased. They can let the chips fall where they may, trusting their own ability to sustain themselves in the face of the unpredictable or customary.

(4) *Sharpening of the contact functions*

We spoke earlier about the importance of making the distinction between what is ourself and what is not ourself. Basic to this ability is the rhythm which exists between the individual's *sense* of his or her own organic identity and the *functions* through which he or she makes and maintains contact. The seven basic contact functions (5) are talking, moving, seeing, hearing, touching, tasting, and smelling. In focusing on these functions, the gestalt therapist seeks to improve such qualities as clarity, timing, directness, flexibility. All of these contact functions have been subjected to the erosive deteriorations of cultural prohibitions and interruptions. Growing up often seems like a long process of learning what not to see or touch or say or do. Each time a function is interrupted in its natural course, its impetus has been challenged. It is true that some others may be inspired by hardship, like Demosthenes. But, more likely, most deficiencies are not so dramatic and will go unrecognized. Many people have overlooked their own contact functions for so long that, although dismayed about their lives, they have little awareness of the simple, but far-reaching, deficit. Gestalt therapists are alerted to these interruptions and deficiencies; they must develop a safecracker's sensitivity to what is missing as well as to what is too much.

In working with a man who speaks incessant gobbledygook, the therapist may ask him to limit himself to simple declarative statements. Or the therapist may respond to the circumvented meaning behind circumlocutions. The therapist might ask a verbally stingy man to add a few words to his sentence once he feels he has completed it. Therapists must have as much variety in their inventiveness as there are linguistic poisons. Following this tack, therapists will frequently meet with objections to making direct contact. Patients may fear they will offend people. They may believe that in order to be understood they have to give the full background to every statement. Or they may make curt statements, sourly requiring that if people want more, they must ask for it.

These objections must be faced. The circumlocutious man may find it objectionable to say what he means to say in fear of discovering he is far more critical than he wishes. When brought face to face with his own critical nature, he may feel pinched by anxiety. The therapeutic task is to turn this anxiety into excitement. How might the patient's critical facility be used right now, for example, in contact with the therapist? As the patient warms to his task he may discover a new clarity, a pungent sense of humor or an affection that endures through the expression of criticism. Then the patient begins to respect the liveliness accompanying his critical faculty; he is on the road to magnifying his diminished zest. The original dread of himself as a tyrannical critic may evolve into the discovery of his genuine perceptual powers and the zing of not soft-pedaling them.

So also with the other contact functions. A man who was bombed out of looking because he couldn't stare at his mother's crotch may surprisedly discover the beauty of his therapist's eyes and no longer be willing to give up seeing. A woman having spent her formative years sitting stiffly with hands folded whenever company arrived may learn to fidget and feel the vibrant sensations which movement releases. People who have rarely been touched may be held or may explore the various textures in the therapy room or in their environment. Each time, the fresh recognition of the excitement and fruition inherent in the exercise of these contact functions supports, even inspires, the person to try them out further.

Repetition is crucial for assimilation. It is rare that one experience solves a problem once and for all, but one experience may light the way. Alas, it is also true that full recovery of functions rarely happens. More likely the individual sets new thresholds for the exercise of function and for better recovery from temporary abandonment of function. The circumlocutious man, for example, may return to his use of circumlocutions in situations which are especially difficult, but he comes back to clarity more easily. It takes more to throw him off the track and less to get him back on.

(5) *Development of experiments*

The functional psychology of John Dewey espoused the primacy of doing something in order to learn. It is better to take children to a farm and to a dairy than just to tell them about milk production. So, also, in gestalt therapy we want to turn our aboutist habits into present action. Individuals are mobilized to face the relevant emergencies of life by playing out their unrequited feelings and actions in the relative safety which the therapist's expertise and guidance provide. In gestalt therapy we call this a safe emergency. Although the safety factors are present in the nonpunitive and sensitively guided atmosphere of therapy, there is also a large emergency factor because individuals are enabled to enter into areas of their existence which were formerly out of bounds and which are still laden with fear. For example, a remark about her grandmother easily passed over in ordinary conversation receives new focus when the therapist asks a woman to play her grandmother, whom she remembered sitting like a sparrow with head tilted to one side. She tilts her head, assuming grandmother's posture, and regards the therapist with the same undemanding, completely loving expression which she remembers her grandmother had. Only now she feels what it is like to be such a loving person. She blushes with the animation brought on by the easy affection. Grandmother was like a star in the heavens beaming out from the deep reaches of the universe, but no longer an everyday part of existence. Now she returns to life within the patient's own skin. Reality begins to include unqualified loving. Mourning surfaces also for the lost birthright, misplaced when grandmother died; a lost right because now everyone—spouse, children, colleagues—needs her and when she doesn't give them what they need she feels unlovable. Then she can't love them either. The therapist says, "Be your grandmother and tell them about you." To her spouse, grandmother describes how, as a child, the patient wanted to know everything and was constantly coming to her with stories about new discoveries she had made. Spouse, in fantasied dialogue, responds by saying that's just what he loves too and what he has been missing. To her children, grandmother tells how the patient could always make up games and toys out of the most unlikely materials, a wooden crate, an old quilt. The children respond, turning to mother (the patient), observing the fact that she never just plays with them and would she please, please, and who cares about dinner. The patient, realizing what she has dismissed from her own adult function, is inspired to become again what she had once been, supporting herself even though the support of her grandmother is gone.

This speculation is only one illustration of the consequences of recreating grandmother. The improvisational possibilities are endless. The action is open-ended, transcending accustomed modes for dealing with memories, fears, sadness, and moving the individual into untried and unpredictable directions. In the improvisational cycle which is played out in the experiment, the patient is moved to fresh ways of being. As we have said elsewhere (7):

> . . . the patient in therapy . . . may tremble, agonize, laugh, cry and experience much else within the narrow compass of the therapy environment. He . . . is traversing uncharted areas of experience which have a reality all their own and within which he had no guarantee of successful completion. Once again he confronts the forces that previously steered

him into dangerous territory and the return trip (may) become as hazardous as he had reflexively feared. The therapist is his mentor and
companion, helping to keep in balance the safety and emergency aspects
of the experience, providing suggestion, orientation and support. By
following and encouraging the natural development of the individual's
incomplete themes through their own directions into completion, the
therapist and patient become collaborators in the creation of a drama
which is written as the drama unfolds.

Two major forms which the gestalt experiment might take are enactment
and directed behavior.

In enactment the aim is to dramatize, to enact some important aspect of
the individual's existence. This could be a dramatization of an unfinished
situation from either the past, the present, or the future. It could be the
dramatization of a characteristic of the patient, as, for example, playing out
the monster in oneself which one is otherwise afraid to reveal. It could be
the dramatization of a polarity in dialogue, as where the tough and tender
parts of one individual talk to each other. It could be the dramatization of
an exchange with a fantasied someone sitting in the "empty chair." It could
be the dramatization of a visual fantasy or it could be the dramatization of
the diverse parts of a person's dream.

In directed behavior, the individual is asked to try on a certain behavior.
A man might be asked to try talking with his hands, to call a friend each
day, to fidget in his chair while talking or listening, to say "dear" when he
addresses the people in his group, to speak with the ethnic accent of the
people who reared him, etc. This supports the actions-speak-louder-than-words
credo. He takes his risks through the action, giving him the palpable effect
from which his previous gaps in experience have distanced him. Also, in
present action, he is free to improvise, to take a new tack instead of the
familiarly doomed course of action he may have tried before.

The experiment is also a route by which the unfinished business of the
patient may be brought into the present. This not only fosters more than
a dry narration of past events, it holds opportunities for action and improvisation and for the resolution of persistent but anachronistic limits on
the patient's experiences. The woman who keeps her distance from all men
because her father kept her at arm's length becomes freer to express her
longing for closeness to a man and to find ways in which this longing can be
satisfied—not by sitting on daddy's lap, but by fantasying sitting on his lap
and telling him what that means to her and expressing also what she would
like to have received from him then. She could try moving, at first awkwardly,
into an embrace or a supportive gesture that a man in her life is now willing

and ready to offer, remaking her assumptions about the inevitable distance that must exist between herself and men.

These are some of the fundamentals of gestalt therapy which lead to behavioral change. The functional objective is to heighten present experience; the faith is that the ultimate objective, change, will be accomplished when one optimally experiences the present. Always, the return to experience, to the acceptance and reengagement with what is, leads to a new orientation for behavioral change. Animating these principles is the move beyond the concept of resistance into the view of the individual as a population of ideas, wishes, aims, reactions, feelings, which vie for full expression. Giving voice to these multiple factors is like giving suffrage to a previously disenfranchised segment of the population. It allows these parts of the person to vote and to be attended to rather than relegating them to dissension and sabotage.

Gestalt therapy is a phenomenologically inductive system in which an individual's development unfolds from moment to moment and in which we are more concerned with opening the person to a continuing process of discovery than sending him or her back through time to concentrate on that which has existed before. This distinction is, to be sure, a subtle one. We believe that supporting a person's potentialities for creative improvisation with a contemporary focus rather than an historical one is a basic ability that he or she needs—now in therapy, ultimately, out of it.

ADDENDUM QUERIES

I

DR. BURTON: Gestalt Therapy, at least as Fritz Perls promulgated it, seemed a defiant cry against the historical excesses of psychoanalysis. It now seems, by counterreaction, and by example of the phenomenologist and existentialist, to overreach itself on the intercurrent experience. What do you see as a proper balance between the here-now experience and those historical and hereditary forces which make up the personality?

DRS. POLSTER: Past experience, pungently and vitally relived, gives historical and contextual substance to the individual's present action. What has occurred earlier in his or her life informs, illuminates, and yields to the present if it is freshly reengaged, not dutifully or technically recounted.

The requirement is to accommodate the individual's past experience within the figural development of what is happening right now. To be stuck as though one were *indeed* living in the past promotes staleness and obsession.

So the resolution of unfinished business from the past has a central position in gestalt therapy and the reenactment of such situations has important methodological leverage. The present is the only time slot in which awareness and expression are possible, sensually and motorically. To return to the unfinished situation with these possibilities achieves a new balance between respect for the patient's history and the fresh opportunities for resolution offered in the present.

Presence is ubiquitous; only its quality is uncertain. There are innumerable stories people tell which reveal past experience and which arouse the most poignant union between the teller and the listener. Many other stories may be distractions or bores. The gestalt therapist, in spite of theoretical proscriptions to the contrary, is always faced with discerning the many shades of difference in the quality of presence and moving toward the quality of greatest immediacy that can be evolved.

II

DR. BURTON: I can find nothing in your very fine chapter which alludes to the causes of uneasiness, discontent, or illness in your patients/clients. Can you say something more specifically as to whether you believe in psychic disease and what its causes might be?

DRS. POLSTER: The concept of psychic disease imposes a linguistic tyranny to which we object. Though its fundamental meaning refers to malfunction of some aspect of the person, its implication is to set the pathological apart from the common experience. Obviously there are people whose personal malfunction is at a threshold which may conveniently warrant such separation. Then we say they are ill and take certain desperate measures which disregard the actual choices of the people involved, through hospitalization, medication, shock treatment, etc.

To say that one person is diseased and another not is simply a practical diagnostic and methodological aid and should not be mistaken for the fundamentals of malfunction which apply to all people. Human trouble exists when a person is unable to assimilate that with which he or she is confronted. This original failure to integrate may happen because of overstimulation, as for example, when one is severely frightened, or when necessary release outlets such as crying, objecting, screaming, embracing are shut off. When this kind of overload happens, we may become lopsided, bloated, emaciated, preoccupied, disappointed, disillusioned, disgraced, frustrated, etc. In these instances, individuals need either to get rid of the effects of what they cannot assimilate or to reintegrate these experiences in order to feel whole again. To feel whole, internally united, is a generic human need and good function is intended to bring about this wholeness. With each malfunction, be it of language, movement, seeing, or whatever, individuals are to some degree handicapped in their struggle to feel whole.

III

DR. BURTON: The implication of gestalt therapy without resistance is of a process and a set of people-healers who are more beneficent and presumably less cruel than those who call for a transference neurosis. But is not the resistance Freud talked about as a psychological process equivalent to the basic fear of losing one's boundaries, one's self, in any new intense and creative experience, and precisely a part of that growth experience? How can gestalt therapy short-circuit or change this fact of growth-life by offering *no resistance?*

DRS. POLSTER: Greater beneficence or less cruelty has nothing to do with the position we are taking in respect to resistance. We are dealing with the prejudicial implications of the word. We are not proposing that one ignore the risks inherent to boundary stretching. There is plenty to be frightened about in the inevitable struggles within oneself as well as against what is outside oneself. The internal struggle is inextricably related to these boundaries, which we call I-boundaries,* and which circumscribe the limits of supports or fears concerning any particular behavior or experience. On that score we have no quarrel with Freudians or others in their recognitions of the "intense and creative experience" as a vital part of growth. On the contrary, we intend to renew the necessary internal struggles.

What we are saying is that we do not view that patient's stuckness, evasiveness, blankness, stubbornness, dumbness, blindness, wiliness, etc., as resistances to what some identify as the *real* problems or directions. We view this growth process as including a struggle *between* or *among* parts rather than the unilateral view of the individual resisting what might be in his or her own better interest. The concept of resistance implies preset goals which are frequently stultifying to growth, particularly when these goals are inculcated either by society or by the therapist.

So the gestalt therapist seeks to give full expression, either in fantasy or in action within therapy, to otherwise discredited behavior. We might tell a person to emphasize his dumbness, to let his jaw hang slackly, his shoulders

---

* Polster & Polster. *Gestalt Therapy Integrated.* New York: Brunner/Mazel, 1973.

slump and a vacant, non-fixed stare take over his vision. And lo, the bright, energetic, but driven young man discovers his capacity for relaxing; that being dumb is not the panic-laden state he had dreaded but instead brings with it an ease and an absence of fear that he had not known he could feel. Now, this means that he will be less likely to panic in the inevitable moments of not-knowing that overcome him. This looseness, which he found in being dumb, can make his intelligence an agile and dependable part of him and can open him to accepting his ignorance with grace.

One might say this is merely a change in wording and that we are just calling resistance something else. There is an element of truth in this, but it is also true that changes frequently revolve around just such changes in words. These changes are responses to previous abuses of words. The change of perspective implied in the rewording of resistance to struggle does indeed suggest change in our methodological emphasis as therapists. Many concepts that have influenced behavior are only small turnarounds in perspective. It is too much to expect that a new concept be something altogether new under the sun.

IV

DR. BURTON: In my study of the lives of therapists I have found that they love life-detection and are still unconsciously detecting their own covert and unresolved lives through their clients/patients. Is it possible in gestalt therapy to practice such a pure phenomenology and experiencing as to say that it is without the need to life-detect? Perls himself had this as a greater need than others, as I observed him.

DRS. POLSTER: We have already said in our paper that it is difficult to "transcend the magnetism of the uncovering phenomenon." There is little likelihood of purity in experiencing each moment and remaining altogether open to discovering only what has never been there before. We have described a methodologically useful difference between the uncovering phenomenon and the creativity phenomenon. To expect purity in the process of transformation would be absurd.

It is true that Fritz Perls remained always heavily influenced by his history as a psychoanalyst and that psychological detection probably fascinated him. It is also true that in spite of this characteristic in his work, even casual observation would reveal large differences between his step-by-step processing of experience as it was happening and the psychoanalytic interpretive mode. We must take both our similarities and differences where we can find them instead of discounting differences just because we are not altogether different.

V

DR. BURTON: Do you find other modalities valuable in gestalt therapy? For example, do you do games analysis according to the transactionalists, painting and creative activity according to the Jungians, meditation according to Yoga, etc.? There is no indication in your chapter of what specific techniques are used in gestalt therapy or whether all of them come in sooner or later as required by an intuitive therapy.

DRS. POLSTER: We find many technical modalities very important in our work. The methodological concept of the experiment is our entry into the entire range of exercises and games which have been invented over the past twenty-five years. Not only is this given repertoire valid for us to include in our work but each gestalt therapist also uses his or her inventiveness to develop experiments individually for individual needs. In working with an artist involved in a troublesome painting, we may have the artist enact one segment of the painting talking to another—one color to another, one figure to another, etc. We have used music. We have used movement—dance, shadow boxing, stretching, playing rigid, fidgeting, etc. We have used metaphors, played parts in allegories, told life stories as they might be made into a comedy by Laurel and Hardy or as a film by Bergman or Fellini. We have played out fantasies. We have played out a day's experience as it might have been treated in a soap opera, etc.

Yoga exercises, meditation experiences, free association, mandala drawing, visual imagery, pantomime, group dream workthroughs, etc., are all possible ingredients in the repertoire of any gestalt therapist. All that is required is that the individual experiment with that which may further his or her own awareness and contact powers.

REFERENCES

1. BEISSER, A.: The Paradoxical Theory of Change, in Fagan, J., and Sheperd, L. (Eds.), *Gestalt Therapy Now*. Palo Alto: Science and Behavior Books, 1970.
2. PERLS, F. S.: *Ego, Hunger, and Aggression*. London: George Allen and Unwin, Ltd., 1947.
3. POLSTER, E., and POLSTER, M.: *Gestalt Therapy Integrated*. New York: Brunner/Mazel, 1973.
4. PERLS, F. S., HEFFERLINE, R., and GOODMAN, P.: *Gestalt Therapy*. New York: Julian Press, 1951.
5. POLSTER and POLSTER. *Op. cit.*
6. Ibid.
7. Ibid.

Reuven Bar-Levav

13

Behavior Change – Insignificant and Significant, Apparent and Real

by REUVEN BAR-LEVAV, M.D.

Individuals and societies may both not like the status quo in which they find themselves, yet they generally prefer it to change, since this always entails not only work but usually also the taking of frightening risks and the possible loss of the sense of security. Consider an individual struggling with his snooze-alarm clock very early in the morning, as he is rudely reminded every few minutes of the call of reality, yet wishing to enjoy a little more sleep and the cozy warmth of bed, rather than step into the cold of morning. Waking up is a gradual process extending over time, at first totally resisted. Only slowly and gradually does reality push itself, as it were, into consciousness. The temptation to turn the whole damned alarm clock off is usually resisted, as the guarding superego is nudging the slumbering and drifting ego to overcome the forces of impulse to remain undisturbed.

Repeated intrusions on the part of the alarm clock are necessary before behavior change occurs, especially when a person is very tired and experiences himself as lacking in energy, as is true in both physical and emotional exhaustion. The force necessary to overcome the status quo of the sleeping state is directly related to the strength of the wish to remain undisturbed. This is also true in a more general sense, and suggests how great and persistent the push to reverse basic character traits must be. Political apathy on the part of the population is an expression of the same principle in terms of mass psychology, since individuals in groups similarly tend to take action only when the discomfort of non-acting becomes greater than the effort of action. Politicians try, therefore, to whip up enthusiasm by making promises that each individual can translate into personally meaningful terms, exactly because of such considerations, thus hoping to activate the political process in their own favor.

These principles hold equally true in clinical settings. Patients generally do not really want to *get* well, they want to *feel* well. Getting well always entails prolonged and painful efforts, and regardless of the reward, such efforts and pain are usually not welcome, except when no other choice is left. The popularity of therapeutic fads such as T.A. (Transactional Analysis) or Encounter, or that of quick-help movements such as T.M. (Transcendental Meditation) and the various oriental "religions" and gurus, rests basically on the quest for easier choices. The goal of becoming a separate, whole individual, capable of surviving without totally depending on others, even if the company and closeness of other human beings is preferred to being all alone, seems desirable and enticing in itself. "I Want To Be Me" is the title of a popular song, the slogan of romantic posters, and the subject of many well-selling self-help books. But, it entails the giving up of the unconscious dream of reuniting with an ever-present, ever-loving, life-giving mother. To do so is painful and frightening and requires enormous courage and perseverance on the part of the patient, as well as exquisite intuition, skill, and competence on the part of the therapist. In spite of the popularity of the slogan, the weaning process is rarely completed, separation-individuation is infrequently achieved, and depression, clinical and subclinical, is by far the most common illness of our age.

The theory of behavior change is essentially the same for individuals and groups alike. Although observable behavior may seem to be the most important criterion for measuring behavior change, it is in fact one of the least important. Gross behavior changes are rapidly and easily achievable both in individuals and in groups when enough force is brought to bear upon a situation. Such changes are often superficial, however, short-lived and meaningless in the long run. More subtle and seemingly insignificant changes in observable behavior, on the other hand, may be indicative of major internal shifts, both in society as well as in individuals. The trained eye may see in them the first signs of major and lasting behavioral changes. Consider the following clinical examples:

A woman is brought to the office by her husband in obvious panic. Her associations are loose, her speech rapid, driven, and disorganized, and she is thrashing about in obvious fear. She is almost totally unreachable, not only because of her gross state of disorganization, but also because of a partial congenital hearing loss. Several years later she leaves therapy not only without her panic, which was brought under control without hospitalization within a month or two, but also basically without life-long paranoid tendencies and with a markedly increased capacity to trust and love. More remarkable, however, is a significant and measurable improvement in her hearing capacity. As she no longer needed to block out so much, she could actually hear more and better. Although she always wore hearing aids, no one ever knew that a functional component also existed in her hearing loss.

A psychiatrist in his fifties, suffering from a lifelong depression that inhibited him and limited his success as a physician, reports after two years of therapy that his gross earnings in the previous year have been $9,000 above those in any other year. His self-destructive and occasionally bizarre behavior has also practically disappeared, but his chronic overuse of alcohol persists.

A depressed mother of two teenaged children, who never really accepted her role as mother and adult, had tried for twelve years to finish college, always without success. Her superior intelligence was no match for her mountainous anxiety, and she would start and stop and drop out before the end of semesters. As her lifelong depression began to lift, she was able to graduate and is now successful in graduate school.

Diane comes from a very disturbed family. All her siblings have either committed suicide or are emotionally impaired in a serious way. Several times over a period of three years she has attempted to call for her first appointment only to hang the phone up in panic. It was long before she came to a group session, and for a full six months she uttered not a sound nor did she ever lift her eyes to look at another human being. She still lives by herself and still works in a job below her capacity, but her personal contacts have increased markedly and are much more trusting and loving even as fear still interferes after years of intensive therapy.

Marty displayed bizarre behavior since he was a little boy, and had seen therapists off and on throughout life. He became more confused and withdrawn in his teens, and withdrew into the basement of his parents' home, rocking himself in a semi-catatonic fashion. He would emerge from the basement from time to time to join a religious sect or a political cause, but would soon be disappointed and return to the basement where his mother catered to the whims of her sick "boy." He now works and pays for therapy from his earnings, lives in his own apartment, and is heterosexually involved. He also returned to school and is able to pursue his studies. His manner of speech, gait, and posture have all changed in ways noticeable to those who know him.

Behavior Change Defined

These short clinical vignettes amply clarify the need for defining what meaningful behavior change is, so that any discussion of it remains rational. It may denote dramatic changes in motor activity or such seemingly slight changes as an ability to look straight at another person with less fear. The philosophic orientation and expectations of those measuring behavior change obviously color the evaluation of such changes. As in psychotherapy in general so also in relation to behavior change, what appears as a satisfactory result to one may well be dismissed by others as a relatively minor matter. The ability to perform sexually by previously frigid or impotent individuals may be considered a significant mode of behavior change. If, on the other hand, such frigidity and impotence are considered to be no more than troublesome symptoms, a detail in a larger picture of rage at, or fear of others, then obviously the mechanical performance of the sexual act, although important in itself, does not yet signify behavior change of a magnitude that will enable the person to live "normally."

> Ruth came to therapy in a psychotic state soon after delivering her first live child. She had had several miscarriages, and married relatively late since she was uncomfortable with men and avoided them socially and sexually. She was helped to overcome this fear in several months of counseling and hypnotherapy, but her disabling menstrual cramps continued to plague her even after marriage.

Ruth's frigidity was only symptomatic of a much more serious and disabling problem that probably was also responsible for her miscarriages. Although her behavior changed markedly as a result of her hypnotherapy, such change in observable behavior failed to recognize the continuing battle inside her, and a florid psychotic depression was the result.

In general then, real behavior change is defined in this chapter as representing only those new aspects of behavior that emanate from, and are the result of, shifts within the personality or character structure—the outside observable manifestations of new aspects of personality reorganization. Such changes are termed "real" whether they are minor and insignificant in terms of observable behavior, or major and significant in such terms. Other changes which do not represent internal shifts within the personality are termed "apparent," even when they are major and significant in terms of observable behavior.

Acting-out as Behavior Change

Since behavior change, or at least the freedom to assume new behavior patterns, is the ultimate goal of all psychotherapeutic modalities, it is understandable why both therapists and patients are eager to find and proclaim signs of it, whether real or apparent, and why the distinction between the two is often overlooked. Therapists earn their livelihood from therapy and may have a need to validate their efforts in such terms. Patients, on the other hand, spend much time, effort and often a great deal of money on their therapy, and they have a vested interest in believing that such expenditures were justified in terms of the results.

Behavior change may also be a manifestation of resistance. Patients change to please their therapist in the hope of being loved and given some of his or her magically ascribed powers, or refuse to change out of conscious or unconscious disappointment or anger. Such resistance is also manifested when patients act outside the therapeutic setting to minimize their hurt, pain or fear.

Self-esteem of therapists which is dependent on patients' improvement is obviously endangered when they fail to make progress. Frustration, impatience, and anger are then bound to interfere with therapists' capacity to continue working with such patients. If improvements occur under such circumstances, their value must obviously be questioned, for these behavior changes may represent nothing more than accommodations for the therapists' sake. Behavior changes may thus be the result of direct pressure that some therapists knowingly or unknowingly subject patients to, perhaps with the best of rationalizations. The Jewish Rabbis of old, long before Freud, recognized the flimsy basis and the temporary nature of transference cures and of changes in behavior that result from outside pressure when they stated that "love which is dependent upon some external cause has no endurance nor a separate existence. With the passing away of that cause, the love, too, passes away. But love that is not dependent upon an external cause has a separate existence all its own, and shall never pass away" (1).

If behavior change is considered without its cause and, if the question of its persistence over time is ignored, both the achievement of such a change and its evaluation become markedly easier. Children are known to sometimes carry out in their lives hidden wishes that seem unacceptable to a parent or are openly condemned. Repeated warnings against certain forms of behavior actually draw a child's attention to such manifestly unacceptable modes of behavior, and the child can both rebel against and secretly please a parent by carrying out such forbidden activities. This is also true in some therapeutic relationships where the morbid interest of therapists may in fact encourage patients to change and to engage in forms of behavior for such questionable reasons. When behavior change becomes the major yardstick of therapeutic success, such and similar manifestations of new behavior may be misinterpreted as real.

Some therapeutic modalities assign legitimacy to actual suggestions from therapists to patients as to acceptable and desirable modes of behavior. Even the very continuation of the therapeutic relationship sometimes hinges on patients carrying out the expressed wishes of the therapist, especially those that are labeled as "good," "healthy," "normal," and "indicative of progress." Such behavior changes may or may not have a salutary effect on patients, at least in the short run, but in any event, they must all be classified as apparent and not as real changes.

Individuals subjected to stimuli which eventually result in significant behavior modifications undergo processes that are similar and analogous to those experienced by whole societies undergoing major internal shifts. In general, both individual and societal behavior change can be classified as belonging in one of the following four groupings, each representing more intense, deeper, and more lasting behavior changes than the preceding one:

1. Simple behavior change.
2. Behavior change accompanied by fantasy changes.
3. Behavior change accompanied by physical or physiologic changes.
4. Behavior change representing personality change.

Simple Behavior Change

The application of enough pressure or force to both individuals and groups will cause them to act dramatically, suddenly, and unhesitatingly in totally new ways. "An offer he cannot refuse" made to a bank teller usually produces a willing handing over of previously guarded sums of money. Individuals will likewise accompany a stranger at the point of a gun. With Hitler's rise to power, tens of millions of Germans and eventually hundreds of millions of others altered their entire life-styles and behavior patterns, as respective countries were mobilized, invaded, bombed, and reconquered.

Highly cherished modes of behavior, encompassing important areas of life, are suddenly changed in compliance with the wishes of occupation forces, even though such invading armies are usually hated. But, since such forms of behavior change are dictated by outside forces and not accompanied by internal changes within individuals or society, previously established behavior patterns are resumed as soon as the outside pressure disappears.

Within hours after the German armies were driven out, behavior systems that had functioned successfully for several years came to a sudden halt, and a sharp behavior reversal took place. Similarly, in spite of real compliance at the point of a gun, an individual will revert back to his or her typical behavior the moment the threat is removed.

Behavior Change Accompanied by Fantasy Change

Sudden and dramatic behavior change can also be accomplished when new situations are established as a result of legal or contractual arrangements. For those still abiding by the old and established codes of personal behavior, entering a marriage is accompanied by new modes of previously unacceptable personal and sexual behavior, a new address, perhaps even a new name. Since such alterations in one's behavior are accompanied by parallel alterations in one's self-concept and self-image, these changes are more profound than those adopted in response to an outside force. Yet, the legendary strains of old-fashioned honeymoons suggest that, even though such behavior changes were accompanied by fantasy changes, further modifications were still required before such married individuals were able to comfortably live with each other.

The mass behavior of groups is also grossly and dramatically affected by changes in the legal system. Such was the case when in 1863 slavery was abolished in the United States. While the ownership and holding of slaves was no longer legally acceptable or tolerated, this major change in the economic and social life of the society was relatively sudden and not accompanied by corresponding changes in the fantasy lives of either blacks or whites. The slaves of yesterday continued to experience themselves more often than not as slaves, even after this status no longer had any legal existence, and similarly most whites did not suddenly begin to regard their black brothers as equal in their humanity to themselves. The actual freeing of the slaves in response to an emancipation proclamation from "above" must be regarded as no more than a simple behavior change at that point. The proclamation changed basically the status and the behavior of slaves and of slaveholders and abruptly forced them to act in totally unaccustomed ways. A fantasy change lag is common, and must always be expected, since fantasy changes are never easily come by. They are, however, *always a neces-sary first step for real internal changes* within an individual or within a group.

A full hundred years had to elapse, in fact, before blacks really accepted, in fantasy as well as in fact, that "Black is Beautiful," and before most whites regarded Negroes as persons rather than as things. Many blacks have self-righteously exploited the guilt of many whites over the long overdue closing of this lag, as if it were one-sided and, in reacting to injustices of the past, have become tolerant of gross injustices in the present. Such gross distortions of reality in either direction are behavioral manifestations of the misguided expectation that fantasy may be changed suddenly even by most humane legislation or by political fiat.

Behavioral Change Accompanied by Physical or Physiologic Changes

Even though gross behavior may sometimes be modified in a lasting way when it is accompanied by fantasy change, such changes are limited in scope and in depth as long as previously established patterns of behavior are automatically repeated by an organism, be it an individual or a group. A compulsive individual in effective psychotherapy, for example, may engage in new modes of behavior in fantasy, and may eventually also experiment with new ways of being in reality. But in the presence of fear or rage such a person is likely to revert back automatically to old behavior patterns which were helpful in the past. Basic character traits must be thoroughly worked through over time before they are altered and become really different. Only then can it be claimed that real personality change has begun to occur. At such a point, a basic shift in the patient's defensive structure will also have occurred, and less physical and psychic energy will be spent in obsessive or compulsive preoccupations. The internal economy of the patient will have changed to permit him or her greater flexibility and more choices to pursue his or her real interests.

Meteoric political movements using personal terror as their chief tool, such as South Moluccans in Holland, the SLA in California, and others in the more distant past, have proven to be no more than short-lived flashes in the pan, since they usually lacked a wide enough economic and social base to sustain them. The same was true of the impressive power amassed by Senator Joseph McCarthy in the 1950's. It was based mostly on fear of Communism, and although formidable in its day, it passed overnight. It represented no new power alignments within society, no new economic interests nor social groupings reaching for new positions. Like similar movements throughout history, these too were basically expressions of protest or fear, rather than integral expressions of genuine strain within the societies from which they sprang. Although occupying the headlines of the world and affecting the behavior of millions of people for a short while, such behavior alterations were in a real sense meaningless, except as bizarre historical episodes.

The miraculous revivals of both Germany and Japan after the Second World War, on the other hand, rising from the ashes of almost total destruction to occupy the peaks of world production, are examples of real behavior change based on definite and real internal transformations. As soon as war was over, the productive capacity of both these nations was shifted in a sharp behavioral about-face from an almost total wartime footing to reconstruction and the production of industrial as well as consumer goods.

The demographic presence of millions of highly-skilled Germans and Japanese who suddenly shifted the direction of their productive efforts was also instrumental in the emergence of new societies with new value systems and, in many cases, entirely new modes of individual and group behavior. Behavior change that is accompanied by internal physical or physiologic change is slower and less dramatic, usually requiring years of hard work to achieve, yet it is generally a more stable change and a more permanent one.

The Jews of old also offer a fascinating example of basic behavior change accompanied by basic internal changes within a society. The success of such adaptive changes is attested to by the fact that it helped the Jewish people to survive for almost two thousand years under very trying circumstances. When their land was overrun, their only Temple in Jerusalem destroyed, and their people driven away, they abruptly changed their territorially based religion and imbued it with universal values based on their specific history. These internal changes in their system helped them adopt new observable behavior patterns not possible before. Animal sacrifices, for instance, were replaced by prayer in a newly devised institution, the Synagogue, and while other ancient peoples perished, they survived. The decadent and pleasure-seeking society of old Rome, on the other hand, in so many frightening ways similar to our own modern Western societies, proved to be too rigid in its internal structure and therefore unable and unwilling to modify its modes of living in response to the new military and political pressures from the outside. Like the dinosaurs, and for the same reasons, old Rome with all its power and glory has disappeared from history's stage.

Physiologic changes, totally unrelated to conscious will, must similarly be altered within an individual as he or she undergoes psychotherapy with the aim of changing basic characteristics of the personality. When such changes take place, the behavior changes of such an individual are likely to encompass important aspects of the person's entire mode of adaptation to reality and to its challenges. When no physiologic changes occur, the behavior changes are likely to remain encapsulated in their scope if lasting, or limited in their life span and life expectancy.

Once physiologic changes have begun to occur within an individual or physical changes within a society, an organic process with its own independent existence and pace has been initiated. This process eventually and inevitably leads to lasting personality or societal changes, unless stopped. The continued, independent existence of such a process does, however, require regular refueling from time to time, very much as the process of pregnancy has its own independent stages and rhythm, yet its continuation is dependent on the mother's life and well-being. Slow but steady and continuous changes occur under the visible surface when nations are being built or destroyed as well as in individuals when reconstructive psychotherapy is successful.

Behavior Change Representing Personality Change

Behavior changes based on parallel changes in the personality structure of an individual or of a group appear to be the most lasting and the most reliable of all. Such changes express facets of the changing core of one's whole being, and represent new adaptive modes to the challenge of existence in the universe. Mao's cultural revolution and the tight regimentation of both Chinese and Soviet societies are conscious, deliberate, but probably futile attempts to bring about such profound changes in their respective societies with enough continuous pressure over enough time. The leaders of these societies fail to understand what makes behavior change possible, and assume simply that pressure from the outside will somehow eventually initiate organic processes within their societies, even if willing cooperation and participation on the part of individuals does not exist.

Experience with brainwashing by means of extreme physical or psychologic deprivation may have misled some to believe that character traits can be changed by manipulating entire societies. Such assumptions confuse the sharply limited strength of any one individual with the enormous and limitless resources of the human spirit. Any one individual may be totally broken beyond repair. The spirit of man, like the legendary phoenix, is capable of rejuvenation and revitalization, at least as new generations are born, grow up, and come fresh into the arena to take up the struggle that may have been temporarily lost in the past.

The existence of typical national characteristics of Englishmen, Mexicans, the conservative Swiss, and others is sometimes used to demonstrate that some form of national character may evolve after all, if only sufficient time is allowed for the process to get under way without disturbance. Linguistic peculiarities, temperament, and general social demeanor as well as typical common elements in posture and gait are all expressions of that which is common among people who share similar geographic, climatic, and political conditions. It proves again that character formation and behavior are largely functions of environment and time. Individuals emigrating to foreign and faraway countries do not suddenly lose their ethnic or national characteristics, and usually continue to follow old behavior patterns for a long time. Behavior change is gradual and slow, like character change.

Much more importantly, however, individual variations in character structure within any one national character group always encompass the whole range of possibilities, and they are far more significant than the common national traits. These characteristics, closer to the core of the personality and more intimately associated with basic fears of individuals, are even more resistant to change, and even more gradual and slower than ethnic ones. Real behavior change is always an end result of much effort over a long time.

In summary, behavior always expresses personality, unless some force interferes. By extension, it is reasonable to expect that real behavior change will similarly always express personality change. All other forms of behavior change must necessarily represent a response to external pressure. Such behavior changes are generally only apparent, for when the pressure is removed behavior is likely to revert back to its original form, with minor modifications at best.

Crisis as an Opportunity

Crisis Mobilization Therapy, C.M.T., is a recently developed, integrated system of psychotherapy which deliberately does not focus on behavior change, even though this is its ultimate goal. Behavior change in C.M.T. is considered significant only when it is real, as defined previously, and it is therefore always incidental to personality change. Profound behavior modifications are expected, and in fact the effectiveness of C.M.T. can only be judged by this yardstick, yet no deliberate attempts are made to modify behavior as such. In fact, unexpected changes in behavior of patients are generally looked upon with suspicion, for clinical experience has repeatedly demonstrated that such changes are often manifestations of a resistance. The giving up of personality traits that have always been considered essential for survival is a frightening and painful process, and patients frequently attempt to escape this self-imposed and yet difficult task (2) by behaving as if they had already undergone the personality change that would make such behavior change possible. If undetected, other undesirable personality traits or symptoms often become more prominent and troublesome instead. Manifestations of behavior change are naturally expected during therapy, but they are repeatedly challenged when they first appear to test whether they are real or not.

Crisis Mobilization Therapy, which is described here only to the extent required by a discussion on behavior change, should not be confused with any form of Crisis Intervention. It has, in fact, nothing in common with it except the use of the word crisis, which means different things in both instances. In C.M.T., crisis denotes a peak emotional reexperience of unresolved internalized conflicts, which can now be resolved in new ways, meaningfully different from past patterns. Patients are helped to reexperience all their feelings in a therapeutic setting, a frightening experience which does not develop spontaneously but must be evoked. Special techniques, provocative and other, were developed for this purpose in C.M.T. Such emotional storms are optimally experienced at a level of intensity just short of the point where anxiety would overcome the patient in the form of confusion or an outright refusal or inability to continue. Such peak emotional experiences require the active and willing participation of patients, although such participation and cooperation are always somewhat tentative and hesitant, considering the fear with which such experiences are often regarded as possibly endangering the very survival of those involved in them. Such crises of affect are usually mobilized or brought up in a group setting, but patients are also seen regularly in individual sessions, which are generally more supportive.

A therapeutic split of the ego must already have occurred before crises of affect can be mobilized. This allows therapists to encourage patients to take further risks, if they wish to do so, even as they are supported when they refuse to proceed. The patients in C.M.T. assume full responsibility to get themselves well or not to, even as it is the therapist's responsibility to make it as difficult as possible for a patient to not move in the direction of health. There is *no place for coercion of any kind in C.M.T.*

Patients are expected to clearly understand and unequivocally accept the principle of "isolation of action" from feelings, which should make it easier for them to take the risks involved in experiencing all their feelings. This principle simply reaffirms the unacceptability of any form of acting-out or acting-in, and should not be confused with isolation of affect. No action whatsoever is to be taken on the basis of feelings alone. All actions, both active and passive, must, instead, first be coolly considered and judged acceptable by the patient's cognitive process before they are carried out.

Most individuals in our society, in and out of therapy, fail to understand that intensity of feelings is never really a rational cause for action. This appears to be a culturally determined basic defect in our society with far-reaching and most damaging consequences to many individuals and to society as a whole. Firm establishment of the principle of isolation of action is a continuous task in C.M.T., for acting-out or acting-in comes in many disguised forms, and is a repeatedly attempted route of escape of patients when they are frightened, hurt, or they otherwise wish to escape a difficult confidential situation.

The Therapeutic Alliance as a Base for Behavior Change

A uniquely strong therapeutic alliance is the cornerstone of C.M.T., and it is regularly built up and strengthened, from a tentative and fragile relationship at first to one that can and should be able to withstand major tests. This alliance is stronger in C.M.T. than in other modes of psychotherapy, because of the active role assumed by the therapist and the central position that is consciously assigned to the interactions and relationship between patient and therapist. In addition, deliberate attempts are made by the therapist regularly to couple deprivation of infantile needs with occasional gratification of appropriate adult wishes. Patients who are either unwilling or claim to be unable to assume more complete responsibility for their lives are induced to do so, although not without a struggle, with the aid of this therapeutic alliance.

Patients in C.M.T. learn early that the commitment to therapy is a two-way affair, both therapists and patients making conscious and volitional choices to work with each other. Although the patients pay the therapists for their time, the latter must decide with which patients they choose to work and must be willing to invest of themselves in the patient. Such choices are always conditional in C.M.T. on the patients' reciprocal commitment to treat their lives respectfully, and to assume full responsibility for their being. Suicidal acts or gestures, just like other forms of regressive action, may be likely causes for termination of therapy.

Patients frequently experience the therapeutic milieu of C.M.T. as providing them with "a place in the world" in which they can be heard and understood, a "home," and they are therefore not usually likely to give this up easily, mindlessly, or frivolously. This sense of "belonging" often provides patients with a sense of basic security which many individuals have known only in earliest childhood or in utero. The wish to maintain this sense of security is strong enough a motive in most instances to overcome the impulse to act-out. Even more so than in psychoanalysis, it is necessary in C.M.T. to construct a closed system in the confines of which pressure can be applied upon patients to facilitate characterologic and thus behavioral change in the direction of health. The strength of this closed system must be sufficient to withstand the pressure of patients against it as they wish to escape when pain and hurt seem to become intolerable.

The Concept of Force in Overcoming Resistance to Behavior Change

Present-day psychotherapy that is not directly involved in mechanistic behavior modification is basically descriptive and analytic in nature, as if this, in itself, would bring about behavior change. Much of physicians' time and the time of staff conferences is devoted to diagnostic determinations and to the understanding of underlying dynamics. Freud's unproven and probably mistaken notion that neurotic conflict is resolved by making repressed, unconscious material conscious and by removing the amnesias (3) is largely responsible for this preoccupation with finding and understanding hidden dynamic aspects.

What may perhaps have been true to some extent in Freud's Vienna hardly applies in this psychologically sophisticated age. Patients today often understand basic psychologic configurations, and can often even apply them, correctly if incompletely, to their own situations, and mouth them with varying degrees of confidence. Such understanding is not usually helpful in the process of self-change, and it is often used, instead, in the service of resistance. Additional dynamic interpretations are only useful in a setting in which the relationship itself is intensive enough to involve the patient emotionally in a meaningful way. More than an accurate description of unconscious self-destructive ways and even more than emotional recognition of such uncovered material by the patient are needed to overcome lifelong pathologic personality traits. What is needed is force, a pressure in the direction of health, *derived from the therapeutic alliance and applied with the explicit permission of the healthy part of the patient's ego* against his or her own pathologic part. *C.M.T., alone of all psychotherapeutic modalities, specifically acknowledges this need for force* and has developed special techniques for its exercise. As patients have been "driven crazy" in their formative years, so they must be "driven sane" in psychotherapy.

The Physiology of Psychological Responses

Mobilized affective crises are basically different from spontaneous eruptions of feeling storms as a controlled nuclear reaction is different from a destructive nuclear bomb. Since the therapeutic alliance is not very strong early in therapy, sufficiently intense affective crises cannot be mobilized until later in therapy, when enough reality-based trust has been established between therapist and patient. The mobilized crises must eventually be of an intensity sufficient to cause measurable changes in physiologic parameters such as blood pressure, body temperature, heart rate, breathing depth, muscle tone and others. Mobilized affective crises which fail to reach such levels of intensity must be regarded as only preparatory for more intense experiences later, but generally those close enough to the core of internalized conflicts bring forth affect of such an intensity. By the remobilization of such crises again and again, previously established physiologic reaction patterns based on the relative power positions of infancy are modified, and eventually basically altered. Affective crises lose their critical nature with time, and when they no longer have a crippling grip on the patient they can be handled more appropriately in an adult manner.

The Modification of Preverbal Hunger and Rage

When lifelong depressions are finally lifted, a task that often requires years of hard work and a great deal of patience, sensitivity, and courage, the organism is freed from leaden shackles that have burdened it up to then. Such release always frees much energy that was previously tied up in submerging frightening feelings. This new energy is now usable for living, and usually tips the internal balance between pathological and healthy tendencies so that real personality changes now occur in rapid succession. Objective determinations of changes in a person must necessarily be based upon records of observable behavior, even though other, often much more important but hidden, processes have occurred underneath the surface. What is actually observed may be essentially the same as that observable as a result of mechanistic behavior modifications, although the two are basically different, one representing modifications in depth, the other only superficial ones.

Lifelong depressions can be ameliorated with drugs and with various psychotherapeutic approaches as they can be suppressed with shock therapy. But such depressions will only really lift when the underlying hunger for good mothering has been sufficiently worked-through, and the enormous underlying rage experienced, expressed, and examined. The treatment of this preverbal hunger and rage is a special concern of C.M.T.

The yearning for the erstwhile Mother is expressed by patients as a wish to be given "more" in a variety of forms. Patients ask questions, wish advice, make themselves confused or stupid, develop psychosomatic symptoms, and in general appear helpless and, therefore, in need of help. This multifaceted yearning for help and the desperate desire to be given, and to be taken care of, are openly recognized in C.M.T. as legitimate but are nonetheless repeatedly frustrated, except when the request for help represents appropriate adult needs.

Biologic hunger of the infant, expressed in adulthood as a multitude of demands for gratification of oral and other drives, cannot be directly satisfied no matter how hard we try. All such efforts are always doomed to failure. But, by steadfastly and repeatedly frustrating such demands, *in a setting that holds clear and close promise of gratifying appropriate adult needs,* such demands are turned first into dissatisfaction and eventually into rage. This rage in its myriad forms is treatable, and several unique techniques have been developed in C.M.T. for this purpose. The longing for reunion with a symbiotic mother can thus indirectly be resolved, and both separation and individuation more completely achieved. The repeated experiences of "loving" and "stroking" an adult patient as "corrective emotional experiences," so commonly the case in the newer modalities of psychotherapy, have obviously no relevance to such basic repair of the ego. In classical psychoanalysis, on the other hand, with its relatively tenuous therapeutic alliance, deprivation of infantile needs usually leads to subclinical depression, not to rage. The experience with a nongiving although benign "mother" usually results in frustration and bitterness, but not in true resolution.

Behavior Change as a Pressured Choice

C.M.T., unlike the various behavior therapy approaches and unlike T.A., Encounter, Rational-Emotive Therapy and others, does not aim at changing behavior through unlearning specific pieces of it which the patient consciously wishes to discard. Like psychoanalysis, C.M.T. recognizes the importance of unconscious factors in determining behavior, which is considered to be a function of the personality. Although it is no doubt entirely possible to overcome important segments of undesirable behavior in a mechanistic fashion, closer scrutiny shows that, contrary to popular expectations, much effort is often required to overcome even a single important symptom in direct attempts to modify behavior. The same work may yield greater benefits when aimed at personality change, thus undercutting many symptoms in a widespread area. If done properly this is the shortest and most efficient way in spite of its length.

These differences in approach are not only philosophical and technical, they also have an immediate practical importance for suffering individuals who come for therapy. Attempts to directly modify pathologic behavior patterns not only appear to be much more economical and quicker but are also more in keeping and in step with the value systems of a society in which instant intimacy and immediate gratification are often expected and often promised. Narrow therapeutic contracts made to help an individual overcome a troubling symptom are popular and sought after, yet they are often followed by deep disappointment later on. Millions of ex-patients exist in this country, individuals who have gone from one therapist to another, improving each time so they "function" better, yet never getting well. The basic hopelessness which plagues many such individuals in the first place, and which is temporarily lifted from time to time, deepens and becomes more tenacious as one therapeutic disappointment follows another. When seen in the long perspective, these relatively short-term efforts are not only unkind by offering false hope but also are more expensive in terms of dollars and despair.

The individuality of each person dictates that the patient must grant the C.M.T. therapist explicit and repeated license to be intrusive before any such approach is attempted. The persistent and direct confrontation of resistances is often experienced by patients as a direct attack upon their dignity or even upon them as persons. Exquisite sensitivity and true respect for each patient are required from the therapist, if one is to be differentiated from the other. Patients must be able to clearly see, soon after every confrontation, that the attack was directed at their pathology and not at them. Further therapeutic work on a rational basis becomes impossible unless the situation is entirely clear to every patient after each time he or she is confronted.

Under the pressure of repeated and unrelenting confrontations with self-destructive traits, each patient must eventually make a very painful and difficult choice: to continue holding onto pathologic behavior that is experienced as being an essential part of the personality, thus risking further intrusions and painful interventions, or to experiment with possibly giving up a small part of the self, frightening as such a move must always be. The only way to really find out whether it is literally possible to exist without some part of the self which has always been considered to be vital is to actually take the difficult and courageous step of experimentally giving it up. This terror-producing decision can be attempted only when the therapeutic setting is experienced as being really safe in spite of confrontations, and only when the therapist is experienced by the patient as truly "being-there" to perform the rescue work that might be necessary. A provocative and confronting therapist may be so experienced no less than a supportive one, if he or she is willing and able to risk making real human contact with the patient and with the patient's travail.

Pressure to change is in fact applied by *all* psychotherapeutic systems, although psychoanalysts and several others would probably deny it. Direct observations of the therapeutic setting and of the interchanges between its participants strongly suggest that patients generally invest therapists with magical powers when they ascribe to them the role of healer. Even when the therapists are most careful not to impose themselves and their values on others, patients often act as if they do and "respond" to such imaginary suggestions or directions. The therapeutic setting in itself forces individuals to look at themselves, which makes it more difficult for them to act mindlessly, and it thus constitutes an indirect form of pressure. Some therapeutic systems even apply pressure by almost openly demanding change as a condition for the continuation of the relationship. The pressure in C.M.T. is not of this type. It consists of forcing the patient repeatedly into making the most difficult choice between consciously remaining in the morbid state, or consciously assuming responsibility for stepping away from it.

Consider the analogy of a person with several hot, swollen, and grossly inflamed abscesses. Behavior modifiers, under whatever labels they come, would basically attempt to reduce the tenderness, swelling, and pain of the one abscess that interferes most with the individual's functioning by applying ice or otherwise anaesthesizing the spot. They would also recommend bed rest and a high fluid intake to support the individual in general, expecting that the natural defenses of the body, aided by these measures, would eventually overcome the infections. The various psychoanalytic approaches, on the other hand, would wish to understand the underlying reasons for this condition, identify the organism that is involved and its sensitivity to antibiotics, and would then proceed to treat the individual systemically with antibiotics, in addition to the other supportive measures. They might perhaps also apply slight pressure near the abscesses in the hope that channels would spontaneously form for pus drainage.

C.M.T. would employ all the previous measures, but it would also introduce two additional techniques into the treatment plan:

1. It would apply heat to the area of the abscesses, thus increasing the pressure within each abscess and in the short run also increasing the pain, the temperature, and the swelling.

2. It would incise with a surgical scalpel into the ripe abscesses to create openings though which proper drainage of the pussy material could occur, using meticulous surgical technique to avoid secondary infections. The temperature, swelling, and pain can now all be expected to subside dramatically and without much delay.

The two additional modalities introduced by C.M.T. obviously require a great deal of specialized skill and much forethought and care. Extreme measures can either benefit or hurt a patient, and they should never be attempted by anyone not carefully trained, nor with a patient whose general health has not been monitored and found to permit it. When the conditions are right, on the other hand, the use of such additional modalities may offer the patient a better chance for a complete recovery without recurrences.

The Critical Moment of Change

In physics, just exactly as in the lives of individuals or groups, minute increments of pressure cannot normally be observed by the naked eye, although they are the necessary components that lead to the eventual dramatic event which we call an explosion, a basic observable change from previous states of being. The temperature or pressure of gases within a boiler may slowly increase for a very long time before the critical moment arrives, when metal fatigue or the strength of other materials is no longer capable of withstanding the countervailing force. Although changes have been occurring slowly for a while, an outside observer can only see the explosion.

What is described as behavior change in individuals is likewise only the end point of a longer process. The relationship between President Ford and Secretary of Defense Schlesinger, for instance, was under increasing strain over a prolonged period, but only those very close to the scene were aware of it. Schlesinger's dramatic and seemingly sudden removal from his post was, in fact, only the natural and expected culmination of such tension and strain. The shifting of masses of icebergs, grinding imperceptibly against each other until one or both suddenly change position and roaringly move to new places, is a natural phenomenon with direct parallels in international relations. When, in 1947, the U.S. announced the "Truman doctrine," in effect guaranteeing the defense of Turkey and Greece, clear boundaries of global power spheres were established, and Soviet expansionism to the south was halted. The announcement itself was dramatically made one day, yet the basic change in the conduct of U.S. foreign policy was obviously no more than the culmination of a long series of complex deliberations.

Major and dramatic changes in behavior are usually preceded by a precipitous increase in tension, sometimes noticed as a sudden decrease in motoric activity, during which society or an individual regroups and reorganizes, gathering resources in preparation for the next stage of being. The first, tentative step or two in a young child's life, a major behavioral change from the crawling to the erect position, is always spoiled by a momentous fall, most hurtful physically and psychologically. This is likely to be followed by the child's remaining on its knees for a while before the next steps are attempted. The more regressed position of crawling provides the young child with a sense of security and with an opportunity to regain self-confidence, a requirement for gaining mastery over the frightening sense of imbalance in the erect position.

Patients likewise often experience a recurrence of symptoms just prior to their changing in a major way, frequently becoming physically ill and regressing into a temporary state of complete bed rest, just like the one experienced in infancy. In general, major behavioral changes can be expected to be accompanied by major events in one's life, such as a temporary withdrawal from outside involvements into contemplative isolation. This period of relative or complete withdrawal, in many psychological and physical ways resembling the labor of childbirth, may last days, months and sometimes even years. The significance of such a period in the lives of individuals or societies is often appreciated only after it has passed by, when the fate of the involved organism has already been determined.

Conclusion

The basic concept of Democracy that all men (and women) are created equal is often misunderstood as meaning that all men (and women) are the same, which obviously is not so. Differentiation by role, position and power, age and gender are all questioned and under attack, as if what rightfully belongs to one must become the property of all. Public officials on all levels have catered to such unreasonable and absurd demands, allowing the legitimacy of even grossly bizarre ones, thus encouraging the most extreme and unreasonable voices to become spokesmen for the public.

Almost everything in this society is in a state of constant flux: morals and values, economic and sexual roles, rights and privileges, responsibilities and expectations. But all these changes essentially appear to involve no more than the loosening of internal controls, resulting in loss of a personal or public sense of balance. Recent behavior change in modern, industrial societies has always been in one direction only, that of gratifying more wishes, whether they make objective sense or not. History has repeatedly demonstrated that such a course of events invariably leads to complete destruction of a society or else to the assumption of power by a central, authoritarian figure using brute force to bring about simple behavior change and save his society for a while.

If our society is to escape the fate of other societies under similar circumstances, behavior patterns must be dramatically reversed to balance the one-sided slide towards promising and *getting* ever more. This basic behavior change on the part of tens of millions of individuals entails *giving up* unsupportable and unrealistic privileges that have become expectations. Attempts to bring about such changes are always understandably resisted, in individual psychotherapy as in the political process.

Strong political leadership willing and able to exercise moral and actual force is an essential prerequisite for such changes to occur. Such a course of action has never before been followed in democratic societies, except in war or under conditions of siege by an outside enemy. The leader in such a society, entrusted to wield power and to use force, is in an analogous role to that of the psychotherapist. Both are freely granted the right to use pressure and force for a limited time and under certain conditions, even against those granting them that right. Extreme courage and true integrity are always required if either political leader or psychotherapist is to use such force against resistance, since his very position may be endangered by such use. Some of those resisting change, out of a wish to maintain old habits or old positions, will surely attempt to protect their interests by trying to remove such a leader or therapist, or at least by trying to strip him of his power to use force.

The common aversion in our society to the open use of force and the almost generalized suspicion cast upon those with power have deep roots in early family relations. Yet both the success of psychotherapy and the continued existence of Democracy may depend on not yielding to such aversion and suspicion. Psychotherapists and political leaders who refuse to exercise the power entrusted to them for reasons of personal survival obviously prostitute themselves and the processes in which they play such central roles.

Winston Churchill, in wishing to mobilize the British people in 1940, understood that real behavior change required basic changes in life-styles and the *giving up* of unrealistic wishes to have more and to be given more. "I have nothing to offer but blood, toil, tears and sweat" (4). John Kennedy similarly understood, at least in his public utterances, that the unrealistic but universal wish for reunion with an ever-present and ever-giving mother is incompatible with the continued existence of a society. "The New Frontier . . . is not a set of promises—it is a set of challenges. It sums up not what I intend to offer the American people, but what I intend to ask of them" (5).

In the absence of valid theories of behavior change, societies such as ours have in the past invariably disappeared from the face of the earth. If the theory of behavior change used as a basis for Crisis Mobilization Therapy proves to be valid, then there is no painless way to effect real behavior change either in individuals or in society. Some form of force, physical or moral, is absolutely essential for overcoming the natural resistance to change. The sooner political leaders learn this simple truth, the better the chance this Republic will have of surviving, and this society of remaining intact and viable. The sooner psychotherapists learn this lesson, the better the chance patients will have of really being cured.

ADDENDUM QUERIES

I

DR. BURTON: The word crisis is a significant concept in your discussion of behavior change, and you make very close analogies to the crisis of a physical abscess which presumably contains bacteria, viruses, and so on. How does one define a crisis on a psychological level without taking refuge in clinical terms such as depression, which just as often mask as they scientifically clarify?

DR. BAR-LEVAV: Psychologically, a crisis is the point at which a person experiences a feeling with maximum tolerable intensity. When a feeling such as fear is experienced with an intensity beyond the crisis point, it will overwhelm the patient, and he or she may become temporarily confused or block it out altogether. Sometimes even more primitive defenses will take over. Fainting is to physical pain what psychotic-like symptomatology is to emotional pain. When the crisis point is exceeded, the healthy part of a person's ego is at least temporarily out of function and unable to participate in the tasks involved in the psychotherapeutic work. Such a situation has the effect of an increased resistance and is, therefore, counterproductive. It must be avoided whenever possible. Working below the crisis point is obviously wasteful, but this is nevertheless the place where most psychotherapy occurs, and remaining there is the aim of all resistances. Patients usually experience high intensity feeling-states as endangering their very existence, and understandably tend to avoid them. The concept of crisis in C.M.T. is similar in many ways to the point of impasse of Fritz Perls.

Anxiety threshold and anxiety tolerance are, therefore, intimately associated with the concept of psychological crisis. These two entities are theoretically considered in C.M.T. to often be manifestations of resistance in themselves, and quantitatively changeable by the psychotherapeutic process. In this sense, C.M.T. is closer to behavior therapy than it is to psychoanalysis, but it differs from behavior therapy in attempting to modify the anxiety threshold and tolerance as character defenses, and not as they relate to any set of symptoms.

Patients usually and understandably behave as if the crisis point has been reached long before it is actually approached. This takes place in the unconscious service of resistance, to minimize pain and maximize comfort.

The abscess itself is not analogous to a crisis, it only contains the elements that may lead to one. A crisis is reached when the swelling, pain, and loss of function are maximal, at which point spontaneous or surgically induced lancing and drainage would produce the most dramatic effects. Physically and psychologically, a crisis is not only a moment of great danger but also the point at which opportunities for change are the greatest and the most promising.

II

DR. BURTON: My understanding of behavior change is the same as yours. Behavior itself can easily be altered by a variety of simple treatment techniques, but a basic change in personality or character structure is much more rare and difficult. Yet, cure or change in any sense of the word involves precisely this.

Your chapter is significant in that it does not reveal to what theory of personality you subscribe. Are you in fundamental sympathy with Freud's structural theory, Jung's archetypes, Adler's social inferiority views, Reich's body approach, some other?

DR. BAR-LEVAV: Crisis Mobilization Therapy is based on a theory of personality all its own, derived from, and in many aspects similar to, Freud's structural theory, yet with basic theoretical differences. The basic units of individual personality organization are id, ego, and superego, but the origin of internalized conflicts is usually dated as being much earlier than in psychoanalysis. Birth *as a separation* from an ever-present, protective, and nourishing mother (to be distinguished from the traumata of birth) is considered to be the basic traumatizing event. Consequently, a basic fear of non-being is regarded as motivating man to help himself survive as best he can.

Influenced by existential philosophy, universal anguish of nothingness is translated into terms of personal panic, against the experience of which individuals construct their entire life-styles. Symptom and character formation are thus seen as self-helpful measures based on the realities of early infancy and carried into adult life.

The basic problem underlying both neurotic and psychotic symptomatology is noncompletion of the process of separation-individuation, an adaptation to very early infantile fears. Basically, psychotherapy is the process of working-through and resolving preverbal hunger and rage, without which true personality change is considered to be impossible and at best only apparent.

III

DR. BURTON: From your chapter I assume that you bring the crisis to a "boil" in the conventional ways that we have all been taught. Have you perhaps derived some unique, more efficient or safer procedures for focusing the crisis into choice and responsibility?

DR. BAR-LEVAV: As its name implies, C.M.T. makes a unique contribution to helping patients reexperience repressed conflicts at levels of highest tolerable intensity. The mobilized crises of C.M.T. do not take place in real-life situations but are only crises of feeling within the therapeutic setting. A variety of provocative and evocative techniques have been developed to bring them about. Language, for instance, is used not only for conveying thoughts and describing situations but also for direct elicitation of feelings, using a technique labeled "dredging for affect." Several other innovative techniques are also used for similar purposes in addition to such conventional methods as guided fantasies and occasionally a direct body approach.

In psychotherapy generally, crises are rarely brought to a boiling point. They are, instead, more often than not submerged with the aid of tranquilizing agents or otherwise. In C.M.T. specific affect is indeed repeatedly mobilized, and only when the "boiling point" has been passed does the task of integration begin.

Although the force of pressure to overcome resistance is specifically applied, the patient must consciously give the therapist explicit and repeated license to do so, and may withdraw such permission at any point. The twin elements of choice and responsibility are repeatedly stressed, and they are basic elements in the therapeutic contract of C.M.T.

IV

DR. BURTON: Various encounter groups, marathons, primal scream therapies, and so on seem to have similar goals to those of C.M.T. in the sense of seeking a quicker resolution of conflict, while the psychoanalytic psychotherapies are more paced and slow. Are you sympathetic to these approaches as blood brothers?

DR. BAR-LEVAV: This query provides me a most welcome opportunity to correct a basic misunderstanding that might otherwise not have been corrected. The presentation itself apparently failed to clarify that C.M.T. is in no way a quick-cure method, and that it is basically different from encounter groups, one-shot marathons, primal scream therapy, and all other modalities that claim to bring about personality changes quickly or easily. Marathons, a few encounter techniques, and occasionally screaming are used, but they serve only as tools for the elicitation of strong affects and are considered of little value in themselves.

The completion of a course of therapy in C.M.T. usually requires no fewer than three, and often as many as six or seven years, just as in psychoanalytic therapies. Although the time span is similar, the personality changes in C.M.T. are claimed to be markedly more profound and more lasting. The quick-cure methods are not considered as blood brothers nor even as distant relatives. On the contrary, they are considered to make unfulfillable promises and to offer false hopes to individuals in distress and need. They may on occasion bring temporary relief, to be followed by greater disappointment than ever, and as such they are regarded as dangerously adding to the suffering of those who use them.

V

DR. BURTON: More than any other author in this symposium you make close and appropriate allusions to the social and cultural scene. What then is the relationship between the culture which is psychotherapy and the culture at large in which it is embedded? Is one a microcosm for the other, a refuge from it, a testing font of creativity, or what?

DR. BAR-LEVAV: The "culture of psychotherapy" is unfortunately a widespread phenomenon that stands as a living testimony to the failures of psychotherapy as a method of healing and cure. When separation-individuation is not completed, current and ex-patients become adherents to, and followers of a "psychotherapy cult" which serves as a security-giving mother substitute. The very existence of a "culture of psychotherapy," like the existence of many other social movements and groupings, is a second-rate and historically a temporary solution to Man's search for the security once experienced in utero.

Industrialization, urbanization, and the changing patterns within the modern family have all contributed to a sharp increase in anxiety of the separated, but not yet individuated, Man. This is culturally and sociologically described as anomie and alienation. Man has found economic and political struggles to occupy him, lay claim to his energies, and allow him to forget his anxieties. National and racial rivalries have similarly been used throughout history as successful diversions from internal problems, internal within society and internal within each person. Class consciousness often replaced self consciousness.

The allusions to social and cultural events in this chapter were mainly to illustrate that behavior change within an individual is no less complex and difficult than it is within society. The nature of Man has basically remained the same, even as his societal organization has become more complex, more sophisticated, and sometimes even more just. The veneer of civilization is often frighteningly thin, as is seen when the social order breaks down at times of war or natural disaster.

True revolutions do not take place on barricades but in those very few consulting rooms in which good psychotherapy is being practiced. Man's fears are patiently dissolved there, as he finally achieves true freedom to be.

REFERENCES

1. PIRKE ABOTH: *Sayings of the Fathers*, Mishnat Chassidim, Chap. 5, V. 19.
2. BAR-LEVAV, R.: Do You Love Me, Yafah Booltiyanski? *Voices, J. of Am. Academy of Psychotherapists*, 1975, 41, 16-22.
3. FREUD, S.: On Psychotherapy. *Selected Papers on Hysteria and Other Psychoneuroses*, Authorized Translation, A. A. Brill. New York: J. Nervous and Mental Dis. Publishing Co., 1909.
4. CHURCHILL, W.: First Statement as Prime Minister, House of Commons, May 13, 1940.
5. KENNEDY, J.: Acceptance Speech, July 15, 1960.

life and be in it with him/her during a critical period of growth. This entails attitudes of regard, respect, interest, concern, and partnership in the developmental process, with a full range of feeling responses to a full range of emotional experiences. Thus, as Jung has put it, psychotherapy consists of two whole psychic systems interacting in depth, in which action each is deeply affected by the other.

That is the overall view, and it may be seen under higher magnification if one asks oneself just what it is that one experiences as a therapist in this interaction.

When someone pours out his/her emotional experience to me, I am moved with that same emotion in empathy with it. This leads to my replicating in myself his/her experience with the emotions and images that belong to his/her psychology. By the same token, when I respond with my feeling to these recountings, the client replicates in him/herself my feeling experiences. Also, when I respond with my recognition of the meaning of his/her recountings, the client equally replicates in him/herself my understanding. The two modes are empathetic feeling and understanding clarity.

In this exchange, I develop in myself as therapist a full range of information, of events, meanings, values, outlook, dreams, memories, and other items belonging to the full context of the client's life experience. Hopefully, all these arrive to lodge in my psyche without walls or blind spots that might shut them out. If so, I am accepting the full range of his/her life in a constellation as complete as his/her communications allow. The result is that I hold in my mind a growing mini-model of that person. So much is this the case that I find myself associating recent occurrences with past dreams and old events often more clearly than he/she. This is because I do not hold in myself the same resistances and defenses that he/she does, hopefully. It is up to me to see to it that I am open and without these walls. In that case, my client can assimilate my feeling responses and my cognitive understanding, and thus see things now freed from the walls, blocks, and resistances that might have been there toward these issues before. The image of the therapist becomes the model of his/her potential free consciousness.

It is not unusual for clients to describe the somewhat uncanny sense of the therapist as a personal presence monitoring their consciousness from moment to moment (between sessions) as if sitting on their shoulder, looking on and commenting. Also it is common for me as therapist to have the sense, at the moment my client enters the room, of his/her bringing into it the atmosphere of the whole context of his/her life, as if wakening the dormant shadows of his/her near and distant past, with names, scenes, emotions, and images all springing to life. The intensity of this experience varies with the degree to which I have opened myself to that person, for that facilitates his/her opening up to me. If he/she has met walls in me and "no take" on certain aspects of experience, there is distress and guardedness, leading to impoverishment of the exchange. Wholeness becomes then actualized in the fullness of the interchange.

The analogies here to the relation of loving feeling between two persons cannot escape the eye. It is very difficult for the profession of psychotherapy to know what to do with this awkward circumstance. The way to ease the tension around the issue has been from the beginning to take refuge in the fact of the "transference" which, holding vestiges of previous, parental relationships, minimizes the validity of the presently growing relationship that exists in its own right. The ardor that springs up has been made even more safe by perceiving it as the "transference neurosis," needing a lot of interpretation to keep it under control and finally to dispel it. A term that has been used for this effort is the graphic phrase, "crushing the transference," thereby telling a whole story in epitome. These formulations were made fifty to seventy-five years ago, the space of three generations. Culturally, we now find ourselves in a different place in relation to these emotions. A certain restive objection prevails nowadays against this rationalistic bias that seeks to interpret the transference feelings as anachronistic illusion and projection, allowing rather the possibility that the relationship's ardor has its own meaning and its own goals.

So far I am describing a state of the therapeutic relationship in which the therapist holds in his/her psyche a mini-model of the client, and the client in his/her psyche a mini-model of the therapist. However, that is only part of the story of what occurs in such an interaction of the two psyches. It is more or less the essence of what occurs on the personal level of the psychology of both persons. In a more profound and archetypal dimension, on the other hand, another configuration is at work that involves the image of the center.

If the relationship between the two persons in the process is intimate and open, and each is communicating in an unguarded, authentic vein, there then begins to appear in dreams the image of the center as a framework of the interaction. Jung has written much on this subject, as the phenomenology of the "vessel," of the "opus," in the alchemical symbolism. All the elements of the inner process are poured into this retort and go through transformations as they combine and synthesize. Or the imagery might be that of the "temenos," the sacred enclosed space in which the mysteries are performed. This imagery does not spring merely from Jungian scholarly myth-making, but from the actual phenomenology of work with dreams in therapy.

A frequent expression of the relation between the two persons in this work, as I have seen it, is that of their working together on the creation of an object in the space between them. For example, a round table top is being carved by both parties jointly, fashioned in the image of a mandala of some sort.

The experiential aspect of this imagery, as I see it, is that all the content of the client's process, and all the responses of the therapist, meet and mingle in this mutual emotional field being established between the two persons. In this sense, the integrating effect is produced not only in the ego of the client, with his/her insights and awareness, and not only in the clarifications offered by the therapist, not even only in the archetypal activity of the "self" within the client's unconscious. Rather, it is in this vessel of the relationship between them. If the client is indeed opening up with all his/her experience, and the therapist is truly receiving it all with openness and without limiting blocks and walls, then all the dimensions of emotional, conflictual, and spiritual occurrences in the client can be received into this vessel and processed there.

In this sense, integrating is done first in the vessel, first in the relationship, and only secondarily in the psyche of the client.

It is, then, the relationship that organizes and reorganizes experience. It is this that produces the dramatic effects so often seen in the interview. A client may come into it all in a turmoil of emotion or of anxiety, pour it all out, and magically sense a relief merely in proferring these confidences. A confidence is *con-fide,* an action of mutual faith with someone. It is given because there is the surety of knowing that one's experience is going to be honored and given full credit for the meaning that it holds, even when it is poorly understood or still unknown.

There are many advantages in acknowledging the therapeutic relationship as one of loving feeling. Chief among these is that the emotional charge and heightened intensity induce at the same time a dramatic activation of the unconscious psyche in great depth, so that the archetypal affect-images become vivid and dynamic. They are stirred in this atmosphere of mutual trust and mutual enthusiasm. It is a characteristic of love relations that the archetype of the center is constellated between the two individuals.

Much of the synthesizing and organizing action of the psyche goes on at the level of unknown, that is, of unconscious, process, long before it is a matter, of conscious insight—long before it reaches the ego. This unconscious process is essentially emotional in its quality, and hence the play of emotion is best allowed to do its own work. Too early a recognition of meaning, and formulation of it, may scotch this subtle process that goes on below the surface.

However, the image of the center appears only when it will. It is one of the many elements that may be "projected" in the relationship, but also may not. The occurrence of the image of the center is only one among several possibilities, and other unconscious contents may have to play themselves out in the "transference." However, in the schizophrenic episode I find the center to be quite regularly represented as the focus of the whole process. Inasmuch as we are discussing at present the healing factors in this psychosis, it would be well to note some of the ways in which the image of the center operates in the psychotic ideation.

The central archetype is the factor in the psyche that, according to all the evidence of our observations, has the capacity to transform the self. This change involves not only the self-image in the usual sense, but also the structure of the personality as a whole. The means by which this is brought about in the psychotic episode are those that I have described elsewhere as the "renewal process." When I speak of a kind of "ideation" it should not be thought of as a fanciful play of symbolic ideas. Rather, they occur as powerful, even overpowering, emotional and spiritual experiences. That is the reason for my preferring to refer to these archetypal phenomena as "affect-images," since they are made up principally of emotion and image together as aspects of the same entity.

This process of renewal is ushered in by frightening feelings of death and of the world being threatened with destruction. Forces are believed to be aligned against one another, the one to bring about this annihilation of the universe—or at least of the moral or social order—the other to preserve it. Creation is experienced anew. However, if all goes well, the death leads but to a new birth, the world destruction to a renewed world image, and the clash of cosmic or social powers to a new design of life and a new structure of values and meanings. A messianic image is brought into play whose role is to fashion and proclaim this new state of being-in-the-world.

There is a considerable amount of opinion currently, among the very people who do the most open and receptive work with the therapy of this psychosis, that to maintain such a stance one must not have theories. The argument is that if one has intellectual expectations, these get in the way of the process that otherwise will go its own way and do its own work. There is considerable influence from Laing's writing in this regard.

In my experience, there is a quality of participation in the psychic process that is vital to the client. This is what I would call "informed listening," that is, hearing the client's communications with recognition of them from past experience. This may be either from one's own or from that of others who have recorded the actual occurrences that have taken place. In this regard I find autobiographical materials fully as valuable as the professional ones. The client in the psychosis knows immediately whether the things he/she is communicating are being found meaningful or incomprehensible. In this altered state it makes all the difference when his/her experience is being found not utterly bewildering but recognizable, for that releases him/ her out of the feeling of being isolated in alienation.

One of the most important of the effects produced by informed listening has to do with the knotty problem of labeling. It has become well known in recent years that the disqualifying and negating effect of diagnostic labeling has a seriously disturbing impact upon the person entering an altered state of consciousness. When it is called disorder, psychopathology, and a sickness, and given medical names, the message conveyed is that the state is of no value and that the best thing to do with it is to be pulled out of it as rapidly as possible. Oddly enough, this moment of labeling can visibly be observed to have the effect of making the individual feel insane and, in consequence, be and act insane. The opposite may also be observed, that when the altered state is affirmed as being a perfectly valid mental space to be in, and possibly fruitful for spiritual and psychological development, the individual may very quickly feel intact once more, and be and act quite coherent.

However, some sort of label remains necessary, since the individual undergoing the experience needs to know what is happening in order to get some sort of working relation to it. A more appropriate kind of label, then, should convey the significance of the actual process going on. The phenomenology of the episode has to do with death and birth, world destruction and recreation, and the play of opposites which at first clash but later become reconciled. I have not been able to think of a better term than "renewal process" as a name of the syndrome, and "visionary state" as a designation of the condition of mind.

From this vantage point, then, the process is seen to have its focus upon the self-image with its root in the deepest and most dynamic layer of the psyche, that is, the central archetype of the "Self." It seems to be this factor, the self-image, that becomes transformed during the episode. I will indicate briefly how this seems to come about as I have observed it.

The main difficulty with the individual's previous development before the psychosis is this: because of certain hurts and emotional injuries in early years, the individual has learned to withhold from intimate, mutually open relationships with others. These might otherwise have brought into play the sharing of the center in the manner I have been describing, but instead, the center has tended to be experienced only in aloneness, in a sort of secret relation to it. The self-esteem is low and debased, and the archetypal image of the Self takes on a compensating function of overvaluing, with fantasies of the heroic or superlative "real" nature of oneself that is kept as a precious secret. The result is a psychology of defending one's prestige and power, but not of coming into close and revealing relations of affection.

The split self-image, too low on the ego level, too high on the archetypal, in this way has gone without the corrective experience that would occur if there were frank interchange in intimate relationships. In this interior isolation, it takes only some blow to self-esteem, or some influx of intensity in feeling sensed as dangerous, for the whole balance to be upset and for the unconscious psyche to be roused into hyperactivity. This leads to the precipitation of a "high-arousal state" in which the lower centers and functions are activated at the expense of the higher. Physiologically it induces a high stress or alarm reaction, which some psychiatrists see as the "cause" of the psychotic episode.

In my observations, the central archetype is the factor in the psyche that is extraordinarily activated in this psychosis. For all the reasons I have been mentioning, it is most difficult for the individual in this state to be left alone with it. If, on the other hand, the image content is brought into relationship, the sequence tends to move through the process that gives renewal to this central archetype of the Self.

The chief characteristic of the renewal, as I see it, is that the potentials and capacities of the Eros principle are activated and made available for living. When that happens, then the old split self, heretofore kept in isolation, gets its chance to loosen up and come into relationship. The new form of the self leads to an emotional life capable of some richness of interchange, and to a sharing of the experience of the center with another.

This means that there comes in this process a new valency, so to speak, for relating in depth. This term is borrowed from chemistry but is also very apt for the psychology of relationship. In chemistry it means the quality that determines the number of atoms that a particular atom may combine with; thus, it is a readiness to unite. This readiness of the individual in the psychotic process to relate in depth imperatively requires a corresponding readiness of the therapist to do likewise. Both centers must be prepared to combine, again in the chemical metaphor. When this does occur, the two centers become involved mutually and together undergo an experience of transformation. Things can go well as long as the individual and the therapist are able to tolerate the play of all the emotions that are released—rage, love, agony, exaltation, etcetera—no matter how intense, as well as the play of all the imagery—mythic, religious, political, etcetera—no matter how unfamiliar.

Now in this full interchange I am pointing to affect and image as the two aspects of the process. The affect tends toward expression, toward conveying the high charge to someone so that it may come into relationship. The image renders the meaning of the affect to the understanding. The personal style of a therapist may lead to emphasizing one of these two aspects at the expense of the other. There are those who tend to feel that the play of the emotion mutually in relationship is the "real" objective of therapy, and those who are so fascinated by the richness of symbolism in the process that comprehending it seems to be the "real" substance of the work. In our Jungian framework, these two modes belong to the general categories of experience that we call "Eros" and "Logos" respectively. Eros tends toward entanglement in experience in relationship, Logos towards abstracting out of experience the meaning and the understanding. For balance and wholeness, both should come into play and receive their due.

Returning now to the original question asked at the start of this discussion—what happens in therapy that makes it work—it seems to me clear that only the full readiness of the therapist to receive the whole of the client's experience and to relate to it and interact with it can suffice. Declining to do so seems to me only to thwart what nature is requiring for wholeness. The two effective virtues of therapy may be said to be "claritas" (clarity) and "caritas" (caring).

ADDENDUM QUERIES

I

DR. BURTON: Since your chapter deals with the most difficult behavior change of all, the psychotherapy of schizophrenia, would you first indicate what you believe a psychosis to be and, secondly, what schizophrenia is in particular?

DR. PERRY: Acute psychosis is a state in which, as Jung has suggested, the dream takes the place of reality. That is, the sense of reality shifts from the outer to the inner world or stage of experience. This is brought about by the circumstance that the ego-consciousness has become overwhelmed by the archetypal affect-images of the unconscious; in the case of depression, by the affects, in the case of schizophrenia, by the images. I cannot see this condition as arising out of a defense against reality, or any other defensive maneuver. It seems rather that the whole syndrome represents instead a shift of the energy so activating the unconscious psyche that it deprives the ego-conscious of its usual charge. To me it appears that the more acute the psychotic state, the more are the defenses overridden altogether.

I see the acute schizophrenic episode, after working with it for twenty-five years, as a high arousal state in which the lower centers and functions are activated at the cost of the higher. It is more realistically viewed as an altered state of consciousness than as a play of psychopathology. A comparison of its phenomenology with parallels in the altered states that are culturally accepted in various societies leads me to call it a "visionary state."

This hyperactivation of the unconscious functions also appears in the phenomenology as emerging from that affect-image that represents itself as the center, the archetypal image described by Jung as the Self, which I prefer to call the central archetype. The highly dynamic process that this center undergoes robs the higher centers and functions of their customary energy, leaving both the ego-consciousness and the complexes in a state of fragmentation, giving rise to the characteristic earmarks of the syndrome, the "thought disorder" and the apparent "dulling of affect."

The intent of the activation of the center is observable if one follows the mental content with care. It shows itself to be the psyche's effort to refashion and renew its cultural orientation, value system, and world image, that is, its entire structure of values, meanings, and design of life. Hence the acute process is so comparable with prophetic and messianic visionary states in rapid culture change as to be indistinguishable.

II

DR. BURTON: Empathy and clarification of feeling are important aspects of the mandatory openness in your therapy with psychotic patients. But I have seen situations where such therapeutic "flowing" led to increased anxiety and autism in the patient. Is there perhaps a still additional factor in the personality of the therapist or in his or her situation which catalyzes empathy and clarification and signals them as curative? The empathy and clarification of encounter groups, for example, have never seemed to me sufficient as curative means.

DR. PERRY: In my experience, the increase in anxiety or autism with this sort of therapy may occur in two kinds of situations. Many persons with a paranoid style of make-up resist the inner vision as a subjective experience and desperately strive to keep it externalized, feeling severely threatened if it is brought too close to inner experience. Also in the chronic condition, after the acute visionary state had been undergone and has failed to do its work, a person may be left with only a fear of its recurrence as a sort of nightmare. In both these situations, I feel we as therapists should be willing to admit the possibility that they are the results of our own failure to know how to deal with the acute episodes in various kinds of personality.

The additional factors in the personality of the therapist who can work in this fashion are, as I have found them, openness and sensitivity to subjective events, and a capacity for "informed listening" which arises from some form of personal experience with the inner life of psychic depth. These allow an open receptivity without being overwhelmed by anxiety, and also allow an honesty and freedom of emotional and conceptual response, including even an affectionate intimacy. I feel group relations cannot take in this dimension of fullness of the client's experience because the emphasis must be upon group process and not the subtle inner process going on in psychic depth; it seems very hard to reveal this except to one person at a time, where confidence is unstinting.

III

DR. BURTON: People who do psychotherapy with schizophrenic patients, myself included, have been accused of romanticising a truly malevolent psychopathology and its cure. It is of course not even certain that schizophrenia may not yet turn out to be an organic disease or a secreting toxin, as Jung finally thought. Do you sometimes feel that the encounter with the schizophrenic patient, as described in your chapter, is a poetic rather than a medical thing and that a two-way idealization process is somehow involved?

DR. PERRY: When the question is raised that this may be fundamentally a condition of biochemical origin, as much of today's psychiatric literature would have us believe, we need to remind ourselves that any emotional occurrence has its biochemical as well as its psychic aspect. It would not occur to me as a psychotherapist to say that I fear a monster in a nightmare because my autonomic nervous system's chemistry induces in me the disturbance (James and Lange notwithstanding). In other words, if one were to have a shattering experience of God, I do not believe one could detect a millisecond's lag between the mental and the physical state, to indicate any primacy in time and causation. That is why I like to call these phenomena "affect-images." The whole organism operates as a unity—psyche and soma—and any claim to give priority to one over the other seems to me motivated by the bias of a culture that somehow views somatic events as "real" and their psychic equivalent as "mystical," meaning "misty." This view of mine is in harmony with Jung's, since he suggested that a toxin might be produced by the hyperactivity of a disturbing autonomous complex; this never held him back from handling schizophrenia by conscientious psychotherapy, which would in turn diminish the toxin.

In my opinion the malevolent course of schizophrenia, that occurs often enough, is most probably an outcome of our way of viewing it and handling it. (Jung made this observation also as far back as 1914.) Schizophrenia is strangely chameleonlike, appearing very differently in differing surroundings. Better said, it is like a magic mirror that reflects back to us exactly what we expect to see; in this regard it behaves just the way the archetypal unconscious does, which, if we approach it with fear becomes fearsome, with hostility, hostile, or with awe, awesome. We can always find our expectations of schizophrenia justified somehow. Thus if one in an eighteenth-century manner anticipates bestiality, the psychotic feels and acts bestial; if one expects violent and insane behavior, one has a wardful of patients acting out violently and needing heavy control; if one's view is that this is a degenerative disease, as in the first decades of the century, then one finds many of one's patients showing a downhill course. In the same way, if one sees in this syndrome nature's own way of effecting change, then that is what takes place in the larger number of cases. At Diabasis we give a realistically favorable but not an idealized picture of what our clients are going through, and hence we have a community of clients who need no medication to feel sane again within two to five days, and who enjoy their stay; the atmosphere is spirited, even jovial often; conversations are lively; people are fond of each other; and most are at work on their inner process.

The tenor of the work has much of the poetic about it, inasmuch as one is dealing most of the time with metaphorical expressions of the deep and underlying issues of our lives and our culture. These are the images that, to use Sullivan's phrase, "reorganize whole masses of life experience"; they convey global issues in the large, and steer the psychic energies into new directions.

When we are sometimes referred to as a "Laingian blow-out center" I balk, because I think there is some idealization of craziness in Laing's writing. At Diabasis we cannot romanticize the process in this way, inasmuch as it represents a task of hard work and painstaking effort on the part of both staff and client. It would feel like a falsification to pretty up this picture and make it look light and easy, or even somehow automatic. We are, however, on the basis of a year's experience with severely psychotic clients, optimistic about the process; after all, 85% of them not only improved without medication, but most went on growing after leaving us.

IV

DR. BURTON: The concept of an alchemical vessel as the locus of behavior change is an apt one. Is this simply a metaphor or perhaps a structuralist concept of an actual therapeutic space which heals? In any event, do you feel that a new "mix" comes out of these vessels because the monads or ingredients have been put in flux and must change their shape?

DR. PERRY: I feel, as Jung did, that the image of the vessel is nature's own expression of such a "therapeutic space." The metaphor is then not so much a *façon de parler* as it is an actual phenomenon, an affect-image that does work. The subjective experience of this image is that two individuals feel themselves sharing a center in common; this is perhaps more familiar to persons through psychedelic experiences in which the sharing of a common center space can be an overwhelmingly vivid occurrence, packed with emotion and imagery of meaning.

I find the expression, a "new mix," an apt one. A good therapist, as I see it, allows him/herself to be open enough to let go into a flux of this kind, and thus allow him/herself to be modified by the experience of the other person's psyche. If there is to be real change, the client must be able to let go into the process, that is, to leave hold of the accustomed set and allow the psyche to do what it must. The consequent reordering or reintegrating is a change of shape in the sense that the structure of the psyche is altered by this complicated work of the affect-images.

V

DR. BURTON: You describe the renewal process of psychotherapy in the psychosis very well. Would you say that the principles of renewal apply as well to neurotic and characterological patients as they do to the psychotic, but perhaps with a diminished intensity?

DR. PERRY: This renewal process does indeed take place in the therapy of many other kinds of personality besides the schizophrenic. The essential factor is not the diagnostic category so much as the degree of depth to which the process goes, that is, the degree of activation of the archetypal affect-images. It appears that in the schizophrenic acute episode, i.e., the visionary state, the archetypal process is intensely energized and sped up, so that an entire process runs itself through in approximately six weeks. Forty days has become a number given sanctified recognition in a variety of tradition; one sees it in the historical accounts of mystics and prophets as well as in some techniques of altering consciousness, such as brainwashing. Therefore I am inclined to think there may be a psychological principle determining this time-span. Yet one may observe all the same content and process in persons who have a somewhat activated play of affect-images, only less overwhelming in strength and more strung out in time. There is in this a most intriguing question of the relation of time and intensity, apparently an inverse relation in which greater intensity varies together with diminished time.

My description of the therapeutic interaction in my paper is drawn from my regular practice with "normal neurotics," in which I spend three-quarters of my time and which is largely composed of young professionals. Neurosis usually shows itself to be a defensive cloaking of a growth process that is being warded off by too conventional and constricted a stance in respect to the new moves that strive to occur in depth. When this propriety is relinquished, and the safer "common sense" or "professional" or "moral" safeguards loosened, then this process in the affect-images becomes activated to seek a new orientation. In the schizophrenic episode, the relinquishing is no longer a matter of choice, since one's world-image and self-image fall apart automatically at the outset. Character problems present more difficulties, inasmuch as these habitual ways of deflecting what nature would otherwise prompt an individual to do are apt to be resistant to change; I believe that if such a character structure is to be altered at all, in anything more than the level of symptoms, it must involve the renewal process.

15

The Integration of Behavior
Change Principles

by ARTHUR BURTON, Ph.D.

To discover any trends which fourteen different approaches to behavior change might contain, I cast them into the form of a table. In this table (Table 1) the theoretical bias, the goals, and the healing procedures of each researcher are offered in capsular form so that they can be quickly apperceived as a totality, and as one against another. Insofar as our fourteen authorities represent the most advanced research thought on behavior change, their conclusions bear serious reflection.

It is immediately apparent from the table that classical Freudian psychology has receded. If the index of psychoanalytic classicism is the centrism of the concept of the unconscious, and a distinctive accompanying methodology for the exorcism of its contents, then very few of our fourteen are now strongly impressed by the unconscious. Only Perry and Strupp seem to make the expected obeisance to it, and then only because Perry is involved with schizophrenics, which makes analysis of the unconscious mandatory, and Strupp comes to the concept principally in the sense that he knows that parent and child have an unknown and unresolved agenda between them which may produce symptoms. Yet Jung before he died told me "that man's unconscious would yet be his undoing," and he hadn't changed his ideas one whit about the creative and destructive powers of the unconscious from the time of his association experiments at Burghölzli. Freud as well fought tooth and nail to maintain his hard-won concept of a less-than-conscious psychic entity which bled the organism of energy and displaced conflict to symptoms in a brilliant variety of ways called hysteria.

It is clear from our data that consciousness is now the focus, but without the exhaustion of the unconscious which repression makes mandatory in a slow and evolving way. And as a consequence, infancy and childhood have lost favor as the primary and invincible locus of the neurotic structure. Very few of our research authorities made a point of the infantile genesis of the neurosis. It is of course taken for granted that the child is father to the man, but only as a first movement of a symphony is to the development of the second and third movements. Infancy is apparently no longer that exquisite sensitized period of life when sensual deprivation can grotesquely deform adult forms of growth. I do not mean to imply that infancy does not shape the adult personality but only that the so-called traumatic experience and emotional deprivation popularized by psychoanalysis do not unilaterally lead to anxiety and neurosis. The adolescent/adult, we now believe, has a choice whether or not to become a neurotic, delinquent, or schizophrenic. Choice and will in mental configurations are more and more emphasized by our researchers in both disease and health. Individuals are no longer the captive of their past, of a programmed fate, as Sophocles and Freud envisaged it. They can help determine their fate.

It follows then that personal history as causation no longer has the dynamic it once did, and long hours spent in free association developing an anamnesis has its limits. For Freud the family situation was always "romantic" and problematic, the locus of all analytic work, but our research authorities see as well a healthy integrative factor in family life; and, in the case of Boszormenyi-Nagy, our family therapist, the entire structure of existence revolves around the family fate—as ego, legacy, and obligation.

The transference (and countertransference), the power of the familial past, is by no means abandoned *as a technique*. Its reintegration power, as Strupp points out so well, is still quite substantial. Perhaps without it the patient might never come to therapy to begin with. But most of us now

TABLE 1

BEHAVIOR CHANGE DYNAMICS ACCORDING TO FOURTEEN AUTHORITIES

Name	Healing Focus	Implementation	Working Through	Theoretical Bias
MARMOR	Corrective emotional experience	1. Seeking and trusting a helper 2. Analysis of the unconscious 3. Intrapsychic and cultural integration	1. Suggestion 2. Cognitive learning 3. Support 4. Reality testing	Modified Psychoanalytic
SALZMAN	The choice to change (will)	1. Analysis of unconscious conflicts 2. Interpersonal dialogue	Socio-cultural-ethical integration of feelings and impulses	Reformed Psychoanalytic
BANDURA	Induction through modeling via conditioning techniques	1. Refinement through enactment 2. Guided performance	Reinforcing social experiences	Social Learning
WOLPE	Replace unadaptive habits by adaptive ones. Reciprocal co-ordination of variegated excitation and inhibition	1. Reinforcement of S-R by reward on multi-levels 2. Counter-anxiety tuition	1. Assertive training 2. Hypnosis/Relaxation 3. Support and approval 4. Refresher training	Reciprocal Inhibition
FRANK	Restoration of failed morale	1. A healing setting 2. A rationale 3. A ritual 4. Analytic synthetics	Intense relationship with helping person fostering a revived morale	Research-Eclectic
STRUPP	Helping relationship on parent-child model	1. Suggestion 2. Openness 3. Reward manipulation 4. Interpretation 5. Modeling	1. Parent-child transfer-ence 2. Interpersonal dynamics	Research-Psychoanalytic
BURTON	An emotional crisis focused by therapy to Either/Or choice	Encounter between patient and therapist on deepest symbolic/humanistic levels	1. Hope 2. Suggestion 3. Modeling 4. Transference 5. S-Factor 6. Archetypal continuity	Existential/Humanistic

WARKENTIN/ VALERIUS	1. Patient's awareness of a therapeutic opportunity 2. A therapist who wants to participate 3. A "fortunate collaboration"	Intense experiencing— with and sometimes against the patient / The Collaborative Factor	1. Unmatched honesty of therapeutic encounter 2. Loving and confronting 3. Modeling 4. Ultra-dialogue	Experiential Psychotherapy
ELLIS	Desire to change—and to work at change	Discarding false beliefs and substituting rational modes of thought and behavior	1. Forced confrontation with neurotic or unsuccessful patterns 2. Demonstrating successful modes	Rational-Emotive
RAIMY	Review of cognitive misconceptions about life	Analysis of associated emotion to misconception	Arrival at new concepts and feelings of goals and purposes	Cognitive Review
BOSZORMENYI-NAGY	Homeostasis or balance in family needs: intergenerational welfare	1. Clarifying ethical and human values 2. Applying ethics and values to dis-ease family situations	1. A dialectical view of reality 2. More intact and healthier families 3. Fulfilled individuals	Intergenerational Family Therapy
POLSTER/ POLSTER	1. "What is, is" 2. "One thing follows another"	1. Focusing on present experiencing 2. Defining engagement 3. Promoting creativity phenomenon	1. Setting a new interactive climate 2. Using the personality of the therapist 3. Expanding ego boundaries 4. Sharpening contact functions 5. Development of experiments in living	Gestalt Therapy
BAR-LEVAV	Crisis-stimulus to change basic character structure	1. Fantasy change 2. Physiological change 3. Personality change	Pregnant evocation of affect to crisis situation; resolution and synthesis of crisis to growth	Crisis Mobilization Therapy
PERRY	Primary unconscious resolution of psychosis	Massive feelings of empathy and identification between participants	Alchemical transformation in the "vessel" of the relationship	Psychotic Reintegration

believe that the reality aspects of regular and systematic encounter with a therapist, in its most numinous present, and with him or her as a firm and loving model, has its own healing rationale. The Gestalt therapists, the most extreme in this area, are of course hardly impressed by transference and prefer resolution by what happens in the here-now dialogue. Albert Ellis, while more cognitive-rational, feels about the same. But this is done with some sense of guilt. All of us know that the family romance, with its unresolved longings and tensions, makes the "healing romance" possible, even if the formulations and dissolution of the transference residuals are not strictly according to the psychoanalytic mode. It may yet turn out, as Boszormenyi-Nagy insists, that the nuclear family is the unit of individual personality, and that we are going to become more rather than less wrapped up with families.

There are those researchers who give behavior change over to conceptual-rational processes, diminishing thereby the *complex*, and go about reversing conceptual misconceptions and myths about feeling and behavior. Raimy finds in almost every instance false perceptive-belief systems which keep the neurotic pot boiling and which beautifully reinforce themselves. The therapeutic task then becomes one of interrupting the "misconception" in any way therapeutically feasible, until that point is reached where patients can no longer believe the "misconception" themselves and change it. Ellis goes even further. He demands, by demonstration, persuasion, and suggestion, that *perfection, family devotion, sexual sanctity, fidelity,* etc., all be rephrased so as to be more realistic and actionable in the milieu in which we live. From living in an intrapsychic dream world of their own making, Raimy and Ellis insist that patients enter the real social world and at least force their private fantasies to match up against the joys to be found there. There is very little analysis of a repressed id in such approaches; but the phenomenological ego comes in for a great deal of examination, rearrangement, and social engineering.

Of course, Drs. Bandura and Wolpe, as our representatives of the behavioral conditioning school, see behavior change as a process of facilitation and inhibition, based upon reward and punishment reinforcement, and this is what the social/behavioral world consists of for them. Wolpe is much more biological about it and will make no concession to values, meanings, models, and the social matrix. The rat remains his scientific model and extinction of anxiety his goal. Bandura more easily recognizes that not only the reinforcement but the reinforcer has something to do with behavior change, and comes out timorously, I must say, for the influence of the healer model and the social nexus in which the reconditioning process takes place.

But both are impatient with the mysticism of traditional psychoanalysis/ psychotherapy and, while perhaps agreeing with the now generally known conclusion that all methods are neither better nor worse than others in healing effectiveness, claim that a concealed operant conditioning actually accounts for the good results obtained in psychotherapy. This leads Wolpe to then unabashedly say that he has an 89% success rate with reciprocal inhibition, and to justify his further efforts on the basis of this statistic.

In all of this it would at first appear that the possibility of unifying the myriad therapeutic approaches contained in this book is an impossibility. But closer examination reveals that old methods come back in new guises. If this were a book of video tapes instead of word symbols, we would not be so pessimistic. There is nothing here that was not anticipated by Mesmer, Janet, Bernheim, Freud, Pavlov, and others. We are now more vigorous and insistent in our specific findings as truth, more commercial about offering them up as relief, but when the essential behavior change factor in each system is teased out, it falls somewhere along an ancient understanding and spectrum. Why then have we become so doctrinaire, and so militant in our belief that we have the new curing word? Well, this is a competitive society, and the business of healing is by now big business. We are not necessarily venal, but we all bring to healing a drive, purpose, and affirmation upon which rests our own personality. To deny a healing system is thus to deny the meaning of the healers' life. We are much too grim about this business of healing. In selecting a therapist, I would look for one who can laugh, and thus be reassured about his or her relationship to life and its conundrums. We need less conviction and more appreciation of the paradoxes of life in our therapeutic work.

Regardless of the healing system which is proffered, in order to be healed the patient must accept—yes, have a readiness to believe in—the values, circumstances, and efficacy of that particular system. Faith is a part of every healing system and when faith is lost, healing stops. Healing systems offer a certain mysterium, an awe, an opportunity for exorcism, a set of powerful myths to believe in, a secret ritual which extols and demeans, and, not the least, they dispel the boredom of life. Many people come to therapy because they feel socially left out if they do not and because they cannot at the moment feel sensual anywhere else but in therapy. It offers high degrees of intensity of feeling for a set of people who notoriously lack the opportunity for intense feeling. It organizes, labels, and gives the seal of approval to a notoriously vague set of despised symptoms. It allows the patients to once again become infantile and dependent, but in a socially approved way. Its content is libidinously sexual, and, as one example, aging therapists begin to lose their nubile patients as they gain in wisdom. Therapy is sexuality without sex, but for a set of people who cannot yet handle sex straight on.

It offers hope in a treatment area which has been made notoriously hopeless by medicine, and it changes what Frank calls demoralization, the loss of social purpose and identity, into a new moral possibility. It is necessary to passionately believe in something in order to be psychically healthy. There are a considerable number of people in Western civilization who believe that the dialogue between two imaginations is what ennobles them and allows them to grow. This belief in the dialogue of the imagination comes from the same Greek sources as do our *demos*. Freedom of the mind, of the spirit, of the soul, is the release from the mythical underworld, from religious constraint, and even from gods of various sorts. To become a god in turn is thus to fight fire with fire. The fact that patients unknowingly and wholeheartedly subscribe to the ethos of Greco-Roman healing provides them with a readiness, even a joy, in becoming behavior change patients. They have then only to search out and find that healing personality who can stand *in locum tenens* for them for childhood and adult experiences never completed—their unfinished business, which they must now finish. Patients by no means seek psychotherapy merely for the removal of anxiety or symptoms.

Culture approves of and shapes its healing forms; it even qualifies them by law. It also anoints the healing personnel with distinct privilege, and the healer in Western civilization has always had a special social position. After the first vicissitudes of Freud, psychoanalytic healing, as occupations go, was a highly desirable job. Not only did it pay well, but it was "clean," brought one an upper- and upper-middle-class clientele—the best educated and the most stimulating intellectually—it was in the service of alleviation of pain and distress, and it gave erotic satisfactions as well. I challenge the law, the ministry, education, and other socially-oriented professions to make the same claim to satisfaction. As I have stated elsewhere, it also permitted psychotherapists to personally finish their own unfinished family business.*

The proliferation of psychotherapies (and psychotherapists), the tenacity with which they maintain their healing theses, and the statistics of cure they offer are no happenstance. People who come to therapists want themselves to become therapists, and most certainly before their treatment is completed they openly profess it. Therapy has now become a social institution, and all social institutions compound their own growth. So it is that there has been comparatively little interest in separating fact from fiction in psychotherapy.

---

* Burton, A. *The Patient and the Therapist.* Sacramento: Hamilton Psyche Press, 1975.

But, it must also be pointed out, research does not come easy to clinician/healers who see such research as impinging upon the good they are doing in the world and also resent the time it takes.

Therapists, by their vast presence in society, promise a psychic salvation the religious have by now in 2000 years failed to provide. Through their indirect influence on McLuhan's hot media forms, the majority of such creative people, having themselves been analyzed, carry the message of psychotherapy, albeit at times bitter, comic, or hostile, to hundreds of millions of people, who either find an immediate closure or disgust with it. But in this way, we propagate the faith which, it must be noted, is now ever growing even if under attack. No one has seriously come out for abandoning psychotherapy, not even Thomas Szasz, for then the social dissidents, the unhappy, the depressed, the alienated, would have nowhere to go and we might have true revolution. They might in their desperation become the greatest terrorists yet known. Behavior change is, in my opinion, in no danger of extinction as a professional venture.

Most psychic therapies are pragmatic methodologies with plausible *ad hoc* theories attached. We then fight our battles on the basis of the hypothesized theories, ignoring of course the identity of the operations involved, or the fact that the relationship between the *practice* and the *theory* is often a very loose one. And we rarely ask our patients in a systematic way what they think of their treatment, nor can we follow them up properly. It is no happenstance that the great proponents of the abolition of shock treatment, lobotomy, medication, and similar organic psychiatric treatment forms are former patients.* There is anger at being cured and anger at not being cured. The conclusion, obviously, is that the overwhelming degrees of freedom in the field of behavior change have had secondary gains for us and we have not really looked very closely at what made behavior change possible in the past.

Of course, the intercurrent shift of social base in society is being reflected in and by the psychotherapeutic process. The family is less frequently a family in the old dynamic sense; more and more it is a simple living together, a conjointness, and less a holistic phenomenon. The libidinal family problems so beautifully described by Freud, the seeking after proper pleasure within the family setting, are now more valuative, ethical, and life-style than sexual. As the family changes, as it becomes more loosely agglutinated, the neurotic formations based upon family libido are bound to change. Perhaps the neurosis of the future will be less socially important and not even dignified by a state of diagnostic "being." It depends on the maintenance of its creative force in society.

---

* *The Madness Newsletter*, San Francisco, Cal.

The problem, of course, comes down to lack of a sufficient concept of man. If we could all accept Jung's *religioso homo,* we might then reduce the anarchy in our field to a tangible amity. If we could accept the Pavlovian-Skinnerian concept of man and be satisfied with calmer, regulated people, we could thereby unify ourselves. If in some humanistic way, the true Christian gospel of brotherhood were suddenly and miraculously practiced universally, as the humanistic therapists seem to want, then existence could be pure native phenomenon and love. Even a new concept of man as demon, as Beelzebub, as atomic power agent, would perhaps be more fruitful than our present fragmented images of man.

Thus it is that some of our researchers cling tightly to a biological model for security and base their treatment procedures on the survival and adjustment aspects of life. But there are others who ignore the soma, and its physiology, and count existence and spirit as all. Still others find in reason, intelligence, and cognition—those advanced features which man's evolved brain made possible—not only the answer to remediation but to life itself. It becomes more and more apparent that we are awaiting, if not a new Freud, then one who will give us this new conception of man: his psyche, his purpose, and his spirit. Perhaps he is already among us. When that time comes we will be able to answer with greater precision the question *What Makes Behavior Change Possible?* But the attempts to answer it, as in this book, are of the greatest importance, even if they fail to satisfy us all.

Index

Gath, D., 36
Gellhorn, E., 62
Gestalt therapy, 5, 7, 8, 23, 118, 138,
    182, 183, 215, 217, 259-272, 322
  beyond resistance, 261-264
  composition, 264, 265
  contact boundary, 265, 266
  five piovtal elements, 266-273
  See Perls
Ghost in the machine, 59, 68
Gleitman, H., 61
Goffman, 139
Good patient therapist relationship,
    6, 7, 9, 21
  conscious, 9
  See Rational emotive therapy
  transference, 9, 21
  unconscious, 9
Goodman, P., 265
Greenspoon, J., 60
Greenwald, H., 195
Grodeck, 161
Group therapies, 76, 77, 91

Habits, 59-61
  breaking of emotional habits, 65
  formation, 60
  reciprocal inhibition, 61, 62
Hardy, A., 44, 45
Harper, 181
Haughton, E., 61
Hazards of evaluating treatment, xv,
    xvi
Hefferline, R., 266
Hegel, G., 132, 231, 234, 265
Heidegger, 134
Hemingway, E., 149
Here and now, 182, 244, 273, 322
Hesse, H., 127
Hilgard, E., 62
Hitler, A., 243, 283
Hodgson, R., 45-47
Hoffman, H., 47
Holmes, F., 67
Holt, R., 97
Honzik, M., 67
Horney, K., 221
Hull, C., 4, 61, 64

Idea of control, 105, 106
  ego control, 108
  external, 106
  internal, 106

Identification with therapist, 7
  emotional support from therapist, 7
Implosive therapy, 209
Insight, 20, 181, 182, 212
  cognitive insight, 4
  emotional insight, 31, 32
  insight therapies, 84
  rational emotive therapy, 184-186
Instinct, 16
Interactional view of human behavior,
    15, 16
Intergenerational approach, 251, 252
  dialectical intergenerational ther-
    apy, 252-255
Intrapsychic, 248, 322

Jacobson, E., 63, 211
James, W., 314
Janet, P., 4, 9, 198, 323
Janov, A., 182
Jeffrey, R., 38-40, 47, 52
Jersild, A., 67
Jones, J., 149
Jung, C. G., xiii-xv, 127, 128, 130, 132,
    141, 144-146, 149, 151, 190, 192,
    217, 277, 304, 306, 307, 312,
    314-316, 319, 325
  archetypes, xv, 142, 143, 300, 313
  Jungian, 88, 122

Kelly, G., 181, 221
Kennedy, J., 298
Kimmel, H., 60
Knight, R., 64
Koegel, R., 49
Krasner, L., 59

Laing, R., 309, 315
Lange, 314
Lazarus, A., 211
Learning theories, 4, 102
Leitenberg, H., 36
Locke, E., 210
Logos, 312
London, P., 210, 211
Lovaas, O., 48, 49
Lowen, A., 193
Luborsky, L., 97
Luce, H., 129

MacAlpine, I., 99
MacFarlane, J., 67